THE ISRAELI ARMORED CORPS

HISTORY, EQUIPMENT, OPERATIONS, 1948 TO 2024

Marc Lenzin and Stefan Bühler

Schiffer
Military History
4880 Lower Valley Road
Atglen, PA 19310

Other Schiffer books on related subjects
Ghosts of Atonement: Israeli F-4 Phantom Operations during the Yom Kippur War, Shlomo Aloni, 978-0-7643-4756-6

Instinctive Shooting for Defense and Combat: The Israeli Method, Fabrizio Comolli and SDU Team, 978-0-7643-5311-6

Copyright © 2025 by Schiffer Publishing Ltd.

Originally published as *Die israelische Panzerwaffe: Geschichte, Technik, Einsätze* by Motorbuch Verlag, Stuttgart © 2022 Motorbuch Verlag.

Translated from the German by David Johnston

Library of Congress Control Number: 2024941290

All rights reserved. No part of this work may be reproduced or used in any form or by any means—graphic, electronic, or mechanical, including photocopying or information storage and retrieval systems—without written permission from the publisher.
The scanning, uploading, and distribution of this book or any part thereof via the Internet or any other means without the permission of the publisher is illegal and punishable by law. Please purchase only authorized editions and do not participate in or encourage the electronic piracy of copyrighted materials.
"Schiffer," "Schiffer Publishing, Ltd.," and the pen and inkwell logo are registered trademarks of Schiffer Publishing, Ltd.

Cover design by Molly Shields
Type set in WeidemannEF/District
ISBN: 978-0-7643-6906-3
Printed in China
10 9 8 7 6 5 4 3 2 1

Published by Schiffer Publishing, Ltd.
4880 Lower Valley Road
Atglen, PA 19310
Phone: (610) 593-1777; Fax: (610) 593-2002
Email: Info@schifferbooks.com
Web: www.schifferbooks.com

For our complete selection of fine books on this and related subjects, please visit our website at www.schifferbooks.com. You may also write for a free catalog.
Schiffer Publishing's titles are available at special discounts for bulk purchases for sales promotions or premiums. Special editions, including personalized covers, corporate imprints, and excerpts, can be created in large quantities for special needs. For more information, contact the publisher.
We are always looking for people to write books on new and related subjects. If you have an idea for a book, please contact us at proposals@schifferbooks.com.

Ha'adam she'Ba Tank Ye'na'tzeah

("The man in the tank will win.")

Contents

PROLOGUE 6

INTRODUCTION AND ACKNOWLEDGMENTS 7

CHAPTER 1: *CREATION OF THE ISRAELI ARMED FORCES* 10

CHAPTER 2: *THE JEWISH BRIGADE
IN THE SECOND WORLD WAR* 28

CHAPTER 3: *THE HAGANAH ON THE ROAD TO WAR* 34

CHAPTER 4: *THE FIRST ARMORED VEHICLES:
RENAULT, HOTCHKISS, AND CROMWELL* 40

CHAPTER 5: *THE WAR OF INDEPENDENCE,
1948–49 (FIRST ARAB-ISRAELI WAR)* 48

CHAPTER 6: *THE EVOLUTION OF THE ARMORED CORPS* 58

CHAPTER 7: *THE SHERMAN TANK
AND ITS MODIFICATIONS* 64

CHAPTER 8: *GROWTH FROM FRENCH PRODUCTION:
THE AMX-13* 70

CHAPTER 9: *THE SUEZ CRISIS OF 1956
(SECOND ARAB-ISRAELI WAR)* 74

CHAPTER 10: *THE STRENGTHENING OF THE
ARMORED CORPS UNDER ISRAEL TAL* 84

CHAPTER 11: *THE BACKBONE OF THE ISRAELI
ARMORED CORPS: THE CENTURION (SHOT)* 90

CHAPTER 12: *COLD WARRIOR: THE PATTON TANK (MAGACH)* 98

CHAPTER 13: *THE SIX-DAY WAR,
1967 (THIRD ARAB-ISRAELI WAR)* 106

CHAPTER 14: *INTERLUDE AND THE WAR OF ATTRITION, 1968–70* 118

CHAPTER 15: *CAPTURED TANKS UNDER THE ISRAELI FLAG: THE T-54/55/62* (TIRAN) 126

CHAPTER 16: *THE YOM KIPPUR WAR, 1973: THE SOUTHERN FRONT* (FOURTH ARAB-ISRAELI WAR) 136

CHAPTER 17: *THE YOM KIPPUR WAR, 1973: THE NORTHERN FRONT* (FOURTH ARAB-ISRAELI WAR) 146

CHAPTER 18: *REVOLUTION IN TANK DESIGN: THE MERKAVA* 162

CHAPTER 19: *OPERATION PEACE FOR GALILEE: THE LEBANON OFFENSIVE, 1982* 172

CHAPTER 20: *THE 2006 LEBANON WAR AND THE FIGHTING IN THE GAZA STRIP* 182

CHAPTER 21: *THE TRANSFORMATION OF THE ISRAELI ARMED FORCES* 206

EPILOGUE 222

DIRECTORY OF CHIEFS OF THE GENERAL STAFF AND COMMANDERS IN CHIEF OF ARMORED CORPS 226

DIRECTORY OF ISRAELI ARMORED VEHICLES 227

TANK MARKINGS OF THE ISRAELI ARMED FORCES 228

BIBLIOGRAPHY 229

Prologue

The state of Israel was born in war, which all of our Arab neighbors declared on us and which was supposed to prevent the existence of a Jewish state. Many of them still do this today.

Tanks played a role in our war of independence, and since then their importance within the Israeli army has grown steadily, from the Hotchkiss and Cromwell tanks used in the beginning; to the Sherman, the Shot Kal (Centurion), and Magach (Patton); to our own tank developed in Israel, the Merkava.

During the Six-Day War in 1967, the Israeli Armored Corps fought heroically and played a decisive role in that historic victory. I was therefore proud to be drafted into the armored corps for my military service. After completing my training, I attended the Israel Defense Force's officer's school and was assigned to the 74th Battalion of the 188th Brigade on the Golan Heights as an armored-platoon leader.

We were a group of professional, well-trained tank crews and commanders. We knew our Shot Kal Alef tanks inside out and maintained our armored-weapons systems well, and our officers mastered the tactics of armored operation by tank units from the platoon to the brigade and the division. All these factors showed themselves in the tank battles of the Yom Kippur War of 1973, which were some of the biggest and fiercest in history. Despite the war's difficult and complicated opening phase, the Israeli Armored Corps emerged from these battles with the upper hand.

During this war I experienced the most stressful moments of my life. I was aware of the fact that if we did not succeed in holding our position in defense of our nation, we might not have a home to return to. Former Israeli prime minister Golda Meir once said, "Our soldiers have always had the same secret weapon—we have nowhere else to go."

During such a war, one learned to appreciate, even love, one's tank, as if it had a soul of its own. I found myself talking to my tank and tapping it affectionately, because it protected me, saved my life more than once, and functioned exactly how I wanted and expected it to.

The modern battlefield has changed. Drones and cyber warfare have reduced the importance of elements such as strategic depth. New technologies are changing and improving most weapons systems in the air and on the sea. But wars are still always decided on the ground, and so the tank has retained its dominant role in land warfare.

I am sure that the Israel Defense Forces and its armored corps, which is constantly evolving, will be able to meet any challenge they will face in the future.

Aviv Shir-On (reserve captain)
Armored-platoon leader in the Yom Kippur War of 1973
and former Israeli ambassador to Switzerland and Austria

Introduction and Acknowledgments

The people of Israel, almost destroyed by the Roman sword two thousand years ago, fled their Promised Land and experienced an unprecedented diaspora. It was only with the rise of the Zionist movement toward the end of the nineteenth century that the Jews began returning to their homeland of Palestine and formed the first paramilitary formations to protect the population, such as the Hashomer and later the Haganah.

It was only after the dissolution of the British occupying power, however, that the way was clear to establish the Israeli armed forces in 1948, with the founding of the independent state of Israel. However, the surrounding Arab states were suspicious of Israel's continued growth. They saw Israel as the new enemy in the Middle East, one that had to be fought with all available means.

The Israeli army has had to pass many a test in the course of numerous wars against its Arab neighbors. The Israeli Armored Corps has always played a decisive role in this. Equipped with only a few armored vehicles during the War of Independence in 1948–49, during the Suez Crisis of 1956, Israeli troops undertook larger armored offensives. From there, a direct line of development can be drawn through the delaying battles and ultimately successful counteroffensives in the Yom Kippur War of 1973 and the fighting in Lebanon, to the house-to-house fighting in the Gaza Strip. In these battles of the past seventy years, the Israeli Armored Corps has grown significantly stronger thanks to its experience and professionalization and has thus become one of the most powerful armored forces in the world.

Many Israeli tank soldiers lost their lives in the Arab-Israeli wars. Their sacrifice for Israel underlines the proud mission of the armored corps, to strike back at any aggressor without delay. This mission, with which the soldiers identify, endures — yesterday, today, and in the future.

The authors, members of the Swiss mechanized forces, describe the technical development and historical role of the Israeli Armored Corps in every important campaign from its creation to the present time. The reader will also find numerous little-known images and maps as well as biographies of the most-important commanders of the Israeli Armored Corps.

An exhaustive account of the individual armored battles would go beyond the scope of this work. Rather, the book aims to provide the interested reader, soldier, officer, and historian with a general overview. However, it provides numerous details, particularly in terms of technical history, and is therefore intended as a small reference work on Israeli armored vehicles.

Aviv Shir-On, former Israeli ambassador in Bern and tank commander, and Dr. David Schiller, journalist and former Israeli paratrooper, actively supported us with in-depth information and technical details. Both were active soldiers on the front line during the 1973 Yom Kippur War.

We have tracked down the book's extensive photographic material in numerous archives. We would like to take this opportunity to thank Ted Nevill of AirSeaLandPhotos; the National Library of Israel in Jerusalem; Hagen Seehase, the former director of the Tank Museum in Latrun Michael Mass; and the Library at Guisanplatz in Bern.

We received professional support from numerous members of the dedicated Officers' Association of the Armored Forces (OG Panzer) under the leadership of President Major im Generalstab Erich Muff.

We would like to thank Peter Forster, former editor in chief of the magazine *Schweizer Soldat* ("Swiss Soldier"), with his inexhaustible knowledge of the Middle East, and Oliver Heyn, with his keen eye for grammar and spelling, for their efficient proofreading.

We would also like to thank the editor Joachim Kuch from Motorbuch Verlag in Stuttgart for his valuable support.

Marc Lenzin and Stefan Bühler
Trimstein and Schwanden, September 2022

Chapter 1
Creation of the Israeli Armed Forces

> . . . in the one hand a shovel, in the other a weapon.
>
> —Nehemiah 4:11

In the year 70 CE the Roman Empire crushed the last Jewish uprising in Judea, devastated much of the land, and ended Jewish independence. It was the beginning of the "two-thousand-year banishment" and the dispersion (the Diaspora) of the Jewish people. Not until the rise of Zionism and the associated hope of a land of their own did the Jewish people slowly begin returning to the Promised Land (Eretz Yisrael) at the end of the nineteenth century.

LONGING AND RETURN: THE JEWS AND ERETZ YISRAEL

Since the sixteenth century, the area between the Jordan and the Mediterranean, which had been known as Palestine since British times, had been an insignificant and neglected province of the Ottoman Empire, which in its heyday stretched from the Balkans to Yemen and ruled almost all the North African coastal countries, including Egypt, as well as the Caucasus and Mesopotamia. From the nineteenth century onward, the once-flourishing great power began to erode rapidly. Corruption and decadence among the ruling elite, a stagnant economy, and backward social structures sealed the fate of the multinational empire. At the beginning of the twentieth century, the Ottoman Empire was regarded as "the sick man of the Bosporus."

Even after the expulsion by the Romans, Jews continued to live in the Holy Land, which they referred to in Hebrew as Eretz Yisrael (Land of Israel). Despite all the inconveniences of existing as a second-class minority in a predominantly Muslim dominion, the number of Jewish immigrants in the four holy cities of Jerusalem, Hebron, Safed, and Tiberias grew steadily from the late Middle Ages onward. The old "Yishuv"—the Jewish inhabitants and their settlements—was recruited from all of this.

In the second half of the nineteenth century, new Jewish immigrants began arriving, mainly from pogrom-stricken eastern Europe, seeking their salvation in the Promised Land for political rather than religious reasons. They were the forerunners of the later Zionist movement, which gained momentum around 1900 thanks to publicists such as Martin Buber, Max Nordau, and Theodor Herzl.[1] In line with political Zionism, the Jewish population in Palestine grew from 24,000 to 87,000 between 1870 and 1914 out of a total population of around 600,000.

It was no land of milk and honey that awaited them; rather, an economically and socially backward province with no network of roads, electricity, health services, public security, or order. Highway robberies and attacks on rural communities have been commonplace throughout the Middle East since time immemorial.

The Ottoman forces of order, consisting of gendarmerie and cavalry regiments, could hardly be relied upon. The representatives of the Sublime Porte, the central government in Istanbul—whether governors, district administrators, judges, or police chiefs—were characterized by corruption and constantly increasing demands for protection money. Reliable protection was offered only by armed self-help, as was customary in all Arab villages and in every Bedouin tribe. Large landowners or wealthy communities therefore hired paid night and field guards.

The first Jewish agricultural settlements, which were established in the coastal plain near Jaffa in the second half of the nineteenth century thanks to donors—such as Mikve Israel, Petach Tikva, Rishon LeZion, and Zikron Ya'akov—made use of Arab night watchmen, just as they employed local instead of Jewish fieldworkers for the harvest. Around 1898, there were around twenty-five such Jewish colonies with a total of around five thousand inhabitants, stretching from Metulla at the sources of the Jordan in the north to Be'er Tuvia near Gaza in the south.

On the other hand, there was the romantic-utopian idea of the new Jewish man who would free himself from his ghetto mentality by working in the fields, which was propagated mainly by the socialist-influenced Zionists from eastern Europe.

---

[1] Theodor Herzl (1860–1904) grew up in Austria and studied law at the University of Vienna. He worked as a correspondent for the newspaper *Wiener Zeitung*, published his pamphlet *The Jewish State*, organized the first Zionist World Congress in Basel in 1897, and was eventually elected president of the World Zionist Organization. The Basel Program adopted there formed the basis for the creation of a new homeland for the Jewish people in Palestine. Herzl fought for the establishment of a Jewish homeland in the biblical homeland until his death in 1904.

Now, in addition to the idea of the "conquest of Jewish labor," there was also the similarly revolutionary idea of standing guard oneself, of self-protection: in Hebrew, *Avoda Iwri* and *Haganah Iwri*.

To achieve this goal of protecting the Jewish population and their villages and farm settlements, Yitzchak Ben Zwi[2] and a few like-minded people founded a secret society called Bar-Giora in Jaffa in 1907. The name was derived from Shimon Bar-Giora, a Jewish leader of the uprisings against the Roman Empire in 70 CE. The Bar-Giora core group of about ten men began guarding the two first Jewish settlements in the Lower Galilee—Sejerah and Mes`ha—later renamed Ilanyia and Kfar Tabor.

AGUDAT HASHOMER

A year later, the members of Bar-Giora made a pilgrimage to the village of Mes`ha, soon to be called Kfar Tabor, below Mount Tabor, in order to found a larger organization to combine labor and self-protection. The name agreed upon was Agudat HaShomer (Hebrew for "the Guardians' Association"). Israel Schochat,[3] a twenty-three-year-old from Belarus, was elected to be its first leader. In addition to guarding and defending settlements, the members of HaShomer were also supposed to take over the harvesting work in the fields and barns, while at the same time being able to proactively fend off attacks by Arab gangs.

The next step was to establish their own settlements according to the collective model, which, after some initial difficulties, began in 1913 with Tel Adash near Nazareth. Others moved to Tel Hai, an estate on the edge of the Hule Valley, around 1910. In 1916, the hard core of HaShomer took part in the building of a kibbutz near Metulla, which was later named Kfar Giladi.

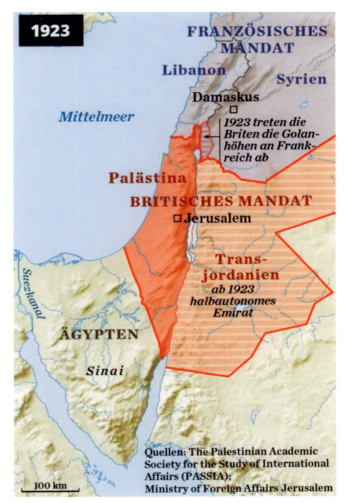

On behalf of the international community, Great Britain took over the administration of Palestine and the future Transjordan after the First World War. France was given a mandate over Syria and Lebanon. *Passia*

[2] Yitzhak Ben Zwi (1884–1963) grew up in Poltava in what is now Ukraine and was co-organizer of the first Zionist Congress in Basel in 1897 and cofounder of the Russian workers' movement "Poale Zion." He studied in Kiev and Constantinople. He arrived in Jaffa in 1907, where he found work as a teacher. Two years later he established the Rehavia High School in Jerusalem. In 1919, together with Ben Gurion, he founded the social-democratic party Achdut HaAvoda, which together with the non-Marxist HaPoel HaTzair provided political support for the Haganah and Histadrut and merged into the new labor party Mapai in 1930. Ben Zwi was one of the signatories of the Israeli Declaration of Independence in 1948 and was elected Israel's second president in 1952.

[3] Israel Shochat (1886–1961) grew up in Liskowa in Belarus. After founding the underground organization Hashomer, he traveled to Constantinople in 1912 to study law. After the First World War, he was one of the founders of the Haganah and served as legal advisor to the minister of police after the founding of the state of Israel.

Despite all the socialist influences, the members of the HaShomer were considered to be disciplined and hierarchically organized. After a short probationary period, candidates underwent paramilitary training, which, despite the background of deterrence, was aimed at deescalation and avoiding the use of deadly weapons in order to prevent the notorious blood feuds.

Shochat and his cofounders dreamed of a nationwide defense system for all Jewish settlements, where the individual guard groups could rush to each other's aid in the event of attacks by marauding gangs.

Fighters of the underground organization Hashomer, the successor to Bar-Giora. Taken in northern Galilee near the Lebanese border at the time of the Ottoman Empire, 1907. *Israel Government Press Office*

THE FIRST WORLD WAR

The period shortly before, during, and after the Great War was probably the most profound period of change in the Middle Eastern region. Before 1914, many people in the Yishuv sought their salvation in cooperation with and loyalty to the Ottoman Empire. Quite a few of the founding generation of Zionists, such as David Grün, who immigrated in 1906, David Ben Gurion[4] from 1909, Yitzhak Ben Zwi, and Israel Shochat, learned Turkish, the official language of the empire, and studied Ottoman law.

On the other hand, dozens of Jews from Palestine enlisted in the Turkish army after the Ottoman Empire declared its entry into the war on the side of the Central Powers on October 30, 1914. However, events soon came thick and fast and shattered the dream of a Jewish integration into the Ottoman Empire: the distrust harbored by the Young Turkish ruling class and its generals toward other ethnic or religious minorities in the empire had been growing for a long time.

Even the Arab officers in the Turkish army were now constantly suspected of being members or sympathizers of a conspiracy against their Turkish brothers in arms. More than 300,000 Arab soldiers served in the Ottoman army — far more than were to fight on the side of the Allies against Turkey in the Arab Revolt that began in 1916.

Ben Gurion, Ben Zwi, and Shochat and many of their party comrades were also arrested by the Turks and driven out of the country. By the end of 1914, over seven thousand Jewish refugees from Palestine had settled in the port city of Alexandria in British-controlled Egypt. It was there in the land of the pharaohs that the politically much more important nucleus of the army of the future Jewish state was formed.

The foundation stone was not laid by the well-known leaders of the worldwide Zionist movement, but by two rebels who, in a sense, opposed utopian Zionism — Joseph Vladimirovich Trumpeldor[5] and Vladimir Zeev Jabotinsky.

From the moment Trumpeldor and Jabotinsky first met in Alexandria, they both recognized the spiritual kinship, the urge to act, and the opportunity that presented itself here in the chaos of the refugee camp: to build an armed Jewish force that could participate in the war against Turkey and thus cement the political claim to the Jewish homeland.

Jabotinsky also found a name for the new force: the "Jewish Legion." It was to be at the forefront of the liberation of Palestine from the Turkish yoke. Within a few days, they had lists of hundreds of volunteers in their hands, and the first groups even got together for a drill.

Trumpeldor and Jabotinsky's request met with a certain amount of goodwill from the British rulers of Egypt and the representatives of the Jewish community of Alexandria. They were granted an audience with the British commander in chief, General John G. Maxwell, who was responsible for the security of the Suez Canal. However, he saw no legal possibility of accepting foreign soldiers into the British army, and the best he could offer was to recruit the volunteers into a transport unit with pack animals. Mule drivers in the rear: this was of course not the frontline assignment that Jabotinsky and the majority of the volunteers had imagined. He flatly rejected the idea and left for Rome, from where he continued to campaign for a Jewish Legion in Paris and London, initially without success. But Trumpeldor took a more pragmatic view of the matter and was finally able to recruit a large group for the replenishment unit, which was set up as the Zion Mule Corps: within four weeks, 650 volunteers had been trained and were sworn in as soldiers on April 1, 1915. Irish lieutenant colonel John Henry Patterson, a veteran of the Boer War, took command, with Captain

---

[4] David Ben Gurion (1886–1973) grew up in Plonsk, Poland, and immigrated to Palestine in 1909. He joined the Jewish Legion during the First World War. He proclaimed the state of Israel in 1948 and became its first prime minister. In 1970, he retired from all political offices and published several books on the creation of the Israeli state. *Time* magazine voted him one of the most important people of the twentieth century. The international airport in Tel Aviv is named after David Ben Gurion.

[5] Joseph Trumpeldor (1880–1920) grew up in Pyatigorsk in Russia, immigrated to Palestine in 1911, and joined the HaSherom and worked for a time in Degania. After the World War, he returned to the Upper Galilee, joined a farmers' collective, and fell in 1920 in a battle for the Jewish settlement of Tel Hai in the Galilee. He became a symbolic figure for Jewish self-defense. He is honored to this day by a memorial day, the eleventh of Adar in the Jewish calendar

David Ben Gurion as a volunteer in the Jewish Legion, 1918. *Wikipedia*

Trumpeldor as his deputy. The unit's languages of communication were Yiddish and Hebrew. As early as the end of April, four companies of the corps landed at Cape Helles, the tip of the heavily contested Gallipoli Peninsula. Until the withdrawal of the landing troops in January 1916, the mule drivers proved themselves beyond all expectations. Exposed to constant Turkish artillery and rifle fire, the Zion Mule Corps transported water, supplies, and ammunition from the landing beaches to the frontline positions and returned with the wounded and the bodies of the fallen.

The small force of 562 men suffered a total of fourteen killed and more than sixty wounded, including Trumpeldor, who took a rifle bullet in the shoulder but refused to be evacuated and remained with the troops. Others, such as Patterson, had to be withdrawn due to illness and were shipped to Egypt to recover. On January 10, the Zion Mule Corps arrived back in Alexandria and was finally disbanded in May 1916. But around 120 men—including Trumpeldor, of course—resisted this decommissioning: after some back and forth, they were transported to England, where the War Office assigned them to the 20th Battalion of the City of London Regiment as its 16th Platoon.

The first of a series of Jewish Legion battalions was finally formed around this group of veterans in 1917. Finally, the months of effort by Jabotinsky and his lobbying of British politicians had borne fruit. As early as November 1917, in the run-up to the announcement of the Balfour Declaration—in which the British government held out the prospect of establishing a Jewish homeland in Palestine—the War Office now permitted the establishment of Jewish volunteer units as line troops for the first time, even as part of the time-honored Royal Fusiliers, also known as the City of London Regiment.

The 38th Fusilier Battalion was the first to be formed in the fall of 1917, recruited mainly from the Russian-Jewish émigrés of London's East End. Jabotinsky, who in the meantime had joined the 16th Platoon as an ordinary soldier, became the unofficial recruiting officer for the 38th, and Colonel Patterson was appointed its commander. Jabotinsky attained the rank of lieutenant and was a platoon leader when the battalion was transferred from London to Egypt in the spring of 1918.

At the same time, the 39th Battalion of the Royal Fusiliers was formed in the United States from American and Canadian volunteers at the instigation of the local Zionist organizations. Ben Gurion and Ben Zwi were among those who organized the recruitment. After their basic training at Fort Edward near Windsor in Canada, this unit was also shipped to Egypt in April 1918, from where it was sent to the front in Palestine that summer.

The "Egyptian Expeditionary Force," consisting of British, Australians, New Zealanders, and Indians, had systematically advanced from the Suez Canal via the north of the Sinai Desert to Gaza. Two major attacks against the Turkish-German lines near Gaza failed in March and April 1917. The use of gas grenades and even eight Mark I tanks specially imported from England did not result in the hoped-for breakthrough. The British commanders Murray and Dobell were dismissed and replaced by the cavalry general Allenby, who rolled up the Turkish front across the southeastern flank near Be'er Sheva in the Third Battle of Gaza (October 31–November 9).

A month later, his troops were in Jaffa and Jerusalem. It was not until the winter of 1917–18 that the Turks again succeeded in establishing a fallback line south of the towns of Tulkarem and Nablus between the coast and the Jordan Valley. This was the front line, which had been frozen for months, where the two Jewish battalions moved in from July 1918 for guard and patrol duty.

Meanwhile, in the southern part of Palestine, which was under British military administration, a third battalion was raised and trained from local volunteers—the 40th Royal Fusiliers, later also known as the "First Judeans." All three units together soon bore the unofficial nickname of the Jewish Legion and together had a total of five thousand men under arms.

On September 19, 1918, Allenby launched a long-prepared offensive, which brought his troops to Damascus, Beirut, and Aleppo by the end of October and finally forced the Ottoman Empire to surrender on October 31. In the front's great swing to the right from the coast of the Mediterranean, through the

CHAPTER 1: Creation of the Israeli Armed Forces

Members of the Jewish Legion training on the Lewis machine gun, Egypt, 1918. *Israel National Collection*

Judean Mountains and over the Carmel Mountains near Megiddo, the 38th and 39th acted as the pivot and anchor point in the Jordan Valley. They occupied bridges and river fords and advanced deep into Transjordan.

In contrast, the men of the 40th who had not yet completed their training saw no action at the front. All the more reason why the "First Judeans" became a rallying point for Jewish aspirations for the Zionist homeland in the following year of 1919. While the warring parties debated the peace treaty in faraway Versailles, Allenby's once-proud army was gradually disbanding: Australians, New Zealanders, Indians, and Britons were shipped home for demobilization. In Syria and Lebanon, French contingents replaced the British occupation troops in accordance with the agreements between London and Paris on the division of the Middle East among the victorious powers (Sykes-Picot Agreement).

FROM THE OETA TO THE MANDATED AREA

The League of Nations, initiated by US president Woodrow Wilson in 1920 and founded as a result of negotiations at Versailles and San Remo, assumed responsibility for the former colonies of the defeated Central Powers. According to Wilson's ideas, the mandate holders in these territories were to establish an administration and autonomous self-determination for the local population as quickly as possible and thus lead these countries to state independence. France took over the Lebanon region and Syria, Great Britain, Mesopotamia (later Iraq), and the Holy Land on both sides of the Jordan River, now officially called Palestine, whose border with the Egyptian Sinai Peninsula formed a straight line between Gaza and the Red Sea near Aqaba.

Neither mandate actually came into force until 1922–23, however, and until then the territory was still under military administration, known as OETA (Occupied Enemy Territory Administration). Naturally, the Indigenous ethnic groups did not like the way their future was being decided in distant Europe. In Damascus, the Hashemite prince Faisal had already proclaimed a pan-Arab kingdom in October 1918. The British secret service officer T. E. Lawrence[6] had made him the leader of the Arab Revolt. According to British promises, he was to rule from Aleppo via the Hejaz to Aden. This naturally met with opposition from other tribal princes and the various ethnic-denominational populations in the Levant.

All of this did not leave people in Palestine indifferent, especially since there were demarcation lines between the old Turkish administrative districts but no clearly defined borders between the mandated territories. In southern Syria and the Lebanon mountains, the Druze continued their uprising against the French until 1927. This also affected their fellow believers living in Galilee and the Carmel Mountains. The same Arab landowners, who for a long time had made and continued to make huge sums of money from the sale of inferior land to the Zionist settlement fund, placed

---

[6] Thomas Edward Lawrence (1888–1935) grew up in North Wales, traveled through Syria and Palestine as a student at a young age, and served in the British intelligence service in Cairo at the beginning of the First World War. Thanks to his local knowledge and language skills as well as his connection to the Hashemite Prince Faisal, he recruited Hejaz Bedouins for the Arab fight for independence against the Ottoman army. When the war ended, he was a colonel. He was involved in a motorcycle accident in 1935 and succumbed to his serious injuries. He became a legend during his lifetime, not least thanks to numerous Hollywood films and books, such as those by Robert Graves and Basil H. Liddell Hart. He was the author of *The Seven Pillars of Wisdom*.

The Negev Brigade Monument, dedicated to the fallen soldiers of the Palmach, created by sculptor Dani Karavan, 1963–68, Be'er Sheva, Negev. *Wikipedia*

themselves at the heads of the new Arab nationalist organizations and now incited their *fellahs* against the Jewish land grab. In the north, Syrian Arabs and Bedouins attacked the Jewish settlements in the Upper Galilee in the spring of 1920. Galilee, Hamarah, and Tel Hai went up in flames.

After the persecutions at the hands of the Turks, as a defensive organization, what remained of HaShomer was only a shadow of its former greatness and a symbol. If Jabotinsky had had his way, the Jewish Legion would have been retained as the core element for protecting the Yishuv and maintaining public order in the mandate territory—but colonialist attitudes and anti-Semitic reservations were increasingly spreading among the officers at British headquarters. The military authorities wanted to demobilize the three fusilier battalions as quickly as possible and banish the remaining units to a camp near Rafah on the Egyptian border.

Jabotinsky also found himself back in Tel Aviv as a civilian in 1920. When the situation in the north escalated, he had to watch helplessly, since the Yishuv as a whole did not see itself in a position to send even a few hundred men with weapons and ammunition to Metulla, Tel Hai, or Kfar Giladi as reinforcements. Incited by inflammatory speeches on the Temple Mount—in particular those of the landowner's son Amin el Husseini, who later became known as the Grand Mufti—pogrom-like conditions broke out on April 4. Hundreds of stirred-up Arabs marched armed through the alleys of the old town, attacking every Jew and foreigner they could find, and invaded the Jewish quarter of the Old City. There they looted homes and synagogues and set fires. Arab police officers refused to intervene and, in some cases, even actively participated in the riots. The British troops had been largely withdrawn from the city before the start of the festival—allegedly to avoid provocations.

THE HAGANAH (HEBREW FOR DEFENSE)

Looking back, the 1920s marked a time of Jewish hopes and illusions. Although the British had succeeded in quelling the riots in Jerusalem after a few days thanks to the massive deployment of troops, peace did not return to the country. Attacks on Jewish settlements and sniper attacks on trucks and buses remained the order of the day.

In the evening, the rebels also tried to storm Tel Aviv but encountered one of the last remaining units of the Jewish Legion, who opened fire and broke up the riot. Shortly before the outbreak of the riots, Tel Aviv had formed a defense committee inspired by the one in Jerusalem. But unlike the self-defense committee founded there by Jabotinsky in 1920, the coastal town lacked trained personnel, weapons, and vehicles.

A nationwide organization was needed that could serve as a foundation for training and weapons procurement. It already had a name: Haganah.

The organization was sponsored by a completely different body that now came onto the scene: the General Workers' Union, founded in Haifa in December 1920, in Hebrew, HaHistadrut HaKlalit shel Ha-Ovdim b'Eretz Israel. With the new third wave of immigration and the strong voices of the Trumpeldor labor legion, the desire arose for a unified trade union that not only was aimed at the classic type of proletarian worker but also wanted to include members of the collective settlements, employees, craftsmen, and even artists.

David Ben Gurion was elected as the organization's first general secretary in 1921. Within seven years, Histadrut had around 22,000 members. In 1939, it broke through the 100,000 barrier and thus represented 75 percent of the Jewish working people in Palestine.

Such an apparatus, which influenced many areas of society, was of course ideally suited as a cover for an underground paramilitary organization. At the same time, it allowed the necessary funding to be raised inconspicuously and gave the activists credible cover stories for their travels around the country.

---

[7] Eliyahu Golomb, born in Waukawysk in what is now the republic of Belarus, attended Herzliya High School in Jaffa and joined the Jewish Legion in 1917. He took on numerous leadership roles in the Haganah, with his home in Tel Aviv serving as a command center for years. He died unexpectedly at the age of fifty-two.

Armored car of the Palestine Police Force with a machine gun mounted in a simple revolving turret, Jerusalem, 1938. *Library of Congress Matson Collection*

The small, secret circle of founders of the new defense organization included leading trade unionists such as Dov Hoz, a veteran of the Jewish Legion, and Eliyahu Golomb,[7] a founder of Kibbutz Degania and also a member of the legion. The third man in the group was Yitzhak Sadeh.[8] In his youth in St. Petersburg, he was a successful competitor in wrestling and other strength events, and he had served in the czarist army during the First World War. Sadeh did not arrive in Palestine until 1920 but quickly became one of the founders and leaders of the of the Labor Legion, where he managed the quarries and road construction projects.

Golomb was appointed as the Haganah's first chief of staff, Sadeh as commanding officer for special tasks. From the ranks of the Jewish battalions and the Labor Legion, Sadeh now selected the first thirty candidates for a Haganah instructor course. The thirty graduates were distributed throughout the mandate area as regional leaders. Under strict secrecy, they trained in the villages of Moshavim and Kibbutzim to set up local defense committees. They trained new volunteers, set up weapons caches ("slicks" in Hebrew) in the settlements, and organized security guards.

Golomb's first and foremost task was to purchase small arms, of which there were plenty to buy in the Balkans after the end of the world war, but which now had to be smuggled overland from Lebanon to Galilee via Beirut. And this went unnoticed by the French and British mandate authorities. At the same time, the Haganah began to set up the first decentralized underground workshops for the repair of firearms and the manufacture of hand grenades.

However, the network also had weak points, which became apparent during a renewed uprising by Arab nationalists in the summer of 1929. The rumors spread by Mufti el-Husseini that the Jews wanted to conquer the Temple Mount were enough to spark Muslim riots in and around Jerusalem. Although the Haganah managed to protect the Jewish quarter in the Old City and the new neighborhoods in the north and west from the Arab mob, in the southwest the Arabs stormed Kibbutz Ramat Rachel, which had been founded three years earlier, on August 23, looting houses and stables and burning everything to the ground.

Wherever Haganah contingents existed, they usually succeeded in fending off attacks by Arab rebels—for example, in Haifa, Tel Aviv, and some of the new settlements in the Jezreel Valley. Histadrut and Haganah took stock of the situation:

- The existing stock of weapons was inadequate, and this also applied to the defenses in the rural settlements. Bulletproof shelters for the fighters and bunkers for the population were needed. Instead of individual isolated outposts, the National Fund was to finance the establishment of settlement blocks, as had been successfully tried out in the Jezreel Valley.
- Help from the Mandate police or British troops could not be relied upon. Security planning could no longer be limited to individual towns and villages but had to be planned regionally and operated according to districts. Neighboring Haganah contingents had to support one another. This was not possible without means of communication.
- Ultimately, the Haganah needed a planning staff and its own intelligence service so that it would no longer be surprised by developments on the Arab side.

But restraint was and remained the motto of the Haganah—a defensive strategy that was the cornerstone of the policy of the World Zionist Organization and its executive bodies in Palestine.

In 1930, the socialist and social-democratic workers' parties merged to form the Mapai, which from then on was to become the strongest political force in the country and also in the Zionist movement.

---

[8] Yitzhak Sadeh (1890–1952), born in Lublin, Poland, began his military career in the Russian army during the First World War. He joined the Haganah in 1936, took command of the Palmach in 1941, and, as a brigadier general, led the first armored unit of the newly founded Israeli Defense Forces (IDF). He died in Tel Aviv in 1952. The Yitzhak Sadeh Prize for Military Literature has been awarded in his honor since 1972.

Joseph W. Trumpeldor in British uniform during the First World War.
National Library of Israel

Ben Gurion was elected Mapai secretary general and was thus head of the two most powerful organizations of the Yishuv. Consequently, he was elected chairman of the Zionist Executive and the Jewish Agency in 1935, succeeding Chaim Weizmann.

He thus rose to become the leading political figure of the ever-growing Yishuv: from 1929 to 1936, 200,000 Jews officially arrived in the country, many of them German and Austrian refugees fleeing Nazi persecution. In September 1940, the Jewish population in the mandate area numbered 488,600 — nine years earlier it had been just under 175,000. At the outbreak of the Second World War, the total population of Palestine thus amounted to 1.5 million people.

In the 1930s, the Haganah changed from a secret security organization based primarily on the agrarian settlements to a national movement that reached all strata of society. And this despite the fact that the British punished underground membership as well as illegal possession of weapons with draconian prison sentences. Nevertheless, there was never a shortage of volunteers, because the need for self-protection not only had been demonstrated in 1929 but was evident in the almost daily raids of the following years

SERVANT OF TWO MASTERS

For the Yishuv and Haganah, the riots were a political breakthrough, since the British, surprised as always by the vehemence of the Arab attacks, were now forced for the first time to involve Jewish auxiliary forces in their defensive measures. The Arab officers of the Mandate police once again proved to be unreliable and unwilling to take action against their compatriots. The British infantry battalions hurriedly brought in by rail from the Egyptian Canal Zone to support the police were neither trained nor equipped to stand up to the Arab gangs.

The Jewish Agency recognized its opportunity as early as 1936 and offered the authorities personnel support. According to the statutes of the Police Law of 1926, the Palestine Police, which had a strength of just under five thousand men, could enlist auxiliary policemen and reservists at any time. The first few hundred Jewish volunteers who joined the newly created "Jewish Settlement Police" (J.S.P.) in the early summer of 1936 became 17,000 men in less than three years, ready to serve as auxiliary and part-time policemen — the beginning of a militia system.

British policemen and soldiers needed local guides who could also serve as translators. They found them in the young people of the kibbutzim and moshavim who, such as the then-twenty-two-year-old farmer Moshe Dayan[9] from Nahalal in the Jezreel Valley, had grown up with the Arab *fellahs* and Bedouins from an early age.

Dayan was given the job of a local auxiliary policeman. His first duty station was the British army camp in Afula, from where patrols were to guard the Kirkuk-Haifa oil pipeline. He now wore a British khaki uniform, carried a rifle, and was paid eight Palestinian pounds a month. He was soon sent to a group leader course, the beginning of a military career that would make him chief of staff of the Israeli army and minister of defense of the Jewish state in the 1950s. Yigal Allon[10] from Kfar Tabor also joined the J.S.P. and was issued his first uniform in August 1936.

Every village, every settlement, and every Jewish town was now given a guard station, led by a noncommissioned officer who, like the auxiliary police, was secretly a member of the Haganah. Supervision was the responsibility of the British police officers at station and district level.

After the initial successes in fending off Arab raids, the Mandate police approved the further expansion of the J.S.P. This happened not least because Ben Gurion's Jewish Agency agreed to cover a large part of the personnel costs. In addition

---

[9] Moshe Dayan (1915–81) grew up in Kibbutz Degania, near the mouth of the Jordan River. He joined the Palmach in 1940 and fought in the Syrian-Lebanese campaign. He lost his left eye and subsequently wore a black eye patch. After serving as commander of various troops in the 1948–49 War of Independence, he became chief of staff in 1953 and commanded the Sinai campaign against the Egyptians in 1956. He served as minister of defense during the Six-Day War in 1967 and the Yom Kippur War in 1973. He was foreign minister under Prime Minister Menachem Begin and played an important role in drafting the Camp David peace agreement in 1979.

[10] For Yigal Allon, see biography on page 24.

to the permanent station guards, the Mobile Guard (M.G.) was now established in the settlement blocks: selected groups of six to ten men each under the command of a sergeant, who patrolled the country roads with the aid of an open flatbed truck (a Model T Ford, called a "Tender") and could quickly bring support in the event of raids. Both Allon and Dayan became leaders of such patrol vehicles, which, in addition to Enfield rifles, usually also carried a Lewis light machine gun and often (illegally) hand grenades.

The mobile patrols were the brainchild of Yitzhak Sadeh, the informal coordinator of the J.S.P. He had long argued against the Havlagah concept in the endless meetings of the kibbutzim, the party committees, and the agency leadership: the defensive behavior condemned the Yishuv's best young people to lie on their stomachs night after night behind the fence in a sandbagged position or to carry out the tedious duty of standing guard. It left the initiative entirely to the Arabs. When the raids on the settlements along the corridor to Jerusalem increased at the beginning of 1936, he gathered the best volunteers in the region into a mobile patrol, known in Hebrew as the Nodedet and in English as the "Flying Column," which took its inspiration from the Boer War and the Irish fight for freedom.

His success proved him right: instead of waiting for the Arab gangs to attack, Sadeh's patrols left the settlements at nightfall and laid ambushes along the approach and retreat routes, which greatly contributed to unsettling the enemy. The Haganah's new initiatives spread like wildfire in the Yishuv. More and more volunteers joined the underground organization.

Sadeh secretly built up his personal network of the most-promising candidates for the future. So, he was ready with everything when, in the early summer of 1937, the Haganah's national command (Hebrew: Mateh Art-zi) and the Jewish Agency agreed, after much debate, to give the Haganah units a new organizational framework:

- Henceforth, the mobile maneuver element of the Haganah was to be grouped into *Posh* (for *Plugot Sadeh*, or field companies) — a selected elite made up partly of the best of the J.S.P., such as the Mobile Guards, but also of Haganah fighters who remained underground. Although they were supposed to cooperate with the Haganah's regional detachments, they were subordinate to their own headquarters, established by Yitzhak Sadeh in a house on Tel Aviv's Rothschild Boulevard. In 1939, the field companies were reorganized into a force called the Chel Sadeh (Field Corps). This active component of the Haganah reached the number of 9,500 members aged seventeen to twenty-five and was now subordinate to the regional commanders.
- Static defense was the responsibility of Him, the Hebrew abbreviation for the words "Chel Mischmar" (Security Corps) and included both the more than five thousand reservists and part-time policemen of the J.S.P. as well as the slowly coalescing home defense units of the settlements and villages, which represented the bulk of the force base in 1939 with 16,000 men and women — although most of them were well over thirty years old.

Less than ten months later, in March 1938, the Posh already had a thousand members in thirteen regional groups, with five hundred more candidates in training.

For the command personnel, special courses were now organized for squad leaders, platoon leaders, and officers, ranging from five days to six weeks and going beyond the previous level of training in an underground organization. Such companies, ready for deployment on call, fitted perfectly into the new territorial defense concept of the Zionist executive bodies.

On the political horizon, the threat of a new British partition plan for Palestine and the possibly of a sudden withdrawal of the Mandate, whose forces would be needed for the conflict with Germany looming in Europe, appeared on the horizon. In 1920, Ben Gurion and the Jewish Agency had seen how individual settlements had influenced the borders of the Mandate territories. In response to Arab unrest and the British partition plans, the ambitious expansion of new fortified villages was now launched in the Yishuv to open previously uninhabited areas as bases and stand up to the Arab rebels — the Tower and Wall Program (Homa u'Migdal).

In less than three years, fifty-seven such settlements sprang up literally overnight in the Galilee and the northern Negev. As first demonstrated with the Kfar Hittim Moshav near Tiberias and in the valley of Beth Shean with the Kibbutz Tel Amal at the beginning of December 1936, hundreds of helpers from J.S.P. and Haganah appeared before dawn with a fleet of trucks and prefabricated building elements, with which a watchtower with a generator and floodlight and a bulletproof fence made of wooden walls filled with rubble and sand were erected by evening. Next, a communal house was built inside the palisades, which served as an operations center, weapons store, and dining hall. The inhabitants initially slept in old military tents. The program continued until the outbreak of the Israeli War of Independence on May 14, 1948, and a total of 118 of these settlements and outposts were built.

A FRIEND IN NEED: ORDE CHARLES WINGATE

After the Peel Commission of Inquiry failed to produce a solution acceptable to all parties in the conflict-ridden Mandate of Palestine, the Arab riots reached a new peak. On September 26, 1937, the district commissioner for the Galilee, Lewis Andrews, and his bodyguard were assassinated in Nazareth by four followers of Izzadin al-Qassam.

Now the velvet gloves of the Mandate power disappeared with regard to the Mufti and his Arab Supreme Committee, which had driven the general strike and the uprising. Those concerned fled to Syria, from where they continued to intrigue. Sir Arthur Wauchope, high commissioner since 1931, asked to leave and was replaced within a few months by Sir Harold MacMichael, who had previously served in the colonial administration in Sudan and as governor of Tanganyika. Unlike Wauchope, MacMichael had no qualms about giving the British troops a free hand in Palestine and taking advantage of martial law and collective punishment. Nor did he object to military intelligence or the army using the intelligence provided by the Jewish Agency or the Haganah.

It so happened that a young artillery captain named Orde Charles Wingate,[11] who had been serving as an intelligence officer with the 5th Infantry Division in Haifa since September 1936, suddenly sought the acquaintance of Zionist officials.

The 5th Division was responsible for the whole of northern Palestine, and running through its area was the oil pipeline, completed in 1935, which was so often sabotaged and set on fire by the Arab insurgents. One of the first Jews that Wingate was able to convince was David Hacohen (1898–1984), a graduate of Herzliya High School, Histadrut functionary, and general director of Solel Boneh. He was also a member of the Haganah leadership. Through Hacohen, Wingate was to get to know the inner circle of the Zionist executive from Moshe Shertok to David Ben Gurion, Abba Eban, and Chaim Weizmann.

Improvised armored vehicles of the Jewish Settlement Police made by the Wagner company in Jaffa, October 1938.
Zoltan Kluger

Eliyahu Golomb gave the British captain, who was well versed in the Bible and soon became a convinced Zionist but was outwardly quite eccentric, pass for every kibbutz and every Haganah division. Wingate traveled all over Palestine, inspected the home defense efforts of the settlements and the J.S.P. police stations, wrote memoranda and analyses for his superiors, and finally appeared at the Lebanese border near Hanita. There, under the leadership of Yitzchak Sadeh, four hundred Haganah men, including one hundred under the command of Moshe Dayan and Yigal Allon, set up an outpost on March 21, 1938 — right on one of the most important Arab smuggling routes.

The British planned a security fence along the border with Lebanon, and its construction took place under Solel Boneh. Hanita was the westernmost anchor point of this installation. No wonder that from then on, hardly a night went by without the Arabs firing on Hanita and its guard posts and exacting a constant toll in blood. Hanita became the legend of the Yishuv and its new will to resist. Wingate arrived, took a look around, and immediately criticized the overly defensive stance of Hanita's garrison. Finally, on a later visit on June 17, 1938, he and Sadeh led a retaliatory attack against an Arab village from which the raids on Hanita originated.

Less than two weeks earlier, Wingate had submitted a memorandum to the British High Command on how to stop the

---

[11] Orde Charles Wingate (1903–44) grew up in Naini Tal, British India. After graduating from the Royal Military Academy in Woolwich and gaining command experience as commander of the Sudan Defense Force, he commanded the Special Night Squad in Mandate Palestine. After the outbreak of the Second World War, he commanded the Gideon Force in Ethiopia and later, as a major general, led an air-transportable commando unit in Burma behind Japanese lines. He died in a plane crash in 1944 near Thilon, in what is now the Indian state of Manipur.

attacks on the pipeline with a mobile, mixed company of British and Jewish volunteers. At the end of June, his direct superior, Brigadier John Evetts, gave him the go-ahead. A force of thirty British infantry, including three sergeants and three lieutenants, were ordered to proceed to Ein Harod. There, where the Bible states that Gideon had once chosen his three hundred warriors for the attack on the Midianites, Wingate set up the headquarters for the three special night squads (SNS).

Each British squad was assigned two ten-man groups for training and handpicked volunteers from the Haganah, each with a J.S.P. sergeant, who brought their police tenders with them and thus ensured mobility. Wingate's SNS operated exclusively at night and were very tough in their commando actions, even though, as a Christian Zionist, he read the Bible to his men after their missions. Successes were achieved and the attacks on the pipeline decreased.

Nevertheless, Wingate's successes and his unconventional manner attracted naysayers and critics, and after a home leave in London, he found himself transferred to an office job in Jerusalem in December. His wish to one day command a Jewish army was not to be fulfilled. In the Yishuv, however, his reputation as *HaYedid*, the friend, remained. His memory is cherished at the national sports college and at the Wingate Institute near Netanya, and as the namesake of one of the most exclusive courses in the Israeli security apparatus.

THE SECOND WORLD WAR REACHES PALESTINE

The Arab uprising collapsed in the spring of 1939, but there was no return to peace and quiet. With its so-called White Paper policy, the government in London now implemented a plan proposed by the Peel Commission in 1937, which froze the expansion of the Jewish homeland and restricted the immigration of Jews to Palestine to 75,000 people over the next five years.

This naturally provoked protests in the Yishuv. However, before clear political lines and possible new alliances between factions of the Yishuv could emerge, another, much-larger conflict broke out in Europe — with the German invasion of Poland in September 1939 and France in May 1940. Palestine, together with Egypt, became a huge logistical base and hub for all operations in the eastern Mediterranean.

Once again, the Yishuv willingly volunteered to serve under the British flag. Over 50,000 men and women from Palestine were to go to war for the empire during the Second World War. Initially, the British armed forces used the highly motivated Jewish volunteers only in technical units and for rear services in the Engineering Corps, in transport units, in workshops, and at logistics centers. Obviously, as in the First World War, the intention was to prevent Jews from serving at the front — something that was undermined by events in North Africa and the Levant.

By July 1940, at the latest, the European conflict had also reached Palestine: after France's surrender, the French garrisons in Syria and Lebanon declared their support for the pro-German Vichy government. German agents appeared in Iraq and Palestine, and the Italian war effort in North Africa was accompanied by bombing raids on Haifa and Tel Aviv; the Italian air force also bombed Acre and Jaffa. Later, German aircraft also carried out attacks.

From September 1940 onward, a cadre group from the 1st Battalion of the Royal East Kent Regiment began training volunteers from the Mandate area at Camp Sarafand and in the Jordan Valley. They were formed into rifle companies of 120–200 men, were given basic infantry training and equipment dating back to the First World War, and were then assigned to guard and security duties in depots and port facilities, on supply lines and strips of coastline. By the beginning of 1943, the number of these companies had grown to fifteen, with around 5,300 Jews undergoing basic training.

As the British situation in the Libyan theater of war deteriorated visibly due to the intervention of Generalleutnant Erwin Rommel's Afrikakorps, British commanders came to the conclusion that the potential of these guard companies could be put to better use. Well-qualified soldiers were transferred to the 51st Middle East Commando, while others were assigned to parachute training or seconded to intelligence duties. Starting in the summer of 1941, the majority of the companies were combined into three battalions, which were now stationed in Egypt as the Palestine Regiment and underwent further training. In 1944, this unit served as the basis of the Jewish Brigade.

DANGER ON THE HOME FRONT: THE ESTABLISHMENT OF THE PALMACH

In the Libyan theater of war, the growing presence of German armored forces of the Afrikakorps alongside the Italians increasingly forced the British army onto the defensive in the summer of 1941. Greece had fallen in April, and by the end of May the Germans had conquered Crete. The closer the Axis powers came to the Egyptian border in Cyrenaica, the more the fear spread that Great Britain might abandon Egypt and Palestine. The invasion of Palestine and the destruction of Yishuv had long since ceased to be an abstract threat.

Who was to defend the Yishuv? Many of the best instructors and fighters of the Haganah and hundreds of the J.S.P. were now serving in the British armed forces. In this precarious

situation, the high command of the underground decided to flee forward: on May 14, 1941, Yitzhak Sadeh was ordered to mobilize six shock companies, known in Hebrew as **Plugot Machaz** (abbreviated Palmach), as a standing force. Unlike the J.S.P. reservists, the Palmachniks were not to be part-time irregulars but were to be permanently available in their platoons and companies. Since the Haganah, as an underground formation, had no barracks in which to house them and no funds to maintain such forces, the Palmach detachments were divided up among the kibbutzim, where their men and women paid for their food and lodging by working part-time in the fields, stables, and kitchens.

At the same time, there was a pragmatic rapprochement between the Jewish Agency and the British military authorities, as if the White Paper and the policy barring Jewish immigration did not exist. The British were urgently looking for personnel with language skills and knowledge of the terrain for intelligence operations behind enemy lines, both in the occupied Balkan states and in the Vichy-controlled part of the Levant. In the Yishuv there were suitable recruits, mostly immigrants from eastern European countries, Austria, and Germany, as well as Jews from Arab countries. Very soon there were specially trained "German" and "Arab" platoons in the Palmach. And when British and Australian units attacked Lebanon and Syria on June 7, 1941, the advance units included around a hundred volunteers from the Haganah, who prepared the invasion as reconnaissance, scouts, and sabotage squads, including many designated Palmach leaders from the Galilee such as Yigal Allon and Yitzhak Rabin, as well as Moshe Dayan, who lost an eye in a battle with Vichy troops at Litani.

Under the auspices of the British intelligence and sabotage organization called the Special Operations Executive (SOE), the British set up a training program in small-scale warfare, through which the first six hundred or so Palmach members were channeled. In the event of a German occupation of Palestine, the graduates were to become part of the resistance movement. However, this cooperation ended in the winter of 1942–43, after the victory at El Alamein eliminated the immediate threat of a German invasion of Egypt and Palestine. The British dissolved

Palmach commander Yitzhak Sadeh (*center*) with Moshe Dayan (*left*) and Yigal Allon (*right*), Kibbutz Hanita, north of Akko, 1938. *Israel Government Press Office*

the joint training camps on Carmel and in Kibbur Mishmar HaEmek and confiscated the weapons that had been issued. The Palmach disappeared underground again and distributed its task forces and platoons to various kibbutzim. The headquarters, which had previously been based in Haifa, also went underground, near Nazareth in Kibbutz Mizra, but continued to recruit in the socialist youth groups of the trade union, scout groups, and agricultural schools.

It was difficult to find new recruits, especially since Palmachniks repeatedly transferred to the British army or to other tasks in the underground, and the majority generally transferred to the reserve after two years of active service. It was difficult to double the number of companies; the seventh company was not formed until 1944 and the twelfth not until 1947. However, there was now also a PalYam naval division and a PalAvir air group. Yigal Allon had little to do with any of this. After his deployment in the Lebanon-Syria campaign, he had taken some time out at Kibbutz Ginossar, which he had founded, was involved in setting up a spy network for the SOE in Syria, and returned to Palmach headquarters only at the end of 1942, where Sadeh made him his new deputy.

CHAPTER 1: Creation of the Israeli Armed Forces | 21

THE GEOGRAPHY OF ISRAEL

Geographically, Palestine is part of West Asia and lies on the eastern edge of the Mediterranean. It is bordered by Lebanon to the north, Syria and Jordan (formerly Transjordan) to the northeast, and Egypt to the south. This area of 10,424 square miles (27,000 square kilometers [km^2]) is home to very different landscapes. Barren hilly country can be found alongside fertile landscapes in the coastal regions, as the Jordan Valley — nestled between the Negev Desert and the Dead Sea — impressively demonstrates.

Israel's Mediterranean coast stretches 143 miles (230 km) from Rafah in the south to Ras al-Naqua in the north. Haifa in the north and Tel Aviv in the center of the coastal strip are the major cities that represent the modern face of Israel today. Other smaller towns such as Ashkelon, Jaffa, and Akko bear witness to a long history and are of historical and archeological interest. In the southern section of the coast lies the Gaza Strip, with the urban centers of Khan Yunis, Rafah, and Gaza.

East of the coastal region, Israel is crossed from north to south by a wide range of mountains and hills in which the fertile Jordan Valley is located. The Jordan River originates from several springs in the Hermon Mountains. Mount Hermon lies at the border triangle between Lebanon, Syria, and Israel and is the subject of territorial disputes due to the importance of its water sources. At the foot of the Golan Heights, the Jordan flows into the Sea of Galilee, which is used extensively for agriculture. In the south, the river emerges from the sea and continues until it flows into the Dead Sea.

The mountainous region and the Jordan Valley are the parts of Israel where most people live. In the northern part, which borders Lebanon and is also known as the Galilee, there are numerous villages and towns of historical and religious significance, especially around the Sea of Galilee, including Nazareth, Tabgha, and Tiberias. The West Bank begins south of the Sea of Galilee and encompasses not only the western bank of the Jordan River, but also a large part of the central and southern mountainous region as far as the Dead Sea. Important cities in the West Bank are Nablus, Jenin, Tulkarm, and Ramallah, the most modern of the Palestinian cities.

South of Ramallah lies Jerusalem, the historical, cultural, religious, and political center of Israel and one of the main obstacles to permanent Palestinian-Israeli peace. All three religions — Judaism, Islam, and Christianity — claim it as their capital. Farther south lies Bethlehem, according to biblical tradition the birthplace of Jesus.

Merkava Mark IV tank of the 188th Armored Brigade on maneuvers in the Negev desert, 2018. *IDF*

The Geography of Israel

Merkava Mark IV of the 7th Armored Brigade guarding a flank on the Golan Heights. In the background is the snow-covered Hermon massif, situated in the border region between Lebanon and Syria, 2012. *IDF*

In the south of Israel lies the triangular Negev desert region, with Be'er Sheva as its capital. In the southeast, the triangle runs toward Eilat, a commercially important port for Israel and therefore also the cause of numerous military conflicts. There are essentially two political entities on the territory of Palestine: the state of Israel and the territories occupied by Israel or autonomously administered by Palestinians. Today's borders are based on agreements between the colonial powers Great Britain and France, which divided up the territory controlled by the former Ottoman Empire after the First World War. The north, with Lebanon and Syria, fell under French rule and the south with Palestine and Jordan under British rule. The southern border, which runs along the Sinai and the Gulf of Aqaba, dates back to an agreement between the Ottoman Empire and Egypt.

Israel's borders with the neighboring Arab states have been subjects of contention by several sides since the founding of Israel in 1948, triggering numerous conflicts and sometimes fierce disputes.

PORTRAIT OF YIGAL ALLON

Allon was a Sabra, a Jew born in Palestine, and not only his parents but his grandparents as well lived there. Allon, born Paicovitch, came into the world in 1918 in Kfar Tabor, a settlement in the Galilee cofounded by his parents. In the turbulent 1930s, he gained his first military experience defending Jewish communities against Arab attacks, but he later grew up in the Haganah and its elite force, the Palmach.

In the final years of the Second World War, he served in the Palmach and became its commander at the age of twenty-six in 1945. Allon was responsible not only for the battles against the Arabs and the British occupying power, but also for the illegal immigration organized against Britain's will and the equally illegal establishment of new settlements. These were often located deep in Arab residential areas and had to be defended even during their construction.

After the expiry of the British Palestine Mandate, the survival of the Jewish population depended solely on the power of its weapons. Allon emerged from the First Arab-Israeli War—the War of Independence of 1948–49—as the most important commander of Israel's armed forces. In the first months of the war, he organized the defense of the Galilee, and later—after being promoted to major general—he led the troops that kept the road to Jerusalem open and prevented the army of Transjordan from cutting the country in two on the central front.

Finally, he led the operations against Egypt that secured the Negev with the port of Eilat, the vital access to the Red Sea, for Israel. However, differences of opinion arose with state founder David Ben Gurion, who wanted to end the advance in the Negev. Allon wanted to continue fighting, and as a result of this dispute Ben Gurion later appointed Yigael Yadin as chief of staff instead of him.

It was Allon's military operations to which Israel owed not only its existence, but also its continued existence as a viable state to a large extent. In those times of uneasy peace, Allon turned to a political career. After five years of study at Israeli and English universities, he was elected to the Knesset in 1955. He went on to hold numerous political offices in the governments of Levi Eshkol, Golda Meir, and Yitzhak Rabin.

In 1967, he negotiated a peace agreement with Jordan, which is still known today as the Allon Plan. This plan envisaged an Israeli annexation of parts of the West Bank, including the Jordan Valley. The predominantly Arab-populated parts of the

After the death of Levi Eshkol, Yigal Allon briefly held the office of prime minister pending new elections. The photo was taken during a press conference in Jerusalem in 1966. *Israel Government Press Office*

Portrait of Yigal Allon

Yigal Allon (*third from left*) with members of his staff at a crossroad in Abu Ageila during the War of Independence of 1948–49. *Israel Government Press Office*

area, on the other hand, were to be brought into a political union with Jordan. The plan attached great importance to secure borders and demanded a certain willingness to make territorial concessions from the parties involved. Allon was also involved in drawing up a peace treaty with Egypt in 1979.

Allon also harbored ambitions for the post of prime minister. After the death of Levi Eshkol in 1969, he took over the reins of government on an interim basis and, along with Moshe Dayan, was one of the favorites to take over permanently. However, he was persuaded to give way to Golda Meir. When Meir resigned in 1974, the next opportunity presented itself, but for internal party reasons he withdrew his candidacy, leaving the post to Yitzhak Rabin.

Allon died on February 29, 1980, and was buried on March 3 at his second place of residence, Kibbutz Ginosar on the Sea of Galilee. The Yigal Allon Museum and Educational Center has been located there since 1987.

CHAPTER 1: Creation of the Israeli Armed Forces | 25

THE ETZEL AND LECHI

Although the Jewish population remained relatively small during the prestate phase, the political landscape was characterized by ideological sectarianism and a patchwork of competing parties and groups. Even in Ben Gurion's social-democratic workers' party Mapai, a leftist wing loyal to the Soviets under Yitzhak Tabenkin, which had a great deal of influence on the Palmach, was making noise.

The Haganah, too, did not present itself as an ideologically united front. There were many supporters of Jabotinsky and his revisionist Betar Zionism in its ranks. The social and political background of many urban Haganah members contrasted too sharply with the broad base of the collective settlements. After the riots of 1929, resistance to the Havlagah policy in the Jerusalem Haganah formed from these ranks around Avraham Teomi, who founded the Haganah Beth in 1931 with some of his followers.

Together with like-minded people from the Betar youth groups in Haifa, Jaffa, and Tel Aviv, the Irgun Zwai Leumi (National Military Organization) developed within a few years, the Hebrew initials of which then became the acronym "Etzel." Unlike the Haganah, the new underground movement established rigid command structures with ranks, organized by groups, sections, and local branches. Formal service and parade drill were replaced by political seminars and sabotage training.

Initially, the Irgun saw itself only as an alternative self-protection militia to the Haganah and succeeded in establishing branches in smaller towns from Rehovot to Rosh Pina. But in the course of the Arab terrorism by the insurgents of 1936–39, individual Etzel cells made a name for themselves with reprisal actions and their own bombings. With increasing British repression against Jewish immigration, the Irgun increasingly directed its activism against the Mandate authorities and their police.

The discussion about this led to an open break within the organization as early as April 1937: more than 1,500 returned to the Haganah, while most of the remaining 1,800 came from the ranks of the Betar. They now joined the leadership of Jabotinksy, who was living in exile and appointed Avraham Stern,[12] David Raziel, and Moshe Rozenberg as new leaders. In November, the Irgun officially declared its renunciation of the Haganah's policy of restraint, which only intensified the British measures and resulted in two assassins being sentenced to death a few months later.

It was only after the outbreak of the Second World War that the Irgun suspended its small-scale war against the British and, like the Haganah, joined the war effort. David Raziel was killed in May 1941 by a German air raid during a commando operation in Iraq. For other activists, such cooperation with England was unacceptable: in 1940, Stern resigned from his Irgun leadership post and founded the Lohamei Cherut Israel, the Fighters for the Freedom of Israel, alias "Lechi," with a handful of radicals in September. The small group continued its underground struggle, financed by bank robberies and declaring itself to be anti-imperialist, in the form of targeted terrorist attacks on individuals and British institutions. Their actions were not well received in the Yishuv; even in its best days after the war, the splinter group, also known as the Stern Gang, had no more than four hundred members. It did not leave behind a political party.

Not so the Irgun: in 1942, General Anders's exiled Polish army corps passed through Palestine, and numerous Polish Jewish soldiers took the opportunity to go into hiding in the Yishuv, including the lawyer and Betar party functionary Menachem Begin, who quickly breathed new life into the Irgun, which had been disoriented by the events of the war, and committed it to an anti-British course.

In February 1944, it broke the ceasefire and declared a revolt against the mandate, which it heralded with bomb attacks against the finance and immigration offices in Jerusalem, Tel Aviv, and Haifa, followed by attacks on police stations ostensibly intended to procure weapons. Probably the most famous Irgun action was the attack on July 22, 1946, on the King David Hotel in Jerusalem, the then headquarters of the British general staff, in which ninety-one people were killed. This terrorist attack led to the final break with the Haganah. British prime minister Winston Churchill also strongly condemned the attack.

In June 1948, the Irgun and Lechi merged into the Israeli Defense Forces. Both groups together had barely more than four thousand men under arms at the outbreak of the war. Politically, Begin survived as the leader of the right-wing conservative Cherut Party, which he founded in August 1948.

---

[12] Avraham Stern (1907–42) grew up in Poland and moved to Palestine during the Bolshevik Revolution. After studying in Jerusalem, he first joined the Irgun resistance movement but founded the Lechi in 1939. Under unexplained circumstances, Stern was shot dead by a British policeman in 1942

OF ARMORED VEHICLES AND SANDWICH TRUCKS

The British military had already demonstrated the advantages of the Rolls-Royce and Lanchester armored car chassis equipped with a machine gun turret in the Middle East during the First World War. They continued to serve well in Mesopotamia, Egypt, and Palestine, putting restless inhabitants or boisterous nomadic tribes in their place. In the Mandate territory, they were considered the *ultima ratio* when it came to securing transportation routes to isolated settlements and bus traffic between cities.

The Palestine police also began fitting light touring cars and flatbed trucks with armor plating for protection against small-arms fire at an early stage. The first armored cars came from the Wagner Brothers iron foundry, a long-established metal workshop of the German Templar community in Jaffa. Later, other companies in Tel Aviv and Haifa also tried their hand at such conversions, and during the Arab uprising of 1936–39, they even armored the buses of the Jewish transport cooperative Egged, which the Yishuv derisively called "Havlagah buses."

Even with the escalation of the internal situation in 1946–47, the Haganah had no legal means of procuring tanks or armored personnel carriers. The Mandate permitted the construction of armored driver's cabs only for trucks or vans, but without armament.

This resulted in a large number of improvised armored vehicles, which were of various shapes depending on the chassis on which they were based. Fortunately, there was a large surplus of trucks after the end of the Second World War.

Because good steel plates were in short supply in Palestine, layered armor was used, consisting of thin steel plates 3–5 millimeters (mm) thick, between which was packed a layer of wood 1–4 mm (0.04–0.16 inches) thick to stop bullets — sandwich style, which gave the vehicles their name.

There was the fully enclosed truck based on the pug-nosed CMP (Canadian Military Pattern) trucks in the 1.5-to-3-ton versions with a sloping roof and two winglike roof hatches, which earned it the nickname Parpar (butterfly). Later, when the Yishuv also bought up decommissioned US Army Dodge WC-52s, these were given a similar body and used as section and radio vehicles.

At the end of the Mandate, there also appeared small manually rotated armored turrets with sloping sides and flexible ball mounts for the passenger seat, with which the armored cars armed with machine guns could actively engage in battle. The man who came up with these things was a certain Joseph "Joe" Kryden, son of Russian emigrants who had come to Palestine before the outbreak of war.

Kryden enlisted in the British army and ran repair workshops for the Eighth Army in Egypt. After the end of the war, he made his knowledge and extensive experience available to the Haganah headquarters. He coordinated the work by the various companies and endeavored to standardize construction methods. By mid-May 1948, over 120 armored cars had left the factories of Magen-Chetwood in Petach Tikva, Ha'argaz in Tel Aviv, Harash near Ramat Gan, and the union-owned metalworks of Solel Boneh in the up-and-coming "Steel City" of Haifa Bay.

A good step toward standardization was taken when a number of the M3A1 Scout Car armored reconnaissance vehicles from the White Motor Company were purchased from France and Italy. Originally designed for American cavalry regiments, during the Second World War the all-terrain, open-top, four-wheel-drive vehicle was always overshadowed by the M3 half-track infantry fighting vehicle with its more powerful engine. Thanks to the improvisational skills of Joe Kryden and his technicians, it became the main combat vehicle used by the armored battalions of the fledgling Israeli armed forces.

Chapter 2
The Jewish Brigade in the Second World War

In the late summer of 1944, Allied armored units finally broke out of the beachheads in Normandy and drove through France and Belgium to the banks of the Rhine. Paris was liberated, and in London the victory bells were ringing. In the east, after the German retreat in the south and the destruction of Army Group Center, in the summer of 1944 Stalin's Red Army was nearing the Balkans. Germany's military situation appeared hopeless. As a result of persistent pressure from the Jewish Agency, British prime minister Churchill finally recognized the right of Jews to serve to serve in the British army.

Chaim Weizmann,[1] the president of the Zionist Congress, had offered Churchill a Jewish military unit under British leadership to support combat operations against Nazi Germany. While the British Cabinet had been debating Weizmann's proposal since the outbreak of the war, it had so far rejected all proposals.

For years, Churchill had been putting off representatives of the Yishuv with excuses such as too little equipment or inadequate training. Behind these excuses was the not entirely unfounded fear that the Jews might once again take up arms against the British in Palestine. Moreover, the politicians in the London ministries feared Arab resentment and a resurgence of protests in Egypt and the other neighboring Arab states.

When plans for the destruction of the Third Reich were presented in the fall of 1944 and eyewitness reports foreshadowed the extent of the Nazi crimes against the Jews, Churchill finally agreed to the formation of the unit. During Rosh HaShanah, the Jewish new year, the British government issued a communiqué announcing the formation of a Jewish brigade. Its headquarters were to be in Cairo, the Star of David on a blue-and-white flag was to serve as its official banner, and British major Ernest Frank Benjamin[2] was to lead the unit.

Most of the soldiers came from the Jewish-Arab Palestinian Regiment, which had already been increased to battalion strength in 1943. These now formed the basic personnel structure of the Jewish Brigade. With additional Jewish volunteers, the 1st to 3rd Infantry Battalions and the 200th Artillery Regiment were formed with around five thousand troops.

Benjamin proudly announced to his officers that these were the first official Jewish combat troops since Roman legions conquered Judea around two thousand years ago. In October 1944, the Jewish Brigade shipped out to Italy, where it joined the Eighth Army as part of General Sir Harold Alexander's Fifteenth Army Group.

On the Italian peninsula, the British Eighth Army formed the right wing of the Allied front, while the US Fifth Army covered the left wing. After the final offensive on Monte Cassino, the Eighth Army, led by Lieutenant General Richard McCreery, pushed through the Gothic Line between Florence and Rimini and continued its march toward the Po Valley.

The situation on the German-Italian front was calm. The Wehrmacht moved into staging areas south of Bologna with elements of the twenty-three German divisions that made up Army Group C under the command of Feldmarschall Albert Kesselring. River courses flowing down from the Apennine mountain range formed a series of natural obstacles, which the German troops turned into a defensive line.

From east to west, in addition to the Reno, this line also included the Irmgard Position on the Senio, the Laura Position on the Santero, the Paula Position on the Sillaro, and the Anna Position on the Gaiana. Further natural obstacles were formed by the northern foothills of the Apennines between Faenza and Modena and the Comacchio lagoons. Half a million soldiers faced each other on both sides of this extended line.

---

[1] Chaim Weizmann (1874–1952) grew up in Motal in what is now the republic of Belarus. He studied at the Technical University in Darmstadt, became a British citizen in 1910, and was director of a munitions laboratory during the First World War. He took an early interest in the writings of Theodor Herzl, and in 1921 he took office as president of the World Zionist Organization (WZO). Following the proclamation of the Declaration of Independence in 1948, the Constituent Assembly elected him as the first president of the state of Israel. He died in 1952 at his home, now the Weizmann Institute.

[2] Ernest Frank Benjamin (1900–69), born in Toronto, Canada, served as a cadet at the Royal Military Academy, Woolwich. After various troop and staff assignments, he was on the staff of the British Middle East Command. After leaving the Jewish Brigade at the end of the war, he continued to serve in the British army as a colonel and later as a brigadier.

Jewish troops in British service marching in a parade along Petah-Tikva Street, September 1942.
Israel Government Press Office

If the Wehrmacht was not exhausted by the end of the winter due to the weather, a final Allied offensive would force a decision in the Italian campaign. First, however, winter was just around the corner, and the Jewish Brigade was impatiently awaiting its first deployment in Fiuggi, around 80 kilometers east of Rome.

Kesselring had confidence in his defensive dispositions and formulated his battle plan as follows:

- In the first phase, the aim is to stall the onrushing opponent on the riverbanks south of Bologna for as long as possible.
- In the second phase, the troops were to withdraw quickly to the fortified defense line in the rear, which followed the winding course of the Reno River north of Bologna. From these elevated positions, artillery and tanks were to be deployed against the approaching enemy to further delay their advance.
- In the third phase, another, third line of defense was to be used to finally halt the enemy advance.

Alexander, on the other hand, planned to push the enemy back to the banks of the Po in the spring with a concentrated thrust. The Allies were to quickly overcome the network of positions around the Reno River, with its natural obstacles, and drive the Wehrmacht out of its defensive positions under pressure in order to thwart a reorganization and renewed counterattack across the Po.

The Fifth Army was to attack west of the Reno by using a classic encirclement, analogous to Hannibal's tactic at Cannae, and hold the enemy's rear defenses in check. At the same time, the Eighth Army would advance into the heart of the defensive system on the Romagna rivers. The battered German army would be trapped in the plain between the two rivers.

CHAPTER 2: The Jewish Brigade in the Second World War | 29

A British poster recruiting volunteers to serve in the Jewish Brigade during the Second World War. *Wikipedia*

The Jewish Brigade consisted of around five thousand Jewish volunteers and was formed in September 1944. It fought alongside the British army in Italy from March to May 1945. The photo shows Jewish soldiers during a break in the fighting in Italy, March 1945. *Yad Vashem Photo Archives*

Before the offensive, Alexander planned a series of smaller advance actions that served two tactical goals:

- Deception: German troops were to mistake the action for the main attack, deploy forces, and thus weaken their main defensive positions.
- Envelopment: By means of advanced river crossings, troops were to get behind the German lines to the east in order to take some of the pressure off the main thrust by the Eighth Army.

The Senio River, which had to be crossed during one of these advance actions, played a decisive role in this plan. McCreery entrusted the Jewish Brigade with the task of crossing the river. On April 10, 1945, the unit crossed the river over pontoon bridges previously built by engineers. American aircraft covered the operation. The soldiers were met by resistance from machine guns on the opposite bank, but this was quickly silenced by Allied artillery, enabling the Jewish Brigade to gain a foothold on the north bank and establish the all-important bridgehead.

CHAPTER 2: The Jewish Brigade in the Second World War

Born in Toronto, Canada, Ernest Frank Benjamin served as a young lieutenant in the Royal Engineers, and later as a captain in the divisional engineers of the 49th Division. After service as a staff officer and promotion to brigadier in Near East Command, in September 1944 he took over the Jewish Brigade as its commander. In the photo he is seen inspecting men of the Jewish Brigade's 2nd Battalion at Alexandria in Egypt, October 1944. *Wikipedia*

The Wehrmacht continued to hold its high, mountainous positions on the other side of the river. The Allied High Command feared that the enemy could threaten the entire bridgehead from this strategically favorable position, especially with its artillery on the crest of Monte Ghebbio.

The general staff of the Eighth Army ordered the Jewish Brigade to eliminate the artillery on this mountain massif in order to prevent the shelling of the bridgehead. The capture was successful, but the Germans were already on the run and even left numerous guns behind on Monte Ghebbio. The Allies now advanced unopposed, overrunning Forli, Imola, and Castel San Pietro, pushing the Wehrmacht toward the Po Valley, and captured Bologna after heavy and costly fighting.

The German plan to reorganize for the final battle in the defensive positions behind the Po line could never be implemented. More and more of the exhausted German soldiers surrendered to the advancing Allies.

On April 14, 1945, the Jewish Brigade was ordered to remain in front of Bologna while the remaining Allied units pushed on after the retreating enemy. However, the decision for the brigade to halt was not based on military considerations, but rather on British policy in Palestine. The brigade had suffered a heavy death toll of fifty-seven dead and 150 wounded during its short forty-eight-day deployment at the front. The British government therefore came to the conclusion that the already strained relationship with the Jewish Agency would be completely

In 1945 the Jewish Brigade fought alongside the British Eighth Army during the Allied spring offensive in Italy. The photo shows men of Company A of the 1st Battalion of the Jewish Brigade on a Churchill tank during a pause in the fighting. *IWM*

Sappers of the Jewish Brigade eating a meal in Italy. Behind them is a knocked-out Panzerkampfwagen V Panther tank, April 1945. *IWM*

shattered if the impression arose that Jewish soldiers would be used only as cannon fodder in the further course of the war.

The war was therefore to end without any further combat operations by the brigade. On May 2, 1945, the German high command in Italy surrendered. The brigade was ordered to take up quarters in Tarvisio—located in the border triangle of Italy, Yugoslavia, and Austria—and set up guard posts. This insignificant town became a stopover for thousands of refugees on their way to the West.

As part of the VIII Corps, the brigade set off on its long journey back to Palestine with six hundred vehicles in July 1945. The brigade passed through bases in the Netherlands and Belgium and also passed through a devastated Germany, with mixed feelings.

For the soldiers of the Jewish Brigade, service in the British army provided valuable experience in the use of armored weapons, artillery, and aircraft. This would have been difficult for those in the Haganah underground army to obtain in any other way. In addition, the framework of a brigade group made it possible for commanders and officers assigned to the staffs to acquire knowledge in the leadership of larger formations.

Two future chiefs of the Israeli general staff, Mordechai Maklef and Chaim Laskov, served as staff officers in the Jewish Brigade.

The then-still-unknown Israel Tal, a section leader in the Jewish Brigade, also achieved honor and fame as a pioneer of Israeli tank doctrine and as the commander of an armored division in the Sinai during the Six-Day War.

CHAPTER 2: The Jewish Brigade in the Second World War | 33

Chapter 3
The Haganah on the Road to War

On November 29, 1947, the General Assembly of the United Nations voted by a majority to end the British Mandate in Palestine. In accordance with the Partition Plan, the land was to be divided into independent Jewish and Arab states as part of a two-state solution, with Jerusalem remaining an international enclave. This was a great moment for Zionism, but a dark day for all the surrounding Arab states, which vehemently voted against this plan. An attack by the Arabs seemed inevitable after the Mandate was revoked in May 1948. This meant that the time had come for the Haganah to leave the underground and form a regular armed force.

The United Nations plan envisaged

- the end of the British Mandate in Palestine and the withdrawal of all armed forces and
- the establishment of the two new independent states and the international administration for the city of Jerusalem no later than October 1, 1948.

The partition plan envisaged the following territories for the independent Jewish state:

- the northern and central coastal plain from Rosh Hanikra to Rehovot
- the eastern Galilee around the Sea of Galilee
- the Negev desert in the south as far as Umm Rashrash (present-day Eilat)

The following areas fell to the new Arab state:

- West Galilee with the city of Akko
- the mountainous region of Judea and Samaria
- the southern coastline as far as Majdal (present-day Ashkalon), equivalent to almost all of the present-day Gaza Strip
- a strip of desert along the Egyptian border

Due to its religious significance, the city of Jerusalem, including the surrounding communities, was to become an international zone under the administration of the United Nations.

All five Arab countries that threatened the future Jewish state with war pursued the enforcement of their own claims to power in Palestine:

- The corrupt and greedy King Farouk of Egypt dreamed of a new great caliphate that would dominate Palestine and wrest control of the Suez Canal from the hated British.
- The Iraqi government was prepared to accept the establishment of the state of Israel if Great Britain allowed Iraq to annex Syria in return.
- The regime in Damascus, Syria, was well aware of these demands and took part in the war against the Jewish state primarily to prevent the strengthening of its Arab rivals.
- Lebanon was more in favor of an immediate guerrilla war than any other Arab state.
- King Abdullah of Transjordan wanted to use the favorable opportunity to expand his empire at the expense of the Arab state envisaged in the UN partition plan. He intended to annex the land west of the Jordan—the West Bank—as well as Jerusalem.

The day after the United Nations decision, Arab insurgents fired on a Jewish bus, attacked supply convoys on their way to Jerusalem, and set fire to shops near Lod Airport (later Ben Gurion Airport). In the three urban zones with mixed populations, Jaffa / Tel Aviv, Haifa, and Jerusalem, Arab snipers opened fire on the Jewish population, often pitting neighborhood against neighborhood.

The British saw little reason to intervene; they were primarily concerned with the smooth evacuation of their forces, with the main focus on the port of Haifa and the military camps at Rafah and the railroad line from there to Egypt.

Haganah's acting commander, Yisrael Galili,[1] recognized that its previous main task—namely, the defense of the Jewish population—now required, under the changed conditions, the formation of an offensive force. This was not a problem in terms of personnel, because after the end of the Second World War, thousands of Jewish soldiers returned to their homes from British military service.

Palmach soldiers of the Harel Brigade riding in an armored truck, part of a supply convoy to Jerusalem, 1947. *Israel Government Press Office*

By the end of March 1948, the Haganah had succeeded in mobilizing about 21,000 men and, with them, formed the first four Hish brigades. For the greater Jerusalem area, in November 1947 the High Command established the Etzioni or Jerusalem Brigade from local field companies.

Next, in December 1947 the Haganah formed the Givati Brigade for the coastal plain and the center of the country. This unit initially fought in the Yaffa-Ramla area and also defended Tel Aviv together with subunits of the Alexandroni Brigade, which was renamed Brigade No. 3 in mid-1948. Shortly before the founding of the state, Givati was reinforced with new recruits and transferred to the northern Negev as the now newly numbered 5th Infantry Brigade.

Meanwhile the Kiryati Brigade, the Haganah's fourth brigade, assumed responsibility for the defense of Tel Aviv and the Gush Dan.

From the Levanoni unit, which was initially intended for the north, in February 1948 there emerged the Golani and Carmeli Brigades, the first and second infantry brigades. Both were initially responsible for the north from the Jordan River to the Mediterranean coast south of Haifa.

In the northern sector, Battalions 1 and 3 merged to form the Yiftach Brigade, which was directly subordinate to Yigal Allon and was headquartered in the Kibbutz Ayelet HaShachar.

The Harel Brigade, the third Palmach, was officially launched by Yigal Allon on April 16, 1948. Its core was formed by the escort troops for the supply convoys from Tel Aviv. Yitzhak Rabin,[2] the former operations officer of the Palmach and Allon's deputy, was placed in command of the brigade.

Protection for the supply convoys was provided by the first mechanized units with armored vehicles. Legally, however, the Haganah saw no possibility of procuring armored vehicles, tanks, or infantry fighting vehicles, since the British Mandate still prohibited the required weapons and equipment. The Haganah therefore procured the following armored vehicles by covert means, subsequently repairing, rebuilding, and upgrading them:

- **PMF Daimler Armored Cars Mark I**
These vehicles weighed about 7.6 tons, reached a top speed of 50 mph (80 kph), and were armed with one 7.92 mm machine gun. The majority were used as reconnaissance vehicles.
- **Ten Hotchkiss H-39 Tanks**
These French-made light tanks weighed 13.2 tons (12 metric tons) and were armed with a 37 mm main gun and one 7.5 mm machine gun. Range on roads was 93 miles (150 km), and the vehicle had a top speed of 22 mph (36 kph).
- **Two Cromwell Mark IV Tanks**
This British medium tank had a crew of five and weighed 30.9 tons (28 metric tons). It was armed with a 75 mm main gun and two 7.92 mm machine guns. Range on roads was 173 miles (278 km), and maximum speed was 38 mph (61 kph).
- **Four M4 Sherman Tanks**
The American-made medium tank weighed about 33 tons

---

[1] Yisrael Galili (1911–86) grew up in Brailov, Ukraine, and immigrated to Palestine with his parents at the age of three. He joined the Haganah in 1927 and was promoted to the high command as early as 1935. In 1946, he took over the office of chief of staff of the Haganah until David Ben Gurion relieved him of his duties when the Israeli armed forces were founded. Galili began a political career in 1949, joining the Knesset and taking on numerous political functions. He served for over a decade as one of the most important advisors to Prime Minister Golda Meir.

[2] Yitzhak Rabin (1922–95), born and raised in Jerusalem, joined the Haganah in 1938, served in the British army during the Syrian-Lebanese campaign in 1941, and took over various Palmach units as deputy commander from 1945. As a major general, he took over the training of the Israeli army in 1953. This was followed by his appointment as chief of staff in 1964 and his triumphant victory during the Six-Day War in 1967. In 1973, Rabin was elected to the Israeli Parliament and served as minister of labor under Golda Meir. This was followed in 1984 by his appointment as minister of defense under Shimon Peres, later becoming prime minister of Israel. He was considered an important advocate of the peace process in the Middle East and was awarded the Nobel Peace Prize together with Yasser Arafat, the chairman of the Palestine Liberation Organization (PLO). He was assassinated in 1995 during a peace rally in Tel Aviv.

(30 metric tons) and was armed with a 75 mm main gun and two 7.62 mm machine guns.

- **Dodge and Chevrolet 4 × 4 Trucks**

These trucks were usually armored with 8.5 mm steel plates in the cargo area and 5 mm steel plates in the driver's cab, but these offered only inadequate protection for the driver and crew. One or two machine guns were usually mounted on simple superstructures. The additional load of around 1.5 tons considerably reduced the top speed of these vehicles, which were also known as "sandwich trucks."

- **M3A1 Scout Car**

This was a light armored vehicle up-armored with steel plates but with only a light armament.

A jeep used in the reconnaissance role, armed with two MG34 machine guns from Czechoslovakian surplus stocks, 1947. *IDF*

The Haganah concentrated its small force of armored vehicles in the 8th Armored Brigade, the first armored unit of the Jewish armed forces. The brigade, which was based in Tel Aviv, was commanded by Palmach officer Yitzhak Sadeh.

Sadeh equipped the 82nd Armored Battalion under the command of Felix Beatus[3] with all his light and medium tanks, and the 89th Mechanized Battalion under Moshe Dayan with the remaining armed vehicles.

The most important armed force during the Arab unrest was the so-called Arab Legion. These were Palestinian Arabs who were effectively subordinate to the British military authorities but were as yet not very structured and relied on spontaneous support from fellow villagers and tribesmen during operations.

M3A1 Scout Car armed with two MG34 machine guns, 1947. *IDF*

With the help of the Arab League, the Palestinian Arabs procured important resources such as money, weapons, and volunteers abroad for military purposes. Among the volunteers were numerous foreign officers, who were spread across the various parts of the country and ultimately formed the hard core of the fighting units.

The decentralized Arab units operated among themselves without a uniform command-and-control organization, and therefore with little coordination. At the head of the Arab population in the mandate area was the Supreme Arab Council, under the leadership of the Palestinian Mufti of Jerusalem Hadj Amin el-Husseini.[4] The leaders of the decentralized units acted

---

[3] Felix Beatus (1917–92) grew up in a Jewish family in Czechoslovakia. He served in the Red Army at the beginning of the Second World War, and later in the newly formed Polish army. Beatus rose from tank driver to brigade commander and moved to Palestine after the end of the war, where he joined the Haganah. Sadeh made use of Beatus's experience in the operation of mechanized formations and put him in command of the 82nd Armored Battalion of the 8th Armored Brigade.

[4] From an influential family, Hadj Amin el-Husseini (1887–1974) grew up in Jerusalem and became the leader of the Palestinians in 1921. During the Arab riots in the 1930s, he acted as a spokesman for all Arabs in Palestine and voiced support for the Nazi government's persecution of the Jews. After the War of Independence in 1948, he lost his political positions and found asylum in Egypt. He was a relative, teacher, and supporter of Yasser Arafat, who later became the leader of the PLO.

Yitzhak Rabin assumes command of the Harel Brigade, 1948. *Israel Government Press Office*)

at their own discretion and turned to the Supreme Arab Council only for financial or military support.

In the early stages of the war, their arsenal consisted mainly of rifles and light small arms. Only the Arab Legion possessed support weapons, heavy equipment, and armored vehicles. Air and naval forces, tanks, and artillery appeared only with the intervention of the regular Arab armies after the withdrawal of the British Mandate.

Toward the end of the Mandate there were around 100,000 British troops in Palestine, with the most-important military bases concentrated on the coastal plain in the middle of the Jewish population centers. Following the decision to withdraw, the British High Command was primarily concerned with ensuring a smooth evacuation in accordance with the evacuation plan. The main focus of the evacuation was on the port of Haifa and the area around Rafah.

Meanwhile, fighting with Arab units continued to increase. In towns with mixed populations, Arab snipers fired on the Jewish population; in Haifa, bombs exploded at the Jewish bus station; and in Jerusalem there were attacks on the editorial office of the Palestine Post and on numerous mosques.

The British military limited its active intervention in the ongoing battles to the bare minimum. Only the British police continued to be a disruptive factor for the Jewish forces, since the police forces were still making efforts to confiscate illegal Jewish weapons and hand over vacated positions to the Arabs.

But the Haganah did not remain idle either and shelled Arab villages such as Salame, near Tel Aviv, and Balad al-Sheik, southeast of Haifa. The situation threatened to escalate further throughout the country. Attacks followed on kibbutzes in northeastern and western Galilee, in the Jewish settlements in the mountains of Hebron south of Jerusalem, in the Sharon Plain, and in the Negev and around Gaza.

During all these events, there was also a need to secure long-distance transportation and supplies on the main routes between Jerusalem and the Jewish settlements in the eastern and western Galilee. The Haganah primarily used armored vehicles to protect the transport convoys.

However, the Haganah soon had doubts as to whether every Jewish settlement could actually be held against the superior strength of the enemy. In addition to military failures, it also faced a new political challenge: the United States announced its intention to no longer support the United Nations partition plan, since it feared that chaotic conditions would prevail in the country after the withdrawal of the British mandate. This American stance significantly boosted the morale of the Arabs but shattered the hopes of the Jews.

At the beginning of April 1948, the Haganah decided to use a military operation to recapture the route to Jerusalem, which had been blocked by the Arabs, and then to keep it open for its own supplies. The operation was code-named Nachshon, named after a chieftain of the tribe of Judah who, according to biblical legend, was the first to walk into the Red Sea during the Hebrew exodus from Egypt.

The plan envisaged the combining of three battalions into a battle group to conquer and secure the area on both sides of the road. A coincidence facilitated the landing of weapons from Czechoslovakia, including Mauser type 98 rifles and MG 34 machine guns. Operation Nachshon began on the night of April 6, 1948.

Numerous Arab strongpoints on both sides of the road to Jerusalem were recaptured by the battle group after fierce fighting and heavy losses. Only a section still occupied by British troops between Latrun and Bab el-Wad remained in enemy hands, since the Jews wanted to avoid a clash with the Mandate. The Jewish convoys were already rolling into Jerusalem undisturbed, ensuring the supply of the city.

Chevrolet CMP (Canadian Military Pattern) truck with Arab insurgents during a push toward Nablus, 1947. *Wikipedia*

CHAPTER 3: The Haganah on the Road to War | 37

M4 medium tank, the first captured Sherman to see action with the Israeli armed forces, 1948. *Israel Government Press Office*

Although not all the objectives of the operation were achieved, Nachshon was an historic turning point in the Haganah's conduct of the war.

For the first time, the Jewish armed forces seized the initiative and fought as a united fighting unit under unified command and with air support, albeit still with improvised weapons. Nachshon meant the transition from disorganized, raid-like offensive tactics to the systematic conquest of Arab-occupied territories.

As a result of the dramatic military situation, the general staff of the Haganah leadership drew up a comprehensive plan for the further conduct of the war. Daleth is the fourth letter of the Hebrew alphabet, and this was therefore the fourth variant of a general war plan. The central idea of Daleth was to achieve control of all the territories of the future Jewish state and secure their defense against a possible invasion by neighboring Arab countries.

The plan was based on a force of 30,000 soldiers. It defined a territorial organization for all units of the army and ensured that there was a battle plan for each brigade. In the course of numerous successful attacks, the Haganah succeeded, on the one hand, in ensuring the territorial unity of the Jewish parts of the country and their connection to one another, and, on the other hand, in also bringing the Arab-held territories under its control and expanding the defenses in anticipation of an imminent invasion.

Colorized photograph of an armored tractor guarding the harvest against attack, Jesreel Plain, 1937. *Israel Government Press Office*

Members of Palmach. *Israel Government Press Office*

The Haganah thus controlled the following areas:

- Upper and Lower Galilee with the Arab centers of Samach and Bet Sche'an and the mixed Jewish-Arab cities of Safed and Tiberias
- western Galilee with Haifa and its mixed population
- the Arab city of Jaffa
- large parts of the new city of Jerusalem, the Jerusalem corridor, and access to the northern Negev.

However, the Haganah also suffered serious setbacks during this time, with considerable losses, the destruction of numerous vehicles, and the destruction of several settlements in the Jerusalem area. Nevertheless, the outcome was not unfavorable. The far-better-fortified defensive positions of the Jewish settlements alone were proof of this.

On May 14, 1948, after the withdrawal of the last British soldiers, the members of the Provisional People's Assembly met in the Tel Aviv Museum. The chairman of the People's Administration and later the country's first prime minister, David Ben Gurion, issued the official declaration of independence and proclaimed the founding of the state of Israel.

Just four days before the proclamation, Golda Meir, as president of the Jewish Agency, had held secret negotiations with the Jordanian king Abdallah, with the intention of keeping the Arab Legion out of the impending military conflicts. However, no common denominator for a peaceful solution was found, and Meir finally declared, "The Arabs want to see us dead. We want to live. There is no compromise."

On May 15, 1948, shortly after midnight and the expiry of the British Mandate in Palestine, the surrounding Arab states of Egypt, Jordan, Lebanon, Iraq, and Syria, supported by the Arab-Palestinian leadership in the country, declared war on the new state of Israel.

Chapter 4
The First Armored Vehicles: Renault, Hotchkiss, and Cromwell

THE RENAULT R-35: DEVELOPMENT

The French tanks produced between the two world wars were already at a high level in terms of quality and quantity. Despite this, French military thinking at that time was rigid and based on conservative thinking.

The French armored forces thus remained subordinate to the infantry, and the new weapon's potential initially went unrecognized. This organization was retained until the outbreak of the Second World War and was reflected both in the development and design of French tanks.

General Jean-Baptiste Eugène Estienne, responsible for French tank development, campaigned with all his might to change this shortsighted concept. Despite his influential position, he was unable to convince the French leadership of the tank's superiority in the context of modern warfare.

In the interwar period, four main tanks were developed in France: the heavy Char B, the medium Somua 35 and the Renault R-35, and Hotchkiss H-35 light tanks. According to French doctrine, these four vehicle types were intended purely as support tanks for the infantry, which was reflected in design features such as short driving range, low speed, and poor radio equipment.

The following requirements were placed on the further development of the Renault FT-17, which had proven itself in the First World War: a two-man tank with a weight of 8 tons and thicker (40 mm) armor that offered the vehicle adequate protection against antitank guns. It was armed with either machine guns or a 37 mm cannon. In view of its traditional role as an infantry support vehicle, the speed was intended to be only 9–12 mph (15–20 kph) and its range limited to 25 miles (40 km).

Renault only partially met these requirements with its new tank concept. One prototype had just 30 mm of armor and weighed 10 tons despite the new specifications.

Due to the constantly deteriorating international situation, this model, the Char Léger Modèle 1935 R, was ordered even before it could be fully tested.

The Renault R-35 was designed with a three-part cast superstructure mounted on an armor plate underneath. The running gear was mounted on the side plates and consisted of five rubber-tired wheels on each side, mounted side by side and suspended on angle levers and springs.

In 1940, a new version of the R-35 appeared. This tank, which bore either the designation R-40 or AMX-40, was a product of the Atelier de Construction d'Issy-les-Moulineaux, a branch of the Renault company.

Between 1935 and 1940, Renault produced 1,600 examples of the standard R-35, of which around 850 saw frontline service.

Although the R-35 was superior to the German Panzer I and II tanks in terms of firepower and armor protection, it achieved little success.

The tank's main gun, with a muzzle velocity of just 1,273 ft./sec. (388 m/sec.), was ill suited to tank-versus-tank combat. As well, the R-35's armor was easily pierced both by the 50 mm gun of the latest version of the Panzer III and by the 75 mm gun of the Panzer IV.

Also, the commander-gunner in his one-man turret was overtaxed in coordinated tank operations. The view from the turret was poor, and in a difficult, complex situation it must have been impossible for the commander-gunner to properly command the tank and operate the manually operated turret and serve the tanks' weaponry.

Even during operations in support of the infantry, achieving this catalog of tasks offered sufficient difficulties. When a radio set was also installed in the turret, it meant simply another burden for the commander.

The Renault R-35 was thus able to achieve little in this new type of warfare.

SERVICE IN THE SECOND WORLD WAR AND AS A CAPTURED TANK IN FOREIGN ARMIES

When the Wehrmacht invaded France, the French army met the attackers with a total of twenty-one tank battalions, whose equipment included the R-35. After the collapse pf France, the R-35 saw further use in the French colonies, including for example in the Syrian-Lebanese campaign of 1941.

A Renault R-35 captured by the Israelis, photographed in the Arab town of Kafr Kanna, June 1948. *IDF*

Renault R-35	
Type	light tank
Manufacturer	Renault
Crew	2 (commander, driver)
Combat weight	10.9 tons (9,900 kg)
Length	13 ft. 9 in. (4,200 mm)
Width	6 ft. 0.8 in. (1,850 mm)
Height	7 ft. 9 in. (2,370 mm)
Engine	4-cylinder Renault gasoline engine, 82 hp (60 kW)
Power to weight ratio	8.3 hp/t (6.1 kW/t)
Maximum speed	11.8 mph (19 kph) [on roads]
Fuel capacity	45 gal. (171 liters)
Range	87 mi. (140 km) [on roads]
Armament	1 37-mm SA 18 (L/21) cannon 1 7.5 mm machine gun
Protection	armor steel structure (32–45 mm frontal, 40 mm on the sides)

Captured R-35 tanks, some after modification, were also used by foreign armies. Some vehicles were fitted with new hatch openings with cupolas and radio equipment housed inside the hull. In 1941, about two hundred examples were used by German troops in Russia in the reconnaissance role—a sign of the acute shortage of tanks on the side of the Wehrmacht, since, with its lack of speed and limited range, the R-35 was completely unsuited to this role. When the German advance in the east stalled in the mud and snow, a significant number of R-35s were converted into ammunition transports and tractors with their turrets removed.

Another version, produced in small numbers, carried a French 47 mm antitank gun. The R-35 was also used to a limited extent as a gun carriage for the German 105 mm field howitzer.

Several R-35s saw combat in Syria during the Syrian-Lebanese unrest. At the beginning of the War of Independence in May 1948, Syrian troops in company strength attacked the kibbutzim of Dagania Alef and Bet, southwest of the Sea of Galilee, with several captured R-35s. The surprised settlers put up fierce resistance, but the tanks were forced to withdraw only when supporting Israeli units of the Golani, Yiftach, and Carmeli Brigades arrived and employed machine guns and Molotov cocktails against them.

Three of the R-35s were captured and incorporated into the Israeli 82nd Armored Battalion. Their subsequent use remains unclear to this day. One R-35 tank destroyed during the attack still sits at the entrance to the village of Bet as a memorial to the heroic actions of the then-still-young Israeli armed forces.

THE HOTCHKISS H-39: DEVELOPMENT

Despite the rejection of the first prototypes from the Hotchkiss company and the introduction of the Renault R-35 for the French infantry, the cavalry still sought a small but heavily armored *char de cavalerie*.

With the same turret as the Renault R-35, a short-barreled 37 mm gun and a coaxial machine gun, production of the H-35 ultimately totaled 1,935 vehicles. The two tanks shared many similarities and differed only in their running gear, the shape of the rear hull, and the arrangement of the driver's seat.

The successor to the H-35 had even fewer differences. The Hotchkiss H-39 light tank had thicker armor, a new six-cylinder engine that produced 120 hp, and a less well-suited engine hood above the hull.

With its improved power plant, maximum speed rose to 22 mph (36 kph) and range to 93 miles (150 km), which predestined it for reconnaissance and security duties. The first H-39s had a short-barreled 37 mm gun (barrel length 21 calibers), which was especially suited for use against soft targets. Later production vehicles mounted the more powerful SA 38 gun (barrel length 33 calibers, muzzle velocity 2,297 ft./sec. [700 m/sec.]) for engaging harder targets.

The H-39's armor protection proved inadequate against German tank and antitank guns, even though its armor was thicker than that of the German Panzers I and II tanks.

Hotchkiss H-39, vehicle number 3990, purchased from France, after the battle for Lod airport, 1948. *Israel Government Press Office*

OPERATIONS DURING THE SECOND WORLD WAR

Since the Char B heavy tank was coming off the production line only in small numbers, the army command placed an order for the H-39 and reorganized its armored divisions. In May 1940, each of the three armored divisions had one battalion equipped with Hotchkiss tanks. Two more battalions—the 13th and the 35th of the French First Army—were each equipped with forty-five tanks to support the infantry. Further vehicles were operated by the independent mechanized infantry companies and the cavalry.

Since the commanders of the French army had little experience in the use of mechanized units, they failed to concentrate their armored units and used them only to support the infantry. From the widely separated defensive positions along the German front through France, Holland, and Belgium to Dunkirk, the French armored battalions were unable to fight anything more than delaying actions. The separate use of foot troops and of mounted and mechanized units decisively weakened the defense's striking power. The shortcomings of the French tanks, particularly their lack of radios, their one-man turrets, and complicated servicing, became all too obvious.

Hotchkiss produced a total of 1,100 H-39 tanks. The Wehrmacht made considerable use of captured examples both in the western and eastern European theaters of war.

In 1942, the H-39 served in German panzer divisions that were in France resting and refitting after heavy losses on the Eastern Front. The Wehrmacht also employed the Hotchkiss for transport and supply duties in the rear area. The chassis of the H-39 with turret removed was also used as a munitions transport and recovery vehicle. A small number fitted with rotating turrets mounting machine guns were also used for limited reconnaissance duties, similar to those assigned to the German type 221 armored car (Sd.Kfz. 221).

The British occupation in Palestine and their ban on weapons for the Jewish underground organizations complicated the procurement of urgently needed armored vehicles. How could such heavy equipment be shipped into the only available port of Haifa and delivered to the Haganah without being discovered?

Since the port of Haifa was still occupied during the British withdrawal and the embarkation of British troops, the port city was out of the question as a transshipment center for the Haganah. The choice therefore fell on the smaller port of Tel Aviv to the south. A supply ship arrived there during the first ceasefire in June 1948, disguised and unrecognized as such by the UN inspectors. The *Borea* unloaded no fewer than ten Hotchkiss H-39 tanks, acquired from stocks of the German or French militaries.

All the H-39s that had been purchased still had their original armament with the more powerful 37 mm gun and coaxial 7.5 mm machine gun. The Wehrmacht had, however, modified the captured H-39s with a rather flatter cupola.

After a comprehensive inspection of the H-39s, it was found that some of their engines had been affected by rust and were in need of overhaul. The original engine-cooling system was also unsuitable for the high desert temperatures and had to be optimized.

All the H-39s were supposed to be incorporated into the 82nd Armored Battalion of the 8th Armored Brigade. The H-39s saw their first combat in the battle for Lod airport, the present-day Ben Gurion Airport. The H-39s saw their last action during the

Hotchkiss H-39 tanks armed with an SA 38 37 mm gun lined up at the Hotchkiss factory outside Paris, August 1949. *Osprey*

fighting for possession of the village of Iraq Al-Manshiyya, located northeast of Gaza, in October 1948. Five of the tanks were destroyed and the rest were disabled by engine failure.

Whether the five remaining Hotchkiss H-39 tanks were repaired and later saw further combat is not clearly documented. Several frontline reports from March 1949 make mention of a single tank still in action. Other unconfirmed sources note isolated actions during the Sinai campaign during the Suez Crisis of 1956.

None of this changed the questionable reputation of the Hotchkiss H-39, however. The last surviving example operated by the Israeli armed forces is in the tank museum at Latrun.

THE CROMWELL MARK IV: DEVELOPMENT

Great Britain's commitment to modern warfare after the First World War can best be described as halfhearted. The British army returned to its traditional role, that of watching over and policing its colonies.

Not until the beginning of the 1930s did the British army's commanders concern themselves with a tank doctrine and form the first mechanized units. Heavy tanks were to provide close support to the infantry, while so-called medium-heavy tanks (cruiser tanks) would be developed for the armored brigades. The cruiser tank designation derived from a class of warship and was supposed to express the opposite of the "land battleships" of the First World War.

Representative of infantry support tanks were the infantry tanks Mark I/II Matilda, Mark III Valentine, and, probably the best known, Mark IV Churchill.

In 1934, tank designer Sir John Carden of the Vickers Company presented the A9 medium tank ordered by the British general staff. It was supposed to be lightly armored and thus more mobile and easier to produce. It was also anticipated that it would be operated in homogeneous tank formations. It was soon followed by the A10 heavy tank.

With the development of more-effective antitank guns, the armor protection of even the A10 was no longer sufficient. Nevertheless, the A9 and A10 served as the prototypes for the future development of the cruiser class of tank. One first such version, designated the A10 Mark II, weighed about 14 tons, had a maximum speed of 16 mph (26 kph), and was armed with a 40 mm gun.

Further development ultimately resulted in the A13 Mark II, which was more heavily armored, with 30 mm of armor plate on the hull and turret front. It was powered by an American Liberty engine built under license, which gave it a top speed of 35 mph (56 kph).

Above and below: Israeli tank soldiers with M4 Sherman and Cromwell Mark IV tanks at Iraq Suwayda on November 7, 1948. *Benno Rothenberg*

The A13 Mark II gave valuable service in the North African desert offensives during the Second World War. It proved effective against the Italian armored forces and later against the Panzerkampfwagens II and II, which formed the mechanized backbone of Rommel's Afrikakorps.

Further development into the A13 Mark III Covenanter resulted from the effort to develop an even-heavier cruiser tank. It was powered by a Meadows twelve-flat, low-profile, twelve-cylinder engine, which proved unsuitable since it tended to overheat. Although this problem was ultimately resolved, the Covenanter did not see action and was replaced by the Mark VI Crusader.

Combat experience in North Africa led to a rethinking of the cruiser tank. The units demanded a more reliable drivetrain, heavier armor with up to 75 mm in the turret, and up to 65 mm of protection on the hull, plus a 57 mm gun.

In June 1941, the Nuffield company executed an order for five hundred vehicles with the designation A24, which was powered by a more powerful 410 hp engine and was based on the design of the Crusader. This vehicle, which was named Cavalier, was also not a success, however.

Meanwhile, the Leyland company began work on the A27 project, likewise, based on the Crusader, for use with the Rolls-Royce Meteor, a development of the Merlin aeroengine intended for use in tanks.

Apart from a new gearbox, the chassis resembled that of the Cavalier. The first A27L Centaur I appeared in June 1942. Like the Cavalier, the Centaur was used only for training purposes.

Production of the A27M Mark I Cromwell began in 1943. The first series were armed with a 57 mm gun. The improved Mark II was produced with wider, 39 cm tracks. Later in the year, new engines were installed in the first series of the Cromwell Mark I. There were designated Mark IIIs.

The tank's crew consisted of the driver, the forward machine gunner, the loader, the gunner, and the commander.

Lessons learned in the North Africa deserts showed that a more powerful armament was necessary to be able to fire both armor-piercing and high-explosive ammunition. The 57 mm gun was therefore bored to enable it to fire American 75 mm ammunition.

The improved gun was installed in the Cromwell III, which, fitted with a new engine, was named the Mark IV. The performance of the tank's 75 mm gun was slightly inferior to that of the M4 Sherman but was superior to the 75 mm gun in the M3 Grant/Lee, both produced in the United States.

As was standard on British cruiser tanks, the Mark IV had a Christie suspension with five large, independently sprung road wheels on both sides. The Rolls-Royce Meteor engine powered the rear-mounted drive sprockets and produced 600 hp, sufficient to give the tank a suitable performance on and off roads. Power was delivered by a Merrit-Brown Z5 gearbox with differential steering.

A 7.92 mm Besa machine gun was mounted in the hull (however, with limited range of traverse), and a second machine gun was mounted coaxially with the 75 mm gun. The 63 mm of armor on the hull front was viewed as insufficient, and therefore additional armor plates were welded onto many vehicles, raising armor thickness to 105 mm. The converted Mark IVs were redesignated the Mark VII and Mark VIII. A final version carrying a 95 mm gun bore the designation Mark VI.

Hotchkiss H-39	
Type	light tank
Manufacturer	Hotchkiss et Cie, France
Crew	2 (commander, driver)
Combat weight	13.2 tons (12,000 kg)
Length	13 ft., 8 in. (4,220 mm)
Width	6 ft., 0.8 in. (1,850 mm)
Height	7 ft. (2,140 mm)
Engine	6-cylinder Hotchkiss gasoline engine, 120 hp (88 kW)
Power to weight ratio	10 hp/t (7.4 kW/t)
Maximum speed	22.4 mph (36 kph) [on roads]
Fuel capacity	55.5 gal. (210 liters)
Range	93 mi. (150 km) [on roads]
Armament	1 37 mm SA 38 (L/33) cannon 1 7.5 mm Model 1931 machine gun
Protection	armor steel structure (22–45 mm frontal, 33–40 mm on the sides)

A further increase in combat capability resulted in the last and most powerful British tank of the Second World War, the Comet.

ACTION IN NORMANDY AND IN PALESTINE

In the war years 1944–45, the Cromwell tank was operated by the British 7th Armoured Division and by several armored reconnaissance regiments and saw action during Operation Goodwood, the Battle of Caen. In the process, elements of the 7th Armoured Division met fierce resistance from the German Panzer-Lehr-Division at Tilly-sur-Seulles and Villers-Bocage.

The successful Allied offensives ended in the pursuit of the Wehrmacht across northern France, Belgium, Holland, and finally Germany. In the process the Cromwell proved itself on account of its reliability, range, and heavy armament.

Because of the latent Arab threat, prior to the outbreak of the War of Independence the Haganah saw itself forced not only to up-armor its existing vehicles (sandwich trucks), but also to procure full-fledged tanks. This was a difficult undertaking, since no Western state was willing to offer the slightest help. The Haganah therefore saw only one way out: the procurement or theft of tanks from the stocks of the British occupying power.

In March 1948, a Jewish agent succeeded in convincing British soldiers Michael Flanagan and Harry MacDonald to help steal armored vehicles from the British arsenal.

The two British soldiers indicated that they wished to remain in Israel after the British Mandate ended, and to make

Hotchkiss H-39 at the Latrun Tank Museum, Israel. *Marc Lenzin Archive*

a new home there. They sympathized with the Israeli fighters and gave them access to a tank hangar in the port of Haifa. In a daring mission, they succeeded in stealing two A27M Cromwell Mark IV tanks.

The fact that these two tanks survived the long trip to Tel Aviv undamaged demonstrated that they were in good condition. One vehicle was armed with the original 57 mm gun, the other with the newer 75 mm weapon.

After their arrival, these two tanks were supposed to be incorporated into the 82nd Battalion of the 8th Armored Brigade. Men of the 82nd Armored Battalion searched abandoned British army bases in Tira and Atlit south of Haifa for spare parts for the vehicles.

The Cromwell tanks saw action during the occupation of Lod airport on July 11, 1948, and in the attack on the police fortress at Latrun several days later. Further combat operations

A27M Cromwell Mk. IV	
Type	cruiser tank
Manufacturer	Nuffield Mechanisation and Aero
Crew	5 (commander, driver, gunner, loader, machine gunner)
Service life	1944–1955
Combat weight	30.9 tons (28,000 kg)
Length	20 ft., 10 in. (6,350 mm)
Width	9 ft., 6 in. (2,908 mm)
Height	8 ft., 1 in. (2,480 mm)
Engine	Rolls-Royce Meteor V, 12-cylinder gasoline engine, 600 hp (440 kW)
Power to weight ratio	28.4 hp/t (15.8 kW/t)
Maximum speed	37.9 mph (61 kph) [on roads]
Fuel capacity	45 gal. (171 liters)
Range	172 mi. (278 km) [on roads]
Armament	1 6-pounder (75 mm) gun 2 7.92 mm Besa machine guns
Protection	armor steel structure (76 mm frontal, 50 mm on the sides)

during the War of Independence were not chronicled and remain in the dark. A situation report of March 1949 lists the Cromwell tanks as still intact and ready to fight.

Michael Flanagan died in February 2014. Michael Mass, director of the Yad Lashiryon Tank Museum at Latrun, praised the soldier Flanagan as a true hero in his eulogy at the Sha'ar HaAmakim Cemetery.

One of the two stolen Cromwell tanks is now on display at the tank museum. Together with the R-35 and the Hotchkiss H-39, these vehicles were among the first tanks of what would one day become the Israeli Armored Corps.

Knocked-out Cromwell Mark IV tanks of the British 7th Armored Division at Villers-Bocage, France. There, on June 13, 1944, Hauptsturmführer Michael Wittmann of the 101st Heavy Panzer Battalion destroyed parts of a British armored brigade with his Tiger I. *IWM*

Cromwell Mark IV (A27M) of the Israeli 82nd Armored Brigade near Latrun, 1948. *World Machal*

Cromwell Mark IV (A27M) at the Latrun Tank Museum, Israel. *Marc Lenzin Archive*

CHAPTER 4: The First Armored Vehicles: Renault, Hotchkiss, and Cromwell | 47

Chapter 5
The War of Independence, 1948–49 (First Arab-Israeli War)

We have always said that we have a secret weapon in our struggle with the Arabs: we have no place to go.

—Golda Meir, prime minister of Israel, 1969–74

In the early morning hours of May 15, 1948, one day after David Ben Gurion declared the independence of the state of Israel on basis of the UN resolution, Egyptian, Jordanian, Syrian, Lebanese, and Iraqi troops crossed the Israeli border. By that time, the Jewish armed forces had succeeded in securing militarily about one-third of the territory promised in the UN partition plan. But Israel's war for independence and existence had just begun.

The Israeli armed forces had previously faced Arab irregular or paramilitary forces. With the start of the invasion, for the first time the Israelis found themselves facing regular troops with advantages in firepower, organization, equipment, and training.

Prime Minister Ben Gurion, who also held the post of defense minister, therefore felt forced to reorganize the Haganah. He formed nine powerful territorial infantry brigades and one armored brigade.

- In the northern sector was the Yiftach Brigade in the Galilee area at Godeb, the Golani Brigade south of Nazareth as far as Beth Shean, and the Carmeli Brigade in the west near Haifa.
- In the central sector the Harel and Etzioni Brigades had taken up position near Jerusalem, and the Alexandroni and Kiryati Brigades between Haifa and Tel Aviv.
- In the southern sector the Negev Brigade and the Givati Brigade and the first armored companies were at the camp in Sarafand.

The Arabs took up offensive positions with the following formations:

- In the north, along the Golan Heights, the Syrian 1st and 2nd Infantry Brigades, supported by French-made R-35 and R-39 light tanks, deployed along the Golan Heights. A reinforced Iraqi infantry brigade and an armored battalion were in the Jordan Valley. A Lebanese mechanized infantry battalion with a supporting battery of artillery massed on the border of Upper Galilee.
- In the area east of Jerusalem, between Jericho and Nablus, was the Jordanian Arab Legion with two mechanized brigades and about 120 armored vehicles.
- Positioned in the Gaza area was the Egyptian 1st Infantry Brigade, and east of Abu Ageila the Egyptian 2nd Infantry Brigade, each bolstered by an armored battalion with British-made Vickers Mark IV light tanks and Matildas.

Thus, in the opening phase of the war, about 51,000 Arab troops with 240 armored vehicles and tanks, 300 armored personnel carriers, and 140 artillery pieces faced just 30,000 Israeli soldiers with just a few armored vehicles and tanks.

THE PHASE FROM MAY TO JUNE 1948: THE NORTHERN SECTOR

The Syrian army began its campaign in the Jordan Valley south of the Sea of Galilee, and it quickly broke through the Israeli defensive positions at the south end of the sea. The Jewish settlers found themselves forced to evacuate their kibbutzes Sha'ar HaGolan and Masada, but even with tanks the Syrians were unable to fight their way into several settlements; for example, at Degania.

The defenders also employed artillery pieces for the first time. They were obsolete 65 mm cannon without aiming mechanisms, from the second half of the nineteenth century, facing modern Syrian guns from the Second World War. Nevertheless, the Syrians were so surprised by the Israeli artillery fire that they broke off their attack and withdrew east of the Sea of Galilee.

The Lebanese army pushed into Israel from the north and occupied the Jewish settlements of Malkiyah and Kadesh. As before, however, the Yiftach Brigade, stationed in Upper Galilee under the command of Yigal Allon, occupied and stubbornly defended the surrounding hills. On May 17, 1948, elements of the Yiftach Brigade retook the police fort at Nebi Yusha, near the international border and the two settlements of Malkiyah and Kadesh. The Israelis blew an important bridge over the Litani River and finally brought about the defeat of the Lebanese invasion.

The Iraqi army drove into the Jordan Valley on the southern wing of the Syrian units between the Jewish settlements of Gesher and Bet-Joseph. Attempts to take the commanding heights of the ruined Belvoir Castle near Kibbutz Gesher were defeated by the stubborn defense put up by the settlers and the Golani Brigade under the command of Moshe Mann.[1] And so, after seven days of bitter fighting, the Iraqi troops withdrew across the Jordan. They then moved south in the direction of Tubas and Nablus, from where an advance into the coastal plain of Sharon was planned, in order to split the Jewish-held area.

After the Jewish troops had successfully repulsed the first wave of invading Arab forces in the north, the Haganah seized the initiative and selected the Arab-held city of Jenin, held by Iraqi units and Arab militias, as its objective.

Three units carried out the attack with the following objectives:

- The 13th Battalion of the Golani Brigade, the unit spearheading the attack, was to take the Arab villages on the hills surrounding the city of Jenin.
- The Carmeli Brigade, under its commander Moshe Carmel,[2] was to invade the city of Jenin and take it.
- At the same time, in the west the Alexandroni Brigade, under its commander Dan Even, was to advance against the city of Tulkarm, where Iraqi forces in brigade strength coming from Nablus were preparing to take Netanya together with Jordanian troops.

When the Iraqi troops on the march from Nablus to Tulkarm received news of the Israeli attack on Jenin, their column halted, and on June 1 advance forces drove into the open flank of the Carmeli Brigade. The main force of the Iraqi 4th and 5th Brigades arrived on the scene on June 3 and, thanks to their use of massed artillery, were able to drive the Israelis from their prepared positions in the city and on the ridges.

THE SOUTHERN AND CENTRAL FRONTS

On May 15, the Egyptian army—and with it forces from Saudi Arabia and Yemen—entered Palestine on two lines of attack: the Egyptian 1st Infantry Brigade moved along the coast road from El Arish in the direction of Tel Aviv, while the Egyptian 2nd Infantry Brigade advanced toward Jerusalem down the Auja al-Hafir–Be'er Sheva–Hebron road.

The attack on the western route by the 1st Infantry Brigade, which was supported by tanks, was directed at the kibbutzim of Nirim and Kfar Darom, as well as Yad Mordechai. The heavy

Givati Brigade convoy south of Tel Aviv, 1948. In the foreground is a jeep armed with an MG34 machine gun. Behind it is an armored truck, one of the so-called sandwich trucks. *Israel Government Press Office*

---

[1] Moshe Mann (1907–2004) was born in Turka in Ukraine and in 1926 immigrated to Palestine. He was soon recruited by the Haganah and was a member of the Jewish Settlement Police (J.S.P.) and the Palmach. After the War of Independence, he took over command of the northern front for a short time. He left the army after the death of his wife in 1948.

[2] Moshe Carmel (1911–2003) immigrated to Palestine in 1924 and was active in Histadrut, the Zionist trade union. He was imprisoned in the central prison in Akko for two years for illegal activities. After the War of Independence, he became a politician and was elected to the Knesset, and from 1948 to 1967 he was the minister of transport.

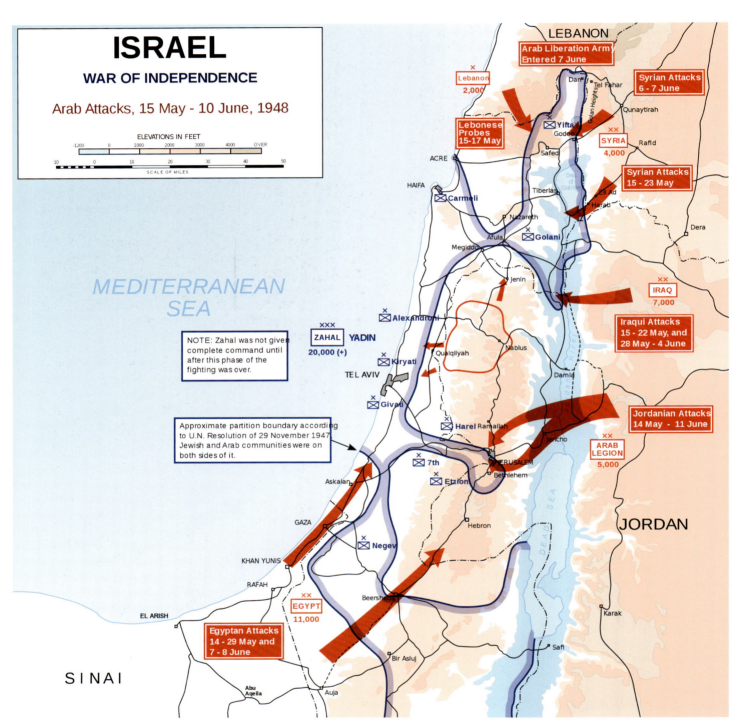

Map showing the positions of Israeli brigades (*blue*) and Arab attacks (*red*) in 1948. *Wikipedia*

One of the first M4 Sherman tanks of the still-young Israeli armed forces in action. It had a retroactively fitted main gun. The photo was probably taken in the northern Negev, 1948. *Israel Government Press Office*

An armored car captured from the Egyptian army, photographed in the Sinai or the Negev, 1948. *Israel Government Press Office*

fighting lasted from May 18 to 24, when the settlers abandoned their positions after a heroic resistance. The Egyptians then resumed their advance north in the direction of Tel Aviv. On the hills of Isdud (modern-day Ashdod), about 20 miles (32 km) south of Tel Aviv, the Egyptian force ran into the Givati Brigade, the 5th Hish Brigade, which had four of its five battalions in a blocking position south of the villages around Rehovoth and in the hill country of the Shefala. One battalion was deployed at Hulda, supporting the defense of the so-called Jerusalem corridor, the only route over which supplies could be sent to the besieged city.

The advance by the Egyptian 2nd Infantry Brigade on the eastern route was less eventful, meeting little resistance. On May 17, the Egyptians reached Be-er Sheva, took the Jewish settlement of Bet-Eschel, drove on through Hebron, regrouped in Bethlehem, and occupied positions in the southern sector of Jerusalem, from where they advanced on the kibbutz of Ramat Rachel.

On May 14, the Arab Legion sent its entire force across the Jordan over the Allenby Bridge and advanced in the direction of Jericho. Its objective was to take all of Jerusalem. On May 15, the Jordanians attacked the Etzion Block—a group of four Jewish settlements on the road between Bethlehem and Hebron—with artillery and mechanized infantry supported by armored vehicles armed with machine guns. The settlements of Atarot and Newe-Jakow, north of Jerusalem, and Hartuv, on the west, fell after fierce fighting. The inhabitants were put into Jordanian POW camps or fled in boats to Sodom at the south end of the Dead Sea.

The Arab Legion occupied all the roads into Jerusalem and began shelling the new city to wear down the inhabitants and force them to surrender. But the siege was only partially successful. The legion's only notable success was the conquest of the completely isolated Jewish quarter in the old city.

The fighting then shifted farther into the "Jerusalem corridor" and the western road into the city. The hills on both sides of the only road into the city were also occupied by the legion and prevented supplies from reaching the surrounded Jewish population of Jerusalem.

---

[3] David Daniel Marcus (1901–48) was born in New York, the son of Romanian immigrants. He graduated from the US military academy at West Point, served on Patton's and Eisenhower's staffs, and in 1944 jumped with the 101st US Paratrooper Division into Normandy as a colonel. With a doctorate in law, he was involved in the preparations for the Nuremberg trials. The Haganah contacted Marcus before the founding of the state to ask him to serve as an advisor for the development of the army. His efforts at Latrun were honored by Ben Gurion, who promoted Marcus to brigadier general (Hebrew: *Aluf*). Marcus thus became the first general of the Israeli armed forces. He was accidentally shot and killed by a soldier on guard duty at 0350 on the night of June 10–11, before the first ceasefire. David Marcus is buried in West Point Cemetery and is the only American officer buried there who died in the service of a foreign power.

CHAPTER 5: The War of Independence, 1948–49 (First Arab-Israeli War) | 51

Ben Gurion immediately ordered a new large-scale operation to open the corridor. The first step was to be the occupation of the key site of Latrun. In 1936, the British had built one of their Tegart forts near the monastery at Latrun, which was now in Arab hands.

Slightly elevated geographically, the police station overlooks the Ayalon Valley and the crossroads of an old trade and pilgrimage route that runs from Jaffa via Ramla and from Gaza to Ramallah and Nablus. Even in Crusader times, there was a watchtower there to protect travelers. The Arab Legion also blocked the supply of water to Jerusalem, since the pipes ran parallel to the connecting road.

The series of so-called Battles of Latrun resumed in the second half of May: several attacks failed and the fierce defense by the Jordanians around and in the fort at Latrun seemed insurmountable. Jerusalem remained surrounded. The local commander David Marcus[3] was an American employed by Ben Gurion as an advisor and instructor. He discovered an alternative route to Jerusalem, a Bedouin trail, behind the Arab lines. This uncertain route led from Bab el Wad to Jerusalem, away from the narrows of the valley, and was built with the help of numerous volunteers in order to ensure that supplies reached the city. The alternative route was called the "Burma Road" and remained undetected by the enemy, so that soon the first convoys were rolling over the new link, delivering supplies to the Jewish population in Jerusalem.

On the night of June 10–11, 1948, the commanders of all Arab and Jewish troops surprisingly ordered a halt to the ongoing operations, since the UN Security Council had ordered a general ceasefire to take effect at midnight.

Although the Haganah suffered more than a few failures during this phase of the War of Independence, and numerous Jewish settlements were evacuated or conquered by Arabs, it did succeed in confronting, delaying, and partially repelling the invasion.

The Egyptians reorganized their forces at Isdud, 18 miles (30 km) south of Jaffa. The Syrians established bridgeheads on the west side of the Jordan in Upper Galilee. The Arab Legion again occupied Ramla and Lydda, including Lod airport.

THE FOUNDING OF THE ISRAELI ARMED FORCES

Heartened by its successes and having learned from its defeats, the Israelis took advantage of the ceasefire brokered by the UN on June 11, 1948, to consolidate their armed forces.

On May 28, 1948, Ben Gurion announced a law for the formation of the Israeli Defense Force (IDF), Zahal in Hebrew,

Negev Brigade convoy with American-made half-tracks armed with British-made 57 mm guns, photographed in the Negev in 1948. *Israel Government Press Office*

an abbreviation of the words Zwa Haganah le-Yisrael. The law was intended to incorporate all paramilitary organizations such as Haganah, Palmach, Irgun, and Lechi into the newly created army.

Furthermore, henceforth there were to be standardized uniforms and simplified structures with new ranks and grades. Ben Gurion organized the existing infantry brigades into four new territorial command areas:

- the northern front, under General Moshe Carmel (Galilee)
- the central front, under General Dan Even (Tel Aviv / Jerusalem)
- the eastern front, under General Zvi Ayalon (Samaria-Sharon)
- the southern front, under General Yigal Allon (Negev, Gaza)

In the process, Ben Gurion promoted Yaakov Dori,[4] the acting commander in chief of the Haganah, to lieutenant general (*Rav-Aluf*) and made him the Zahal's first chief of staff. The commanders

---

[4] Yaakov Dori (1899–1973) was born in Russia. After the pogroms in Odessa, his family immigrated to Palestine in 1905. During the First World War, he served in the British army as a member of the Jewish Legion. In 1939 he became chief of staff of the Haganah and in 1948 commander in chief of the newly founded Israeli Defense Force (IDF). After the War of Independence, he ended his military career and became prime minister of the Science Council, and later president of the Technical University in Haifa.

of the various fronts, the air force, the fleet, and several higher officers in the general staff were promoted to brigadier generals and placed under the chief of staff. He in turn reported directly to Ben Gurion, the prime minister and minister of defense.

With the founding of the Israeli armed forces, the Israeli Armored Corps (Chel Shirion) was formed from the 7th and 8th Armored Brigades under its first commander, Yitzhak Sadeh.

Ben Gurion decided to give command of the badly decimated 7th Brigade at Latrun to the Canadian Ben Dunkelman,[5] a Jewish veteran of the Second World War. Its two infantry battalions, the 71st and 72nd, had taken heavy casualties at Latrun. The 3rd or 79th (later 73rd) Battalion, commanded by Chaim Laskov, described itself as a mechanized formation with half-tracks, flamethrowers, and sandwich-armored vehicles. While it had taken heavy losses outside the reinforced concrete walls of the police fort, it had been able to withdraw in good order. The 7th Brigade was withdrawn from the Jerusalem front and was replaced by the Yiftach Brigade, coming from the north. The 7th withdrew into the Haifa-Akko area and became active again when the ceasefire ended on July 7.

The Israeli units were still inferior to the Arabs in numbers and weaponry and because of their geopolitical situation, but not in command, organization, and discipline. With the small nation under pressure from the Arab states, the fighting spirit of the Israeli soldiers grew, since basically they had no choice but to win or be driven into the sea. This tenet significantly bolstered the Israeli fighting morale and lives on to the present day.

THE PHASE FROM JULY 1948 TO JANUARY 1949

The next phase of the war, the so-called Battles of the Ten Days, brought a radical change in tactics and logistics on the part of the Israeli army. With the enemy close to the Jewish population centers, the Israelis could not use purely defensive tactics. Once on the offensive, the invading armies would have been able to break through the thin Israeli lines, overwhelm their limited forces, and take the rest of the country, which without tactical depth would have been easy to overrun.

---

[5] Ben Dunkelman (1913–97) grew up near Toronto, the son of Polish Jewish immigrants. At the age of eighteen he immigrated to Palestine and as a convinced Zionist joined a kibbutz. He served in the Canadian army during the Second World War and fought in the Normandy offensive at the Battles of Caen and the Falaise Pocket. After returning to Palestine, he served in the Israeli army and fought on the central and northern fronts during the War of Independence in 1948–49. After the war, he returned to Canada and worked in the textile, furniture, and art fields.

Half-tracks of the 89th Armored Battalion of the 7th Armored Brigade with mounted infantry. These troops were photographed in the Upper Galilee during the advance to Sasa after the taking of Nazareth, 1949. *Israel Government Press Office*

The war could basically not be won unless the enemy was struck a devastating blow. In this situation the Israelis surprised everyone by taking the offensive.

The Lebanese army still controlled the front line between Rosh Hanikra and the Bint Jbeil coast, ensuring the logistical link and keeping the avenues open to supply reserve units and new volunteers to the Arab liberation army.

The Syrian army occupied the Mishmar HaYarden bridgehead on the Jordan River with an infantry brigade supported by armored units and infantry. Another brigade held the hills of the Golan and watched over the east side of the Jordan River.

With the renewed outbreak of fighting, the attempt to crush the Syrian bridgehead initially failed. However, the fierce Israeli resistance also prevented the Syrians from expanding the bridgehead and from launching an offensive strike in the Hule Valley.

In order to clear up the situation in the western Galilee, the 7th Brigade moved to the northern front, launched a frontal attack against the Syrian units, and captured Nazareth. The Syrians then withdrew.

In the central sector, around Jerusalem a massive attack was now needed to retake and keep open the roads leading to Tel Aviv, which were held by two battalions of the Arab Legion. The occupied cities of Ramla and Lod, with its airport, were also to be liberated.

Haganah soldiers training in house-to-house fighting in Tel Aviv, 1948. *Israel Government Press Office*

The Israeli plan of attack, code-named Dani, went as follows:

- In the first phase the Arabs in the occupied territories around Ramla and Lod were to be attacked by the Harel and Yiftach Brigades and the 8th Armored Brigade and destroyed.
- In the second phase the areas surrounding Latrun and Ramallah were to be occupied with support from elements of the Kiryati, Alexandroni, and Etzioni Brigades.
- In the third phase the main roads to Jerusalem were to be opened.

The attack's main strike was to be delivered by the armored brigade, which consisted of two units; namely, the 82nd Armored Battalion, under Felix Beatus, and the 89th Battalion, under Moshe Dayan. The former had ten Hotchkiss H-39s, two Cromwell Mark IVs, and one M4 Sherman. Dayan's unit was essentially a commando unit and was equipped mainly with Jeeps armed with machine guns and a few armored vehicles.

Since crews were difficult to recruit, most of the men were veterans of the British and South African armies. Yitzhak Sadeh planned to liberate Lod airport with a simultaneous attack by the two battalions. The advance began promisingly, with the English-speaking armored company, which had both Cromwell tanks and the M4, in particular, making progress. The attack force broke through the front lines and quickly advanced onto the airport grounds.

The Russian-speaking armored company with its H-39 tanks lost its way, however, stumbled upon the enemy, and came under fire from the Jordanian units. The Yiftach Brigade was heavily engaged, so tying up the enemy that Dayan was able to drive through the enemy's front lines, take the city of Lod, and encircle the surprised Jordanians. Sensing victory, he ordered his unit to continue its advance and, after a fierce battle, also liberated the nearby town of Ramla, capturing one of the Arab Legion's armored cars, a Marmon-Herrington Mark IV F, which was immediately put to use against its former owners, the first of a whole series of ex-British armored cars that were soon to reinforce the armored corps.

The bloody battle for the liberation of Ramla and Lod was a triumph of combined arms and the first success by an Israeli armored brigade. Mobility, maneuverability, and concentration of firepower was the key and formed the cornerstone of the doctrine of the Israeli Armored Corps.

Ramla and Lod, the latter with its international airport, were in Israeli hands. The direct threat to Tel Aviv had been lifted, and parts of the "Jerusalem corridor" were secured. The Israelis failed, however, to penetrate the walls of the city of Jerusalem and take the old city.

On the southern front, the Egyptians attacked before the ceasefire expired, using the element of surprise to take the Negev Brigade's positions at Kaukabah and Hulikat, deepening the area that separated the Negev from the north. The Egyptian 1st Brigade pushed ahead along an alternative route farther inland, in order to reach Tel Aviv by way of Rehovoth, west of Latrun.

The Egyptians coordinated all their attacks from the Iraq Suwaydan fort, an old British police station, successfully repulsing numerous Israeli attacks. In preparation for another incursion, the Givati Brigade attacked the hills with the commanding village of Ibdis, held by the Egyptians, and put the enemy to flight, capturing heavy equipment such as antitank guns, armored personnel carriers, and even a light tank, and occupied new defense lines to reorganize the unit.

Negev Brigade convoy carrying Palmach soldiers. The jeeps are armed with MG34 machine guns. Photograph taken in the Negev in 1948. *Israel Government Press Office*

On July 10, the Egyptians launched a counterattack. The battle for the hills near Ibdis lasted all day. The Egyptian infantry attacked wave after wave, with artillery and air support, but the attacks failed.

After the failure by the Egyptians, the Israeli forces seized the initiative and counterattacked to restore contact with the Negev. Dayan's 89th Battalion, which was available after taking Ramla and Lod, was to lend support and move to the southern front.

On July 19, 1948, a second UN ceasefire took effect. The Israeli armored forces played a significant role in the "Battles of the Ten Days," supporting the infantry brigades, breaking through the enemy's lines, and launching successful counterattacks.

After the resumption of hostilities on the night of October 18–19, 1948, the Harel Brigade began an attack against the Egyptian troops in the Judean foothills, successfully expanding the "Jerusalem corridor" to the south. On October 27, the troops of the Harel Brigade linked up with those of the Givati Brigade, which had meanwhile retaken the settlement of Bet Jibrin, in order to regroup.

In the western combat area, on October 22, the UN observer staff succeeded in extending the ceasefire.

In the eastern sector, the fighting continued until October 28. The Egyptian troops abandoned the coastal plain from Isdud to the vicinity of Gaza. On October 27, the Israeli forces retook the settlements of Isdud and Nizanim. Medschdal and Yad Mordechai followed on November 5 and on November 11, and the 8th Armored Brigade occupied the police fort at Iraq Suwaydan.

The Egyptians subsequently abandoned the town and their positions south of Karatiyah and assembled in Falujah and Iraq Al Manshiyah. The result was the so-called Falujah Pocket, in which an Egyptian reinforced infantry brigade was encircled for months.

While the troops of the Arab Legion prepared for another attack in central Galilee, the Israeli commander of the northern front, Moshe Carmel, decided to finally end the threat from Jordan and Syria.

Operation Hiram, in which the Golani, Carmeli, and the 7th Armored Brigades took part, lasted sixty hours. The Israeli forces drove the Jordanian troops out of Palestine and cleared the entire north as far as the international border. Israeli troops then advanced into Lebanese territory as far as the Litani River. This ended the fighting on the northern front.

The Egyptian army occupied positions in the south of Israel as follows:
- An Egyptian brigade held the Falujah Pocket.
- Two brigades defended the area around Gaza.
- One brigade secured the connecting axis between Abu Ageila and El Arish.

The Israeli army's 8th Armored Brigade and the Negev, Golani, and Harel Brigades, the latter after being withdrawn from the "Jerusalem Corridor," took up positions along the front line between Rafah and Sodom on the Dead Sea. The Alexandroni Brigade continued besieging Falujah.

Yigal Allon gave the order for Operation Horev, with the intention of ultimately driving the Egyptians from Israeli territory, since their presence would endanger the security of the Negev and the entire country.

CHAPTER 5: The War of Independence, 1948–49 (First Arab-Israeli War)

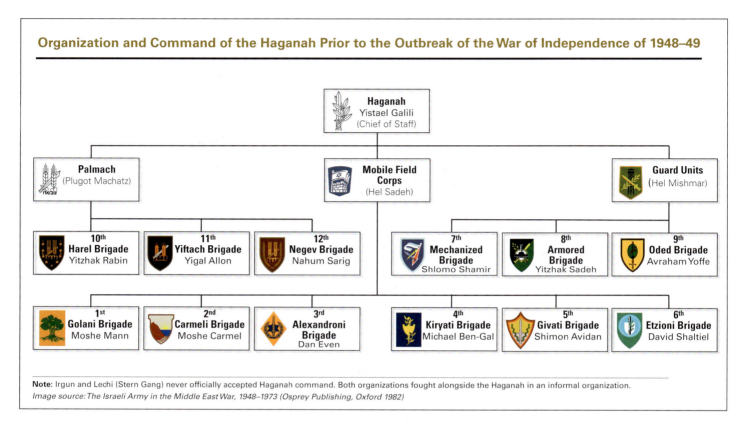

Organization and Command of the Haganah Prior to the Outbreak of the War of Independence of 1948–49

Note: Irgun and Lechi (Stern Gang) never officially accepted Haganah command. Both organizations fought alongside the Haganah in an informal organization.
Image source: The Israeli Army in the Middle East War, 1948–1973 (Osprey Publishing, Oxford 1982)

The battle plan envisioned

- the destruction by the Alexandroni Brigade of the Egyptian troops encircled in the Falujah Pocket;
- tying down the enemy in the Gaza area by the Golani Brigade;
- elements of the Harel Brigade and the 8th Armored Brigade covertly moving along the old Roman road between Bir Asluj and El Auja and driving into the enemy rear at Abu Ageila, enveloping and destroying the enemy; and
- the Negev Brigade and elements of the 8th Armored Brigade simultaneously moving out of the area east of Gaza on the road to El Auja, breaking through the Egyptian defensive lines, and linking up with the Harel Brigade advancing from the north near Abu Ageila.

On December 22, the commander of the southern front, Yigal Allon, unleashed the offensive in heavy rain and a fierce sandstorm. Contrary to expectations, the Egyptians were able to repulse numerous attacks by the Alexandroni Brigade. The Egyptian 6th Infantry Battalion, under Major Gamal Abdel Nasser, who later became Egyptian prime minister, put up particularly stubborn resistance. The pocket remained closed and was not cleared until the ceasefire agreement was reached between Egypt and Israel.

The Golani Brigade's command battalion surprised the Egyptians with heavy artillery fire and tank assaults, securing important hills around the strip of coastline in Gaza, but after meeting heavy resistance it was also forced to fall back. The advantage of this action was that at that moment the Egyptians focused their attention on Gaza and sent additional troops into that area.

On December 25, the Negev Brigade attacked the Egyptian positions on the Be'er Sheva–El Auja road and took them after fierce fighting. The Egyptians quickly moved reserves from El Arish, but they were stopped and the threat of an enemy attack against the Israeli rear was eliminated.

The Egyptian front slowly collapsed, with parts of the army taken prisoner or fleeing. The Israeli units pushed south into the Sinai, with the intention of also taking Abu Ageila and the coastal city of El Arish. At the same time, elements of the Harel Brigade moved farther east from Al Auja and took the oasis villages of Kusseima, Bir Hassana, and Bir Hama in the Sinai.

While a fierce sandstorm raged, which paralyzed all combat activity, on January 6, 1949, the Egyptian government announced that it was prepared to enter ceasefire negotiations with Israel. The fact that Egypt, the most powerful Arab state, entered negotiations with Israel was an important success, which subsequently brought the other Arab states, with the exception of Iraq, to the negotiating table.

Israeli GMC 6×6 truck with armored driver's cab and light side armor, 1948. *IDF*

THE PHASE FROM JANUARY TO JULY 1949

While the Arab troops withdrew over a wide area from the entire Israeli battle zone, the last Jordanian troops also left the eastern part of the Negev and the southern tip of the Red Sea. From March 5 to March 10, a column from the Negev Brigade and one from the Golani Brigade advanced on two different routes toward the Red Sea. At three o'clock in the afternoon on March 10, a company under Captain Avraham Adan reached the police station at Umm Rashrash, present-day Eilat, which had been abandoned by the Arab Legion, and hoisted the banner of victory—the Star of David on a white background. A third column from the Alexandroni Brigade had moved northward from the Arava Depression toward Sodom and Kibbutz Ejn Gedi on the Dead Sea in order to secure this part of the Negev for Israel.

A ceasefire agreement was signed with Egypt on February 24, 1949, with Lebanon on March 23, with the kingdom of Jordan on April 3, and with Syria on July 20. The Iraqi troops handed the territory they occupied over to the Arab Legion and left the country, without Iraq ever concluding a ceasefire with Israel. Thus ended the Israeli War of Independence.

In keeping with the terms of the ceasefire, the Israelis withdrew from Lebanon south of the Litani River and the Syrians from their bridgehead in Upper Galilee. The Egyptian brigade encircled in the Falujah Pocket was allowed to leave. Transjordan annexed the Samaria-Hebron area and the old city of Jerusalem and renamed the country the kingdom of Jordan. The Gaza Strip remained under Egyptian occupation.

In the War of Independence, the Israeli side lost about four thousand soldiers and approximately two thousand civilians killed. It is thought that casualties on the Arab side were about 3,700 to 7,000 soldiers and approximately 3,000 to 13,000 Palestinians killed.

In addition to the shortcomings of the individual Arab militaries, their effectiveness was primarily diminished by the remarkably poor command coordination. At no time did the Arab states act as a unified alliance. Mutual mistrust and individual interests prevented effective military operations.

With the formation of a new cohesive military force, Israel succeeded in concentrating its strength. The country had stood its ground and won not only the longest but also the costliest war in its history.

While the Jewish armed forces operated mostly in platoon and only sometimes in company strength during the Arab uprisings in the prestate phase, during the War of Independence, the battalion, and in some places the brigade, was the most important unit.

The battles were fought mainly by infantry, and the use of armored forces was rather the exception. However, the successful actions by the 7th Armored Brigade in Galilee and the Negev demonstrated without exception tactical strengths such as mobility, concentrated firepower, and formation of a point of main effort inherent in this weapon. To some extent, combined arms operations (i.e., the combination of infantry, armor, artillery, and airpower)—for example, during Operation Dani—showed the potential that mechanized units offered the newly formed Israeli Defense Force.

With victory in the War of Independence, Israel consolidated its existence as a state and improved its situation through territorial gains. These territories helped form Israel, which would have consisted of several separate units within the borders of the original UN partition plan, into a compact and defensible state territory.

Chapter 6
The Evolution of the Armored Corps

The end of the War of Independence marked the beginning of a new phase in the history of the young state of Israel. The ceasefire was not followed by peace treaties with the neighboring states. On the contrary, the Arab governments bolstered their arsenals of weapons and fueled the fire in the tense war atmosphere. Realizing that its enemies were at a heightened state of military readiness, Israel initiated a comprehensive reorganization of its armed forces. The armored corps was also reorganized, and its arsenal was expanded.

Due to the difficult economic situation—the country was engaged in reconstruction after the war—it could afford neither a large regular army nor a force of professional volunteers. The solution that is still practiced today was the continued existence of a small core of professional soldiers for instructional services and highly technical branches of the armed forces such as the air force and the navy, coupled with general compulsory service of two years for all able-bodied young people. Well-organized reserve units with annual refresher courses and an efficient system for rapid troop mobilization completed the new structure of the Israeli armed forces. A corresponding military service law was passed by the Knesset on August 15, 1949.

The highest military command body was the United General Staff. It consisted of the commanders of the army, air force, and navy as well as the three territorial commands of the northern, central, and southern fronts. Following the resignation of Jaakov Dori, Yigael Yadin[1] assumed the position of chief of the general staff.

---

[1] Yigael Yadin (1917–84), born in Jerusalem, joined the Haganah at the age of fifteen, commanded various combat units during the War of Independence, and became chief of staff of the Israeli armed forces in 1949. He ended his military career at the age of thirty-five after disagreements with David Ben Gurion over defense budget cuts. He later devoted himself to archeological studies and undertook numerous important excavations. Even as an archeologist, Yadin never completely withdrew from politics, serving as a military advisor to Prime Minister Levi Eshkol during the Six-Day War and in 1973 as a member of the Agranat Commission, which investigated the government's mistakes during the Yom Kippur War. During Menachem Begin's government, he served as deputy prime minister and played a key role in the negotiations that led to the Israeli-Egyptian peace treaty (Camp David Accords). He died in Hadera in 1984.

TRAINING AND REORGANIZATION OF THE ARMORED FORCES

The Israeli armed forces attached great importance to a comprehensive network of military schools and training facilities. In doing so, various partnerships were established with foreign countries. Within this framework were to be trained specialists, unit commanders from platoon leaders to brigade commanders, and general and staff officers.

For example, the army command sent a group of handpicked cadres to the French regular army's tank officer training course in Saumur, France. Paradoxically, officers from the Syrian army also took part in this course, some of whom, after initial reluctance, became friends with the Israelis and even exchanged experiences from the battles of the War of Independence.

The Israeli military attached great importance to the general education of its soldiers. For example, learning Hebrew was compulsory for immigrants, and the military also provided basic education for soldiers who came from less developed countries. Career officers were even given the opportunity to obtain an academic degree at universities in Israel or abroad.

Of the twelve infantry brigades that served during the War of Independence, nine were disbanded and converted into reserve brigades. The Golani and Givati Brigades remained in active service. The 7th Armored Brigade, which had a remarkable combat record, also remained as an active unit but took over the 82nd Armored Battalion from the 8th Armored Brigade as well as the 9th Infantry Battalion and a reconnaissance company from the Negev Brigade.

The 82nd Armored Battalion was stationed west of Jerusalem in Ramla and was divided into four tank companies. They had only the remaining M4 Sherman tanks, which were only partially combat ready. The less proven Hotchkiss H-39 and the two Mark IV Cromwell tanks were no longer included in the new structure.

IMPROVED SHERMAN TANKS

The battalion's Company A consisted of a number of M4 Sherman tanks without guns, which came from surplus Italian stocks. The idea was to mount the Krupp M1911 75 mm gun in these tanks. Surprisingly, the Israeli armaments services found what they were looking for in Switzerland, because that country had acquired the guns for use as towed field howitzers but had never used them, having placed them in storage in ammunition depots in mountain caves. With a great deal of effort and technical creativity, Israeli armorers mounted the guns, which had never been used in this form, in the Sherman tanks.

In the course of this, the M4A2 and M4A3 Sherman tanks of Company B were also fitted with the 75 mm gun, for which, however, only sparse ammunition supplies were available. One Sherman tank received the more powerful 76 mm gun, for which no ammunition was available.

The other two companies were equipped with half-tracks and had no tanks. The status of the newly established armor school at Ramla was also less than euphoric, since it had just three Sherman tanks of different types with minimal practice ammunition.

The shortage of senior instructors and trained crews was also a serious problem. The only experienced volunteer was a British tank officer, who was named the armor school's chief instructor, with the rank of major. The other instructors—including Russians, Czechs, and Israelis—had great difficulty communicating with one another or understanding the available training manuals—mainly older American publications on handling the Sherman tank.

At the beginning of the 1950s, Colonel Moshe Pasternak, the newly named head of the armored corps and successor to Yitzhak Sadeh, began training the armored corps.

Initial exercises and maneuvers by the armored corps showed little confidence in the effectiveness of this type of weapon. In 1951, for example, a gunnery demonstration took place that was supposed to impress high-ranking officers with the capabilities of the armored corps in supporting infantry in battle. As the Shermans advanced loudly and the projectiles from their poorly maintained gunnery systems detonated about 100 feet in front of the tanks, the cadre of inspectors left the demonstration unimpressed and outraged, but the tank crews were left baffled.

Maneuvers with the infantry were also only moderately successful at first, for while the tank crews were made up of regular soldiers, the infantrymen were usually recruited from reservists, who had a much-poorer level of training.

However, an important incident was to abruptly change the armored corps' status and difficult image. The 7th Armored Brigade attacked the flank of a defensive line during a maneuver in the Negev in 1952. The exercise went according to plan until

The emblem of the Israeli Armored Corps depicts a Cromwell Mark IV tank on a red field. *Wikipedia*

Lieutenant Colonel Uri Ben Ari[2] caused a surprise. He energetically drove his formation of tanks and half-tracks over 80 miles (130 km) to the front and initiated an attack on the defensive line. In the manner of the cavalry, he advanced in line formation and put to flight an entire infantry brigade, which defended the sector in vain.

Even though they knew that it was only an exercise, the infantry nevertheless fled in panic before the approaching tanks. The surprising maneuver completely disrupted the carefully prepared exercise plan. Chief of Staff Yadin was less than pleased, but Prime Minister Ben Gurion, who was also attentively watching the battle, came to the conclusion that the armored corps must be supplied with more combat resources immediately.

In the mid-1950s the Arabs began equipping their mechanized units with more-modern tanks. The Egyptian army, for example, purchased tanks made in Great Britain, the United States, and the Soviet Union, including Centurion Mark 3s, M4A2 Shermans, T-34/85s, SU-100 tank destroyers, and SU-152 self-propelled guns. The arms race in the Middle East had begun.

---

[2] Uri Ben Ari (1925–2009), born in Berlin, immigrated to Palestine in the 1940s and joined the Palmach. He fought as a company commander in the Jerusalem sector during the War of Independence, led the 7th Armored Brigade in the Suez Crisis, and rose to become commander of the armored corps in 1956. During the October War of 1973 he served as deputy commander of the southern front.

M4A3 Sherman tank, the Israeli M1 version with a 76 mm gun. *IDF*

The Israeli Armored Corps meanwhile profited from the friendly attitude of the French. This is explained mainly by the escalation of the Algerian conflict. While Egyptian prime minister Nasser sent weapons to aid the Algerians in fighting the French occupying power, the French declared themselves ready to provide Israel with modern tanks. Even if, in most cases, these were surplus M4A1 Sherman tanks with 76 mm guns, which were being replaced by more-modern types in the French army, these vehicles were regarded as being sufficiently advanced. They were also in good condition and were supplied with sufficient quantities of ammunition. The Israelis renamed their M4A1s the M1.

France also sold Israel several hundred AMX-13 light reconnaissance tanks armed with the powerful 75 mm gun (L 61.5), which was clearly superior to the 76 mm F-34 gun (L42) of the Soviet T-34. The procurement of the fleet of AMX-13s turned out to be a complicated and strictly secret undertaking, of which even in Israel only a select few had knowledge.

While the newly procured AMX-13s and M1s arrived secretly in the port of Haifa, the Israelis tinkered with further improvements to the performance of their aging Sherman tanks. The first task was to install a more powerful gun. This idea was based on a British concept, which saw the Sherman converted into the Firefly version with which to go up against the German Panzer V Panther and Panzer VI Tiger tanks in Normandy.

Israeli engineers installed the powerful CN 75-50 gun carried by the AMX-13 into their obsolete M4A1s, thus creating the M50 Sherman, whose development is regarded as a classic example of technical inventiveness and cooperation between armor experts. In mid-1956 a company of the new M50 Shermans was added to the 82nd Armored Battalion.

The fact that the ceasefire agreements were very vaguely worded led to ongoing skirmishes between Israel and its neighbor states. At the end of November 1950, for example, there were armed clashes with the kingdom of Jordan's Arab Legion on the road to Eilat, which were a consequence of different interpretations of the demarcation line. Further areas of conflict were the Latrun area and the "Jerusalem corridor," where Jordanian troops repeatedly violated the terms of the ceasefire. There were further provocations by the Syrian side in the demilitarized zone in the Jordan Valley and at Auja al-Hafir and by the Egyptians in Gaza.

The first deterioration in the security situation came with the beginning of the so-called Fedayeen infiltrations (terrorist groups made up of former Palestinians). They sought not only to inflict material damage but also to carry out strikes against the Israeli population. These raids were carried out from every Arab nation bordering Israel and were supported by local military authorities.

Since in some cases uncoordinated Israeli revenge strikes against the Fedayeen proved unsuccessful, a special formation with the designation Commando Unit 101 was given the task of carrying out more-effective counterstrikes. The new chief of the general staff, Mordechai Maklef,[3] named Ariel Sharon[4]

---

[3] Mordechai Maklef (1920–78) grew up in Motza near Jerusalem. Maklef lost his entire family in the Hebron massacre of 1929 and joined the Haganah. During the Second World War, he fought in the Jewish Brigade in Italy and was commander of the Carmeli Brigade during the War of Independence in 1948–49. At the age of thirty-two, he became the youngest chief of staff of the Israeli armed forces. However, Maklef resigned from the military after just one year in this position and from then on worked in leading positions in the public sector.

Exercise involving an armored company of the 82nd Armored Battalion of the 7th Armored Brigade, early 1950s. *IDF*

commander of this unit of about fifty specially selected and trained soldiers. Sharon began carrying out retaliatory strikes against the insurgent fedayeen, in some cases under difficult geographical and tactical conditions.

Despite its controversial tactics, Commando Unit 101 is regarded as the prototype Israeli special unit. In January 1954 the general staff combined Commando Unit 101 with the 890th Paratrooper Battalion and thus formed the 202nd Paratrooper Brigade, which would several times play a decisive role in future Arab-Israeli conflicts.

The fedayeen attacks and the closure of waterways to Israeli shipping traffic in the Suez Canal and the Gulf of Eilat were only several of the causes that led to the second open war between Arabs and Israelis. The newly organized Israeli Armored Corps with its expanded arsenal of weapons was about to face its first test.

---

[4] Ariel Sharon (1928–2014), born in what is now Belarus, served in the Haganah at the age of thirteen and later in the Jewish Settlement Police. In the 1948–49 War of Independence, he fought as a platoon leader in an infantry company of the Alexandroni Brigade in the Latrun battles. In the Suez Crisis in 1956, he led the 202nd Paratrooper Brigade, and during the Six-Day War in 1967, he commanded a division in the Sinai campaign. In 1969, he became commander of the Southern Command and led the 143rd Division during the Yom Kippur War in 1973. His political career began in 1974 as a member of the Knesset, later serving as minister of agriculture under Menachem Begin, then minister of defense and prime minister in 2001. He suffered a stroke in 2005, fell into a coma, and died in 2014. After a state funeral, Sharon was buried on the family farm Havat Shikmim in the north of the Negev desert.

Members of the 890th Paratrooper Battalion, which was later combined with Commando 101 to form the 202nd Paratrooper Brigade. It became an unparalleled producer of military leaders, since several of the officers seen here led major units during later Arab-Israeli wars. *From left, standing*: Lieutenant Meir Har-Zion, Major Ariel Sharon, Lieutenant General Moshe Dayan, Captain Dani Matt, Lieutenant Moshe Efron, Major General Asaf Simchoni. *From left, seated*: Captain Aharon Davidi, Lieutenant Ya'kov, Captain Rafael Eitan. *Israel Government Press Office*

CHAPTER 6: The Evolution of the Armored Corps | 61

PORTRAIT OF HAIM LASKOV

Haim Laskov was born in 1919 in the Belarusian city of Baryssau and grew up in poor conditions there. In 1925, he immigrated to Palestine with his family, who settled in Haifa. Laskov joined the Haganah as a teenager and served in Orde Wingate's paramilitary organization special night squads (SNSs), among others. This unit comprised around two hundred soldiers and primarily fought against the Arab uprising in the Galilee. During the Second World War, Laskov served as a company commander in the Jewish Brigade, which supported the British army during the campaigns in Italy in 1944.

After the outbreak of the War of Independence in 1948–49, Laskov led the 79th Armored Battalion of the 7th Armored Brigade during Operation Nachshon, part of the Latrun battles. It succeeded in opening up some supply routes to Jerusalem and fighting for the first time as a united, albeit improvised, combat unit with infantry, simple armored vehicles, and air support. After being promoted to brigadier general, Laskov took command of the 7th Armored Brigade and fought together with parts of the Golani Brigade during Operations Dekel and Hiram in the Galilee region.

Chief of the General Staff Chaim Laskov congratulates a cadet after successfully completing officer school, July 1959. *Israel Government Press Office*

Although Laskov had never been a combat pilot, he took command of the Israeli air force after the War of Independence in 1951. Under his leadership, the Israeli military leadership procured twin-engine Gloster Meteors from the British, Israel's first jet fighter aircraft. After studying abroad, including at Oxford University, Laskov took up the post of deputy chief of staff in 1955. After differences of opinion with his superior Moshe Dayan, the latter transferred him to the armored corps, which he commanded until the outbreak of the Suez Crisis.

During the invasion of the Sinai Peninsula in 1956, Laskov commanded the 77th Division, which forced the breakthrough through Rafah with infantry and armored forces and fought on the front line at El Arish–El Kantara. In 1958, at the age of just thirty-nine, Laskov succeeded Moshe Dayan as chief of staff of the Israeli army and was promoted to lieutenant general.

His tenure as chief of staff included a controversial military parade in Jerusalem, which was held to mark the tenth anniversary of the Israeli armed forces, and a surprise mobilization of the reserves, which caused panic in the country after coded call-up signals were broadcast by radio and also put the armed forces of neighboring Arab countries on high alert.

Laskov resigned from his post in January 1961 and served as director of the Israel Port Authority. During his tenure, the port of Ashdod was built, which is still an important cargo-handling center for Israel today. Laskov also served as a member of the Agranat Commission, which investigated the misconduct of Israel's political and military leadership after the Yom Kippur War.

Laskov died in Tel Aviv in 1982.

Portrait of Haim Laskov

Brigadier General Chaim Laskov (*seated, left*) with officers of his staff, photographed in the Rafah area, November 1956. *Israel Government Press Office*

CHAPTER 6: The Evolution of the Armored Corps | 63

Chapter 7
The Sherman Tank and Its Modifications

In the period between the two world wars, the United States neglected its armored forces more than any other major power, because as a nation dominated by isolationism it paid little attention to land forces.

Not until the early 1930s did the US Army begin experiments with armored vehicles, forming its first armored battalions, each with two tank companies and single infantry, combat engineer, and support companies. The newly created tank units were placed under the cavalry, which was then based at Fort Knox.

Fort Knox thus became the cradle of the modern American armored force. With the production of new tanks and under the influence of progressive cavalry officers such as Adna R. Chaffee and George S. Patton, the first American armored brigades were formed.

With the outbreak of the Second World War, Congress made available funding for an expansion of the armored forces, and under Chaffee various cavalry and infantry divisions were combined to form the American Armored Corps, with an initial strength of two divisions.

DEVELOPMENT HISTORY OF THE M4

The American armaments industry increased production of tanks in the first years of the war and produced the M3/M5 Stuart light tank and the M3 Lee/Grant medium. When the United States entered the war in December 1941, three armored divisions were ready. Eleven more would follow by 1943. The M3 was always an interim solution, since it was only lightly armored, and its short 75 mm gun (31 calibers) was ineffective against the German Panzer IV in direct combat.

A requirement was therefore issued for a new tank that would have more-powerful armament and better armor protection and be simpler to maintain. The first prototypes were based on a cast hull and a turret with a 75 mm M2 cannon. The cannon, which had a barrel length of 28.5 calibers, was an interim solution until the M3, with a longer barrel (37.5 calibers), became available. The turret armament also included a coaxial .30-caliber machine gun. There were three more machine guns in the hull, two fixed and the third in a ball mount.

The new tank was similar in design to the M3. Equipped with a Wright-Continental R-975 engine and Cletrac steering, the tank's drive sprockets were front-mounted.

The first production examples of the M4A1 left the production line of the Lima Locomotive Company in February 1942. The companies Detroit Tank Arsenal, Baldwin, Alco, Pressed Steel, and Pullman, which had previously produced the M3, switched production to the M4 and achieved an output of two thousand vehicles per month.

To quickly increase production, the various factories also produced different engine and transmission types.

These included

- M4A2, with a General Motors 6046 twin diesel engine, producing 410 hp;
- M4A3, with a Ford GAA V-8 engine built specially for this purpose, producing 500 hp;
- M4A4, with a thirty-cylinder Chrysler Multibank engine, producing 425 hp; and
- M4A6, with a Caterpillar D-200 nine-cylinder diesel radial engine, producing 460 hp.

At the time it entered service, the M4 was equal to most German tanks then in production. It had 51 mm of frontal armor and a 75 mm gun, which was capable of penetrating 60 mm thick armor plates sloped at an angle of 60 degrees at a range of 1,500 feet (460 m). However, the appearance of the more powerful Panzer V Panther and Panzer VI Tiger made improvements to the M4, especially in firepower and armor protection, of vital importance.

At the beginning of 1944 the existing M4A1, M4A2, and M4A3 fleet began to be retrofitted with a more powerful 75 mm gun. Its improved armor-piercing performance — with a muzzle velocity of 693 m/sec., the gun was able to penetrate 110 mm of armor plate sloped at 60 degrees at a range of 1,500 feet — proved very useful in combat against the more heavily armored German tanks.

Introduced at the same time as the heavier armament were so-called "wet" ammunition racks, with a hollow outer casing

Overhauling Sherman tanks, some early acquisitions by the Israelis. The machine guns have already been mounted on the turrets, while those for the forward hull wait to be installed, 1949. *Israel Government Press Office*

M1 Super Sherman with 75 mm gun during maneuvers in the Negev in the 1960s. *IDF*

M4A1 Sherman (Original version)	
Type	Medium tank
Manufacturer	Lima Locomotive Works, Pressed Steel Car Company, Pacific Car and Foundry Company, Pressed Steel Car Company
Introduction	1942
Number made	49,234
Crew	5 (commander, gunner, loader, driver, machine gunner)
Service life	1942 – 1957
Combat weight	33.4 tons (30,300 kg)
Length	19 ft. (5,800 mm)
Width	8 ft., 6 in. (2,600 mm)
Height	7 ft., 6 in. (2,300 mm)
Primary armament	M3 L40 75 mm gun (97 rounds)
Secondary armament	1 × M19191A4 7.62 mm machine gun (5,050 rounds) 1 × M2 12.7 mm machine gun (600 rounds)
Engine	Wright Continental R-975-C1 9-cylinder gasoline engine 400 hp
Transmission	Spicer Synchromesh (5 VW, 1 RW)
Power-to-weight ratio	13.2 hp/ton
Ground clearance	17.4 in. (0.443 m)
Wading ability	39 in. (1.0 m)
Trench crossing	90.5 in. (2.3 m)
Obstacle	24 in. (0.610 m)
Gradient	60%
Maximum speed	25 mph (40 kph) (on roads)
Fuel capacity	158.5 US gal. (600 liters)
Range	124 miles (200 km) (on roads)
Protection	Armor steel structure (51–76 mm frontal, 38–51 mm on the sides)

filled with a mixture of water and glycerin, which in the event of a hit prevented the ammunition from cooking off. For further protection in combat, the crews attached spare track links, sandbags, wood, and even elements of concrete to the armor plates.

The British army also approved the M4 and gave the tank the name "Sherman," after the American general William T. Sherman. They quickly shipped the first production M4A1 tanks to North Africa to reinforce the British Eighth Army in its defensive struggle against Rommel's Panzer Group Africa. About 270 Sherman tanks took part in the Second Battle of El Alamein in 1942.

In February 1944, the British began producing a converted Sherman called the Firefly to enable it to match the firepower, in particular, of the latest German tanks. This model was armed with the British 17-pounder gun (76.2 mm, L55), enabling it to penetrate 120 mm of armor plate sloped at 60 degrees from a range of 1,500 feet.

The British converted a total of about six hundred Shermans into Firefly models. They formed the backbone of the Allied forces in the Normandy offensive, in Alsace, in the Battle of the Bulge, and in the final battles in western and northwestern Germany after the crossing of the Rhine.

CHAPTER 7: The Sherman Tank and Its Modifications

THE FIRST USE OF SHERMAN TANKS IN PALESTINE

While the British were withdrawing their troops from Palestine, and Arab attacks on the Jewish population were increasing, the Haganah sought to acquire tanks to supplement its arsenal of half-track vehicles. Most of the tanks used by the British were supposed to be scrapped. In addition to two Cromwell Mark IV tanks, with the assistance of several British soldiers the Haganah was also able to steal a Sherman tank near Tira, located south of Haifa. It had most recently belonged to the Royal Wiltshire Yeomanry Regiment. The tank had fought in the Battle of El Alamein in 1942 and was finally shipped to Palestine.

A thorough inspection of the captured M4A2 Sherman was soon followed by disappointment. The diesel engine's starter was unreliable, and the main gun, the turret ring, machine guns, and the optical sight were missing, as was the radio equipment and lighting.

Mechanics repaired the Sherman as best they could so that it could be thrown into the ongoing fighting of the raging War of Independence. The missing main gun was initially replaced by a 20 mm Hispano-Suiza cannon. The General Motors twin diesel engine was repaired in a makeshift manner, and missing components were replaced with available spare parts. The tank was given the name "Meir," after the newborn son of workshop commander Shimshon Reznik.

Taken on strength by B Company of the 82nd Armored Battalion of the 8th Armored Brigade, "Meir," together with the two Cromwell Mark IVs, saw its first action in the battles for Latrun, Lod, and Ramla.

Despite technical difficulties, the Israeli general staff evaluated the first combat experiences with armored vehicles as successful, and it sent teams of experts around the globe to procure additional tanks. Doing so proved difficult, however, since few countries offered help due to the difficult international conditions. The Czechs broke off negotiations for the acquisition of Panzerkampfwagen 38(t) light tanks and Jagdpanzer 38 Hetzer tank destroyers. In the United States the Israelis tried to purchase the M3 Stuart light tank, but negotiations failed over administrative differences with the exporting authorities. They had better luck in Italy. The Italian army had a large number of tanks, including Shermans, left over from the Allies' offensives of the final years of the war. Most of the Shermans lacked armament, however.

The Israelis purchased 130 M4A1s from the Italians that were supposed to be scrapped, and under the greatest secrecy shipped them to Haifa. The lack of guns was compensated for by an unusual acquisition from Switzerland, where old, never-used 75 mm Krupp cannon from towed howitzers from the First World War were stored in munitions depots. "Meir" was one of the first tanks to be fitted with one of the newly acquired guns.

Making the M4A1s imported from Italy ready for use in combat proved a daunting task. The tanks were in poor condition, and time was of the essence. Nevertheless, in a short time the following three M4A2 tanks were converted to carry the Krupp 75 mm guns:

- a Sherman tank named after Tamar Horen, the female assistant of a staff officer of the 8th Armored Brigade
- a Sherman of the 82nd Armored Battalion employed as a command vehicle and given the name "Ruth II"
- A Sherman without armament employed as a recovery vehicle in the second phase of Operation Horev was given the name "Ada," after Ada Sereni, a fighter in the Palmach.

The tanks "Meir" and "Tamar" did not survive the War of Independence. Both drove over mines during an attack on Egyptian units during Operation Horev, which wrecked their drive sprockets, transmissions, and mountings and parts of the tracks.

At the beginning of 1955, Israel reacted with alarm to the armament programs of the surrounding Arab states, which were procuring modern, more-capable tanks. On behalf of the Soviet Union, Czechoslovakia supplied postwar versions of the T-34. They were not the models with the original 76 mm gun, but tanks produced under license in Czechoslovakia with the much more powerful 85 mm gun. Another threat was the SD-100, a Czech-produced version of the SU-100 self-propelled gun, which was capable of destroying any tank in the Israeli arsenal from a significant range.

THE M1

At that time, France was the only nation prepared to supply tanks, and it sold Israel sixty M4A1 and M4A3 Shermans with the more powerful M1 76 mm gun. In the course of standardization of the existing tank fleet and the newly acquired types, it was agreed to adopt the name "M1 Super Sherman."

With only a few modifications, the M1 took part in the Sinai campaign during the Suez Crisis of 1956, encountering Egyptian Shermans. A few M1s also supported the 10th Armored Brigade's attack on Jerusalem during the Six-Day War in 1967. After victory in 1967, the Israelis converted some M1s into recovery tanks and retired the rest from service.

While preparing the M1s to enter service, the Israelis realized that they needed a tank with a more powerful gun to

M50s, modified M4A2s, moving through the Negev while on maneuvers, 1965. *Israel Government Press Office*

keep pace with the tanks acquired by the Arab states. With support from the Bourges Arsenal in France, Israeli engineers began working on a further-upgraded version of the Sherman. It was to be based on the M4A1 Shermans with the cast steel hull and the M4A3 and A4 versions with welded hulls.

THE M50

The central element of the upgrade was replacement of the tank's main armament. The Israelis were impressed by the capabilities of the 75 mm CN 75-50 carried by the French AMX-13 light tank. Its technology was based on the legendary gun carried by the German Panzerkampfwagen V Panther from the Second World War. With a barrel 62 calibers in length, it was very long and had an outstanding-for-the-time muzzle velocity of 3,280 ft./sec. (1,000 m/sec.), and with Model 1951 ammunition it was capable of penetrating up to 110 mm of armor plate.

However, the length of the cannon led to space problems and necessitated technical modifications to the turret. The engineers moved the gun so far forward that it shifted the center of gravity, and an extension was added to the rear of the turret to serve as a counterweight. Instead of the automatic loader used by the AMX-13, it was decided to use a manual loading system. The conversion was completed with the installation of a standard smoke extraction system from a French manufacturer. With these modifications the turret weighed in at about 5 metric tons. The tank was given the designation M50, a reference to the name of its gun. The Israeli engineers modified all the Shermans on hand to M50 standard, which led to a large number of variants, especially when it came to power plants. The tank was powered either by the 400 hp Continental R975 C4 radial engine, the 400 hp General Motors engine, the 500 hp Ford engine, or the 425 hp Chrysler power plant. All these variants had a top speed of about 25 mph (40 kph).

Twenty-five vehicles reached the units just in time for the start of the Suez Crisis of 1956. Thirteen of the upgraded M50s formed a company of the 82nd Armored Battalion of the 7th Armored Brigade, while another twelve formed a company of the 277th Armored Battalion of the 27th Reserve Brigade.

M51s advance on Egyptian positions in the Sinai following an Israeli airstrike, 1967. *Israel Government Press Office*

In this pressing situation, the Israelis decided to equip the Sherman with the new QV-105-F1 105 mm gun, which was carried by the French AMX-30 tank. The gun, which had a muzzle velocity of 3,280 ft./sec. (1,000 m/sec.), was, however, too large for the standard Sherman turret. They adapted a larger version of the M23 turret from the M1, reduced the barrel length by 4.9 feet (1.5 m), fitted a muzzle brake to reduce recoil forces, and installed a turret counterweight for stability, similar to that of the M50.

These changes also led to adjustments to the turret control system and the suspension. The manual aiming device was to be replaced by the French hydraulic design of the AMX-13. The M51 weighed approximately 35 tons and was powered either by the 460 hp Cummings engine or by the original engines of the companies Continental or Ford. The tank's top speed of 25 mph (40 kph) was similar to that of the M50 or the original Sherman.

The development and testing phase was completed in 1960, and the first batches of the new tank with final approval were handed over to the units in July 1962. By 1967, 175 M51 tanks were in service.

They saw action on the Sinai Peninsula and around Jerusalem during the Six-Day War in 1967 and on the Golan Heights during

New, more-modern tanks with more-powerful guns such as the American M48 Patton and the Soviet T-54/55 outclassed the upgraded M50. Despite this, the M50 took part in fighting during the Suez Crisis and the Six-Day War in 1967. A few examples were even still in service with reserve units at the time of the Yom Kippur War in 1973, but by then they were of little more than symbolic value and were retired after the war.

THE M51

A further increase in the M50's combat capabilities was necessary to meet the threat posed by the latest Soviet and American tanks being delivered to Egypt, Syria, and Jordan. Against the background of political relations, it still seemed unlikely that Israel would be able to procure more-modern tanks in the foreseeable future, at least not in large numbers.

In 1958, France offered to sell Israel fifty-five American-made M47 Patton tanks, but the United States rejected the sale, and it would not be until years later that the first M48A1 and M48A2 Patton tanks were secretly delivered to Israel. It was also problematic that the M50 was leaving the workshops in small numbers only. The Israelis produced just one hundred M50 Shermans between 1956 and 1961.

M51s of the 14th Armored Brigade, 38th Division (Ugda Sharon) on the advance at the Suez Canal during the Six-Day War, 1967. *Israel Government Press Office*

the Yom Kippur War in 1973. Despite its upgraded gun, the M51 proved obsolescent in both wars, and the Israeli military slowly replaced it with M48s and M60s supplied by America and British-made Centurions. Despite this, the M51 was still in service with several reserve units in the early 1990s.

The fact that the numerous modified Sherman tanks remained in service with the Israeli Armored Corps alongside more-modern tanks for so long is due to the high quality of their original design, reliability, and considerable firepower.

An M51 (*foreground*) and an M50 (*behind*) on display at the Israeli Tank Museum at Latrun. *Marc Lenzin Archive*

M 50 Sherman	
Type	Medium tank
Service entry	1956
Number made	300 (50 M50 Degem Alef, 250 M50 Degem Bet)
Crew	5 (commander, gunner, loader, driver, machine gunner)
Combat weight	38.6 tons (35,000 kg)
Length	20 ft., 4 in. (6,200 mm)
Width	7 ft., 10 in. (2,400 mm)
Height	7 ft., 2 in. (2,200 mm)
Primary armament	SA 50 L/61 75 mm gun (62 rounds) as carried by the AMX-13
Secondary armament	1 × 7.62 mm M1919 machine gun mounted coaxially (4,750 rounds) 1 × 12.7 mm M2HB machine gun mounted coaxially (600 rounds)
Engine	M50 Degem Alef: Wright-Continental R-975-C4 9-cylinder gasoline engine, 400 hp M50 Degem Bet: Cummins VT-8-460 8-cylinder diesel engine, 460 hp
Transmission	Spicer Synchromesh (5 forward gears, 1 reverse)
Power-to-weight ratio	M50 Degem Alef: 11.4 hp/ton M50 Degem Bet: 13.2 hp/t
Ground clearance	17.4 in. (0.443 m)
Wading ability	39 in. (1.0 m)
Trench crossing	90.5 in. (2.3 m)
Obstacle	24 in. (0.610 m)
Gradient	60%
Maximum speed	25 mph (40 kph) (on roads)
Fuel capacity	160 US gal. (606 liters)
Range	186 miles (300 km) (on roads)
Protection	Armor steel structure (63–76 mm frontal, 38–76 mm on the sides)

M 51 Sherman	
Type	Medium tank
Service entry	1962
Number made	180
Crew	5 (commander, gunner, loader, driver, machine gunner)
Combat weight	44 tons (40,000 kg)
Length	20 ft., 4 in. (6,200 mm)
Width	7 ft., 10 in. (2,400 mm)
Height	7 ft., 2 in. (2,200 mm)
Primary armament	D1508 105 mm gun (47 rounds)
Secondary armament	1 × 7.62 mm M1919 machine gun mounted coaxially (4,750 rounds) 1 × 12.7 mm M2HB machine gun mounted coaxially (600 rounds) M51 Degern Daleth: 60 mm mortar
Engine	Cummins VT-8-460 8-cylinder diesel engine, 460 hp
Transmission	Spicer Synchromesh (5 forward gears, 1 reverse)
Power-to-weight ratio	11.5 hp/ton
Ground clearance	17.4 in. (0.443 m)
Wading ability	39 in. (1.0 m)
Trench crossing	90.5 in. (2.3 m)
Obstacle	24 in. (0.610 m)
Gradient	60%
Maximum speed	25 mph (40 kph) (on roads)
Fuel capacity	160 US gal. (606 liters)
Range	186 miles (300 km) (on roads)
Protection	Armor steel structure (63–76 mm frontal, 38–76 mm on the sides)

Chapter 8
Growth from French Production: The AMX-13

From 1956 onward, the Israelis procured and operated about four hundred AMX-13s. The first modern light tank operated by the Israeli Armored Corps was delivered to the units just before the Sinai campaign and supplemented the first-generation Centurion tank from Britain. The AMX-13 took part in the Sinai campaign of 1956 with one battalion and later with three battalions during the Six-Day War.

DEVELOPMENT

The development of a new light tank suitable for reconnaissance and covering the flanks was determined by French tank doctrine, which emphasized firepower and mobility. This doctrine called for a light, fast-tracked vehicle with the most effective gun possible, in which German experience in mounting high-velocity guns on various light chassis was to be combined with the promising concept of the oscillating turret. The design firm Atelier de Construction d'Issy-les-Molineaux began work in 1946, and two years later the first of a series of prototypes was completed. Quantity production by the Atelier de Construction Roanne (ARE) finally began in 1952 and continued until 1964 (French production) and 1987 (license production in Argentina), with a total of 7,700 vehicles completed. This made the AMX-13 the most produced tank of any western European nation and by far the most successful French tank of all time. Of the 7,700 vehicles produced, 4,300 served with the French army, while the remaining 3,400 were exported to twenty-five nations. The name AMX-13 consists of an abbreviation of the Atelier de Construction d'Issy-les-Molineaux and the tank's operational weight of 14.3 tons (13 metric tons). In the French army, however, the vehicle was designated Char 13t-75 Modèle 51.

Whereas in conventional tank turrets the gun is moved independently of the turret in the vertical axis, in an oscillating turret it is fixed to the turret structure. The movement in the vertical axis is achieved by tilting the entire turret. The main advantage of this is that, compared to the size of the chassis, a smaller and lighter turret with a larger gun could be mounted—similar to the tank destroyers from the Second World War.

The French army developed a whole series of experimental heavy tanks equipped with oscillating turrets and heavy guns, such as the AMX-50, the Somua SM, and the Lorraine 40t. The concept was adopted for use in only two light vehicles, the Panhard EBR and the AMX-13. At the same time, experiments with the oscillating turret (T69, T54E1, T57) were also being carried out in the United States, but the concept was ultimately abandoned. Despite its high production numbers, in action the AMX-13 demonstrated the limits of the concept, which was difficult to integrate into a conventional tactical structure and was therefore no longer pursued by France. In 1966 the AMX-13 was rearmed with a CN-90-F3 L/52 90 mm tank gun for the French army, and later even with a CN-105 L/57 105 mm gun for export (Dutch army).

TECHNICAL FEATURES

The crew of the AMX-13 consisted of the tank commander, the gunner, and the driver. The tank commander was on the left side of the turret and had a commander's cupola with seven L794B periscopes, which gave him an all-round view even with the hatch closed, and a telescopic sight with magnification factors of 1.5 and 6. The gunner was on the right side of the turret and had two L794D aiming devices with 7.5 magnification and a TCV 107 laser rangefinder. The driver sat forward on the left side of the hull, next to the engine.

The lower part of the hull was cast and connected to the chassis by a conventional turret ring, which enabled the turret to be rotated 360 degrees. The upper part of the turret was a combination of cast steel and welded armor steel plates and was placed on the lower part in such a way that it could move freely in the vertical axis (−8 degrees to +12 degrees). The turret's azimuth and elevation were controlled by hydraulic motors, with maximum traverse speed of 30 degrees per second and elevation speed of 5 degrees per second. The system was not stabilized, and thus aiming and firing while on the move was not possible.

The 75 mm SA 50 L/61 gun and the 7.5 mm coaxial MAC 31 machine gun were fixed to the turret. The main gun was a development of the German 75 mm KwK 42 L/71 gun used in the Panther tank during the Second World War. The AMX-13 employed an automatic loader with two revolver magazines, each holding six rounds. The rate of fire was up to twelve rounds per minute. When the two revolver magazines had been emptied, the tank had to withdraw into cover, where they were reloaded from outside the vehicle. The vehicle carried a total of thirty-two rounds of ammunition (twenty-one in the turret, eleven in the hull). Ammunition was loaded through the turret roof, and the spent casings were thrown out a hatch in the rear of the turret. The 7.5 mm coaxial machine gun was loaded with two-hundred-round belts, and 3,600 rounds of machine gun ammunition were carried.

Compared to its firepower, the AMX-13's armor protection was very weak. The frontal armor consisted of welded steel plates with a thickness of 40 mm, the side armor was 20 to 25 mm thick, the rear armor was 15 mm, and the turret and hull top as well as the bottom armor was only 10 mm. Thus, only the frontal armor was capable of standing up to heavy machine guns (12.7 or 14.5 mm) and light cannon (up to 20 mm). For self-defense there was a smoke grenade discharger system on each side of the turret (2 × 3 smoke grenade dischargers). There was no NBC protection system.

The power plant was positioned forward on the right side of the hull and consisted of an eight-cylinder SOFAM gasoline engine (250 hp) and a transmission with five forward and one reverse gears. The drive sprockets were in front, and the first and last road wheels were sprung by torsion bars with a hydraulic shock absorber. The steel tracks, which were 13.8 inches (350 mm) wide, consisted of eighty-five links and had to be fitted with rubber pads for driving on asphalt roads.

Maximum speed was 37 mph (60 kph), and with a full tank (480 liters) a range of 249 miles (400 km) was possible. The AMX-13 had a ground clearance of 14.5 inches (370 mm) and was able to cross a trench 5.25 feet (1.6 m) wide, a vertical obstacle 2.1 feet (0.65 m) tall, or a 60 percent incline and wade bodies of water up to 2 feet (0.6 m) deep.

The NIMDA upgrade saw the installation of a new Detroit Diesel 6V-53T six-cylinder diesel engine (275 hp), a NIMDA N303 automatic transmission, a mechanically activated dry clutch, a new cooling system, and a new Elbit LANCELOT fire control system. In addition, the tank was given thicker

AMX-13 tanks taking part in a military parade in Jerusalem to mark the anniversary of Israel's independence, 1958. *Israel Government Press Office*

armor, and a fire suppression system was added. The modernized drivetrain increased range to 341.75 miles (550 km), and the digital fire control system improved first-shot accuracy and shortened the target acquisition and engagement times through the addition of second-generation day- and night-vision aiming devices for the gunner and a control unit for the commander.

IN ACTION

Israel received the first 180 AMX-13s from France in 1956 as part of an agreement to reinforce the Israeli army and maintain the balance of power in the region after an Egyptian-Czechoslovakian arms deal on 1955, which saw weapons valued at more than eighty-three million USD delivered to Egypt by the USSR. In addition to the AMX-13, France delivered additional 75 mm tank guns to Israel with which to equip its existing M4 fleet. Because of the shortage of battle tanks, the ZMX-13, which had been conceived as a reconnaissance tank, had to serve as a replacement. The vehicles were assembled into a tank battalion in the 7th Armored Brigade and experienced their baptism of fire the year they entered service, during the Sinai campaign.

CHAPTER 8: Growth from French Production: The AMX-13 | **71**

AMX-13 tank of the 60th Armored Brigade, 84th Division (Ugda Tal) near El Arish during the Six-Day War, 1967. *IWM*

AMX-13 tank of the 37th Armored Brigade, which has just refueled and rearmed and is standing by for another attack on the Golan Heights during the Six-Day War, 1967. Like the M50 Sherman, the AMX-13 was armed with the powerful 75 mm SA 50 gun developed from the German KwK 42 L/70, which armed the Panzerkampfwagen V Panther during the Second World War. *IWM*

AMX-13	
Type	Reconnaissance tank
Manufacturer	Atelier de Construction d'Issy-les-Moulineaux, France
Service entry	1956 (with the Israeli armed forces)
Number	400 (in service with the Israeli armed forces)
Crew	3 (commander, gunner, driver)
Combat weight	16 tons (14,500 kg)
Length	16 ft., 1 in. (4,900 mm; not counting barrel), 21 ft. (6,400 mm; with barrel)
Width	8 ft., 2 in. (2,500 mm)
Height	7 ft., 6 in. (2,300 mm)
Primary armament	SA 50 L/61 75 mm gun (32 rounds)
Secondary armament	1 × 7.5 mm MAC 31 coaxial machine gun (3,600 rounds) 2 × 3 smoke grenade launchers
Engine	SOFAM 8-cylinder gasoline engine, 250 hp
Power-to-weight ratio	17.2 hp/ton
Ground clearance	14.5 in. (0.37 m)
Wading ability	23.6 in. (0.6) m
Trench crossing	63 in. (1.6) m
Obstacle	25.6 in. (0.65 m)
Gradient	60%
Maximum speed	37 mph (60 kph) (on roads)
Fuel capacity	127 US gal. (480 liters)
Range	248 miles (400 km) (on roads)
Protection	Armor steel structure (400 mm frontal, 20 mm on the sides)

AMX-13 tank on display at the Israeli Tank Museum at Latrun. *Marc Lenzin Archive*

During the Six-Day War, four hundred AMX-13s organized in three battalions took part in combat operations. One battalion was committed against the Jordanians and advanced through the West Bank, took Taluzi and Tubas, and finally occupied Nablus. Another battalion fought against the Egyptians in the Gaza Strip and along the coast road in the north of the Sinai Peninsula. The AMX-13 suffered its heaviest losses on this front, including at Jiradi Pass and at Rafah. The third battalion attacked Syrian troops on the Golan Heights.

The Israelis recognized that the AMX-13 was too lightly armored and that its main gun was relatively ineffective against the more modern Arab T-54/55 and IS-3 tanks supplied by the Soviet Union. Although the Israeli Armored Corps began gradually withdrawing the AMX-13 from service after the Six-Day War in 1967, its use by Israel was nevertheless one of the greatest combat successes by the AMX-13.

CHAPTER 8: Growth from French Production: The AMX-13 | 73

Chapter 9
The Suez Crisis of 1956 (Second Arab-Israeli War)

The nationalization of the Suez Canal was a dangerous chess move by Egyptian president Gamal Abdel Nasser.[1] The governments of Great Britain and France sounded the alarm, while Israeli prime minister David Ben Gurion saw that the time had come to counter the threat posed by the Arab state on the Nile and conquer the Sinai Peninsula, in which tank units would play the decisive role.

The Mediterranean and the Suez Canal increasingly became the focus of public attention in the 1950s, since the waterway provided an important strategic link, especially for the Western powers of Great Britain and France to their Asian colonies. At the same time, the Suez Canal served as a raw-materials route, especially for crude oil bound for Europe.

This lifeline was soon to become the focal point of world affairs and trigger a war that further inflamed tensions between East and West in the midst of the Cold War.

The Arab states, especially Egypt, suffered a serious defeat against the Israeli armed forces. Opposition to the government spread, and on the national holiday in 1952, the Free Officers Movement led by Gamal Abdel Nasser overthrew the reigning Egyptian king Farouk I.

Nasser enjoyed a high level of acceptance and popularity among the people, rising rapidly in the political arena and gaining further power. He saw Egypt taking a leading role for both the Arab and the African-Islamic world.

As a result of his devotion to Arab nationalism, Nasser took an aggressive stance toward Israel. Although he negotiated a peace settlement with Israel that included the Palestinians, he soon saw the talks as sabotaged, since Ben Gurion rejected proposed solutions and rearmed the Israeli army with arms supplied by West Germany and France.

In order to secure water supplies for future periods of drought, Nasser pushed for further expansion of the Aswan Dam in Upper Egypt. This regulates the water level on the Nile and ensures the irrigation of fields via a widely distributed network of canals during periods of drought.

However, the dam proved to be too small despite several stages of expansion. There was a threat of famine if the growing Egyptian population had to endure periods of drought lasting one or more years.

In 1954, German companies offered to expand the dam and construct a new power plant for 2.1 billion dollars, with the United States initially agreeing to provide partial financing but then withdrawing its offer. The World Bank also withdrew its offer in view of the fact that full financing was no longer guaranteed.

Nasser, who was forced to complete construction of the dam for reasons of power legitimacy alone, saw only one way out of this situation: he nationalized the Suez Canal in order to use future revenues to finance the construction of the dam. He also turned his back on all Western governments and finally received additional financial and military support from the Soviet government.

The alliance of Great Britain, France, and Israel planned a violent response to this action. Against the backdrop of the Cold War, the future invaders invoked the danger of the spread of communism in the region and the need to secure Israel's borders.

British prime minister Anthony Eden saw Nasser's pan-Arabism as a threat to his nation's interests in the Middle East and therefore firmly rejected any policy of appeasement. France stood by the British, since it was disturbed by Egyptian support for the insurgents in Algeria, who had been fighting against the French colonial power for years.

Two scenarios appeared to offer a way out of the crisis:

- toppling Nasser's government with air attacks and a land offensive

---

[1] Gamal Abdel Nasser (1918–70) grew up in modest circumstances in Alexandria. He attended the military academy in Cairo in 1936 and fought as commander of an infantry battalion in the Israeli War of Independence in 1948–49. Nasser founded the Committee of Free Officers in 1949 and led the coup d'état against King Farouk I in 1952. Four years later, Nasser was elected president of Egypt. The defeat in the Six-Day War in 1967 took its toll on his health. He died in 1970, immediately after mediating a ceasefire between Jordan and the Palestinians. His successor as president was Anwar el-Sadat. The reservoir behind the Aswan Dam is named after him.

- ending the crisis by calling for a resolution by the UN Security Council with the condition that Egypt return the Suez Canal unconditionally or reverse its decision to nationalize the waterway

The United States under President Eisenhower initially adopted a cautious stance and tried to mediate with foresight in order to avoid a confrontation with the Soviet Union.

In order to put a stop to the latent threat posed by Egypt, Ben Gurion saw the opportunity to take the Sinai, which was only partially occupied by the Egyptians, in a military campaign—especially since Eden saw an invasion of the Sinai by Israeli forces as an ideal pretext for Anglo-French intervention. A joint ultimatum was to call on Egypt and Israel to cease hostilities and accept a temporary occupation of the canal.

The British government formulated five conditions that would be considered a casus belli and justification for a preemptive strike:

- Terror attacks by the fedayeen made normal life impossible in Israel.
- The Arabs blocked the connection through the Gulf of Aqaba and the Strait of Tiran.
- The Arabs tried to shift the balance of power between Israeli and Arab militaries in their favor.
- Iraqi or Syrian expeditionary forces (or both) appeared in the kingdom of Jordan.
- A military pact was formed among Egypt, Syria, and Jordan, along with the creation of a joint Arab high command.

All five conditions occurred in late 1955.

During the Israeli War of Independence, many Arab inhabitants had fled Palestine to Jordan, Syria, Lebanon, and Egypt. As a result, more and more groups came together to carry out infiltrations and terrorist attacks across the border on Israeli territory. One of the best-known groups was Fatah, which began operating in 1965 under Yasser Arafat, the later leader of the Palestine Liberation Organization (PLO).

In September 1955, the Egyptians tightened their naval blockade of Israel. The Israelis had long been denied passage through the Suez Canal and, for two years, access to the Gulf of Eilat. This was followed by the closure of the Strait of Tiran and thus the connection to the Red Sea, accompanied by the installation of heavy coastal artillery at Ras Nazrani.

The balance of power shifted to Israel's disadvantage through the rearming of all the surrounding Arab states with equipment primarily produced in Russia and supplied by Czechoslovakia.

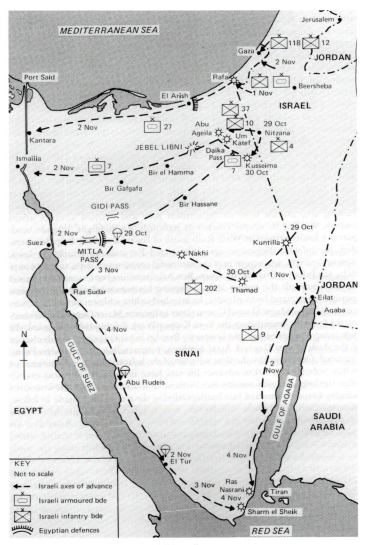

The Sinai campaign, 1956. *Wikipedia*

These deliveries included fighter bombers, reconnaissance aircraft, medium and heavy tanks, and artillery of various calibers. These arms deliveries influenced the balance of forces in the region and set in motion an ongoing arms race in the Middle East.

The arms deliveries were accompanied by a number of different Arab military alliances, culminating in an agreement among Egypt, Syria, Jordan, and Saudi Arabia.

To the Israeli government, this development justified an incursion into the Sinai. In fact, it seemed that the timing could hardly have been more favorable, because

- Soviet forces were occupied with the popular uprising in Hungary and the unrest in Poland,

Senior officers inspecting the troops after the taking of Sharm El Sheik. *From left to right*: General Asaf Simchoni (commander of the southern front), Chief of Staff Moshe Dayan, and General Avraham Yoffe (commander 9th Infantry Brigade), November 1956. *Israel Government Press Office*

Centurion heavy tank of the British 6th Armoured Regiment disembarking at Port Said in the opening phase of Operation Musketeer. Visible in the background is the statue of Ferdinand de Lesseps, the builder of the Suez Canal. November 1956. *Wikipedia*

- the United States was occupied with the heated presidential election campaign that was taking place, and
- cooperation with Great Britain and France offered advantages because a concentration of allied troops on the Suez Canal would force Egypt to withdraw forces from the Sinai, leaving weakened defensive positions on the peninsula.

Moshe Dayan, by then chief of staff of the Israeli armed forces, gave the operation the code name Kadesh. The name is a reference to the biblical episode of the exodus from Egypt, when the Israelites rested in Kadesh in Sinai before they set off for the Promised Land.

The Sinai Peninsula, whose area of 60,000 km² was three times larger than that of Israel at that time, forms a triangular shape and connects the African and Asian continents. It borders the Mediterranean Sea to the north, the Red Sea to the south, the Suez Canal to the west, and, to the east, the Israeli Negev and the Gulf of Aqaba. The Suez Canal runs along the western border of the peninsula, connecting the Mediterranean Sea with the Red Sea.

In the north and central Sinai there are vast areas of sand dunes and hard soil and, in places, long, dried-up watercourses. The terrain in the south is hilly and barren, with its dominant feature being Mount Sinai.

The population, which includes some Bedouin tribes in the south, is concentrated in the town of El Arish on the Mediterranean, west of Gaza City.

The poorly developed and badly neglected road network had last been used on a larger scale by the British during the Second World War to supply their Eighth Army in North Africa. An important road in the north leads from El Kantara on the Suez Canal along the coast via El Arish to Rafah, south of Gaza. Another road leads via Abu Ageila centrally through the Sinai and connects Ismailia on the Suez Canal with Al Qusaymah. From the city of Suez, another more southerly connection leads via Nakhl to Kuntilla. The connection crosses the Mitla Pass, which was to become of strategic importance during the crisis.

The Egyptian army units under Chief of Staff Abd al-Hakim Amer[2] were in defensive positions on the peninsula even before nationalization of the canal:

- In the northern sector was the 3rd Infantry Division, with the 5th Infantry Brigade in Rafah and the 6th Infantry Brigade in Abu Ageila, and the 4th and 99th Infantry Brigades in reserve.
- In the Gaza Strip was the 8th Infantry Division, with the 86th and 87th Palestinian Brigades.
- The 21st Infantry Battalion had taken up position on the Gulf of Aqaba at Sharm El Sheikh.
- The 1st and 2nd Armored Brigades of the 4th Armored Division were in the Ismailia area.

The Egyptian armored forces consisted mainly of M4 Sherman medium tanks armed with 75 mm guns. They also had Soviet equipment — T-35/85 medium tanks, Josef Stalin (IS-3) heavy tanks with 122 mm guns, and Archer tank-destroyers, based on the chassis of the British Valentine tank and armed with a 17-pounder (76.2 mm) antitank gun. Approximately 115 tanks and 110 artillery pieces were present in the Egyptian defense positions.

Meanwhile, the Israeli armed forces formed powerful reserves and optimized their mobilization. Whereas in the War of Independence the largest unit was the infantry or armored brigade, Dayan now created divisional battle groups (called *Ugda* in Hebrew), to which infantry, armored brigades, or support weapons could be added as required.

The Israelis had about 45,000 troops available for the campaign in the Sinai. There was the 38th Division, under the command of Jehuda Wallach,[3] the 77th Division, under Chaim Laskov,[4] and the 202nd Paratrooper Brigade, under Ariel Sharon. Armored units were to be employed on a large scale for the first

Troops of the British 3rd Parachute Battalion during the occupation of the El Gamil airport, November 1956. *IWM*

time, supporting the two divisions in the attack. The Israeli armored force, which had grown significantly in the past few years, consisted mainly of M4 Sherman tanks, which had been upgraded to various degrees:

- 125 M1 medium tanks with 76.2 mm guns, eighty-five M4 medium tanks with the earlier 75 mm gun, and twenty-five M50s with the French-made 75 mm from the AMX-13
- 180 AMX-13 light tanks
- 730 half-tracks armed with machine guns or antitank guns

There were not enough trained tank crews for the AMX-13 and M4 Sherman tanks that had been quickly procured in 1955–56. Therefore, only about 280 of the 460 tanks took up attack positions for the imminent action in the Sinai.

The 7th Armored Brigade under Colonel Uri Ben-Ari[5] was organized as follows:

---

[2] Mohamed Abd al-Hakim Amer (1919–67) was born in the Egyptian province of Minya and attended the military academy in Cairo. After serving in the Arab-Israeli War of 1948, he played a leading role in the 1952 coup d'état against King Farouk I. As chief of staff, he commanded the Egyptian army during the Suez Crisis in 1956 and the Six-Day War in 1967. However, he fell out of favor after the war and took his own life by poison in 1967.

[3] Jehuda Wallach (1921–2008) was of German origin and grew up in southern Germany. He immigrated to Palestine and joined the Palmach in 1938. Wallach commanded the Givati Brigade during the War of Independence in 1948–49. After the Suez Crisis, he left the army due to conflicts with Moshe Dayan in order to study world history and sociology at the Hebrew University in Jerusalem. He earned a doctorate from Oxford University in 1965 and taught at various universities until his death in 2008.

[4] See portrait of Chaim Laskov on page 62.

[5] Uri Ben-Ari; see portrait on page 83.

- the 82nd Armored Battalion, with three companies of M4A3 Sherman medium tanks with 75 mm guns and M1 Super Shermans with 76.2 mm guns
- the 52nd Mechanized Infantry Battalion, with three companies equipped with half-tracks armed with machine guns or antitank guns
- the 9th Armored Battalion, with three companies of AMX-13 light tanks

The hastily assembled 27th Armored Brigade under Brigadier General Chaim Bar-Lev[6] consisted of

- one armored battalion with two companies of M1 Shermans and one company with M50 Shermans, both armed with 75 mm guns;
- one armored battalion with two companies of AMX-13 light tanks; and
- one mechanized infantry battalion with half-tracks armed with machine guns and antitank guns.

Before taking command of the armored brigade, Bar-Lev was responsible for the Israeli army's training. His tactics were based on mobile warfare, fighting at long distances, and long-range envelopment maneuvers, as well as surprise encirclements and the resulting destruction of the enemy.

Dayan was of a different opinion. He regarded the invasion of the Sinai as an infantry attack, with the armored forces acting solely in a support role. His misgivings about the armored forces would prove to be unfounded in the course of the operation, however.

As per discussions with the British and French, the Israeli forces were to begin the campaign with an airborne landing near the Suez Canal, to provide the invaders with a pretext for issuing an ultimatum to Israel and Egypt to quickly withdraw their forces.

The choice fell on the Mitla Pass, located about 18.5 miles (30 km) east of Suez. Blocking this bottleneck was interesting from a strategic point of view, since it made it possible for the Israelis to cut the Egyptian supply lines to Ras Sudar as well as to Abu Ageila and El Arish.

Other war aims were the destruction of the Egyptian forces in the Abu Ageila—El Arish—Rafah area, the clearing of the occupied Gaza Strip, and the capture of Sharm El Sheik in the south, in order to reopen the Gulf of Eilat to Israeli shipping.

Daya formulated his plan as follows:

Colonel Uri Ben-Ari, commander of the Israeli 7th Armored Brigade, issuing orders prior to the attack on Abu Ageila, October 1956. *Israel Government Press Office*

- In the first phase, the 890th Battalion of the 202nd Paratrooper Brigade was to carry out an airborne landing operation against the eastern exit of the Mitla Pass. The rest of the brigade was to simultaneously advance on the Kuntilla–al-Thamad–Nakhl axis toward the Mitla Pass, to relieve pressure on the paratroopers. In the central sector, coming from Nitzana, the 38th Division, with its 4th and 10th Infantry Brigades and the 37th Mechanized Brigade held in reserve, was to drive west to destroy the enemy forces in the Abu Ageila-Al Qusaymah-Um Katef area.
- In the second phase, the 1st Golani Brigade, the 11th Infantry Brigade, and the 27th Armored Brigade of the 77th Division were to move out of their starting position near Be'er Sheva, break through the defensive ring around Rafah, and destroy the enemy forces in the El Arish area. Meanwhile, the 9th Infantry Brigade was to advance south along the coast of the Gulf of Aqaba and take Sharm El Sheik.
- The 7th Armored Brigade was then to stand ready to support either the attacks by the 4th Infantry Brigade to Al Qusaymah or the attack by the 10th Infantry Brigade at Um Katef.

---

[6] Chaim Bar-Lev; see portrait on page 124.

AMX-13 light tanks of the 9th Armored Battalion, 7th Armored Brigade, on the Al Qusaymah–Ismailiya axis, November 1956. *Israel Government Press Office*

OPERATION KADESH

Dayan launched Operation Kadesh on the night of October 29, 1956. About four hundred paratroopers of the 890th Battalion under Lieutenant Colonel Rafael Eitan[7] landed at the eastern entrance to the Mitla Pass. The jump was completed without incident, and the paratroopers immediately took up positions or set up ambushes and blocked all open access roads. Air drops supplied the battalion with additional weapons, such as antitank guns, mortars, ammunition, and reconnaissance vehicles.

The remaining units of the 202nd Paratrooper Brigade crossed the Egyptian border at Kuntilla; broke through the enemy positions in the center of the Sinai Peninsula at Kuntilla, Al Thamad, and Nakhl; and, on the evening of October 30, linked up with the isolated parachute battalion at the Mitla Pass.

The Egyptians reacted on the morning of October 31. Egyptian chief of staff Amer sent elements of the Egyptian 2nd Infantry Brigade to the eastern exit of the Mitla Pass to prevent the Israelis from advancing on the Suez Canal. He also sent units of the 5th Infantry Brigade into the Ras Sudar area to guard the oil fields there. He subsequently dispatched the 1st and 2nd Armored Brigades with T-34/85 tanks and SU-100 tank-destroyers from Ismailia to the Bir Gifgafa area to block the northern exit from the Mitla Pass.

The threat to the Suez Canal had thus become a fact. Great Britain and France demanded that the two warring parties immediately stop all fighting, withdraw from Sinai, and evacuate

---

[7] Rafael Eitan (1929–2004), son of Ukrainian parents, grew up near Nazareth. He served as a young officer in the Palmach and fought in Jerusalem during the 1948–49 War of Independence. After commanding the 890th Battalion during the Suez Crisis in 1956, he led an airborne brigade in the Gaza Strip during the Six-Day War in 1967. In the 1973 Yom Kippur War, he led the 36th Division, which, among other things, stopped the Syrian advance on the Golan Heights. In 1978 he was appointed chief of staff of the Israeli armed forces under Prime Minister Menachem Begin and led them in the 1982 Lebanon campaign. After leaving the army, he pursued a political career under various prime ministers, last as minister of agriculture.

7th Armored Brigade insignia. *Wikipedia*

the strategically vital locations of Port Said and Suez.

Nasser's rejection of these demands caused the British and French to launch Operation Musketeer. It was a previously conceived plan to attack key positions around the Suez Canal and envisaged a linkup with the advancing Israeli forces.

The situation did not develop as the British and French had hoped, however. The hoped-for political support from the United States was not forthcoming, and a United Nations resolution even demanded that the three alliance partners immediately withdraw their forces from the Sinai. But the immediate veto gave Dayan an important time advantage, with which to continue the campaign in the Sinai.

On the morning of October 30, Wallach ordered the 37th Division to advance out of the Nitzana area. The spearhead of the 7th Armored Brigade broke through the Egyptian positions around Al Qusaymah and kept this important crossroads open. The possibility now existed for the Israeli forces to drive into the Sinai from the east in a southerly, westerly, or northerly direction. Israeli possession of the crossroads also posed a threat to the flank of the Egyptian 3rd Infantry Division in the northeast of the peninsula and enabled the Israelis to fall upon its rear.

Meanwhile, the 7th Armored Brigade, still unnoticed, moved through the Deika Pass behind the enemy lines and split up into several columns. One moved south to Bir El Hasana; the other pushed north to the crossroads of Gebel Jebel Libni. This advance cut the Egyptian supply line from Ismailia to Abu Ageila.

Abu Ageila was defended by a series of fortifications, infantry trenches, bunker systems, and minefields. Towed artillery, howitzers, and dug-in antitank guns completed the defenses of this key area, so important to the Egyptians. This defensive ring blocked access to the connecting road through Bir Gifgafa to the Suez Canal as well as the road via Bir El Hasana to the Mitla Pass. If the Israelis were to break through there, the outcome of the campaign would largely be decided in favor of the Israelis.

While elements if the 7th Armored Brigade attacked the ring of fortifications at Abu Ageila from Jebel Libni in a westerly direction, the 10th Infantry Brigade launched a frontal attack on the defense positions from the east. After heavy fighting, which lasted one day and night, the Israeli units broke through the defense ring and occupied Abu Ageila.

The main burden was borne by the armored battalions of the 7th Armored Brigade. In heavy fighting they destroyed numerous Egyptian Sherman tanks and Archer tank-destroyers. The Egyptian troops trapped in Abu Ageila surrendered or fled west in the direction of the canal.

During this phase there was a costly collision in the Mitla Pass. The paratrooper brigade was advancing west and in the narrow pass fell into a well-prepared ambush. It developed into a fierce battle waged bitterly by both sides. As darkness fell, the Israeli paratroopers closed in and in hand-to-hand combat conquered the mountainous terrain and the heights on which the Egyptians had entrenched themselves.

The Mitla Pass had been cleared, and the way to the Suez Canal now seemed open.

While the fighting for possession of the Mitla Pass and the town of Abu Ageila surprised the Egyptians, their 6th Infantry Brigade and the 3rd Infantry Division awaited the Israelis in well-fortified defensive positions surrounding the city of Rafah.

Laskov issued orders for the attack on Rafah during the night of November 1. The Israeli 3rd and 4th Infantry Battalions were to break through and keep open the southern defense ring, while the 27th Armored Brigade broke through the ring of positions and secured the road between Rafah and Gaza City, to enable the remaining units of the Golani Brigade to take the city by storm. The well-prepared attack struck with full force, and Rafah fell on November 2 after heavy fighting.

Laskov then reorganized his units at the northern exit from Rafah, sent the 27th Armored Brigade in the direction of El Arish, and likewise took the city on the Mediterranean by storm. The unit even advanced beyond the city and stopped only about 15 km from El Kantara on the Suez Canal.

The conquest of Rafah ultimately sealed the fate of the Gaza Strip. It was defended by the Palestinian 8th Infantry Division, while its 86th Infantry Brigade held Khan Yunis in the south of the strip and the Egyptian 26th National Guard defended the city itself.

The Israeli side gave responsibility for occupying the Gaza Strip to the 11th Infantry Brigade, under Aaron Doron.[8] It had two infantry battalions and an armored battle group with one company of M4A1 medium tanks and one of armed half-tracks. On the morning of November 2, the battle group launched its direct attack on Gaza City with artillery support. It penetrated the southwestern defense ring and covered the advance by the following infantry brigades. After a brief battle, the Israelis took the inner city and forced the Egyptians to lay down their arms.

---

[8] Aaron Doron (1922–2016) grew up in Ludwigshafen, Germany. His family immigrated to Palestine in 1939, where he joined the Haganah. He fought as an officer in the War of Independence in 1948–49, commanded the Yiftach Brigade during the Sinai campaign in 1956, and later led the Golani Brigade. After his retirement from the army, he became director of Tel Aviv University.

M50 medium tanks of the 82nd Armored Battalion, 7th Armored Brigade, near Abu Ageila, November 1956. *Israel Government Press Office*

The Israelis now turned their attention to Khan Yunis, located at the south end of the Gaza Strip. The Palestinian 86th Infantry Brigade stubbornly defended the coastal city, but it was soon hopelessly outmatched and surrounded by Israeli units. The defenders finally laid down their arms on the morning of November 3 and surrendered.

The final phase of the campaign was to be the capture of the southern part of the Sinai Peninsula. Dayan dispatched the 9th Infantry Brigade under Avraham Yoffe,[9] which was to advance down the west coast along the Gulf of Eilat. The unit reached Kuntilla on October 31, and the following day the motorized advance continued along the Gulf of Eilat. Difficult terrain and clashes with the enemy slowed the pace of the advance.

---

[9] Avraham Yoffe (1913–83) joined the Haganah at the age of sixteen, served with the special night squads under Orde Charles Wingate, and fought as a captain under the British flag in the Second World War. In the 1948–49 War of Independence, he was commander of an infantry battalion of the Golani Brigade. After his command of the 9th Infantry Brigade in the Sinai Campaign in 1956, he briefly took command of the southern front. He later moved to command of the northern front and left the army in 1964. He was recalled to service at the outbreak of the Six-Day War in 1967 and led one of the three divisions in the Sinai campaign. After leaving the army again, he took part in archeological expeditions under Yigael Allon and began a political career in the Likud Party.

Dayan therefore dispatched elements of the 202nd Airborne Brigade as well, to advance along the Suez Canal through Ras Sudar to the southern tip of the peninsula and take Sharm El Sheik from the east.

Dayan carried out this southward advance as a pincer movement from two directions. Under Israeli pressure, the Egyptians finally abandoned their positions around Raz Nazrani and fled from Sharm El Sheik.

This brought Operation Kadesh to an end, and the guns fell silent. The Sinai Peninsula was in the hands of the Israelis.

While Israeli troops eliminated the remaining nests of resistance in the Gaza Strip and the defeated Egyptian units left Sharm El Sheik, the Anglo-French attack and the recapture of the Suez Canal were taking place.

On November 5 and 6, the British committed an infantry division, an armored regiment with Centurion heavy tanks, an airborne brigade, and a commando brigade. At the same time, the French followed with an airborne brigade plus a light mechanized-infantry division equipped with M47 Patton medium and AMX-13 light tanks.

The powerful Anglo-French forces began taking key objectives on the canal, including Port Said, Ismailia, and Suez. The Anglo-French plan was initially crowned by success, as the Egyptian army withdrew in the face of the enemy's air superiority and rapid advance.

With Port Said in flames, the Soviet Union stepped in and threatened the two European powers with military invention, including the use of nuclear weapons. The Soviets also accused Israel of acting as a vicarious agent of the colonial powers and called on Ben Gurion to withdraw from the Sinai. The United States subsequently brought a peace resolution before the United Nations that, after a ceasefire, was to allow the formation of a UN peacekeeping force in the battle zone. The threats were effective, and the antagonists ceased hostilities on November 6, 1958.

The Egyptian president Nasser can be seen as the clear winner of the war. Despite the military debacle, he succeeded in cementing his position in Egypt and presenting himself in the role of a heroic resistance fighter against Western-Israeli imperialism. All of this also significantly increased his prestige in the surrounding Arab states. As well, as a result of the war the Soviet Union provided Egypt military and economic support and thus enhanced Nasser's position even further.

For the colonial powers of Great Britain and France, the Suez Canal crisis led to their definitive loss of influence in the region and the withdrawal of their troops from the Middle East. The events resulted in the resignation of Anthony Eden as British prime minister in January 1957.

Ultimately, however, Israel also emerged from the war as a winner. The Israeli military had achieved an impressive military success. Although the Egyptian army's retreat saved it from being struck a destructive blow, the Israelis solidified their reputation as the most powerful military force in the Middle East.

After the war, politically and militarily Israel increasingly turned to the United States, which as a result gained influence in that strategically and economically important region. Israel also secured direct access to the Red Sea by way of the Gulf of Aqaba and was thus no longer dependent on the Suez Canal.

As a result of the UN resolution and an ultimatum from the Soviets and Americans, which demanded a withdrawal to the ceasefire line from the War of Independence, the Israeli government decided to withdraw from the Sinai. It did so, however, on the condition that the Israeli forces would be replaced by armed United Nations peacekeeping troops.

On January 15, 1957, the Israeli forces pulled back behind the international border. On March 6, 1957, they left the Gaza Strip and, two days later, the southern part of the Sinai with Sharm El Sheik. The United Nations Emergency Forces (UNEF I) formed a buffer zone between Egypt and Israel. It sent a garrison to Sharm El Sheik and thus guaranteed free passage through the Straits of Tiran into the Gulf of Eilat.

Due to allied pressure on the key areas around the Suez Canal, Nasser withdrew two divisions from the Sinai. As a result, the Egyptians faced the Israeli army with no strategic depth and with only reduced mechanized units and troops in static defensive positions.

The fact that the Israelis had been able to take the Sinai Peninsula within just one hundred hours was in no way due to inadequacies on the part of the Egyptian military, but on its concept of waging war. In the three main battles of the campaign — the battles for Abu Ageila, Rafah, and the Mitla Pass — the Egyptian forces demonstrated an astonishing will to fight and stubbornly resisted the Israelis.

The Israelis, however, demonstrated clear superiority in mobility, their use of combined arms, and their employment of armored forces. While the War of Independence had clearly assumed the form of an infantry war, and even Moshe Dayan had harbored doubts about the use of armored forces, the war in the Sinai resulted in the emergence of a promising Israeli armored doctrine.

This was demonstrated by encirclement of the opponent and by clever maneuvering that enabled attacks from unexpected directions. In addition, the Israelis attacked from on the move, with only short reorganization phases at the intermediate objectives and a clever alternation of mounted and dismounted combat. The leaders were also given extensive freedom of action down to the lowest ranks.

In one week of fighting, the Israeli armed forces conquered an area three times as large as Israel, inflicted more than two thousand casualties, and took about six thousand prisoners, including many officers. Hundreds of tanks, artillery pieces, armored vehicles, and huge quantities of ammunition, as well as other items of equipment and war materiel, fell into Israeli hands.

In contrast, the Israeli army's losses, 171 killed and several hundred wounded, were comparatively minor.

Since Operation Kadesh, the Israelis have celebrated October 29 as "Armored Forces Day," since the campaign on the Sinai Peninsula led to an indisputable turn in the armored corps' doctrine.

PORTRAIT OF URI BEN-ARI

Uri Ben-Ari was born in Schönefeld, southeast of Berlin, in 1925. His parents did not survive the National-Socialist regime, but they were able to shield Ben-Ari from the Holocaust, sending him to British-occupied Palestine before the outbreak of the Second World War. After the war he joined the Palmach and fought as a company commander in the War of Independence in 1948–49 in the Jerusalem sector against Arab units invading from Trans Jordan.

When the Suez Crisis began in 1956, Ben-Ari was promoted to colonel and assumed command of the 7th Armored Brigade. There was, however, disagreement in the general staff about the use of armored forces, which in the Sinai were to support the infantry. Tanks were originally envisaged at best for reconnaissance and security against invading Jordanian forces. Ultimately, Uri Ben-Ari and Chaim Bar-Lev, the commander of the 27th Armored Brigade, were able to convince the general staff to employ tanks in the Sinai. The armored corps would be better able to exploit its potential there than in the rocky, hilly terrain east of Jerusalem. The capture of Al-Qusaymah and Abu Ageila, probably the most important Egyptian-held fortress, was largely thanks to Ben-Ari's prudent use of armored forces.

Ben-Ari's success as a commander did not go unnoticed, and that same year he took command of the armored corps. In the Six-Day War in 1967, Ben-Ari commanded the 10th Harel Brigade, whose task it was to break the Jordanian resistance north of Jerusalem and open the main road to Ramallah. Ben-Ari subsequently succeeded in driving to Ramallah and securing the northern and southern exits from the town.

During the Yom Kippur War of 1973, Ben-Ari served as deputy to Major General Shmuel Gonen, commander of the southern front. After the war he took over the Office of the Consul General in Washington. In 1978, he left the Israeli army and subsequently wrote books on military history.

His book *Follow Me*, a story about a company commander who fought in the Battle of Jerusalem, was awarded the Yitzhak Sadeh Prize in 1995. His novel *In a Stranglehold*, based on his own experiences, tells the story of five Jewish youths who grew up in Nazi Germany before the Second World War.

A press conference during the Yom Kippur War, 1973. *From left to right*: Lieutenant General Avraham Adan (commander of the 162nd Division), Ephraim Katzir (Israeli president), and Uri Ben-Ari (deputy commander of the southern front). *Israel Government Press Office*

Ben-Ari died in 2009 and is buried in the cemetery of Kibbutz Shefajim, 1.2 miles north of Herzliya.

Chapter 10
The Strengthening of the Armored Corps under Israel Tal

The success of the Israeli Armored Corps in the Sinai campaign influenced the doctrine of the Israeli armed forces in the late 1950s and 1960s. Chief of Staff Dayan had become the most important advocate of a powerful armored corps, and as a result, some of the best infantry officers were transferred to leading positions in the armored forces. Among these commanders were Colonel David Elazar (later chief of staff) and Colonel Israel Tal, who would become one of the most influential commanders of the Israeli Armored Corps and gain worldwide fame as a tank expert.

REORGANIZATION OF THE ARMORED CORPS AFTER THE SINAI CAMPAIGN

The newly assigned officers underwent a protracted retraining course under the direction of Major Shmuel Gonen. Colonel Elazar became the deputy to Major General Chaim Bar-Lev, who took over command of the armored corps, while Colonel Tal became commander of the 7th Armored Brigade. Learning from experience gained in the war, the Israeli military undertook its second major restructuring and transformed an army dedicated almost exclusively to infantry into a mobile armored force. Several new armored brigades were formed, several of which were built upon tanks, others on mechanized infantry. After much consideration and many experiments, there was a reduction in the number of tanks in the companies, initially to three platoons each with four tanks and two command tanks (fourteen tanks per company), and later to three platoons each with three tanks and two command tanks (eleven tanks per company).

These changes were based on combat experience when the need was recognized to keep as many tanks as possible on the move. In a tank company with seventeen vehicles and two platoons in position, eleven tanks would fire while six remained in movement. Using the same tactic, in a company of eleven vehicles, eight tanks could fire, while only three tanks were in movement. Furthermore, controlling seventeen tanks in combat considerably exceeded the capabilities of the less experienced company commanders, while a smaller company with eleven tanks was easier to lead and allowed more officers to command tanks in combat. This solution also proved itself in light of the fact that mechanical breakdowns and combat losses meant that a regrouping of units was often necessary during battle—a practice that would be used frequently in later wars.

At the beginning of the 1960s, the Soviets equipped the Arab armies with modern tanks, including the T-54 and T-55, which were superior to the existing Israeli tanks. The new Soviet tanks had more-powerful engines and their powerful 100 mm guns were superior to the 75 mm guns of the Israeli Sherman M50. Urgent requests for more-modern tanks went unanswered by the United States, and in the end only the British government declared itself willing to sell Israel some of its Centurion tanks.

Although it had seen action in the Korean War in 1950–53, it was in the Middle East that the Centurion would make its name. In the future it would form the backbone of the Israeli Armored Corps and prove itself to be a reliable weapons system. The Centurion entered service with the Israeli Armored Corps in 1960, when the first company equipped with Mark 3 Centurions (armed with the 20-pounder, or 84 mm, gun) was formed.

Although the Centurion was an impressive tank in its day, it took a long time before the tank was fully accepted by the Israeli tank crews. They had long been used to the simple Sherman tank. This enthusiasm became more pronounced following the introduction of the M50 model with its high-velocity gun.

Initial experience with the newly procured British tanks was disappointing, however. In the barren, dusty Negev desert, the principal training area for Israeli armored units, the Centurion performed poorly. Its radiator became clogged with sand and dirt, causing engines to overheat. The prestart and shutdown checks worked out by the British down to the smallest detail were far too complicated for the inexperienced Israeli tank crews. This led to many mechanical breakdowns, which were allegedly due to the inadequate technical standard of the tank. The brakes burned through and caused serious accidents. To make matters worse, the improperly calibrated 20-pounder guns were inaccurate compared to those of the Sherman tanks; hits on targets were regarded by the crews as pure luck. All in all, it is not surprising that tank officers turned down offers to join Centurion units and instead preferred to remain with the old Shermans.

The general staff recognized that solutions were required to overcome the problems with the Centurion. Therefore, a team of experts from the Ordnance Corps, which had amassed a great deal of experience modifying the Sherman, was tasked with working out a plan to bring the British tank up to Israeli requirements.

At that time, there was an escalation in firefights with the Syrians, which was later called the "War over the Waters." Positioned high atop the Golan Heights, the Syrians regularly shelled Israeli settlements and brought work to a halt in the entire Hule Valley. Retaliatory measures were difficult, both militarily and politically, since neither side wanted to go to war. An effective tank gun was needed to be able to strike the Syrian positions with pinpoint accuracy. Experts regarded the Sherman tank as inadequate for this task.

At that time, the Israeli tank workshops had mounted the newly acquired British 105 mm L7 gun in a Centurion Mark 5. The first prototypes, manned by specially trained crews, soon saw action on the Syrian border. High-ranking officers tensely awaited the results of the first combat. As usual, the Syrians opened fire on an Israeli patrol, which was moving along the border road while providing cover for a tractor working in the nearby fields, at about noon. After the Syrians had fired, the concealed Centurions advanced into their firing positions and opened fire with their 105 mm guns. All hell broke loose when the shells struck the enemy positions. The Syrians responded with artillery and mortar fire on nearby settlements. Several Panzer IV tanks of World War II vintage that were dug in on the hills were also committed. Their German 75 mm guns were still very effective despite their age. The Centurions fired almost without pause but had difficulty seeing their targets, since exploding Syrian artillery rounds had covered much of the valley with clouds of dust. The Syrians, firing from the Heights, still had good visibility and could observe the effect of most of their rounds.

After a battle lasting several hours, a ceasefire was reached at the urging of the United Nations. The evaluation of the results was, however, extremely disappointing for the Israeli Armored Corps.

The crews, already skeptical prior to the battle, were now completely disgusted with the new tank. The nearby Sherman crews looked on with joy at the fate of their "rivals" and disheartened the Centurion crews even further by knocking out several enemy tanks in another action against the Syrians.

This all came to an end, however, when another staff officer for the armored corps was named. Major General Israel Tal was not the man to see a tank shortcoming as an impossible problem. On the contrary: because of his technical experience, it was clear to him that not only could he defend the Centurion against all its critics, but that he had to defend it once and for all. After the action in the north, he assembled all the senior officers and gave them an encouraging speech. The general lectured them on their shortcomings, pointed out in detail the shortcomings he had personally observed in the gunnery and maintenance procedures, and issued precise instructions aimed at nothing less than perfection.

Special maintenance personnel were named to calibrate the tank guns precisely to British specifications. Gunnery courses were prepared to retrain both the regular and reserve tank crews. This was followed by the meticulous development and implementation of maintenance procedures, which were enforced with strict discipline. In addition, newly constructed tank gunnery ranges with long firing distances enabled innovative shooting competitions, which served as obligatory performance tests. The promotion of officers was also linked to professional performance tests. As the results steadily improved, the poor morale in the Israeli Armored Corps likewise rose significantly.

At 0145 on August 1, 1960, the Syrians again opened fire, this time on a tractor working the fields at Almagor, north of the Sea of Galilee. A rescue team sent to rescue the tractor was also fired on. The Israeli Centurions immediately opened up with accurate fire from their concealed positions. A number of Syrian tanks were put out of action within minutes, several of them on fire. One of the Israeli tank gunners was none other than General Tal himself. Then the Centurions advanced to attack the Syrian excavators. Their crews thought themselves safe and assumed that the Israeli tanks, which were miles away, could not reach them. They were proven wrong, however, and the Israeli tank units systematically destroyed all the Syrian equipment. After this successful engagement, the Syrians halted their work on the water diversion project on the Golan Heights and left control of the valley below to the Israelis. General Tal and his armored soldiers had achieved a great victory—both technically and in terms of morale. The Centurion appeared to have been vindicated!

Meanwhile, another type of tank entered service with the Israeli armored forces. After unsuccessful negotiations with the American government for direct deliveries of tanks, a request was made to the German government to supply Israel with a number of M48 A2 Patton tanks that were being replaced by newer models in the Bundeswehr.

A selected group of Israeli tank officers took part in a conversion training course at Münster in West Germany, under conditions of great secrecy. Its conclusion coincided with the arrival of the first tanks in Israel. The 79th Armored Battalion was formed, using the Pattons, and it was integrated into the 7th Armored Brigade. Its first commander was Lieutenant Colonel (later major general) Jackie Even, an experienced tank soldier who had previously served in the 82nd Armored Battalion. The

M4A1 Shermans during a military parade on the occasion of the victory in the Sinai Peninsula, December 1956. *AirSeaLand Photos*

Patton's 90 mm gun showed itself to be clearly inferior to the Soviet 100 mm gun. Since the Israeli armaments industry was already engaged in equipping the army's Centurions with the L7 105 mm gun, it was only natural that it was immediately decided to also arm the Patton with it. Plans were worked out to upgrade the M48 A2s that had been acquired to the standard of the later M60. This included the installation of a standard diesel engine. Modernization of the Centurion had priority, however, and in fact most of the Pattons were not upgraded until the end of the decade.

Meanwhile, the operational doctrine of the Israeli Armored Corps slowly took shape. Prior to the war in the Sinai, the headquarters of the armored corps was primarily concerned with organizational, training-related, and logistical tasks, while the operational or even tactical aspects under which the troops would operate in combat received little attention.

After the success in the Sinai campaign, the new tank commanders achieved a higher status in the military chain of command: the commander of the armored corps, now a major general, became a member of the general staff and thus had the opportunity to express his views on mobile warfare. The first in line was Major General Chaim Ber-Lev, who not only advocated a complete restructuring of the corps with new formations but also introduced new combat doctrines such as tank-versus-tank combat, mountain warfare, and night combat technology.

Several large exercises were held to test the new concepts. At the beginning of the 1960s it was known that the Arabs—in particular the Egyptians—had adopted the Soviet doctrine of warfare with its linear, in-depth defense system and powerful tank reserves in the rear. In view of this challenge, the new commander of the armored corps, Major General David Elazar, set about finding a suitable answer to this problem. As a result,

the armored corps trained its units in the techniques of attacking fortified defenses — both by day and by night.

In 1964, when General Tal assumed command, the work of the armored corps reached its peak, as numerous newly created units were integrated and extensive war games were carried out.

During Israel Tal's time in command from 1964 to 1968, the Armored School also received a great deal of attention. The school, built in 1949 near Ramla in modest circumstances, had moved to Khan Julis in the south in order to further expand its various facilities. It was divided into the basic training areas of tank gunnery, communications, driving, and maintenance. Later a tactical section was added, as were sections for tank commanders and officer training. When it became necessary to organize special courses for Sherman, Centurion, and Patton tank crews in the 1960s, there was a separate department for each type of tank, which was responsible for developing the technical aspects of the respective tank. The school also set up decentralized training bases, in which reserve tank crews could be retrained from one type of tank to another.

By 1965 the armored corps already had nine brigades (five armored and four mechanized brigades). The 7th Armored Brigade was divided into the 82nd Centurion (modified) Battalion and the 79th Patton Battalion, while the 9th Battalion, which was originally equipped with AMX-13 light tanks, became a mechanized infantry unit.

Two of the older reserve armored brigades were formed with one Sherman battalion, consisting of two companies of M50s and one of M51s, plus a battalion of AMX-13 light tanks and a half-track battalion. Apart from a limited core of career soldiers, who looked after logistics, the entire brigade was staffed by reserves. Two newly formed armored brigades each received two (later three) battalions with up-gunned Centurions, while the mechanized brigades were formed with an M50 Sherman battalion of four companies and two armored grenadier battalions on half-track vehicles. Artillery support was provided by a medium 120 mm howitzer battalion on half-tracks. The newly formed 14th Mechanized Brigade was assigned the 52nd Sherman Battalion, while its two armored grenadier battalions were reserve units. This organization made it possible to form battalions with several types of tanks from men who completed their military service in the regular companies. Finally, each territorial command received a reserve armored battalion equipped with M1 Shermans, which had to undergo special training for the armored infantry support role in the border regions.

Developments in the field of armored technical equipment such as mine-clearing tanks, combat engineer tanks, and special equipment were also incorporated into the armored units.

Improved communications systems were also introduced, with the tanks initially switching from the obsolete SCR 608 series (with the separate SCR 300 series for communication between tanks and infantry) to the GRC series, which improved communication. Ultimately, however, the modern VRC series, which reintroduced the excellent predefined ten-button layout, was adopted, making life much easier for tank crews.

A short time later, the first armored division headquarters was established so that the armored corps was fully operational in 1967. It was a well-trained, motivated force with experts in various fields. This meant that the corps was able to face the Arab armored forces with full confidence. The test would not be long in coming.

PORTRAIT OF ISRAEL TAL

Israel Tal was born in northern Galilee on September 13, 1924, and grew up in a kibbutz in Mahanayim. Tal began his military career at the age of seventeen, when he joined the British army's Jewish Brigade. He served as a machine gunner in North Africa and Italy, and it was there that he first came into contact with tanks. He was made an NCO (noncommissioned officer) in 1945, and after the disbandment of the Jewish Brigade he joined the Haganah. Tal served as an infantry officer in the War of Independence in 1948–49 and rose to become deputy to Brigadier General Chaim Laskov. After the war, Tal studied armor tactics in Great Britain and in the Sinai campaign commanded a brigade that advanced down the central axis to the Suez Canal.

After the war in Sinai, Tal was promoted to commander of the armored corps, and he convinced the political leadership that Israel must massively strengthen its armored forces and carry the war to the enemy. With his doctrine he laid the foundation for victory in the Six-Day War in 1967, in which he successfully commanded the 84th Division on the southern front under the command of Yeshayahu Gavish.

There was great euphoria in Israel after the triumph in the Six-Day War, which led to a wanton underestimation of the neighboring Arab states. In the doctrinal dispute over the rigid "Bar-Lev Line" on the Suez Canal, Israel Tal and Ariel Sharon were ultimately defeated by Chief of Staff Chaim Bar-Lev. Neither Tal nor Sharon believed in a stationary defensive battle in the sense of a new Maginot Line and instead argued in favor of mobile warfare.

To his men, Israel Tal was known affectionately as "Talik." His leadership skills and expertise made him both legendary and popular. He usually knew every single component of new weapon systems — and systematically asked his troops about this knowledge. The respect that Tal enjoyed even led to some of his soldiers consulting him about private problems. But Tal also demanded rigorous discipline from his troops, because to him only a highly disciplined army was a good army.

In 1972, Chief of Staff David Elazar made his trusted Israel Tal his deputy. In the Yom Kippur War, Tal coordinated operations in the headquarters, while Elazar directly commanded the troops on the two fronts. With losses to the enemy's new antitank weapons — namely, the AT-3 Sagger and RPG-7 — rising steadily, the two officers quickly switched to the doctrine of combined arms — a masterstroke that ultimately led the Israeli armed forces to victory.

After retiring from the army in 1974, Tal joined the Israeli Ministry of Defense and was given the task of developing a new tank to replace the old Centurion, Patton, and Sherman tanks.

Major General Israel Tal. In 1997, he became the only soldier to receive the Israel Prize, the highest honor his country bestows each year on the eve of its founding day. The Tank Museum at Fort Knox, Kentucky, in the United States honors Tal together with Moshe Peled, Erwin Rommel, George Patton, and Creighton Abrams as one of the five most capable tank commanders in the world. *Israel Government Press Office*

Tal thus performed a final service for his country not only as a highly decorated soldier, but also as an intelligent project manager. Engineers, designers, and mechanics did not work separately in different offices and workshops, but together in a single large room, in the middle of which was the Merkava prototype in the making. The new tank was produced in record time, entered service in 1979, and, in its Mark IV version, is now one of the best battle tanks in the world.

Weakened by a stroke he suffered in 1999, Israel Tal remained frail until his death and died on September 8, 2010, in Rehovot..

PORTRAIT OF DAVID ELAZAR

David Elazar was born in Sarajevo in the kingdom of Yugoslavia in 1925. In 1940 he immigrated to Palestine, where he joined the paramilitary organizations of the Jewish settlers. Elazar's leadership qualities were quickly recognized in the Palmach, and he soon began climbing the military career ladder. During the War of Independence in 1948–49, he fought as a commander on numerous fronts and, among others, took part in the battle for the San Simon Monastery in Jerusalem.

With the unification of the Haganah and the Palmach after the founding of the state of Israel in 1948, Major Elazar took over an infantry battalion of the Harel Brigade in the Jerusalem sector. Later, during the Suez Crisis in 1956, he led the 12th Infantry Brigade, which as a reserve unit was part of Chaim Laskov's 77th Division, with the task of supporting the clearance of the Gaza Strip.

In 1958 he served in the Israeli Armored Corps, first as Chaim Bar-Lev's deputy and then, beginning in 1961, after promotion to major general, as its commander. When the Six-Day War broke out in 1967, he was given responsibility for the northern front and played a major role in the defeat of the Syrian army and the conquest of the Golan Heights.

After the war, Elazar briefly served as head of the operations department of the Israeli general staff, then in early 1972 he was promoted to chief of staff. The beginning of his term was marked by numerous difficult decisions related to the combating of terrorist activities by the Palestinians, including the hijacking of aircraft, the taking of hostages, and attacks. Equally difficult was his decision to authorize the shooting down of an unidentified Libyan aircraft that had entered Israeli airspace. It later turned out that it was a passenger aircraft whose pilot had simply made an error. More than a hundred civilians lost their lives in the incident.

Elazar's further term of office was marked by the Yom Kippur War, which broke out in 1973. After initial misjudgments by the political leadership and the general staff about the timing of the attack by the Egyptians and Syrians, as well as other disagreements, Elazar nevertheless led his army to victory with great determination.

However, the so-called Agranat Commission, set up after the Yom Kippur War to investigate the political functionaries and military commanders who had made inadequate preparations for the war, came to a different conclusion. Although it gave a sympathetic review of Elazar's consistent leadership during the war, it came to the devastating conclusion that he alone bore personal responsibility for the misjudgment of the situation and the readiness of the Israeli armed forces. Elazar criticized the

David Elazar as chief of the general staff of the Israeli army (1972–74). *Israel Government Press Office*

verdict, which took too little account of his successful command during the war, and then voluntarily submitted his resignation.

Elazar left the army and died of a heart attack in 1976. Despite the harsh findings of the Agranat Commission, Elazar was remembered by posterity as a commander who led the armed forces to victory during the difficult Yom Kippur War with a cool head and consistent determination.

Chapter 11
The Backbone of the Israeli Armored Corps: The Centurion (Shot)

The Centurion entered service with the British army in 1945. Because of its armor protection, which was upgraded several times, relatively effective armament, and its modern fire control system, it is regarded as one of the most successful postwar tanks, due in large part to its successful use by the Israeli armed forces between 1959 and 1992 under the designation Shot (whip). After initial setbacks, the Israelis came to appreciate the Shot and subsequently incorporated many of its proven systems into the design of their Merkava tank.

DEVELOPMENT OF THE CENTURION

Development of the Centurion began in 1943 as the A41 Cruiser Tank. It was designed to be the British answer to the German Panzerkampfwagen V Panther and Tiger VI. The first six prototypes of the Centurion Mark 1 reached Belgium in May 1945, after the German surrender.

The original requirements envisaged the installation of the proven Ordnance QF 17-pounder (76 mm). With a specified weight of 40 tons, the frontal turret armor was to provide effective protection against a direct hit from the German 88 mm ammunition, while the hull was to be able to withstand the explosion of an antitank mine. High speed was considered to be of secondary importance, and mobility was to be similar to that of the A34 Comet. The underpowered Rolls-Royce gasoline engine plus the high fuel consumption in combination with the tank's low maximum speed were the most-significant shortcomings of the otherwise advanced design.

The demonstration model produced by the Associated Equipment Company (AEC) was inspected in May 1944, and twenty prototypes were subsequently produced in various configurations: ten with a QF 17-pounder and a 20 mm Polsten cannon, and five with a modernized QF 17-pounder (77 mm HV) and a bow machine gun.

Development continued after the end of the Second World War. Production of the Centurion began in November 1945 with a contract for eight hundred vehicles. The Centurion Mark 1 / Mark 2 officially entered service with the 5th Royal Tank Regiment in December 1946. Soon after the new tank entered service, Royal Ordnance completed development of the QF 20-pounder (84 mm), which was installed in a completely cast turret with a coaxial .30-caliber Besa machine gun. The new Centurion Mark 3, production of which began in 1948, also had an improved engine and was the first tank in history with a fully stabilized weapons system, which enabled the crew to fire accurately while on the move, which drastically increased its combat effectiveness. A further improvement in combat performance was achieved with the introduction of the 105 mm Royal Ordnance L7 gun in the Mark 5/2 (the Mark 4 was not produced).

Development work on the Centurion Mark 7 came to an end in 1953. One disadvantage of the earlier versions had been their limited range of about 62 miles (100 km) on roads; consequently, the Mark 7 had a third fuel tank incorporated into the hull to increase range to 93 miles (150 km). The Marks 8 to 13 incorporated nonvital changes and optimizations, primarily concerning the tank's armor protection and night-fighting equipment. The Chieftain was supposed to begin replacing the Centurion in British service in 1962. Due to serious shortages of the new tank, this process began only in 1965, and the Chieftain did not become available in numbers until 1967.

Other operators of the Centurion in addition to Great Britain and Israel included Australia, Austria, Canada (347), Denmark (106), Egypt, India, Iraq, Jordan (293), Kuwait, Lebanon, New Zealand (12), the Netherlands (662), Sweden (240), Switzerland (300), Singapore, South Africa (203), and Somalia. Between 1946 and 1962, a total of 4,423 Centurion tanks (Mark 1 to Mark 13 and foreign variants) were produced.

THE CENTURION ENTERS SERVICE WITH THE ISRAELI ARMED FORCES

With the end of the War of Independence in 1949, the newly founded state of Israel had been preserved. It emerged victorious from a war on five fronts against six nations that had previously invaded—on the day Israel declared its independence. The Arab armies were defeated by supposedly weak Israel, which had only a few obsolete Sherman, Hotchkiss, and Cromwell tanks. The Arab leaders could not comprehend that their well-trained

armies equipped with modern weapons could have been beaten by the young and poorly equipped Israeli armed forces.

Immediately after the war, the Arab nations began acquiring large quantities of modern weapons, including tanks and aircraft. The military of Egypt, the largest and most powerful of the Arab nations, was still influenced by British doctrine, as were the Jordanian and Iraqi armies. Although there was an arms embargo against the warring nations of the Middle East—including by Great Britain and the Soviet Union—many countries sold unlimited quantities of weaponry to the Arabs, while Israeli was subject to a strictly enforced embargo. This was a result of the political situation, in which several of the dominant countries, especially Great Britain, favored the Arab side over the Israelis.

The Arab nations continued to bolster the materiel and personnel of their armed forces in the 1950s, forming new battalions and brigades. At the end of 1951 the Egyptians placed the first nine of a total of forty Centurion Mark 2s from Great Britain in service. This delivery upset the delicate balance of forces created after the War of Independence, since the Egyptians had now received a modern battle tank impervious to every weapon in the Israeli antitank arsenal.

The sale of the Centurions to Egypt was just one of many examples that illustrate the double standard applied by different British governments against Israel. It was therefore a lucky coincidence for Israel that delivery of the remaining thirty-one Centurions from the Egyptian contract was temporarily stopped as a result of the diplomatic crisis between Egypt and Great Britain over control of the Suez Canal.

The introduction of the Centurion into the Middle East accelerated the reequipment of the Israeli Armored Corps and led to the purchase of the French AMX-13, whose 75 mm gun was capable of penetrating the Centurion's frontal armor. The up-gunning of obsolete Sherman tanks to M50 standard, which was also capable of successfully engaging opposing Centurions, also took place against this background. Both initiatives were only interim solutions, however, since the Israelis would actually have preferred to purchase more-modern versions of the Centurion from the British for use against the Egyptians. Several official inquiries to Great Britain received a negative response, however.

Diplomatic relations between Israel and the British government improved over the course of time, however, and in mid-1953, Israeli submitted another request for the purchase of twenty Centurions. As expected, the British played for time and delayed discussing the request, and in the end the British government itself decided the matter. In 1955, two years after the original request, the British Foreign Ministry approved the sale of Centurions to Israel. The approval was, however, given only after the exertion of considerable political pressure and after evidence was provided that the British had already sold Centurions to the Egyptians and Iraqis but still refused to supply them to Israel. Israel's chief negotiator was Shimon Peres, later president of Israel, who was then director general of the Defense Ministry. But even the desired authorization proved to be a disappointment, since the British government ultimately approved just six tanks instead of the twenty originally requested by Israel. This was a significant affront; anyone with a knowledge of modern tank warfare must have seen that the sale of so small a number of tanks made little sense, since it was not enough to equip a company, to say nothing of a battalion. The British were probably also certain that Israel would never purchase the tanks under these circumstances. To everyone's surprise, however, the Israelis accepted the British government's offer, but only after an analysis of the pros and cons of the agreement:

A Shot Kal Alef during a combat exercise on the Golan Heights. The side skirts were removed during training to avoid damaging them. *Israel Government Press Office*

- The number of tanks for sale was too small for their effective use and was not even sufficient to equip two platoons.
- The tanks were ten times as expensive as the Sherman.
- The Centurions were the older Mark 3 and not more-modern models.
- The tanks were already all badly worn and not new; consequently they would have to be massively overhauled prior to entering service with the Israeli military.
- The Israelis already had the AMX-13, which with its powerful 75 mm gun was capable of penetrating the frontal armor of the older Centurions procured by Egypt. There was therefore no immediate requirement for the large-caliber gun of the Centurion.
- The Centurion was a highly modern tank that would force the Israelis to train a completely new logistical and maintenance unit, including new technicians.
- The Centurion was armed with a new 20-pounder gun, with which the Israelis were not familiar; therefore, putting the tank into service would require the procurement of extensive stocks of new ammunition of various types.
- The Centurion's gasoline engine used a great deal of fuel; therefore its range was limited, and the tank also caught fire easily.

Against the background of these disadvantages, investing in such a small number of tanks seemed neither logical nor practical. There were, however, other strategic considerations:

- The Israelis wanted to avoid giving the British grounds for rejecting future arms sales. It was thought that the British would not enter into negotiations the next time if the Israelis turned down this deal, since they had to assume that Israel would ultimately not conclude the deal anyway.
- Service use of the AMX-13 light tank had revealed many problems; consequently, the procurement of a new tank still had priority.
- The original schedule drawn up for development of the M50 Sherman, which was to have the powerful M50 tank gun, could not be kept to, which delayed the vehicle's entry into service.

A Shot Kal Gimel in the outer districts of Beirut during the First Lebanon War, June 1982. *IDF*

- The pro-Arab French foreign ministry threw up roadblocks to the export of M50 tank guns to Israel and declared that it was prepared to sell only two dozen of these guns, which were envisaged for installation in the first batch of M50 Shermans.

After an analysis of the advantages and disadvantages listed above, the Israeli authorities authorized the purchase of six Centurions, even though the number was insufficient.

Just as Israel and Great Britain were finalizing the Centurion sales agreement, the Suez Crisis among Great Britain, France, and Egypt was gaining in scale and momentum. While the British and French began planning an invasion of Egypt to take the Suez Canal, the blocking of the Strait of Tiran also made war between Israel and Egypt appear likely. After the war of 1956, during which Great Britain and Israel were on the same side, relations between the two states improved considerably. Israel took advantage of the new conditions to again request the supply of twenty Centurions, and this time the British were ready to supply them. While the number of tanks was still insufficient to equip a company, the British promised to deliver more-modern but still not brand-new Mark 5s. Despite these disadvantages, Israel agreed to the purchase, but two years were to pass until the first Centurions were in fact delivered in mid-1959.

At the beginning of 1959, Major Mendi Maron, adjutant to Chief of Staff Chaim Laskov, was selected to lead a delegation to Great Britain to study the new tank. In addition to Maron, the delegation consisted of Captain Shmuel Gonen, the

> ### CODE NAME SHOT
>
> The purchase of Centurions by Israel was top secret, since neither the British nor the Israelis wanted this information to become public. The British wished to avoid damaging their relations with the Arab nations, while the Israelis wanted to keep their potential enemies in the dark about their new weapon.
>
> In Israel, this matter was taken so seriously that even a special code name was chosen, which was to replace "Centurion" in all official documents or conversations. The chosen code name was Shot (Hebrew for "whip") and was ultimately retained by the Israeli armed forces for more than three decades as the name of the vehicle.
>
> The first company to use the Shot in action was the so-called Zayin Company of the 82nd Battalion. Interestingly, the weapon that appears in the company emblem is not a whip, but a spiked mace, since at that time the whip was obviously not martial enough for the company!
>
> Because the spiked mace had been an especially effective weapon against enemy armor during the Middle Ages, the choice of the company symbol was nevertheless very appropriate. Furthermore, it was already too late to possibly change the code name to Morag (Hebrew for "mace"), especially since this name had already been given to the mine-clearing vehicle based on the Sherman.

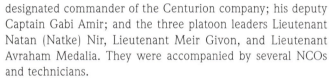

designated commander of the Centurion company; his deputy Captain Gabi Amir; and the three platoon leaders Lieutenant Natan (Natke) Nir, Lieutenant Meir Givon, and Lieutenant Avraham Medalia. They were accompanied by several NCOs and technicians.

The delegation received instruction at Bovington, headquarters of the British Armored Corps. Since the members of the Israeli delegation primarily had experience with the older 75/76 mm guns of the Sherman, the Centurion's high-velocity gun presented a new problem: the muzzle blast when the gun was fired threw up so much dust that an immediate evaluation of the effectiveness of the shot was impossible. The British had developed two solutions to this problem:

- Use of tanks in pairs: while one tank fired, the second observed the effect and vice versa. This in fact reduced the firepower of a platoon by half, however.
- Firing of three rounds in quick succession with different distances. For example, the first round was fired at a distance of 2,625 feet (800 m), the second at 1,970 feet (600 m), and the third at 3,280 feet (1,000 m). This meant that every target in the line of fire would be hit by at least one round, although this solution resulted in high ammunition consumption.

The Israelis quickly got to grips with the new techniques, and after several days of training they were faster than the best British crew. The Israeli team saw itself as trailblazers: laying the foundations for a new era in the Israeli Armored Corps that would begin with the arrival of the Centurions in Israel and would revolutionize the corps. For the Israelis, Centurions had capabilities that had been long awaited, including the ability to shoot while on the move, the introduction of new types of ammunition, and the achievement of improved mobility.

While the main delegation was studying in Great Britain, a small party of four experienced technicians were sent to Germany under Master Sergeant Arieh Ben Dror to learn and practice servicing the Centurion at a British NATO base. The instructors were experienced German technicians who had served on the British model. Master Sergeant Ben Dror was very satisfied with the training base, since the tanks were constantly kept in motion there and the team had the opportunity to train in nearly real-life conditions. During the three months they spent there, the Israelis not only were able to gain experience in various areas of Centurion maintenance but also spent many hours driving the tanks. This gave them a good understanding of the complicated and sometimes problematic drivetrain of the Centurion. When the course was over, the trained soldiers returned to Israel to join the companies to work with the Zayin company's maintenance team.

In 1959, the first sixty Centurions were finally delivered to Israel. Of these, sixteen were Mark 5s with the 10-pounder gun, and forty-four were brand-new Mark 8s armed with the 105 mm gun. Between April 1959 and October 1962, Israel received another 135 Mark 5 Centurions, and from 1965 onward, another 250 vehicles: 190 used Mark 5s and sixty brand-new Mark 6s.

A Shot Kal Gimel stands guard over a convoy of M113 APCs during the First Lebanon War, June 1982. *IDF*

Prior to the outbreak of the Six-Day War in 1967, the Israelis had 385 Centurions, and during the war thirty of the forty-four Jordanian Centurions were captured by the IDF. Additional vehicles were later purchased from the Netherlands and South Africa, and over the years the number of Centurions in Israeli service rose to 1,080. The tanks entered service with the designation Shot.

The Israeli Armored Corps initially had considerable difficulties with the Centurion, and the first modifications were undertaken soon after it entered service. These included the conversion of all older vehicles to the British 105 mm gun, which was built under license in Israel; the adaptation of the cupola ring to accommodate a mount for a .50-caliber machine gun; modifications to the firefighting system, the electrical system, and the brakes; and an increase in fuel capacity. The original power plant was retained for the time being, and the unmodified vehicles were later named the Shot Meteor after the tank's Rolls-Royce Meteor engine.

A major conversion program followed in the years 1967 to 1970 with the introduction of a more powerful Teledyne Continental AVD-S-1790-2A diesel engine and the Allison CD850-6 automatic transmission as installed in the M48/M60. This led to a logistical harmonization of the fleet and overcame one of the original Centurion's most serious disadvantages. The new version was called the Shot Kal (Kal being an abbreviation for "Continental") and was easily distinguishable from other variants of the Centurion by its raised rear decking resulting from the larger power plant, the added turret basket on the rear of the turret, and its two air filters.

The first version, the Shot Kal Alef, proved itself to be very reliable during the Yom Kippur War of 1973, and consequently the remaining Shot Meteors were in turn converted into the new version. Despite the successful employment of the Alef, there were several setbacks, especially with the electric turret drive system, which was not very capable and quickly drained the vehicle's batteries. It was decided to develop a new turret drive system that was based on the hydraulic system of the M48 (Cadillac Gage). Fears on the part of tank crews that the hydraulic lines would explode when the tank was under fire and set the vehicle on fire were at least partially countered by the introduction of a new hydraulic fluid with a higher ignition temperature. The new version with additional bow armor was designated the Shot Kal Beth and entered service in 1976.

The new system was only a provisional solution, however, and was unable to overcome other problems. In particular, the absent and urgently needed two-plane stabilization, which was essential for precise shooting on the move, led to only limited use of the system. When the Israelis introduced the M60A1, which had an improved turret drive system and the longed-for two-plane stabilization, this was quickly integrated into the Shot Kal. The new version also received, among other things, a new fire control system, replacement of the alternator with a powerful generator, an external first-aid kit, and modified tow hooks. This model, designated the Shot Kal Gimel, entered service in 1979.

The final version, the Shot Kal Daled, was introduced in 1982. In this case the modifications included the addition of Blazer explosive reactive armor modules on the hull and turret fronts and an updated fire control system with a laser rangefinder. Although not all older versions were completely reequipped, at least the attachment points for the reactive armor were gradually mounted on the Alef, Beth, and Gimel vehicles. For this reason, the reactive armor is not a clear identification feature for the Shot Kal Daled.

The Shot Kal remained in active service as a battle tank until 1992 and was them retired from service and sold (e.g., to Singapore as the Tempest) or was reequipped for new roles, as in the case of the Nagmashot, Nagmachon, Nakpadon, or Puma armored personnel carriers.

TECHNICAL FEATURES

The Shot had a crew of four: driver, gunner, loader, and commander.

Compared to the Comet, the Centurion had a longer hull with an additional, sixth road wheel. The Christie suspension with vertical springs was replaced by a Horstmann suspension with three horizontally sprung, externally mounted, two-wheel bogies. Ease of maintenance was improved at the cost of ride quality, and the amount of work required to repair mine damage was clearly reduced.

THE DIFFERENCE BETWEEN BRITISH AND ISRAELI DESIGNATIONS

It is important to understand that there is a difference between the original British and the adjusted Israeli designations for the various versions (marks). In the British system, the only difference between the Mk. 3 and the Mk. 5 was the replacement of the former's 7.92 mm Besa coaxial machine gun with a .30-caliber Browning. The British completely ignored the differences between the various turret types (i.e., emergency escape hatch, loader's periscope, plate shape, and slope). To the Israelis, however, the loader's periscope on the horizontal part of the turret roof was the most significant distinctive feature. All Israeli vehicles in this configuration were given the designation Mk. 3, while all vehicles with a loader's periscope moved forward into the sloped part of the turret were identified as a Mk. 5.

The twelve-cylinder gasoline engine mounted in the rear of the tank (Rover Meteor Mark 4 B1) produced 650 hp. With a combat weight of 51.8 tons, the tank had a relatively poor power-to-weight ratio of 12.5 hp/ton. Off roads, the Centurion achieved a speed of 12 mph (20 kph), on roads 22 mph (35 kph). The Mark 1 to Mark 6 versions had a fuel capacity of just 144 US gallons (546 liters), which limited range to 35 miles (56 km) off roads and 50 miles (80 km) on roads. The Mark 7 version of the Centurion was given a third niche tank in the rear, which raised operational range to 62 miles (100 km) off roads and 93 miles (150 km) on roads. In addition to the main engine, the Centurion had a four-cylinder auxiliary engine that produced 16 hp (Morris USHNM, A 41 Mark 2A./1).

The transmission (Merrit-Brown Z51R) had five forward and two reverse gears, and power was transmitted by means of a mechanical superposition steering system.

The Shot Kal version was powered by a twelve-cylinder diesel engine (Continental AVDS-1790-2A) producing 750 hp. In contrast to the original Centurion, the transmission (Allison CD 850-6) had just two forward and one reverse gears. The prototype of the original Centurion Mark 1 had a sloped 76 mm glacis plate, and the turret front was well protected, with 152 mm of armor plate. On the Mark 2 the glacis armor was increased to 118 mm, and the sides and rear were up-armored from 38 to 51 mm, and the 5/1 had even-thicker armor. The Centurion was equipped with smoke grenade dischargers for self-defense. If necessary, the Shot Kal could be equipped with Blazer reactive armor modules. The Centurion Mark 1 was armed with an Ordnance QF (quick-firing) 17-pounder (76.2 mm), which could fire high-explosive and subcaliber ammunition with a caliber of 76.2 × 583 mm R with an effective operational range of 1,640 yards (1,500 m). Mounted coaxially was a 20 mm Polsten cannon (Polish copy of the 20 mm Oerlikon, 450 rounds per minute) with an effective range of 1,093 yards (1,000 m). A Besa machine gun was mounted for engaging enemy infantry (7.92 × 57 mm, 500–800 rounds per minute). From the fifty-first production vehicle of the Mark 2, the tank was fitted with an electrical two-plane stabilization system from the Metropolitan-Vickers company, or Metrovick for short. The Centurion was thus less vulnerable than battle tanks of other nations (including the M48 and M60), since all hydraulic systems could be eliminated from the fighting compartment. The latter tended to explode when hit due to their high pressure and flammability of the hydraulic fluid. The 20 mm cannon was replaced by a coaxial .30-caliber Besa machine gun. The Mark 3 was fitted with a more powerful Ordnance QF 20-pounder gun (84 × 618 mm R).

The Mark 5 version saw the Besa machine guns replaced by .30-caliber Browning machine guns (one coaxial, one on the commander's cupola), and the 5/1 version finally received a reinforced glacis plate. The 5/2 was rearmed with the much more powerful Royal Ordnance 105 mm L7 gun, increasing effective firing range to 1,968 yards (1,800 m). Beginning with the Mark 6, a .50-caliber Browning machine gun was also fitted with ballistics comparable to the main armament. This was supposed to make it possible for the weapons system to take the range of the target before use of the main gun, thus saving ammunition. The Mark 6 introduced infrared equipment, giving the Centurion a limited night combat capability.

ACTION WITH THE ISRAELI ARMED FORCES

In the Six-Day War of 1967, a total of 293 Centurions fought on the Israeli side along with M50 Shermans, upgraded M51 Shermans, and AMX-13s, successfully engaging Egyptian T-34/85s and more-modern T-54/T-55 tanks as well as Jordanian M47 and M48 Pattons and Syrian Panzer IVs. Both Egypt and Jordan had Centurions too, but all thirty of the Egyptian tanks were destroyed due to inadequately trained crews and poor tactics. The thirty Jordanian Centurions were captured by Israeli forces. When the fighting began, the 7th Armored Corps had fifty-eight Shot tanks and sixty-six M48s and advanced from the Gaza Strip along the Mediterranean Sea to the Suez Canal. Farther south, nine Shot tanks blocked the Mitla Pass, but four of them ran

Shot Meteor	
Type	Battle tank
Manufacturer	Royal Ordnance, Great Britain
Service introduction	1959 (with the Israeli armed forces)
Number	1,080 (with the Israeli armed forces)
Crew	4 (commander, gunner, loader, driver)
Combat weight	57 tons (51,800 kg)
Length	25 ft., 7 in. (7,800 mm; not counting barrel), 34 ft., 5 in. (10,500 mm; with barrel)
Width	11 ft., 2 in. (3,400 mm)
Height	9 ft., 6 in. (2,900 mm)
Primary armament	Centurion Mark 5: Ordnance QF 20-pounder gun (84 mm), 64 rounds), Royal Ordnance L7 105 mm gun (64 rounds)
Secondary armament	1 × L3A1 7.62 mm coaxial machine gun (3,600 rounds) 1 × M2HB 12.7 mm machine gun (1,000 rounds)
Engine	Rolls-Royce Meteor Mark 4 B1 12-cylinder gasoline engine, 650 hp
Transmission	Merrit-Brown Z51R (5 forward gears, 1 reverse)
Power-to-weight ratio	12.5 hp/ton
Ground clearance	20 in. (0.51 m)
Wading capability	51 in. (1.3 m)
Trench crossing	132 in. (3.35 m)
Obstacle	35.4 in. (0.9 m)
Gradient	60%
Maximum speed	31 mph (50 kph) (on roads), 12 mph (20 kph) (off roads)
Fuel capacity	145 US gal. (550 liters)
Range	93 miles (150 km) (on roads), 62 miles (100 km) (off roads)
Protection	Armor steel structure (120–195 mm frontal, 38–51 mm on the sides)

Shot Kal	
Service introduction	1967
Number	390 (with the Israeli armed forces)
Crew	4 (commander, gunner, loader, driver)
Combat weight	59.5 tons (54,000 kg)
Length	25 ft., 7 in. (7,800 mm; not counting barrel), 34 ft., 5 in. (10,500 mm; with barrel)
Width	11 ft., 2 in. (3,400 mm)
Height	9 ft., 6 in. (2,900 mm)
Primary armament	Royal Ordnance L7 105 mm gun (72 rounds)
Secondary armament	1 × M2HB 12.7 mm machine gun (1,000 rounds) 1 × FN MAG 60-40 7.62 mm coaxial machine gun (1,200 rounds) 2 × FN MAG 60-40 7.62 mm machine guns (3,500 rounds)
Fire control system	Shot Kal Gimel: two-plane stabilization Shot Kal Dalet: laser rangefinder
Engine	Teledyne Continental AVD-S-1790-2A diesel engine, 750 hp
Transmission	Allison CD850-6 (5 forward gears, 2 reverse)
Power-to-weight ratio	13.9 hp/ton
Ground clearance	20 in. (0.51 m)
Wading capability	51 in. (1.3 m)
Trench crossing	132 in. (3.35 m)
Obstacle	35.4 in. (0.9 m)
Gradient	60%
Maximum speed	31 mph (50 kph) (on roads)
Fuel capacity	780 liters
Range	250 km (on roads), 150 km (off roads)
Protection	Armor steel structure (120–195 mm frontal, 38–51 mm on the sides); Shot Kal Beth: supplementary armor (composite).

out of fuel and had to be towed into firing position by other tanks. Nevertheless, these few tanks were able to keep the pass blockaded against three retreating Egyptian divisions.

The Shot earned its legendary reputation in the tank battles on the Golan Heights; for example, in the fighting in the Valley of Tears, during the Yom Kippur War in 1973. There a total of 105 Shot Kal tanks of the 7th Armored Brigade and twenty of the 188th Armored Brigade stopped an advance by about five hundred Syrian T-55s and T-62s. About half the enemy tanks were destroyed before the Syrians retreated. The reason for this success lay in a combination of carefully planned firing positions on the hills, the accuracy of the 105 mm gun at long ranges, and outstandingly accurate shooting, the result of intensive training by the Israeli tank crews. The 100 mm guns of the Soviet tanks used by the Syrians were not as accurate. In three days, the Syrians lost the majority of their T-55s and T-62s, some of which were later put into service by the Israelis as the Tiran (see chapter 15, "Captured Tanks under the Israeli Flag"). This compensated at least in part for the heavy losses in the Sinai, which were in part inflicted by the massive use of AT-3 Sagger guided antitank missiles and RPG-2 and RPG-7 rocket-propelled grenades by Egyptian infantry at the Bar-Lev Line. Altogether, the Israelis lost about two hundred tanks, about 40 percent of their southern armored groups, in the first two days of war. In the course of the entire war, 1,063 Israeli and 2,250 Arab tanks were damaged or destroyed. To make good the Israeli losses, after the war the

A Shot Kal Gimel on display at the Israeli Tank Museum at Latrun. *Marc Lenzin Archive*

Americans supplied two hundred M48 and M60 tanks, and the United Kingdom four hundred more Centurions.

The following experiences by the IDF in the Yom Kippur War confirm the high effectiveness in combat of the Shot:

1. The 105 mm gun made it possible for the Shot to open fire with HEAT ammunition from a distance of 1,750–2,405 yards (1,600–2,200 m) (in some cases, up to 4,374 yards, or 4,000 m) and with HESH ammunition even from 3,280 yards (3,000 m). By comparison, the Soviet T-62 was able to open fire only from 437 to 1,312 yards (400 to 1,200 m) with HEAT ammunition. The Shot's main gun was thus superior to those of all Arab tanks.
2. Despite the tank's stabilization system, to exploit its superior range a halt was always made before firing. As a result, first-shot hits were achieved as a rule, which was decisive in view of the Arabs considerable local numerical superiority.
3. The superior depression of the tank's main gun made it better able to exploit cover and partial concealment and compensated for the Shot's larger silhouette.
4. The ammunition capacity of seventy-two rounds resulting from the Shot's enlarged ammunition space proved decisive in many combat situations.
5. The Israelis found the tank's heavy armor particularly effective.
6. The tank's effectiveness was due in large part to the excellent level of training and the skilled tactical and battle conduct of the Israeli tank crews.
7. According to statements by various high-ranking Israeli officers, the Shot best met Israeli requirements.

Shot Kal tanks also played a major part in the invasion of Lebanon in 1982, where the tank's reactive armor proved effective against antitank weapons wielded by infantry in particular. Tanks of the 460th Brigade encountered Syrian tank units at Jezzine, and in the ensuing tank battle a quantity of Syrian T-62s were destroyed, while the Israeli forces lost eight Shot Kals and decided the battle in their favor.

A Shot tank from the first delivery batch (registration number 813875) during a gunnery exercise. *Israel Government Press Office*

CHAPTER 11: The Backbone of the Israeli Armored Corps: The Centurion (Shot)

Chapter 12
Cold Warrior: The Patton Tank (Magach)

While the Arab states were equipping their armored units with Western and Soviet tanks, Israel tried reinforcing its existing fleet of tanks with more-modern models. In addition to the British Centurion, these efforts centered on acquisition of the American M48 Patton tank. After initial political setbacks, a small number of these vehicles finally became available, launching the successful career of the Magach, which would remain in Israeli service for more than half a century.

DEVELOPMENT OF THE M48

The US Army received its first M26 Pershing tanks during the fighting in Germany in the final months of the Second World War. Despite its classification as a heavy tank, in terms of weight, protection, and firepower it was very similar to the German Panzer V Panther medium tank. After the war the M4 Sherman was replaced as the standard tank by the M26 Pershing and was reclassified as a medium tank.

With the beginning of the Cold War in the late 1940s, the army began a general modernization of its armored forces. In 1948, an upgraded model of the M26 entered service as the M46 Patton. A significant element of the M46 modernization program was the use of a new propulsion system consisting of a Continental AV-1790-5A twelve-cylinder gasoline engine and an Allison CD-850 tank transmission. With minor modifications, this combination was to remain the centerpiece of American tank production until the introduction of the M1 Abrams in 1981. About 2,400 Pershings were converted to M46 Patton standard by 1951.

By the beginning of the Korean War, the M46 had already reached the limits of its capabilities. The new long-term standard tank with the project name T42 was still in the preliminary development stage. As an interim solution, the turret of the T42, development of which had been completed, was mounted on the M46 chassis. This new vehicle entered production at the Detroit Tank Arsenal and the American Locomotive Company in 1951 as the M47 Patton. Even before production began, in December 1950 the US Army tasked the Chrysler Corporation with development of a regular successor, the M48 Patton. The new vehicle was to retain the earlier tank's engine and transmission but have heavier armor and a larger turret ring to accommodate a heavier gun.

As well, the crew was to be reduced from five men to four. The first M48 prototype was developed and produced in just one year. The first production vehicle left the line in April 1952. The M48 entered service with the American 2nd Armored Division as the new standard tank in 1953. Except for a few hundred examples, the M47 was exported as part of the Military Assistance Program (MAP) starting in 1955.

The M48 was followed by about 3,200 examples of the M48A1, whose greatest innovations were the M1 commander's cupola with integrated .50-caliber machine gun and a larger driver's hatch with the ability to accommodate an infrared night vision device. One of the greatest disadvantages of the M48 and M48A1 was its limited range of just 70 miles (112 km). This could be increased with use of externally mounted 55-gallon drums on the rear of the hull, but these had to be jettisoned before entering combat. This shortcoming was finally eliminated by the M48A2, which introduced a more efficient and compact version of the Continental engine and larger fuel tanks, more than doubling range.

Many M48s and M48A1s were exported by MAP, while the M48A2 became the standard tank of the US Army and the Marines in the late 1950s and 1960s. The latter remained the most produced version among the total of 11,703 Pattons of all models until production ended in 1959.

The M48A2C featured minor improvements. The separate tensioning idler wheel between the last road wheel and the drive sprocket was eliminated, and the track was tensioned by means of a return roller. The fire direction computer was modified and the number of usable types of ammunition was increased.

DEVELOPMENT OF THE M60

The lessons learned in the conflicts in Korea, India-Pakistan, and the Middle East and information about Soviet tank design impacted the development of the next generation of American battle tanks. Examination of a Red Army T-54A by the British military attaché in Budapest during the Hungarian Revolution of 1956 created a shock in Western military circles. The Soviet

Magach 3 tanks of the 252nd Division (M48A2C with L7 gun), October 1973. *Israel Government Press Office*

tank was 9.9 tons (9 tonnes) lighter than the M48 but was better armored. Both vehicles had a 100 mm glacis plate, but that of the T-54 was more sloped. With its 100 mm gun, the T-54 was also better armed than the M48 with its 90 mm gun.

In 1954 the T95 prototype became the focal point of future tank development by the US Army. The vehicle had a low chassis, similar to the T-54. The program included the T53 Optical Tracking, Acquisition and Ranging (OPTAR) system—a forerunner of the laser rangefinder—and a composite armor of steel and ceramic (silicon dioxide), which offered improved protection against hollow charges. The total of eleven T95 prototypes was also used to test different hydropneumatic suspension systems, a cross-drive transmission, and even a gas turbine power plant.

The T95 could have led to a revolutionary American battle tank, but costs and the associated technical requirements led to a decision to continue production of the M48A2 until at least 1961. The T95 project was finally shelved in favor of the XN60 program, which combined the chassis of the M48A2 with the new Continental AVDS-1790 twelve-cylinder diesel engine, the composite armor tested on the T95 combined with a more powerful armament (90 mm gun with improved T300 HEAT ammunition, X15E8 105 mm gun, and T123E6 120 mm gun). The composite armor was dropped due to technical problems and replaced with conventional steel armor (cast steel). The M68 105 mm gun developed in Great Britain was selected as the tank's main armament.

Production of the M60 began in 1959. The first 360 vehicles were made at the Chrysler factory in Newark Delaware, after which production was transferred to the Detroit Tank Arsenal, where the remaining 2,205 M60 tanks were built.

The first prototypes of the modernized M60 tank (Pilot 1 and 2) were completed in May 1961, the third (Pilot 3) not until June 1961. Pilot 1 was sent to Eglin Air Force Base for environmental testing, while Pilot 2 was tested at the Yuma Test Station and Pilot 3 underwent field trials at Fort Knox. Production of the M60A1 began on October 13, 1962.

The modified turret of the M48 was replaced by a completely redesigned version that was longer and narrower and through its shape offered better protection (250 mm or armor on the turret front, 140 on the sides). The gun was moved forward by 5 inches (12.7 cm) to provide more room for the crew. The ammunition load rose from 57 to 63 rounds.

The engine also received a variety of modifications, as a result of which this version used less fuel and produced fewer visible exhaust gases. The commander and gunner now had infrared night vision devices, which relied on an active infrared source. This was provided by an infrared illuminator on the gun barrel, which crews sometimes used to heat their field rations during maneuvers. The mechanical brakes gave way to hydraulic models to make work easier for the driver. The coaxial M73 machine gun was also replaced by the M219 model.

ENTRY INTO ISRAELI SERVICE

In 1960, the Israelis tried unsuccessfully to purchase M48 tanks from the United States to compensate for the growing numbers of T-54s in the Egyptian and Syrian armies. For political reasons the American government was not ready to supply these tanks, but it did agree to the transfer of two hundred M48s from the Bundeswehr as part of German reparations to Israel. The first forty M48A1s arrived in the port of Haifa on the night of December 10, 1964, with men of the 7th Armored Brigade standing guard as the tanks were unloaded.

When this transfer became public knowledge, under pressure from the Arab states the German government found itself forced to halt further deliveries. In 1965, however, Israel was able to reach a negotiated settlement with the United States for the delivery of a further 250 M48s. By the start of the Six-Day War in June 1967, Israeli had in service a total of 140 M48A1s (Magach 1) and 110 M48A2Cs (Magach 2). The M48s could not be used in combat due to their poor condition, and they were initially placed in storage for future conversion to Magach 3 standard.

The conversion into Magach 3s — with the British 105 mm gun, a lower commander's cupola, and the new Continental diesel engine — began in 1966, and during the Six-Day War, Israeli was able to equip only one company with the new vehicles. During the war about a hundred Jordanian army M48s and M48A1s also fell into Israeli hands.

The Magach was basically very popular with the troops, since it was more reliable and faster than the Shot and was easier to maintain. Although the Magach's hull was more heavily armored than the early versions of the Shot (120 mm compared

Magach 1, from 1964	M48A1 in original configuration
Magach 2, from 1965	M48A2C in original configuration
Magach 3, from 1970	Modernized M48A1/A2 with 105 mm L7 gun (like the Shot), lower turret profile, new communications system, and a Continental AVDS-1790-2A 12-cylinder diesel engine (750 hp) with an Allison CD-850-6A transmission, later also equipped with reactive armor (Blazer)
Magach 5, from 1975	M48A5 in original configuration
Magach 6, from 1971	Modernized M60/M60A1/M60A3 with lower commander's cupola and reactive armor (Blazer).
Magach 7, from 1986	Modernized M60/M60A1/M60A3 with a Continental AVDS-1790-5A diesel engine (908 hp), additional armor, and a fire control system based on that of the Merkava.

Overview of the versions of the Magach

to 76 mm), overall the Shot was better armored thanks to its heavier turret armor (195 mm vs. 180 mm), since in battle a higher number of turret hits had to be expected. The most unpopular feature of the Magach was the tall M-1 commander's cupola, which left the commander very exposed. On the Magach 3 this was replaced by the lower "Urdan" version.

By the time of the Yom Kippur War in 1973, the American arms policy had changed, and Israeli took delivery of approximately nine hundred M48/M48A1/M48A2 tanks and several hundred M60A1s. The Magach battalions now formed the backbone of the Israeli Armored Corps in the Sinai, while the Shot battalions saw action primarily on the Golan Heights.

Thanks to modernization with the 105 mm gun and the well-trained and highly motivated Israeli tank crews, the Magach was more than a match for the Egyptian T-55s and T-62s. The heavy tank losses suffered by the Israelis were caused mainly by Egyptian infantry armed with the 9M14M Malyutka guided antitank missile (AT-3 Sagger) and RPG-7 rocket-propelled grenades.

The M60 entered service with the Israeli Armored Corps as the Magach 6 and over the years received numerous modifications:

- Magach 6 Alef: modernized M60A1
- Magach 6 Bet: new AVDS-1790-2C diesel engine (750 hp) and new tracks
- Magach 6 Bet Gal: new Gal fire control system (developed in Israel)
- Magach 6 Bet Gal Batash: modern passive armor, new AVDS-1790-5A diesel engine (908 hp)

Magach 1 (M48A1), Magach 2 (M48A2C)	
Type	Battle tank
Manufacturer	Chrysler, Fisher Body, Ford Motor Company, American Locomotive Company, USA
Service introduction	1952 (USA), 1965 (with the Israeli armed forces)
Number	12,000 (USA, export, all variants) 100 M48A1 (IDF), 150 M48A2C (IDF), 100 M48/M48A1 captured from Jordan
Crew	4 (commander, gunner, loader, driver)
Combat weight	M48A1: 51.15 tons (46,400 kg), M48A2C: 52.5 tons (47,600 kg)
Length	30 ft., 6 in. (9,300 mm)
Width	11 ft., 9 in. (3,600 mm)
Height	10 ft., 2 in. (3,100 mm)
Primary armament	M41 90 mm gun (M48A1: 60 rounds, M48A2C: 64 rounds)
Secondary armament	1 × M73 7.62 mm coaxial machine gun (M48A1: 5,570 rounds, M48A2C: 5,500 rounds) 1 × M2HB 12.7 mm machine gun (M48A1: 600 rounds, M48A2C: 1,400 rounds)
Engine	M48A1: Continental AV-1790-5C gasoline engine, 650 hp M48A2C: Continental AV-1790-7C gasoline engine, 690 hp
Transmission	Allison CD-850-4A (2 forward gears, 1 reverse)
Power-to-weight ratio	M48A1: 14 hp/ton, M48A2C: 14.5 hp/ton
Ground clearance	16.5 in. (0.42 m)
Wading ability	47 in. (1.2 m)
Trench crossing	102 in. (2.6 m)
Obstacle	35.4 in. (0.9 m)
Gradient	60%
Maximum speed	M48A1: 28 mph (45 kph) (on roads), M48A2C: 31 mph (50 kph) (on roads)
Fuel capacity	M48A1: 200 US gal. (760 liters), M48A2C: 335.5 US gal. (1,270 liters)
Range	M48A1: 68 miles (110 km) (on roads), M48A2C: 112 miles (180 km) (on roads)
Protection	Armor steel structure (110–178 mm frontal, 51–76 mm on the sides)

Magach 3 (M48A3)	
Service introduction	1970
Number	540 (with the Israeli armed forces)
Crew	4 (commander, gunner, loader, driver)
Combat weight	53.5 tons (48,500 kg)
Length	30 ft., 6 in. (9,300 mm)
Width	11 ft., 9 in. (3,600 mm)
Height	10 ft., 10 in. (3,300 mm)
Primary armament	Royal Ordnance L7 105 mm gun (54 rounds)
Secondary armament	1 × M73 7.62 mm coaxial machine gun (5,950 rounds) 1 × M2HB 12.7 mm machine gun (1,200 rounds)
Engine	Continental AVD-S-1790-2A diesel engine, 750 hp
Transmission	Allison CD-850-6 (2 forward gears, 1 reverse)
Power-to-weight ratio	15.5 hp/ton
Ground clearance	16.5 in. (0.42 m)
Wading ability	47 in. (1.2 m)
Trench crossing	102 in. (2.6 m)
Obstacle	35.4 in. (0.9 m)
Gradient	60%
Maximum speed	31 mph (50 kph) (on roads)
Fuel capacity	1,460 liters
Range	298 miles (480 km) (on roads)
Protection	Armor steel structure (120–195 mm frontal, 38–51 mm on the sides), Blazer reactive armor (from 1981)

Magach 3 tank with reactive armor modules. *Israel Government Press Office*

- Magach 6 Bet Baz: new Baz fire control system (similar to that used in the Merkava Mark III)
- Magach 6 Gimel: modernized M60A3

The last model of the series entered service as the Magach 7 in 1985 and was largely based on the Magach 6 Gal Batash. Because of its newly developed supplemental armor (analogous to the Merkava Mark II and III), the tank is barely recognizable as an M60.

TECHNICAL FEATURES

The M48/M60 or Magach had a crew of four consisting of a driver, gunner, loader, and commander.

The rear-mounted twelve-cylinder gasoline engine of the original M48/M48A1 (Continental AV-1790-5C) produced 650 hp, which gave the tank, at a combat weight of 51.15 tons (46.4 tonnes), a power-to-weight ratio of 12.7 hp/ton (14 hp/tonne), which was superior to that of the Shot. A more powerful engine (Continental AV-1790-7C, 690 hp) was installed in the M48A2, but because of its increased weight (52.5 tons, or 47.6 tonnes) its power-to-weight ratio was roughly the same (13.15 hp/tonne). The Magach 3 ultimately had a twelve-cylinder diesel engine (Continental AVD-S-1790-2A), which produced 750 hp — the same engine that powered the Shot Kal.

The M60 or Magach 6 was powered by a slightly modified diesel engine (Continental AVD-S-1790-2A), which also produced 750 hp. Off road, the Magach achieved a speed of 18.5 mph (30 kph), while on road it was capable of 31 mph (50 kph) and was thus 50 percent faster than the original Shot. Because of its relatively inefficient gasoline engine, combined with a relatively low fuel capacity (200 US gallons, or 760 liters), the maximum operational range of the Magach 1 was just 68 miles (110 km), while that of the Magach 2 was 112 miles (180 km) thanks to external fuel tanks. Not until the introduction of the diesel engine and a larger fuel tank did the later models (from the Magach 3 onward) achieve a range of about 300 miles (480 km) on roads.

The transmission (various versions of the Allison CD-850 transmission) had two forward gears and one reverse gear, and power was transmitted to the tracks by means of mechanical superimposed steering.

The Magach's hull was better armored than that of the Shot (76 mm), with 120 mm (M48) or 155 mm (M60) of armor plate. The turrets of the first versions (Magach 1 and 2), however, were still rather less well armored than that of the Shot (180 mm compared to 195 mm in the Shot). On the Magach 3 the turret

Magach 5 (M48A5)	
Service introduction	1975
Number	2,069 (with the Israeli armed forces)
Crew	4 (commander, gunner, loader, driver)
Combat weight	54 tons (49,000 kg)
Length	30 ft., 6 in. (9,300 mm)
Width	11 ft., 9 in. (3,600 mm)
Height	10 ft., 2 in. (3,100 mm)
Primary armament	M68 105 mm gun (54 rounds)
Secondary armament	1 × M240 7.62 mm coaxial machine gun 1 × M60 7.62 mm machine gun (10,000 rounds)
Engine	Continental AVDS-1790-25 12-cylinder diesel engine, 750 hp
Transmission	Allison CD-850-6A (2 forward gears, 1 reverse)
Power-to-weight ratio	15.3 hp/ton
Ground clearance	16.5 in. (0.42 m)
Wading ability	47 in. (1.2 m)
Trench crossing	102 in. (2.6 m)
Obstacle	35.4 in. (0.9 m)
Gradient	60%
Maximum speed	31 mph (50 kph) (on roads)
Fuel capacity	385 US gal. (1,460 liters)
Range	285 miles (460 km) (on roads)
Protection	Armor steel structure (120–195 mm frontal, 38–51 mm on the sides), Blazer reactive armor from 1981

Magach 7 tank during a combat exercise. *Israel Government Press Office*

armor was likewise reinforced to 195 mm, while the Magach 6 had significantly heavier turret armor (250 mm) when it was introduced.

Unfortunately, there is no information available on the performance of the composite armor with which the Magach was later equipped. It can be assumed that the armor was designed to be effective against fire from the then-current generations of Soviet tanks (first the T-62 with its 115 mm gun; later the T-62, T-72, and T-80 series with the 125 mm smooth-bore gun) and as of the Magach 6 Bet Gal Batash was at least 250 mm of RHA against armor-piercing shot (APFSDS) and 500 mm of RHA against hollow-charge ammunition (HEAT).

As a result of losses to antitank weapons during the Six-Day War, in the late 1960s Israel developed its own Blazer reactive armor, which was used on almost all variants of the Magach after it entered service. Newer versions from the Magach 6 onward had smoke grenade launchers for self-defense.

One major disadvantage of the Magach compared to the Shot was its hydraulic gun / turret drive system, which when hit tended to explode and thus set the tank on fire and, in the worst cases, could kill the crew—something the Israeli crews experienced during the Yom Kippur War of 1973.

The Magach 1/2 was still armed with the M41 90 mm tank gun, which could fire high-explosive (HE), hollow-charge (HEAT), and subcaliber armor-piercing (APCR) ammunition with an effective range of 1,640 yards (1,500 m). It was capable of penetrating 240 mm of armor with armor-piercing ammunition and 320 mm with HEAT ammunition. An M73 7.62 mm machine gun was coaxially mounted, and there was also an M2HB 12.7 mm machine gun mounted on the commander's cupola. The Magach 3 finally had the Royal Ordnance 105 mm L7 tank gun from the Shot Kal, which greatly improved its effectiveness. The Magach 7 had a 12.7 mm machine gun mounted on the gun mantlet, and 7.62 mm machine guns were added both for the commander and loader.

In addition, from the Magach 6 onward, more and more developments from the Merkava program, such as its fire control system, were adopted, on the one hand, to create logistical similarities between the different vehicle fleets, and, on the other hand, to make Israel more independent of the foreign arms industry.

Magach 6 (M60, M60A1, M60A3)	
Type	Battle tank
Manufacturer	Chrysler Corporation Delaware Defense Plant, Detroit Arsenal Tank Plant
Service introduction	1971
Number	360 (with the Israeli armed forces)
Crew	4 (commander, gunner, loader, driver)
Combat weight	58 tons (52,600 kg)
Length	22 ft., 9 in. (6,946 mm)
Width	11 ft., 9 in. (3,600 mm)
Height	10 ft., 10 in. (3,300 mm)
Primary armament	M68 105 mm gun (63 rounds)
Secondary armament	1 × M240 7.62 mm coaxial machine gun (6,000 rounds) 1 × M85 12.7 mm machine gun (900 rounds)
Fire control system	Magach 6B Gal: Gal fire control system (Israel) Magach 6B Baz: Baz fire control system (Israel)
Engine	Continental AVDS-1790-2C 12-cylinder diesel engine, 750 hp
Transmission	Allison CD-850-6A (2 forward gears, 1 reverse)
Power-to-weight ratio	14.3 hp/ton
Ground clearance	17.7 in. (0.45 m)
Wading ability	48 in. (1.22 m)
Trench crossing	35.8 in. (0.91 m)
Obstacle	102 in. (2.60 m)
Gradient	60%
Maximum speed	30 mph (48 kph) (on roads), 20 mph (32 kph) (off roads)
Fuel capacity	375 US gal. (1,420 liters)
Range	298 miles (480 km) (on roads)
Protection	Armor steel structure (258–276 mm frontal, 74–140 mm on the sides) Magach 6B Gal Batash: supplemental armor (composite) Blazer reactive armor (from 1981) NBC defense system Nachel Oz fire-warning and fire-extinguishing system

Magach 7 (M60)	
Service introduction	1986 (with the Israeli armed forces)
Number	1,040 (with the Israeli armed forces)
Crew	4 (commander, gunner, loader, driver)
Combat weight	60.6 tons (55,000 kg)
Length	30 ft., 11 in. (9,430 mm)
Width	11 ft., 9 in. (3,600 mm)
Height	10 ft., 10 in. (3,300 mm)
Primary armament	M68 105 mm gun (63 rounds)
Secondary armament	1 × MAG 7.62 mm machine gun (10,000 rounds) 1 × M85 12.7 mm machine gun (900 rounds) 2 × 6 smoke grenade launchers
Fire control system	Knight Mark 2 (as in the Merkava)
Engine	Continental AVDS-1790-5A 12-cylinder diesel engine, 910 hp
Transmission	Allison CD-850-6A (2 forward gears, 1 reverse)
Power-to-weight ratio	16.5 hp/ton
Ground clearance	17.7 in. (0.45 m)
Wading ability	48 in. (1.22 m)
Trench crossing	35.8 in. (0.91 m)
Obstacle	102 in. (2.6 m)
Gradient	60%
Maximum speed	30 mph (48 kph) (on roads), 20 mph (32 kph) (off roads)
Fuel capacity	375 US gal. (1,420 liters)
Range	298 miles (480 km) (on roads)
Protection	Armor steel structure (258–276 mm frontal, 74–140 mm on the sides) Magach 6B Gal Batash: supplemental armor (composite) Blazer reactive armor NBC defense system Nachel Oz fire-warning and fire-extinguishing system

A Magach 6 Bet Gal tank. *Israel Government Press Office*

IN ACTION WITH THE ISRAELI ARMED FORCES

At the beginning of the Six-Day War, just two battalions were equipped with the Magach: the 79th Armored Battalion of the 7th Armored Brigade, under the command of Major Ehud Elad, and an independent armored battalion of the Special Operations Group under the command of Colonel Uri Barom.

The two battalions functioned as the spearhead of the attack by the Tal Division in the Gaza Strip. During the fighting for Rafah, Barom's battalion destroyed at least twelve Egyptian T-34/85s and fifteen IS-3M heavy tanks. One of the fiercest battles in which its Magach tanks took part occurred at the Jiradi Pass, where the Israelis lost a number of vehicles to mines and antitank guns.

Despite this, the tanks succeeded in overrunning the entrenched defensive position; however, the commander of the 79th Armored Battalion and several of his officers were killed in this battle. The Israelis did not commit their Magach tanks on the Jordanian front since the Jordanian army was equipped with the same type.

In the Yom Kippur War of 1973, the Israeli armed forces committed 540 Magach 3 and Magach 6 tanks, more than half of which were knocked out in combat—the majority by hits from Soviet antitank weapons (9M14M Malyutka wire-guided antitank missiles and RPG-7s).

By the time the war ended, just two hundred tanks were still operational. These losses were made good by the modernization of older models until the end of the 1970s, which were successively equipped with reactive armor. Israel was the first nation to use this technology operationally, in Lebanon starting in 1981.

The Israeli-made Merkava tank later replaced the Magach, but as before the armed forces kept the older vehicles in reserve. According to various sources, there are currently still about 200 Magach 5s (M48A5), 360 Magach 6 Aled (M60A1) and 1,040 Magach 6/7 (M60A3 or more modern) in the inventory.

Chapter 13
The Six-Day War, 1967 (Third Arab-Israeli War)

A new state of Israel with broad frontiers — strong and solid — which extend from Jordan to the Suez Canal.

— Moshe Dayan, 1967

Despite Egypt's ignominious defeat in the war in the Sinai in 1956, President Gamal Abdel Nasser further solidified his political power and made himself into the undisputed leader of the Arab world. He armed his military with weapons from the Soviet Union and other Eastern Bloc states and in 1958 formed the United Arab Republic together with Syria.

As of early 1967, with his arsenal of weapons, Nasser was in a position to launch an attack on Israel at any time, depending on its military readiness.

In May 1967, the Soviet government informed Cairo about Israeli troop concentrations not far from the Syrian-Israeli border. This force allegedly consisted of more than ten brigades, but in fact there was no more than a company in that area, in waiting to ambush Syrian saboteurs. This report caused Nasser to move Egyptian and Syrian units into the border area to be ready for an offensive against Israel.

He also demanded that the United Nations withdraw all UNEF (United Nations Emergency Force) peacekeepers for their own security, since Egyptian troops had already moved into assembly areas on the eastern border of the Sinai and in the Gaza Strip. The UNEF had been policing the Egyptian-Israeli border since the end of the Suez Crisis, and it now appeared that it might become caught between the fronts. Without waiting for a formal response from the secretary-general of the United Nations, Sithu U Thant, on May 17 the Egyptians unceremoniously took over all the border observation posts. It was thus too late for the secretary-general to save the integrity of the UN force, and he withdrew it.

Meanwhile in Cairo, Mohamed Abd al-Hakim Amer, who had led the Egyptian formations in the previous Sinai campaign and was now defense minister, ordered the call-up of additional reserves.

When Nasser announced the closure of the Straits of Tiran to Israeli shipping on May 22, by Israel's definition this was a casus belli. The Straits of Tiran linked the Gulf of Aqaba with the Red Sea and gave Israel vital access to the Indian Ocean. Blocking this access struck the young state in its most sensitive spot.

Israeli prime minister Levi Eshkol[1] regarded the Egyptian actions as an act of war against Israel, and he dispatched his foreign minister, Abba Eban, to Paris, London, and Washington with a request for support. Political efforts to defuse the crisis failed, and Eshkol realized that Israel would have to act alone.

Meanwhile, fear of another war grew among the Israeli population, and loud voices demanded a stronger leader — someone they knew and trusted. With pressure on the government continuing to grow, at the end of May 1967, Eshkol named Moshe Dayan to the post of defense minister. A successful commander during the Suez Crisis in 1956, he had been highly decorated and had since been regarded as a legend.

Dayan decided to launch a preventive strike to knock out the Arab air forces. Defensive positions were to be occupied along the Jordanian and Syrian borders. The plans for this had been prepared in every detail by the chief of the general staff, Rabin, years before.

Since Israeli territory was ill suited for waging mobile warfare, an incursion was to be made into the Sinai and if necessary western Jordan and the Golan Heights as well. According to Dayan's plan, superiority on the ground would have to be brought about by achieving air superiority.

At 0745 on June 5, 1967, Dayan ordered the beginning of Operation Focus. Israeli Mirage IIIC, Mystère IV, and Super Mystère combat aircraft, all French made, surprised the Arab forces and bombed airfields, air defense positions, and radar

---

[1] Levi Eshkol (1895–1969) grew up in the Ukraine. He immigrated with his family to Palestine in 1914 and served in the Jewish Legion on the British side during the First World War. In 1940, Eshkol became a member of the Haganah and coordinated its illegal arms buildup as finance minister. His political career in the Knesset began in 1951 as a member of the Mapai Party, which he founded. After Ben Gurion's resignation, he assumed the office of president in 1963. He was the first Israeli prime minister to visit the United States and establish diplomatic contacts with the government of the Federal Republic of Germany. In 1968, he also founded the Israeli Labor Party Avoda and died a year later of a heart attack.

installations in Egypt, Syria, and Jordan. By evening the Israelis had destroyed the bulk of the Arab air forces, which were equipped mainly with MiG aircraft from the Soviet Union. Hundreds of aircraft, some of them among the most modern in the world, lay as burning wrecks on the ground.

THE CAMPAIGN IN THE SINAI PENINSULA

The Egyptian army had previously occupied the Sinai Peninsula with two divisions. Until shortly before the Israeli airstrikes began, Chief of Staff Mohamed Fawzi[2] reinforced the front with a further five divisions. This meant that at the outbreak of the war, the following Egyptian units were in the Sinai Peninsula:

- in the Gaza Strip, the 20th Division of the Palestinian Liberation Army
- south of the Gaza Strip, between Rafah and El Arish, the 7th Infantry Division
- in the key area of Abu Ageila, the 2nd Infantry Division
- in the Jabal Libni-Bir Hasana area, the 3rd Infantry Division
- between Bir Gifgafa and Bir Thamada, the 4th Armored Division
- south of Al Qusaymah and El Kuntilla, the 6th Infantry Division
- west of El Kuntilla Battle Group Shazly, an armored force in division strength

Since the Soviet Union had in 1956 begun equipping the Egyptian army with an arsenal of weapons valued at far more than a billion dollars, in 1967 its total strength was about 100,000 men, 1,200 tanks, 200 self-propelled guns, and 1,000 armored personnel carriers.

The armored brigade is the Israeli army's basic tactical unit. It is an independent fighting unit with about three thousand troops; its own armored, infantry, or paratrooper battalions; and artillery and heavy mortar batteries plus engineering, communications, and reconnaissance units. Each Israeli division, or *Ugda*, consists of two or three such fighting units.

---

[2] Mohamed Fawzi (1915–2000) grew up in Cairo and attended the Royal Military Academy. During the Suez Crisis in 1956, he led the military academy and later served as secretary general of the Arab Legion. During the Six-Day War in 1967, he commanded the Egyptian army in the Sinai. In 1968 he took over the office of minister of defense under Nasser and later Anwar el-Sadat. Suspected of having had a leading role in a coup attempt, he was placed under house arrest but was acquitted in 1974. He died in Cairo in February 2000.

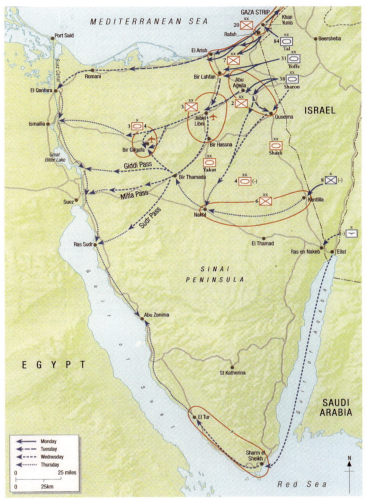

Map of the campaign in the Sinai, June 5–10, 1967. *Osprey*

For the offensive into the Sinai, the chief of the Israeli general staff, Yitzhak Rabin, assembled the following units on the Israeli-Egyptian border:

- in the northern sector at Rafah, the 84th Division, under Brigadier General Israel Tal, with the 7th and 60th Armored Brigades plus the 202nd Paratrooper Brigade and the 215th Artillery Regiment
- in the central sector, the 31st Division, under Brigadier General Avraham Yoffe, with the 200th and 520th Armored Brigades
- opposite Abu Ageila, the 38th Division, under Brigadier General Ariel Sharon, with the 14th Armored, 99th Infantry, and 80th Paratrooper Brigades plus the 214th Artillery Regiment

- south of El Kuntilla, the 8th Armored Brigade, under the command of Brigadier General Avraham Mandler[3]

The Israeli analysis of the enemy's assembly areas revealed favorable conditions for an attack and also for defense. In the event of an attack, the Israelis expected the Egyptian 6th Infantry Division to advance east through the Negev, in order to cut off supplies from Eilat and link up with the Jordanian army. In the event of a defense posture, however, the Egyptian units would use deeply echeloned defensive positions to block all main lines of advance through the desert.

Rabin and Major General Yeshayahu Gavish,[4] commander of the southern front, therefore formulated their battle plan as follows:

- In the first phase, the 84th Division (Tal) was to break through the enemy defensive lines at Khan Yunis-Rafah and occupy the interim objective of El Arish. This was to be followed by a simultaneous attack with the 38th Division (Sharon) to the south against the defense lines at Um Katef-Abu Ageila.
- In the second phase, the 31st Division (Yoffe) was to break through the defensive lines at Bir Lahfan.
- In the third phase, the 31st Division (Yoffe) was to drive to the Mitla, Gidi, and Sudr Passes and cut off the enemy's avenue of retreat to the Suez Canal. Meanwhile the 84th Division (Tal) would advance farther west and cut the supply line to El Kantara on the Suez Canal. The 38th Division (Sharon) was to destroy the encircled enemy at Jebel Libni, while Mandler's 8th Armored Brigade opened the barrier at El Kuntilla and thus liberated Eilat and Sharm El Sheik.

---

[3] Avraham Mandler (1929–73) grew up in Linz, Austria. After immigrating to Palestine, he served in the Haganah at a young age and later as an officer in the IDF. After commanding the 8th Armored Brigade during the Six-Day War in 1967, he commanded parts of the armored corps in the 1973 Sinai offensive during the Yom Kippur War. He was killed by an Egyptian artillery strike on October 13, 1973, after his radio message was intercepted by the enemy and the position came under fire.

[4] Yeshayahu Gavish (1925–2024) grew up in Tel Aviv and attended school in the kibbutz Givat Ha Shlosha. He served in the Palmach at the age of eighteen and fought under Yigal Allon in the Latrun offensives during the 1948-49 War of Independence. His rapid rise saw him become commander of the southern front during the Six-Day War in 1967. Despite successfully leading the three divisions in the Sinai campaign, the glory of victory belonged to the commanders Tal, Sharon, and Yoffe.

THE OUTCOME IS DECIDED IN THE SINAI PENINSULA

This peninsula is little more than a wasteland of sand seas, dunes, and barren mountain ranges, where as early as 1956 the battle for dominance of the Suez Canal raged. Now there was to be an even more violent clash between the forces of Zionism and those of Arab nationalism.

At that time, the 7th and 60th Armored Brigades were the elite of the Israeli Armored Corps. The former had fifty-eight upgraded Centurions (Shot) and sixty-six M48A2 Patton (Magach) tanks, while the latter fielded fifty-two M51 Shermans and thirty-four AMX-13s. The two brigades were attached to the 84th Division, commanded by Israel Tal, and together they had a combined force of about three hundred tanks. This force was now to force the decisive breakthrough at Rafah and El Arish. Tal knew that he would have to be victorious in this first battle if Israel was to win the war. The armored corps was therefore to strike like a clenched fist, and his appeal to his men was unmistakable: "Break through or die."

The campaign in the Sinai began with a fierce artillery barrage on the positions of the Egyptian 7th and 20th Infantry Divisions. The Israeli 7th Armored Brigade, led by the 79th and 82nd Armored Battalions, smashed through the Egyptian positions, took Khan Yunis, and pushed on in a westerly direction to Schech Sued, where it encountered fierce resistance. At the

Israeli general staff press conference after the successful Sinai operation on June 8, 1967, at Bir Gifgafa. The map on the right shows the Suez Canal and the western sector of the front, which was taken on June 7. The arrows mark where the divisions under Tal, Sharon, and Yoffe reached their respective objectives. *From left*: Ariel Sharon, Yishayahu Gavish, Israel Tal, and Avraham Yoffe. *Israel Government Press Office*

Israel's approximately two hundred M50 and M51 tanks were upgraded M4 Shermans. Their increased effectiveness was largely due to their more-powerful Continental eight-cylinder engines and more-powerful guns, such as the French-made 75 mm CN-75-50 of the M50 and the 105 mm CN-105-F1 of the M51. In the photo can be seen M51 tanks of the 60th Armored Brigade (84th Division under Tal) moving in the direction of Rafah, June 5, 1967. *Israel Government Press Office*

Approximately five hundred T-54/55 medium tanks formed the backbone of the Egyptian armored forces. A development of the T-44, the T-54/55 had up to 75 mm of armor, reached a top speed of 30 mph (48 kph) on roads, and was armed with a powerful 100 mm gun. The photo shows a T-54 burning after the battle for Bir Lahfan in the Sinai. It was knocked out by a Shot of the 200th Armored Brigade (31st Division under Yoffe). *Israel Government Press Office*

same time, Tal committed his second armored brigade to outflank and attack the enemy artillery positions west of Rafah. However, in difficult terrain the unit missed the Egyptian troops and were themselves taken by surprise from the rear. A fierce tank battle developed, during which numerous Egyptian T-34/85s were set on fire and burned on the battlefield. An Israeli tank battalion held in reserve was finally able to break through and destroy the enemy forces. On June 8, all Egyptian troops still in the Gaza Strip surrendered.

At El Arish the attackers again encountered Egyptian resistance, which was characterized by a deeply echeloned defensive position with antitank guns. While Tal's units fought their way forward against the Egyptian 7th Infantry Division in the firefight at El Arish, General Yoffe's 31st Division marched toward Bir Lahfan.

Yoffe's mission was to cut the main road to the north between Abu Ageila and Jabal Libni and prevent the Egyptians from reinforcing their troops in El Arish. In fact, an Egyptian armored battalion moved in the direction of El Arish and for an entire night engaged Yoffe's armored brigade in fierce fighting in the blocking position.

The next morning the 84th Division, under Tal, took El Arish. Elements of his division linked up with Yoffe's unit in Bir Lahfan, while the remaining troops advanced further in the direction of El Kantara. The drive through the first Egyptian defense line had succeeded.

The taking of the second defense line at Abu Ageila fell to Sharon's 38th Division. This position had been regarded as one of the most powerful defensive bastions in the 1956 campaign and the junction of all the roads in the Sinai. The positions, with deeply echeloned trenches, numerous minefields, antitank guns, artillery, and flanking units of heavy tanks, were manned by the Egyptian 2nd Infantry Division.

The Israelis could not afford to advance deeper into Sinai with such powerful forces in their rear. Like Tal's victory at El Arish, this attack was also vital and had to be successful at all costs.

Heavy artillery fire began the attack, and Sharon's armored brigade smashed into the Egyptian positions. The enemy defended himself fiercely, waiting until the Israeli troops were almost upon their positions and then opening fire point-blank with tanks, some of them dug in. The Egyptian defense had little success, however, and was overcome by the charge carried out by the heavy Centurions. Less than twenty-four hours later, Sharon reported that he had broken through the second defense line and taken the fortress of Abu Ageila. He regrouped his armored brigades in preparation for a further advance in the direction of Al Qusaymah.

After both Egyptian defense lines had been breached, the Egyptian troops began fleeing in panic west through the desert. Both of Yoffe's armored brigades drove southwest in the direction of Jebel Libni, where the Egyptian 3rd Infantry Division,

A status report in the Negev desert on the eve of the Six-Day War. *From left*: President Levi Eshkol, Labor Minister Yigal Allon, and General Israel Tal, June 1967. *Israel Government Press Office*

The Israel arsenal included about 250 British Shot Meteor tanks. Weighing about 50 tons, with a maximum speed of 21.5 mph (34.6 kph) on roads and armed with the 105 mm L7 gun in place of the original 84 mm gun, the Shot was the backbone of the Israeli Armored Corps. Here, tanks of the 7th Armored Brigade (84th Division) at the Gaza Strip shortly before the outbreak of the war, June 1967. *Israel Government Press Office*

reinforced by a battalion of T-34/85 tanks and several SU-100 tank-destroyers, stood guard over a major air base. His tanks followed in column formation behind the two armored brigades under Tal. The first tanks arrived on the hills on the outskirts of Jebel Libni at four in the afternoon. While Yoffe's tanks swung west, Tal's brigades turned right and formed a pincer formation around the airfield. The defenders' resistance crumbled under pressure from the attackers.

After the airfield had been taken, the two divisions separated again. While Yoffe's force drove south to Bir Hassana, Tal's brigades moved toward Bir Gifgafa to block the road to Ismailia. After passing weakly held Bir Hasana, Yoffe's armored units reached the narrow passageways of the Mitla and Gidi Passes. They represented an important operational link in the direction of the Suez Canal and were defended by the Egyptians — as they had been in 1956 — with great determination. Yoffe's tanks, artillery, and infantry fired on the retreating Egyptian 6th Infantry Division. Soon the entrances to the passes resembled a giant scrapyard, filled with numerous wrecked armored vehicles. In the fading daylight, few enemy vehicles escaped the inferno and fled west.

With Yoffe's units guarding the exits from both passes, the retreating Egyptians could only fall back through the Ismailia Pass. Tal used the opportunity and assembled every available tank in the still-open pass. A huge dust cloud signaled the approach of the Egyptian 4th Armored Division, which had orders to take up position on the central massif east of the Ismailia Pass. There followed a bloody battle, in which numerous T-55 tanks and armored personnel carriers burned, and Tal's unit also suffered significant losses. Not until the following day, after regrouping and rearming, did the Israeli force again advance on the Egyptian positions and finally smash the enemy. In the course of this battle, the Centurion tank once again demonstrated its superiority over the Soviet-made T-54 and T-55 tanks.

Soon afterward the Egyptian forces withdrew their tanks and tried to retreat through the pass. The Israelis subsequently met almost no opposition between the Ismailia Pass and the Suez Canal. Early on the morning of June 9, when Tal's Patton tanks approached the Suez Canal, the Egyptians on the bank fired signal flares in the belief that they were Egyptian tanks looking for the bridge over the canal.

At the same time, Yoffe pushed his units from the eastern exits from the Mitla and Gidi Passes to the western exits. One of his armored brigades drove back the Egyptian units and pushed through the narrows in the direction of the Suez Canal. The second brigade moved north about 18 miles (30 km) to cut off the Egyptians' avenue of retreat through the Gidi Pass.

Meanwhile, the leading units of Sharon's 38th Division met in Al Qusaymah, which had already been evacuated by the Egyptians. Not until they resumed their advance did they meet resistance from elements of the Egyptian 6th Infantry Brigade, which was trying to retreat to Nakhl. Since it was already getting dark, Sharon decided to order a lull in the fighting, refuel, and wait for daylight to continue the advance on Nakhl.

He got there before the Egyptian 6th Infantry Brigade, blocking the pilgrimage route east of the city with a battalion of Sherman tanks, and occupied the northern entrance with Centurion tanks and mechanized infantry.

The Josef Stalin (IS-3) was the heaviest tank in the Egyptian arsenal, weighing 45.8 tons and armed with a powerful 122 mm gun. It had impressive armor protection up to 120 mm in thickness and achieved a maximum speed of 23 mph (37 kph) on roads. Its shortcomings included a tendency for its engine to overheat, which made it ill suited to the high temperatures in the desert, and its special two-part ammunition, which made rapid reloading and a high rate of fire impossible. The photo shows an IS-3 in the Israeli Tank Museum at Latrun. *Marc Lenzin Archive*

The Egyptian troops of the 6th Infantry Brigade fell into the trap, caught in crossfire from Israeli tanks and under attack by the Israeli air force. The Egyptian unit tried in vain to extract itself from the Israeli trap. Many of its troops fell in the firestorm.

Sharm El Sheik fell just one day later to a combined sea and paratrooper landing operation, and seventy-two hours after the start of the attack, the Israeli flag was flying everywhere along the Suez Canal.

The victors allowed the defeated to withdraw — but without their weapons and equipment — so as not to burden themselves with tens of thousands of prisoners.

BATTLE OF JERUSALEM AND THE WEST BANK

During the offensive in the Sinai, Dayan ordered the commander of the central front, Uzi Narkiss,[5] initially not to commit any ground troops against the Jordanian units in the West Bank.

Narkiss, whose area of responsibility included Jerusalem, Tel Aviv, and the densely populated coastal plain of Israel, found himself facing two possible enemy responses in the West Bank: on the one hand, a Jordanian attack into the Israeli sector west of Jerusalem, and on the other hand, with a breakthrough in the north to the coast of Netanya and the associated interruption of the Israeli supply lines. In the latter case, Israeli supplies for the ongoing campaign in the Sinai would be severely disrupted.

From the beginning of the conflict, the city of Jerusalem was the focal point and Dayan's greatest military challenge. Placed under international administration by the UN in 1947, later, during the 1948–49 War of Independence, the city was divided into the Jewish western and Jordanian-occupied eastern quarters. Access to the Temple Mount and the Wailing Wall, the holiest sites in the city, remained closed to Jews from then on.

The Egyptian general Riad[6] was chief of staff of the Jordanian forces, which occupied positions along the West Bank — north

---

[5] Uzi Narkiss (1925–97), who grew up in Jerusalem, joined the Palmach at the age of sixteen. During the 1948–49 War of Independence, he led the 4th Infantry Battalion of the Harel Brigade. After his deployment as commander of the central front and the historic capture of the Old City of Jerusalem during the Six-Day War in 1967, he left the army and held leadership positions in civilian organizations such as the Jewish Agency and the World Zionist Organization.

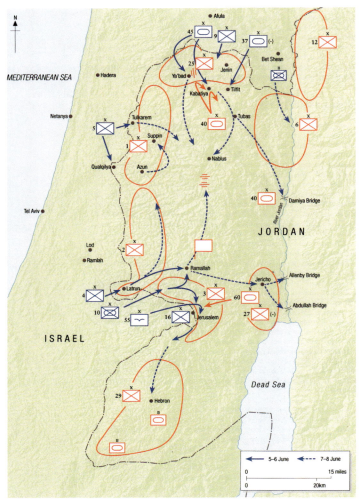

Map showing the conquest of the West Bank, June 5–10, 1967. *Osprey*

into the Jenin area and south as far as Hebron — as follows:

- In the north between Jenin and Latrun were the 1st, 2nd, and 25th Infantry Brigades.
- In the south between Ramallah and Hebron were the 3rd, 27th, and 29th Infantry Brigades.
- In reserve in the rear east of the Jordan were the 6th and 12th Infantry Brigades.
- West of the Jordan, the 40th Armored Brigade was positioned at the Damya Bridge, and the 60th Armored Brigade was in the Jericho area.

While the 55,000 Jordanian troops were not a particularly large force, in terms of training and combat readiness they represented one of the most capable military forces in all the Middle East. The Jordanian army was organized according to the traditional British model and trained its soldiers in all weapons systems with great efficiency. Until 1946, what was then Transjordan was under British colonial control, and with their help Jordan formed the legendary Arab Legion, which proved to be a stubborn opponent for the Israeli forces in the war of 1948–49.

Narkiss concentrated his Israeli units on the central front as follows:

- the 16th Etzioni Brigade in the Jerusalem corridor
- the 4th Infantry and 10th Harel Brigades southwest of Latrun
- the 5th Infantry Brigade in the Netanya area
- in the Jenin area, the 36th Division, under the command Elad Peled,[7] with the 9th Infantry Brigade and the 37th and 45th Armored Brigades

Under pressure from continuous Israeli air attacks, Egyptian general Riad ordered the artillery positioned on the hills to open fire on the Jewish part of Jerusalem and the suburbs of Tel Aviv. Not a single district in the Jewish part of the city was to be spared, and the hail of shells even destroyed the houses of the prime minister and the mayor of Jerusalem.

Only when units of the Jordanian 29th Infantry Brigade occupied the UN's Government House was there no stopping the Israeli defense minister. Dayan recognized the historic opportunity to conquer Jerusalem and revise the 1949 Partition Agreement.

On the morning of June 5, Israeli M50 Sherman tanks of one of the point companies of the Etzioni Brigade crossed the

---

[6] Abdul Munim Riad (1919–69) grew up in Tanta near the Nile River delta. He joined the Egyptian army at an early age and completed his officer training at the Royal Military Academy, at the same time as Gamal Abdel Nasser, Anwar el-Sadat, and Saad el-Shazly. After general staff training and commanding battalions, he took command of the artillery corps in 1960. During the Six-Day War in 1967, he was chief of staff of the Jordanian army in the West Bank. After the war, he drew up the attack plans to destroy the Bar-Lev Line, the Israeli defensive front along the Suez Canal. A visit to this front line was his undoing on March 9, 1969, when Israeli artillery opened fire on Riad and his staff. He died on the battlefield. Nasser posthumously awarded Riad the highest Egyptian military decoration.

[7] Elad Peled (1927–2021), who grew up in Jerusalem, served as a soldier in the Haganah and later as an officer in the Yiftach Brigade during the 1948–49 War of Independence. It was involved in the Latrun offensives. After his divisional command in the Six-Day War in 1967, he left the Israeli armed forces and became minister of education and minister of culture. He died in July 2021.

Colonel Mordechai Gur (*in the middle, seated*) issuing orders to commanders of his 55th Paratrooper Brigade. The photo was taken on the Mount of Olives looking toward the Dome of the Rock, June 1967. *Israel Government Press Office*

demarcation line and moved on Government House. The Jordanians blocked the streets, dug in on Radar Hill, and blocked the road to Mount Scopus, the Jewish enclave. The Sherman tanks opened fire on the Jordanian Patton tanks from close range, and at about 1500 the Israelis finally retook the residence. Riad subsequently deployed his armored forces: the 60th Armored Brigade moved from Jericho toward Jerusalem, and the 40th Armored Brigade left the Damya Bridge for Jericho.

To prevent the relief of the Jordanian troops in Jerusalem, Narkiss ordered an attack from Jenin in the direction of Nablus, accompanied by a southward advance toward Hebron. Uri Ben-Ari's 10th Harel Brigade, which was between Tel Aviv and Jerusalem, advanced north out of the Jerusalem Corridor to take position on the hills between Jerusalem and Ramallah. At the same time, the Israelis barricaded the main roads leading south from Jerusalem to Bethlehem. The 55th Paratrooper Brigade, under Brigadier General Mordechai Gur,[8] which was envisaged for an airborne operation at El Arish in the Sinai, was subsequently rushed to Jerusalem.

Toward evening on the first day of fighting and after fierce enemy resistance, the Jordanian towns of Bayt Surik and Biddu fell into Israeli hands. The way to the hills at Bir Nabala and Qalandiya, which in places rose to 2,300 feet (700 m), lay open before the brigade. No sooner had it arrived when the column ran into about thirty Jordanian Patton tanks, of which seven were destroyed. The rest withdrew in the direction of Jericho, pursued by the Israeli air force.

Ben-Ari then ordered the capture of Ramallah. The first armored battalion was ordered to break into the city and to fire in all directions to eliminate resistance from machine guns and antitank weapons. After successfully clearing the city, the tanks took up positions at the northern and southern exits. The brigade later followed the same procedure in the occupied town of Jericho, farther east on the Jordan. An advance in the direction of the Allenby Bridge and the Dead Sea and a second push in the direction of Nablus ended the operation. The Israelis had occupied the area around Jerusalem to the east and the strategically important bridge over the Jordan.

It was not only the troops of the central front who contributed to the victory in Jordan, since units of the northern front supported the liberation of the West Bank. Peled deployed his 36th Division with the 9th Infantry Brigade and the 37th and 45th Armored Brigades, occupied the town of Jenin in a first concentrated action, and then pushed on toward Nablus. The Jordanian 40th Armored Brigade, positioned in the area of the Damya Bridge, was routed by Peled's units by using envelopment and deception tactics. Nablus fell, which meant that the entire northern sector was also in Israeli hands.

At the same time, the battle for the old city of Jerusalem had begun. The Jordanian 27th Infantry Brigade held all the fortifications around the demarcation line and also mined the streets. The Eztioni Brigade continued its attack, on one hand, in the direction of Sur Bahar, and, on the other hand, against the southern outskirts of Jerusalem. Israeli infantry cleared a path with explosive charges, engaged the enemy in hand-to-hand fighting, and in this way cleared trenches and houses in which the Jordanians had entrenched themselves.

On Tuesday the Israelis took the Abu-Tor quarter and the Mount of Olives, which dominated the Old City, and in fierce house-to-house fighting advanced to the Kidron Valley. On Wednesday they cleared the south wall of the Old City to relieve the pressure on the 55th Paratrooper Brigade, which was also fighting in the city center. After receipt of the news that the northern and eastern sectors of the West Bank were in Israeli hands, elements of the Etzioni Brigade and the 16th Infantry

---

[8] Mordechai Gur (1930–95) grew up in Jerusalem and joined the Haganah as a teenager. He served as a company commander in the Negev Brigade during the 1948–49 War of Independence and commanded a paratrooper company during the Suez Crisis in 1956. He took command of the Golani Brigade in 1961, led the 55th Paratrooper Brigade in the conquest of Jerusalem during the Six-Day War in 1967, and later replaced David Elazar as commander of the northern front. In 1974, Gur was promoted to lieutenant general and succeeded David Elazar as chief of staff. After leaving the army, he took on political functions and acted as a representative of the interests of the Labor Party or as minister of health. Under Prime Minister Rabin, Gur served as deputy minister of defense. He committed suicide in July 1995 after his health continued to deteriorate.

General Uzi Narkiss (*left*), Defense Minister Moshe Dayan (*center*), and Chief of Staff Yitzhak Rabin (*right*) in Jerusalem shortly after the taking of the Jordanian part of the city, June 1967. *Israel Government Press Office*

M47 and M48 Patton tanks formed the backbone of the Jordanian armored brigades. With a crew of four, a weight of 47.2 tons, and a twelve-cylinder Continental engine, this heavy tank reached a maximum speed of 30 mph (48 kph) on roads. It was originally armed with a 90 mm gun, and the Jordanians upgraded their M48s with a 120 mm weapon. In the photo is a Jordanian M47 of the 12th Armored Brigade that was captured by crews of the Israeli 45th Armored Brigade in Jenin, June 1967. *Osprey*

Brigade set out in the direction of Hebron. The bulk of the enemy forces had abandoned Hebron, however, and so there was minimal fighting.

With support from an armored battalion, the 55th Paratrooper Brigade pushed toward the Jordanian-occupied area of the Old City. Houses that were not taken by the paratroopers were destroyed by Sherman tanks from close range. After dark, searchlights illuminated targets, and Israeli flags marked buildings already taken. Ammunition Hill, the Police Academy, Rockefeller Museum, the enclave of the Hebrew University, and the Augusta Victoria Hills, with the Mount of Olives, quickly fell into Israeli hands.

General Gur finally ordered the assault on the Temple Mount and the Wailing Wall, after the paratroopers had broken into the Old City through the Lions' Gate. The last Jordanian units withdrew, and the Israelis removed their helmets out of respect before the Wailing Wall. The Star of David flag waved over the government building, and Dayan spoke words of victory to the exhausted troops. Jordanian king Hussein admitted defeat and finally asked for a ceasefire.

BATTLE FOR THE GOLAN

Since the founding of the Israeli state, Syria has laid claim to the Golan Heights. This strategically important hilly area sits astride the Damascus–Kuneitra–Haifa axis and controls all east–west links in the region.

The Syrians recognized the importance of the Golan Heights and developed part of the hill chain into an impregnable fortress. These fortifications stretched for around 18 miles (30 km) from the Sea of Galilee to the north and dominated the Israeli lowlands

An M51 of the 37th Armored Brigade (36th Division, under Peled) moving in the direction of Kuneitra. In the background are the Hermon Mountains, June 1967. *Israel Government Press Office*

to the west. There were forward strongpoints and observation posts in the Jordan Valley, and behind them company positions with underground bunkers, deep trench lines, and concealed fighting positions securing the first hilltops, while wire obstacles blocked the entrances, and minefields prevented an attacker from going around. On the chain of hills itself, there was an almost continuous line of fortifications, which again featured trenches as well as fighting and observation positions. Positioned farther to the rear were the first mortar and artillery positions, as well as assembly areas for tactical reserves.

A total of 250 artillery pieces and dug-in tanks, most of them Soviet products, were in position on the hills and were capable of firing more than 10 tons of shells per minute. Even German Panzerkampfwagen IV tanks, supplied by the CSSR post-1945, were positioned there.

A deceptive calm reigned on the Israeli-Syrian front after the successful Israeli airstrikes on Syrian air bases on June 6. The Israeli forces also remained quiet when Syria began shelling Israeli settlements. Pressure rose on the Israeli government to finally strike back. Prime Minister Eshkol, who himself had once lived in a kibbutz near the Jordan, finally demanded that the army take action against Syria.

Chief of Staff Rabin ordered Major General David Elazar,[9] who was acting as commander of the northern front, to work out the mission orders. Only Dayan still showed reluctance, for he feared possible intervention by the Soviet Union in Syria. He wanted to avoid at all costs a wider war involving the Soviets.

At 0600 on June 9, Dayan woke the sleeping commander of the northern front with a telephone call. "Can you attack?" asked the minister of defense. Elazar replied that he could. In fact, he was eager to do so, especially after the Egyptians had been defeated in the Sinai and Jordan in the West Bank.

---

[9] David Elazar; see portrait on page 89.

CHAPTER 13: The Six-Day War, 1967 (Third Arab-Israeli War) | 115

Dayan's reservations had disappeared, and he ordered Elazar to launch Operation Hammer, the attack and capture of the Golan Heights.

The Syrian army was commanded by Chief of the General Staff Ahmed Suidani,[10] who had no fewer than twelve brigades—organized in three brigade groups—posted along the Israeli-Syrian border:

- North of Kuneitra was the 12th Brigade Group, with the 11th, 80th, and 132nd Infantry Brigades and the 44th Armored Brigade.
- South of Kuneitra was the 35th Brigade Group, with the 8th, 19th, and 32nd Infantry Brigades and the 17th Mechanized Brigade.
- In reserve in the rear was the 42nd Brigade Group, with the 25th, 50th, and 60th Infantry Brigades and the 14th Armored Brigade.

Approximately 40,000 Syrians with 260 T-34/85 and T-54 tanks plus a large number of artillery pieces were in good tactical positions on the heights. Even though the positions on the heights offered some advantages, the Syrian troops and equipment were in highly inadequate condition.

Elazar issued his attack orders at 1100 on June 9 and accordingly deployed the Israeli troops for the offensive as follows:

- The 1st Golani Brigade and the 2nd Infantry Brigade moved up to the front line north of Shamir. The 45th Mechanized Brigade and the 37th Armored Brigade were taken from Peled's 36th Division and served as the reserve. Mandler's 8th Armored Brigade also moved from the Sinai to the Golan front.
- The 3rd Infantry Brigade advanced south of Hulata. It was reinforced by the 55th Paratrooper Brigade, with the 80th Paratrooper Brigade in reserve.

The Israeli force that would attack the Syrian defensive positions consisted of about 20,000 men with 250 M50 and M51 Sherman tanks.

---

[10] Ahmed Suidani (1932–94) grew up in Daraa, Syria. He quickly rose through the military ranks and commanded the Syrian secret service as director in the early 1960s. In 1966, Prime Minister Jadid promoted him to chief of staff. After the defeat on the Golan Heights during the Six-Day War in 1967, Suidani held Defense Minister al-Assad responsible for the debacle. The latter issued an arrest warrant for Suidani, whereupon he planned to flee to Iraq. However, this failed and Suidani was sentenced to twenty-five years in prison. He died shortly after his release in 1994.

The Israeli plan envisaged that

- in the first phase, airstrikes would take out the Syrian artillery positions;
- in the second phase, the main invasion routes would be cleared of mines, and the 8th Armored and the 45th Mechanized Brigades would break through the front lines in the north and the 37th Armored Brigade in the south; and
- in the third phase, the 1st Golani Brigade would advance north and the 3rd Infantry Brigade south, secure the Golan Heights, and take Kuneitra with the bulk of their units.

After concentrated airstrikes against the Syrian artillery positions, in the north the 8th Armored Brigade launched its drive through Zaoura to Qala. Mine-clearing bulldozers led the way, but they soon found themselves under heavy counterfire from the dug-in Syrian tanks and artillery.

Meanwhile, the Golani Brigade crossed the border and attacked Banias, resulting in the costliest fighting of the offensive.

Farther south, the 37th Armored Brigade crossed the Jordan and attacked the Syrians on the Rawiya–Nafakh–Aliqa axis. By Friday evening the Israelis had broken through the northern part of the defensive line between Zaoura and Kala, establishing a bridgehead 5 miles (8 km) in width, and were nearing the outskirts of Masade.

At dawn on June 10, the Israelis resumed the offensive on all sectors of the front; however, Syrian resistance waned, and they lost one position after another. In the afternoon the Sherman tanks leading the Golani Brigade reached Kuneitra. They found it a ghost town, in which the Syrian crews had abandoned their tanks with engines running and radios on and fled.

In the southern sector, elements of the 3rd and 37th Infantry Brigades fought their way toward Butmiya to occupy the hills to the south. Parts of the battle group struggled up the only road through Yarmuk Gorge, negotiating narrow curves up to the hills, and in the process engaged Syrian units entrenched in bunkers and trench systems. Syrian resistance ultimately collapsed, and the Israeli troops advanced in the direction of Damascus.

CONCLUSIONS

The Six-Day War ended on June 10, and it bestowed upon the Israeli armed forces the myth of invincibility. Israel had established itself as the strongest power in the Middle East, but the price had been high: 750 killed and 2,500 wounded. The losses

suffered by the Arab states were even higher: about 30,000 soldiers killed.

The Gaza Strip, the Sinai Peninsula, the Old City of Jerusalem, the West Bank, and finally the Golan Heights—Israel won all these areas, and these impressive gains quadrupled the area of the country, which from a military-strategic point of view was an enormous gain. Buffer zones from the original borders now gave the Israeli army the opportunity to meet enemy forces before they reached the key areas of the country.

Tanks played a decisive role in the fighting in the Sinai Peninsula as well as in the West Bank and the Golan Heights. The M50 and M51 tanks deployed in Jerusalem supported the attacking infantry singly and in groups. All in all, this action had once again proved the decisive significance of armored units in fighting in built-up areas.

The Israelis conceived and executed their attacks following classic tank doctrine:

- break through the defense lines
- drive into the enemy's rear
- encircle and destroy the enemy

The consistent leadership by the officers from the front also had a decisive influence on the battle. Israeli tank commanders, even under the heaviest fire, often led while standing exposed in their turrets, in order to have a better view of the battlefield. This resulted in a significantly disproportionate loss rate among commanders compared to the total losses.

Wherever Israeli armored spearheads were halted by minefields, the following vehicles always cleared new paths without losing time. The mopping-up of enemy positions took place later because the decisive factor was the rapid seizure of traffic junctions and the key terrain, in order to gain control of the area.

The effectiveness of the tanks used by Israeli differed. The French AMX-13 light tank proved inferior to Soviet tanks. The Israelis were conscious of this inferiority; therefore this type was used primarily against infantry. The M50 and M51 upgraded Sherman tanks, on the other hand, proved themselves as a result of their mobility in almost impassable terrain. The M48 Patton (Magach) again proved itself superior to the T-54/55 in terms of armor and effectiveness of its main armament, since even at a shallow angle of impact, its armor-piercing rounds reliably penetrated the armor of the Soviet tanks. The Centurion (Shot) heavy tank likewise earned an outstanding reputation, since its additional 20 tons of steel was as highly prized as its gun, which distinguished itself through its accuracy and range.

Speed and aggressiveness of command, together with the use of combined arms, formed the decisive basis for the Israeli

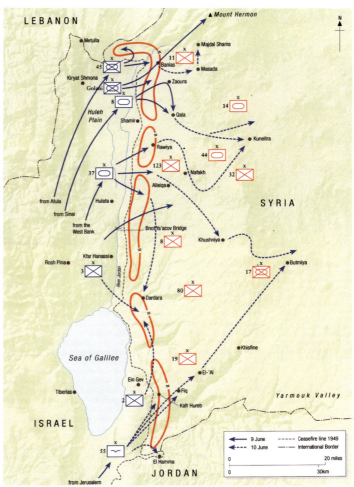

Map of the taking of the Golan Heights, June 5–10, 1967. *Osprey*

victory. Also noteworthy were the night battles fought in Ramallah and Jericho. There, armored battalions drove through the towns and fired to all sides until enemy resistance faltered. The Israelis did not risk occupying the towns during the night.

Concerning the storming of the Golan Heights, it is noteworthy that tanks began exchanging fire with the enemy while climbing the hills, rather than on the plateau itself. In the northern sector the tanks that were used were primarily AMX-13s, which supported the advance by the infantry but in some cases also led the way.

In the Third Arab-Israeli War, the Israelis confirmed the old truths of basic military principles. They had speed, created moments of surprise, demonstrated their ability to maneuver, and were able to concentrate their forces. But what made the Israeli waging of warfare so extraordinary was their perfect and consistent application of these principles.

Even today, the Six-Day War is regarded as a lesson in modern warfare.

CHAPTER 13: The Six-Day War, 1967 (Third Arab-Israeli War)

Chapter 14
Interlude and the War of Attrition, 1968–70

>> It quickly became obvious that the total defeat of the Egyptian army and the heavy losses suffered by the Jordanian and Syrian armies had not put an end to the fighting. These defeated armies began an accelerated reconstruction with the active help of the Soviet Union.

— Lieutenant General Chaim Bar-Lev,
general staff of the Israeli armed forces, 1972

After its overwhelming victory in the Six-Day War, Israel hoped that the Arab states would finally recognize the reality of its existence and enter into peace negotiations. The Jewish state signaled that it was prepared to give up significant parts of the occupied territories as the price of peace. However, these hopes were dashed in August 1967, when the Arab leaders agreed to a ceasefire agreement but rejected peace in three ways: "No peace with Israel, no negotiations with Israel, and no recognition of Israel."

On the contrary, the surrounding Arab states, in particular Egypt, began rebuilding their armed forces. The older T-34, T-54, and Josef Stalin (IS 3) tanks were replaced by hundreds of T-55s, armored personnel carriers, and artillery pieces, likewise made in the Soviet Union. In April 1968 the Egyptian general staff presented a plan to President Gamal Abdel Nasser for the retaking of the Sinai Peninsula.

REORGANIZATION OF THE ISRAELI ARMED FORCES

The Israeli armed forces also drew lessons and consequences from the Hundred-Hour Offensive, reorganized their formations, and optimized the following operational principles:

- Formation of armored brigades with a single type of tank, each with three battalions of Centurion or Patton tanks
- Incorporation of the armored infantry and heavy mortar formations into the mechanized brigades, since they could not keep pace with the battle tanks of the armored battalions
- Assignment of half-track vehicles to the elite infantry units of the Golani Brigade and paratrooper brigades to increase their mobility

The new doctrine envisaged opening the battle at long range with the artillery and punching through enemy positions with mechanized brigades, while the armored battalions engaged the enemy's tanks. The commander of the Israeli Armored Corps, Major General Israel Tal, was of the opinion that tanks were not only the leading tactical combat element, but also the decisive strategic weapon. Consequently, a mechanized attack combined with the air force could force the outcome of the war, as the offensives of the Six-Day War impressively proved.

Tal argued that the last war had shown that the tank could overcome almost any opposition due to the accuracy of its armament and its mobility.

The argument for modernizing the mechanized infantry was even more consistent. The general staff criticized the fact that Tal had allowed the infantry to take excessive casualties in the Sinai. This necessitated the support of the paratroopers, as the example of the battle for Rafah (before the drive on El Arish) showed.

The claim of excessive casualties was explained by the fact that most infantrymen were drafted from the reserves without combat experience and therefore had a lower level of training and experience. This was in contrast to the tank crews, who spent most of their service and training time in regular armored units.

The mechanized infantry was equipped with new armored personnel carriers for greater mobility, and these replaced the M3 half-tracks. The most effective solution at that time was the American M113 APC. It could follow the tanks into battle but was unable to provide fire support for the infantry under battle conditions. The procurement of combat troop carriers or even the production of a domestic armored troop carrier was not up for debate at that time.

The armored corps continued its reorganization at the beginning of the 1970s and optimized the structure of its

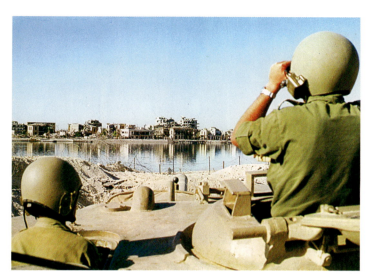

In a firing position on the Bar-Lev Line. From their M48 Patton, a commander and his loader observe the city of El Qantara, September 1973. *Israel Government Press Office*

divisions (*Ugda*). A division now consisted of three armored brigades, which in addition to the upgraded Centurion (Shot Kal and Shot Meteor) and the M48 Patton (Magach 3) now also incorporated newly procured M60s (Magach 6) from the United States and captured T-54/55 (Tiran) tanks. The divisions reinforced their battalions with 155 mm M109 SP self-propelled howitzers and combat engineer units, as well as armored vehicles for better protection while operating specially developed mine-clearing equipment.

With the new tanks also arrived the first M113 APCs. These integrated themselves seamlessly into the regular mechanized infantry battalions. Specially converted vehicles were used as armored command vehicles in the command staffs of the larger units. In the following years, M50 and M51 Sherman tanks were also assigned to the mechanized brigades.

The latent threat to Israel posed by the surrounding Arab states forced the Israelis to maintain a constant state of combat readiness. Of the 2.4 million Israelis, more than 300,000 were available for compulsory service in the land army (not counting the air force and navy). Of these, 40,000 served as regular soldiers in the standing army, the rest in the reserve. Because of the necessity of maintaining constant readiness along the frontiers, these reservists were not called up for maneuvers or courses as they had been in the past; instead, somewhat more than one-twelfth of the reserve served four, five, or more weeks "at the front."

Entire reserve units were often called up at one time, so that the cadres that would have to lead their companies or

Map showing the Bar-Lev Line, which extended along the east bank of the Suez Canal. According to a plan by Defense Minister Moshe Dayan, in the event of an attack by the Egyptians there would be no static defensive battle for the canal front. Instead, the Egyptians would be allowed to cross the canal unopposed, enabling them to advance into the interior of the peninsula. This advance was intended to draw the Egyptians beyond the coverage of their antiaircraft systems and expose them to classic counterattacks, encirclement, and destruction by the Israeli forces. *Osprey*

batteries in time of war got to know the men assigned to them under battlefield conditions.

Enhanced by the glorious victory in the Six-Day War, the Israeli Armored Corps, along with the paratroopers, was the elite of the Israeli armed forces. Basic training included military

CHAPTER 14: Interlude and the War of Attrition, 1968–70 | 119

An Israeli infantryman, his face marked by the multiday artillery bombardment of the Bar-Lev Line, August 1973. *IDF*

forms, handling personal weapons, and physical training and lasted eleven weeks. This was followed by a two-month course at the Armored Academy, where drivers, loaders, gunners, and radio operators were trained separately. Two months of unit training in the Sinai or the Negev at the company-battalion level completed the training. The official swearing-in ceremony was usually held at historic Masada.[1]

The trained tank soldiers were assigned either to the 252nd Armored Division, the 7th Armored Brigade in the Sinai, or the 188th Armored Brigade on the Golan Heights, where they did a further two years of service. Assignment to a reserve unit and regular follow-up courses completed the military training.

The general staff concerned itself with the question of how to effectively defend the expanded territories on the Golan Heights, the West Bank, the Gaza Strip, and the Sinai Peninsula. With its newly won strategic depth, the Israelis could position their forces both right on the front line as well as echeloned to the rear.

The responsible officers held different opinions about the waging of war along the Suez Canal. If the Egyptians decided to cross the canal and hold a limited strip of territory as a bridgehead, the Israeli defensive strategy would be undone. This forced the general staff to design a concept of active defense for the east bank of the Suez Canal.

In the opinion of Defense Minister Moshe Dayan, there should be no stationary battle fought for the canal front; rather, the Egyptian army should be allowed to cross to the east bank unopposed, enabling a first attack to be made in the interior of the Sinai Peninsula. This advance would draw the Egyptian army beyond the protection of its surface-to-air missile batteries and enable the Israeli armed forces to carry out classic pincer attacks.

Ariel Sharon, the general staff officer responsible for training, proposed that a line of strongpoints be maintained right on the bank of the canal, with a simultaneous crossing to the west bank and the elimination of the Egyptian air defense system by tank and infantry attack. He had a suitable crossing location scouted and prepared north of the Great Bitter Lake. In fact, Sharon's 143rd Division crossed the canal at this location on October 15, 1973. His plan was, however, based on an Israeli preventive strike and was therefore politically doubtful.

The chief of the Israeli general staff, Chaim Bar-Lev, expected the best result from a sustained defense right on the east bank. A relatively weak line of strongpoints was to be sufficiently strengthened with forty-eight hours warning. Cooperation between strongpoints and tanks from blocking positions and local counterattacks in company and battalion strength were supposed to prevent the Egyptians from crossing the canal or digging in on the east bank.

Golda Meir,[2] the prime minister of Israel since March 1969, decided in favor of the chief of the general staff's plan as the basis for defensive preparations along the canal.

The result was a 112-mile-long chain of about thirty strongpoints that extended north to the Mediterranean coast and south to the Gulf of Suez. The so-called Bar-Lev Line was named after the then chief of the general staff and was supposed to be able to withstand heavy artillery fire, protect the troops, and, overall, function as an advanced warning system.

---

[1] Masada is an archeological site and is enthroned as a summit plateau on the edge of the Judean Desert high above the Dead Sea. During the Jewish War (66–70 CE), the Jews retreated from the Romans to Masada. Besieged there, the Jews found themselves in a hopeless situation and chose suicide. Since 1956, the Israeli armed forces have been using the excavation site for military ceremonies and recruit swearing-in ceremonies. Since 1968, paratroopers have been sworn in at the Wailing Wall in Jerusalem, and the armored forces at Latrun since 1991.

Shot (Centurion) tanks in the assembly area behind the Bar-Lev Line. The tanks maintained constant readiness in order to intervene immediately in case of an Egyptian attack on the east bank of the Suez Canal. February 1970. *AirSeaLand Photos*

It was not, however, a continuous line of fortifications, but rather a system of individual fortified positions with open areas between them. The general staff tasked the deputy commander of the armored corps, General Avraham Adan,[3] with construction of the defensive line. He created a defensive line that was regarded as Israel's biggest military construction project and went down in history as such.

---

[2] Golda Meir (1898–1978) grew up in Kiev. During the pogroms against the Jews there, she and her family immigrated to the United States, where, after leaving high school, she studied to be a teacher at the Milwaukee State Normal School. Not until 1921 did she move to Palestine, where she became a delegate to the Zionist World Congress, and from 1946 led the Jewish Agency's political department. She was labor minister in Ben Gurion's cabinet and foreign minister under Prime Minister Levi Eshkol. In 1969 she was chosen to be Israel's prime minister. She died in 1978 and is buried at the Mount Herzl National Cemetery in Jerusalem.

[3] Avraham Adan; see portrait on page 161.

THE WAR OF ATTRITION

Strengthened by weaponry supplied by the Soviet Union, the Egyptian army established a defensive line on the west side of the canal, manned by about three divisions with roughly 150,000 troops. From March 1968 to January 1969, the general staff rebuilt shattered units, replaced many older officers, introduced more-effective training, and reorganized its formations. This was intended to restore the morale of the troops and improve their fighting spirit for a renewed offensive against Israel.

A first series of blows against the Bar-Lev Line began with sporadic sniper fire and then increasingly heavy artillery fire. Starting in March 1969, a higher intensity of artillery fire fell on the Israeli positions than anything previously seen. The Israelis returned fire, and the Egyptian chief of the general staff was killed in a forward observation post.

While Israel agreed to a UN proposal for a renewed ceasefire, Egypt initially rejected the idea. In response, the Israelis shelled Egyptian oil refineries and carried out additional acts of retribution against Egypt; for example, in Upper Egypt on April 29,

Israeli prime minister Golda Meir during a visit to the Bar-Lev Line. On the left is Ariel Sharon, who commanded the 143rd Division (Ugda Arik) in the Yom Kippur War, Sinai Peninsula, 1973. *Israel Government Press Office*

against the coastal defense position at Al Adabiyah on June 22, and on the power distribution center at Sohadsch on June 30.

Many foreign observers and the Israeli army command questioned the sense of the Egyptian military actions. Among the explanations offered were an attempt to increase the hostility of the army and the people against Israel, and the assertion that the Middle East should be a permanent source of unrest in order to keep the pressure on Israel to evacuate the Sinai Peninsula.

In reality, Nasser hoped that the artillery barrages on the Bar-Lev Line would prevent the Israelis from expanding it and exhaust Israel's military forces. He explained his strategy in a speech on May 1, 1969: "We will not allow Israel to turn the ceasefire line into a permanent border. Either Israeli will withdraw or there will be constant fighting!"

The War of Attrition had begun.

Beginning in July 1969 the armed conflict intensified, taking on a further dimension. After the Israelis were subjected to further Egyptian artillery strikes, Israel committed its air force for the first time, following the doctrine of extending the fighting to enemy territory.

The air force's commander, General Mordechai Hod,[4] began with retaliatory strikes on selected targets carried out by French-made Mystères and Mirages and A-4 Skyhawks and F-4 Phantoms supplied by the United States.

The air attacks soon produced results. The Egyptian artillery bombardments slackened noticeably, but on the other hand, there were fierce air battles everywhere, in which the Israeli pilots demonstrated their superiority over the Egyptians.

The Israeli fighters subsequently punched large holes in the newly established air defense system of the Egyptians, outmaneuvering the air defenses and destroying numerous S-75 Dvina (SA-2 Guideline) surface-to-air missile launchers and MiG-21 fighters. The successful use of airpower ultimately resulted in Israeli air superiority over the canal zone and deep inside the Egyptian rear.

The Israelis followed with amphibious landings; for example, on September 9, 1969, when a combined operation was carried out on the west side of the canal, in which tanks, armored infantry, naval vessels, and the air force took part. Amazingly,

---

[4] Mordechai Hod (1926–2003) was born in Kibbutz Degania, southwest of the Sea of Galilee. He joined the Jewish Brigade as a driver and served in the Italian campaign in 1945. After the end of the Second World War, he became a member of the Haganah. After completing training as a pilot, he flew Supermarine Spitfire fighter planes to Israel, where they were used by the newly founded Israeli air force. In 1960 he became chief of operations in the air force staff. He led the Israeli air force (IAF) during the 1967 Six-Day War before ending his career in 1973. In 1977 he became president of the El Al aviation group.

S-75 Dvina surface-to-air missile (SA-2), developed by the Soviet Union in 1953, range 4.3 to 27 miles (7 to 43 km), 430 lb. (190 kg) fragmentation warhead with proximity or impact fuse. Surface-to-air missiles of this type were part of the Egyptian protective screen against Israeli Mirage, Skyhawk, and Phantom combat aircraft. *Wikipedia*

Prior to the outbreak of the Yom Kippur War, there were two armored battalions of the 188th Barak Brigade and two infantry battalions of the 1st Golani Brigade on the Golan Heights west of the ceasefire line. They were divided among seventeen positions, which were guarded by nine armored platoons. In the photo is a Shot (Centurion) near Kuneitra, summer 1973. *AirSeaLand Photos*

no enemy troops intervened during the Israeli force's ten-hour presence in Egyptian territory.

Despite Egyptian propaganda, losses on the Israeli side were not serious. In 1969 these totaled 240 killed, nine aircraft shot down, and two tanks destroyed. No defensive positions were destroyed, taken, or occupied. In contrast to claims by the Egyptians, the Bar-Lev Line's pioneering technical design had proved a success.

Nasser now slowly lost patience and that same month undertook a secret trip to Moscow to press for further arms deliveries. The Soviet Union responded by immediately supplying the latest materiel and military personnel. In response, the Egyptians opened various ports and airfields to the Russians. The deliveries included 150 MiG-21J interceptor fighters and eighty-five batteries of the S-125 Neva (SA-3 Goa) surface-to-air missiles. With this arsenal of weapons, the Soviets sent about two hundred pilots and fifteen thousand surface-to-air missile personnel to the Nile and the Suez Canal, where there were already four thousand Soviet advisors.

Egypt expanded its air defense system in the Cairo-Alexandria-Ismailia-Suez area, its defensive screen extending from the Suez Canal up to 9 miles (15 km) deep inside the ceasefire zone on the Israeli-occupied east bank. In April 1970, a storm of artillery fire again broke over the Israeli positions.

Diplomatic steps were taken in addition to these military escalations and attacks. In July 1970, Nasser announced that he was prepared to accept a ceasefire, which began on August 7, 1970.

With this, a deceptive peace settled over the Suez Canal, seven hundred days after the start of the War of Attrition and about a thousand days after the conclusion of the Six-Day War.

The War of Attrition between Egypt and Israel lasted about eighteen months and was the longest conflict between the warring parties. On September 28, 1970, Nasser died of a heart attack. His successor, Anwar el-Sadat, subsequently continued preparations for a resumption of hostilities against Israel.

The Fourth Arab-Israeli War was about to begin.

PORTRAIT OF CHAIM BAR-LEV

Chaim Bar-Lev, born in 1924 under the family name Brotzlewsky, grew up in Vienna, the son of a Yugoslavian family. At the age of four he and his parents returned to Yugoslavia, where his father took over as manager of a textile company. In 1939, shortly before the outbreak of the Second World War, his family immigrated to Palestine, where he attended an agricultural college. He served in the Haganah while attending school and later in the Palmach, where he trained to become a paratrooper.

Prior to the outbreak of the War of Independence, as a captain he led a special unit of the Palmach whose mission it was to blow up the Allenby Bridge. This happened during Operation Markolet, a major action by the Palmach that took place on June 16–17, 1946. No fewer than eleven bridges were destroyed in this action, to prevent Arab troops from invading Palestine.

In the War of Independence, Colonel Bar-Lev first commanded an infantry battalion, and later a regiment during Operation Horew. After further training at Sandhurst in Great Britain, during the Suez Crisis he commanded the 27th Armored Brigade, which was under the 77th Division. His brigade was responsible for the invasion and clearing of parts of the Gaza Strip and distinguished itself in the subsequent advance to the Suez Canal.

Bar-Lev led the Israeli Armored Corps in the years from 1957 to 1961. After further studies at universities in New York and Paris, he returned to the army and during the Six-Day War initially served as deputy chief of the general staff and starting in 1968, after promotion to lieutenant general, as chief of the general staff.

In the following years of the so-called War of Attrition from 1968 to 1970, Bar-Lev was the spiritual father of the large-scale defensive line along the Suez Canal. The system of fortifications of the "Bar-Lev Line" extended the entire length of the canal and served both as a hindrance to an Egyptian breakthrough across the canal into the Sinai, and as a springboard to allow Israeli forces to cross the canal at any time. The Bar-Lev Line, which cost about $500 million, consisted of twenty-five bunker positions made of concrete and extending several stories deep in the sand. Camouflaged with sand, numerous minefields protected the forts against attack by infantry or armored vehicles. More than three thousand Israeli troops manned the positions, confident that this defensive system would enable them to fight off any attack by the enemy.

The bunker system gave cause for doubt in the Israeli general staff, however. Major General Israel Tal, spiritual father and creator of the flexible Israeli Armored Corps, in particular was

Chaim Bar-Lev, chief of staff of the Israeli army from 1968 to 1972. Photo taken in 1968. *Israel Government Press Office*

opposed to any sort of static defense. He observed that the fortifications were a modern version of the Maginot Line of the Second World War and therefore not suitable for armored warfare. Major General Ariel Sharon also did not hold back critical statements and assessed the defense system as worthless. When the Egyptian attack came in the following war, the system of fortifications was in fact quickly overrun.

Even before the outbreak of the Yom Kippur War, Bar-Lev left the army and served as minister of trade and industry in Golda Meir's government. This post was to be of short duration, however. After the Egyptian army stormed the Bar-Lev Line and

Portrait of Chaim Bar-Lev

Defense Minister Moshe Dayan (*left*) with the retiring chief of staff Chaim Bar-Lev (*right*) at the swearing-in of the new chief of the general staff David Elazar (*second from left*) in 1973. *Israel Government Press Office*

pushed the Israeli army back into the Sinai, Chief of General Staff David Elazar recalled the capable Bar-Lev and placed him in command of the southern front. This ousted Bar-Lev's overtaxed predecessor Shmuel Gonen. Bar-Lev forcefully led the Israeli counteroffensive and, with the crossing of the Suez Canal and the encirclement of several Egyptian armies, brought about the Israeli victory.

After the war, Bar-Lev served in the Knesset, this time as secretary of the Worker's Party, and from 1984 to 1988 as minister for police affairs. He died in Tel Aviv in 1994 after a lengthy serious illness.i

Chapter 15

Captured Tanks under the Israeli Flag: The T-54/55/62 (Tiran)

During the Six-Day War in 1967, the Israelis captured several hundred Syrian and Egyptian T-54 and T-55 tanks. During the Yom Kippur War in 1973, Israeli captured more tanks, including T-62s. Since all these tanks had powerful guns, and there was at that time a critical shortage of battle tanks, they were overhauled, upgraded, and placed in Israeli service under the designation Tiran.

DEVELOPMENT OF THE T-54/T-55

In 1943, the Kharkov Machine Building Design Bureau undertook the T-34M development project, a further development of the T-34 from the prewar period, and from it created the T-44. Thanks to a space-saving torsion bar suspension, novel transverse engine placement, and the elimination of the hull-mounted machine gun position, the T-44 was at least as capable of off-road operation as the T-34 but had significantly better armor protection and a more powerful ZiS-5-53 85 mm gun.

By the time the T-44 had achieved production readiness, the T-34 had already been modified to carry the same gun, and although the T-44 was superior to the T-34 in many respects, the leaders in Moscow decided to continue production of the T-34 series (T-34/85) and produced only limited numbers (1,823 vehicles) between 1944 and 1947.

In 1944, experiments were carried out with the 122 mm D-25-44 gun. Because of the limited ammunition load of twenty-four rounds, this concept was discarded, and focus was placed on installing the 100 mm D-10T gun, which was already in successful use by the SU-100 tank-destroyer. Two prototypes, one with the 100 mm D-10TK and one with the 100 mm LB-1, were completed in 1945 and put through extensive testing. The design with the D-10T was accepted in April 1946, and in the following year the first examples of the vehicle, now designated the T-54, were produced at Nizhny Tagil and Kharkov.

Trials carried out in White Russia revealed numerous shortcomings, and production had to be halted after 1,200 examples had been produced. Not until the tank was completely redesigned as the T-54-2 did production resume at Uralvagonzavod in Nizhny Tagil in 1949. The tank was subsequently built in larger numbers than any other in the postwar period, with a total of more than 50,000 examples leaving the production lines.

The T-54A, which entered production in 1954, had an improved 100 mm D-10TG gun with the STP-1 stabilization system, which stabilized the gun in the vertical axis. The T-54B appeared two years later with STP-2 Tsyklon two-plane stabilization for the main gun, which was now designated the D-10T2S. In April 1959, infrared searchlights and sights were added for the commander, the gunner, and the driver. Amazingly, the first models of the Centurion from 1947 had a complete gun stabilization system, while those of the T-54/55 series did not enter service until 1957. Conversely, Soviet tanks were equipped with IR night vision equipment several years prior to their NATO counterparts. About 24,750 examples of the T-54 series were produced in the Soviet Union. 5,465 examples were produced in the nations of the Warsaw Pact, and another 9,000 in China, where it was designated the T-59.

In October 1955 a comprehensive improvement program was begun for the T-54 under the designation "Object 155." The most important innovation was the addition of an NBC protection system, which the Soviet planners regarded as essential in any future conflict. The new design received its operational certification in May 1958, and production ran from June 1958 to July 1962 in the Soviet Union and subsequently in Czechoslovakia and Poland.

DEVELOPMENT OF THE T-62

The Soviet Union was forced to consider a successor to the successful T-55 following the introduction of new battle tanks by the Western forces in the mid-1950s (M48, Chieftain). Two development paths were taken: one was the "Object 165," an improved T-55 with a more powerful 100 mm L62 gun, and the other was the "Object 166," a new vehicle armed with a then-unique 115 mm U-5TS Molor smooth-bore gun. From the latter was developed the T-62.

Like the American M60, the T-62 was created as a reaction to tank developments by the other side and was originally designed as an interim solution pending the service introduction of the "Object 430," which later became the T-64. With the

An Egyptian army SU-100 tank-destroyer after the Sinai campaign, November 1956. *IDF*

U-5TS, the T-62 had the most modern tank gun in the world, but because it cost 50 percent more than the T-54/55, production in similar numbers was out of the question. The Soviet T-62 first saw action in the invasion of Czechoslovakia in 1968 and the border clashes with China in the same year.

The T-62 underwent several modernization phases beginning in 1973; however, these were carried out only in stages and only for parts of the armed forces. The first upgrade was carried out in 1972 and included the installation of a DShkM 12.7 mm heavy machine gun as a reaction to the increasing threat posed by combat helicopters and improved wading capability.

As of 1975 some T-62s were also equipped with an externally mounted KTD-1 laser rangefinder. In the late 1970s, T-62s were fitted with T-72 tracks and drive sprockets plus improved power plants. A complete modernization finally became possible at the beginning of the 1980s with the T-62M program. In addition to improved protection through the use of composite armor, additional track skirts, and improved mine defense, the most-important upgrades were the new W55-U engine, producing 602 hp, improved offensive capabilities with the addition of the 9K116-2 "Sheksna" guided weapons system, and a new fire control system with a laser rangefinder.

CAPTURED TANKS IN SERVICE WITH THE ISRAELI ARMED FORCES

Shortly before the Six-Day War in 1967, Israel feared total destruction and anticipated a combined attack by three Arab armies. While its worst expectations materialized, in this war Israel achieved a totally unexpected, history-making victory. In just six days it defeated three hostile nations and conquered the Golan Heights, the Sinai Peninsula and the Gaza Strip, and the West Bank.

Analyses of the war focused not only on the question of how Israel won the war, but also on how its Arab opponents had lost it. During their disorderly retreat, the latter abandoned vast quantities of vehicles, ammunition, fuel, and rations. At least some of the captured equipment had the potential of reinforcing the Israeli armed forces, both quantitatively and qualitatively. When it came to the more advanced weaponry such as tanks, artillery, and aircraft, it became apparent that it could not simply be put to use. In addition to required maintenance, ammunition in particular caused headaches for the engineers. If ammunition was not captured in sufficient quantities, producing it in quantity was impossible. Consequently, in some cases considerable resources had to be invested for a limited number of weapons systems.

A T-34 tank knocked out by tanks of the Israeli 14th Brigade during the last major tank battle in the Sinai during the Six-Day War. *IDF*

This was a totally foreign situation for the Israelis, using captured enemy weapons to increase one's own strength. During the 1948–49 War of Independence, much of Israel's arsenal had been made up of stolen and captured equipment, which came primarily from the British army. In fact, for the military of a new state, there was no other viable option. Seven years later, the Israelis captured additional weapons systems during the war in the Sinai in 1956. In addition to the warship ***Ibrahim el Awa*** and a MiG-15 fighter aircraft, these included the capture of mainly obsolescent tanks and APCs: 16 T-34/85 tanks, 4 SU-100 tank-destroyers, 36 Sherman tanks of various models, several Valentine-Archer tank-destroyers, 56 BTR-152 armored personnel carriers, 231 Universal Carriers, and several dozen command tanks, APCs, and engineering vehicles. Some of the captured vehicles, however, were little more than charred scrap metal.

Several months later, the Israelis realized that the captured Valentine-Archer tank-destroyers were useless due to a lack of spares. Likewise, no unit wanted to use the Universal Carriers, which is why they were issued to the local militias of several border settlements, even though the militiamen had neither spare parts nor sufficient training. The SU-100 tank-destroyers were also unusable from the outset, even though there was plenty of 100 mm ammunition available. As a result, these systems were used for propaganda purposes or as targets on firing ranges.

The situation was different when it came to the T-34 and Sherman tanks. Since the Israeli armed forces were already using large numbers of Sherman tanks, the ones they captured were given a general overhaul and brought into line with the existing fleet. They were either quickly put into service or were cannibalized for spare parts.

The T-34 was the more interesting of the two types, since at that time it was one of the most powerful and advanced tanks in the Egyptian arsenal. The Israelis used the opportunity to study the vehicle's technical details and train a group of soldiers in its use. On the eve of the Six-Day War, the Israelis were therefore familiar both with the tank's characteristics and its capabilities.

Mechanical engineer Arkadi Timor was a real stroke of luck for the young Israeli army. During the Second World War, he had served in the Red Army as a tank officer, rose to the rank of colonel, and led a T-34 brigade during the Battles of Leningrad and Moscow. After the war, he immigrated to Israel, and in the mid-1960s he joined the logistical corps of the Israeli armed forces, where he quickly made a name for himself as an expert in armored vehicles—especially those made in the Soviet Union.

On the fourth day of the Six-Day War, Timor was invited to a meeting with the chief of the general staff, Yitzhak Rabin, and the pair discussed the possibility of using captured tanks. At that time, neither Rabin nor Timor knew the full scale of the booty: it was just the tip of the iceberg. The Egyptian army announced the retreat on the morning of June 6, the second day of the war. Within twenty-four hours of this declaration, the Israeli units maneuvered deeply and quickly into the Sinai and blocked several main roads leading to the Suez Canal.

The west bank of the Suez Canal was taken on the fifth day of the war, and more than 550 armored vehicles, almost two-thirds of the original Egyptian force, had to be abandoned by their crews: 256 T-54/T-55 tanks, 127 T-34/85s, 56 SU-100s, 55 Shermans (of two different models), 19 IS-3M tanks, 14 PT-76s, 8 Centurion Mark 2/3 tanks, and about 20 command and recovery vehicles based on the T-34.

On the night of June 6, the Jordanians also announced that they were retreating, after most of their tanks and aircraft had been destroyed and the majority of the West Bank was under Israeli control. There too the attackers were forced to abandon 190 of their original 255 tanks, including 129 M48 Pattons, 30 M47s, and 30 Centurion Mark 3s.

On June 7, Syria switched from an offensive to a defensive strategy and withdrew a considerable part of its forces to protect its capital, Damascus. On June 9 the Israel forces also marched into Syria and took the Golan Heights—capturing about 120 of the 190 Syrian tanks deployed there, including 55 T-34/85s, 25 Panzer IVs, 20 T-54/T-55s, 15 SU-100s, and several StuG IIIs and AMX-13s.

All told, during the Six-Day War the Arab armies surrendered about 860 tanks, which was equivalent to about 80 percent of the Israeli tank fleet during the war. Also captured were 390 armored personnel carriers, 740 artillery pieces and antiaircraft guns, 4,000 trucks, and 28,700 light weapons, assault rifles, and machine guns, plus 18 tons of ammunition. Locating all this "booty" was no easy task and required thousands of hours of work and several months to complete the search. Some tanks had been abandoned beneath camouflage netting and were difficult to find, a considerable number were damaged and had to be towed, and of course counting and identifying the specific types and models of previously unknown equipment was an additional challenge.

It was clear to the Israelis that the defeated Arabs would not accept the outcome of the war and would equip themselves with new and improved Soviet weaponry to resume the struggle. This coming war would also be fought primarily with mechanized means, and thus the result would depend directly on the quantity

Israeli troops examine a Valentine-Archer tank-destroyer of the Egyptian army, November 1956. *IDF*

and quality of the tanks employed. It took some time until the armed forces were reorganized and the addressing of these challenges could begin. The newly conquered territories were set up as strategic buffer zones in which a renewed enemy attack could be parried and the battle then carried across the border into the neighboring state. In practice, this new agenda meant the building of a much-larger army and the development of new capabilities to enable a crossing of the Suez Canal, the Jordan, or the Red Sea. The next war, at least as the general staff saw it, could end with the conquest of an Arab capital, probably Cairo, but perhaps Damascus or even both.

The armored corps was a decisive part of this new strategy. In the next six years the number of tanks and armored brigades was to double, and their fighting capability improved. Hundreds of new tanks were to be put into service, and a considerable number of the tanks already in service were to be upgraded or replaced. With the help of standardization, it was intended that the tank fleet, which during the Six-Day War consisted of eight different models of tank with five different gun calibers and five different engine types, would in essence be reduced to two standard types, the Shot (Centurion) and Magach (M48 Patton). Both were to be armed with the British 105 mm gun. It was envisaged that the remaining 151 Sherman tanks and the 178 AMX-13s, which were no longer capable of dueling with enemy tanks, would play a secondary role in the mechanized infantry brigades.

As more main battle tanks were needed, the armed forces began looking at various options. Of course, the purchase of new tanks from the Western nations was regarded as the best option, but this required great political efforts and would not necessarily be successful, as Israel had learned from past experience. Great Britain was a possible supplier, and in 1965

Syrian T-54 knocked out on the Golan Heights during the Six-Day War, June 1967. *IDF*

Israel began evaluating the British Chieftain as a future battle tank. Although Israel had the intention of purchasing several hundred vehicles or producing them locally under license, Great Britain dragged out the negotiations and finally canceled them in 1969. Israel was, however, able to continue purchasing the Centurion tank and, between 1959 and 1973, acquired almost a thousand vehicles, which it converted in Israel to meet its requirements.

Another possible supplier was the United States. Since 1948 it had traditionally refused to supply Israel with modern weapons. This position changed in 1964—probably because the Americans recognized that Israel could be an important partner in the region—and several hundred M48 Patton tanks were supplied to Israel. The United States wanted an Israel that was neither too weak nor too powerful, in order to avoid an escalation in the Middle East or a direct confrontation with the Soviet Union. With each tank the Soviets delivered to Syria or Egypt, Israel's desire for Western tanks grew stronger. Ultimately a situation of mutual dependence formed between the two nations: Israel supplied the United States with important information about Soviet activities in the region, while the US in return met some of Israel's vital diplomatic and military requirements, including the delivery of 136 M60 tanks in 1972. France backed away from being a secondary supplier when the government of President Charles de Gaulle imposed an arms embargo on Israel several days before the start of the Six-Day War.

Under these circumstances, the use of captured vehicles became an unavoidable method of achieving a rapid and relatively cheap buildup of the Israeli Armored Corps. The simplest step was the integration of the forty-two Centurion tanks captured by the Israelis (Mark 2/3), which were immediately sent to the conversion facilities. The Sherman tanks could also be used relatively easily, either as sources of spare parts or as conversions into support vehicles. The situation when it came to the Jordanian M48 tanks was more complex: bringing these vehicles up to the same logistical standard as the Israeli Magach tanks required special conversion kits from the United States, which was unhappy to see Israel taking over tanks it had originally supplied to Jordan to maintain the military balance in the region. Ultimately, however, 108 of the captured M48 tanks were returned to service as Magach 3s.

By far the greatest dilemma, however, concerned the Soviet T-54 and T-55 tanks. Redesign would require a considerable outlay of time and resources with no promise of success. The Israelis therefore tried to recruit knowledgeable mechanics and technicians from among the Russian Jews who had immigrated to Israel, but none of these persons had experience with the T-54/55. No technical handbooks or replacement-parts lists had fallen into Israeli hands on the battlefields. Spare parts could be obtained by cannibalizing other tanks, but that was only a temporary solution. It was also unclear if, in the midst of the Cold War, the necessary parts could be obtained on the international market. In this situation, the only solution was to make the parts in Israel.

Therefore, immediately after the war, two T-54/55 tanks were taken to a workshop and taken apart piece by piece. Each individual component was examined, sketched, cataloged, cleaned, and reassembled. In a slow process, the mechanics became familiar with the foreign technology and were finally able to define three main subtypes: the T-54, the T-54 with gun stabilization, and the T-55. It turned out that some tanks of the same model had been made in different factories and were not identical, which made the identification of parts even more difficult.

Apart from the technical aspects, introducing the tanks into active service was associated with a very complicated formal process. It had to be authorized by the chief of the general staff and the defense ministry and required its own budget. In particular, however, it needed someone who was high ranking and dogged enough to see the project through. In the case of the T-54/55, it was Major General Israel Tal, commander of the armored corps and one of the most esteemed officers in the general staff.

Tal was enthusiastic about the idea of converting and reusing captured tanks. Shortly after the war, he met with several officers of the armored corps, including Arkadi Timor, to discuss the future of the captured tanks. He understood that further research was necessary, and asked Arkadi to head the research team that would analyze the idea's potential and opportunities. At this meeting the tanks were also given the name Tiran, which referred to a Hebrew tyrant of old and was meant to be an allusion to the Communist government of the Soviet Union.

Two Tiran tanks disembarking from a landing ship capable of transporting up to eight Tirans. *IDF*

The T-54/55 tanks undoubtedly had great potential, but the Israelis required standardized engines and gun calibers, and there were far too many types of tank already. In light of this point, a question arose: Was another tank really necessary? The Soviet art of engineering was a problem, since the absence of a turret floor in the T-54 models and the loading with the left hand complicated the job of the loader. The tank's shock absorption system was also minimal; operation of the gearbox, brakes, and steering was difficult; the internal arrangement of the hull and turret was uncomfortable; and maintenance was a nightmare. Although some parts were extremely durable, a relatively simple task such as the replacement of an engine required more than a day's work and thus about ten hours more than for the Shot and Magach tanks.

Another problem was the Soviet tank's inferior ability to depress its main gun compared to Western tanks. Because the gun could not be depressed as far, the ramps in the prepared tank positions had to have a different angle than those for the standard Western tanks, to enable them to fight as effectively from partially concealed positions.

All these features pointed to a completely different battle tactic. Soviet doctrine was based primarily on numerical superiority. According to this reading, whether the enemy destroyed ten, twenty, or a hundred tanks made no great difference to the overall operation. Knocked-out tanks would be towed to the rear, repaired, and returned to service. The comfort of the crew was considered of no importance, and repairs on-site were not worth wasting resources such as combat engineers or armored sappers during the battle.

The Israeli battle tactic, on the other hand, was based on Western concepts: the crew was one of the most important elements in tank combat and should therefore feel relatively comfortable in order to enable it to endure longer periods of combat and make possible the maximum possible exploitation of human resources. Furthermore, every single tank was regarded as important, and the ability to quickly repair a damaged tank in combat acquired a decisive significance.

For these reasons, the Soviet tanks could not be placed in service without eradicating some of these disadvantages. On the other hand, some of the Soviet technologies offered clear advantages. Their night vision systems were much better than the Xenon infrared searchlights carried by the Israeli tanks, which gave them a clear advantage in night fighting. The T-55's smoke-generating system, with which the tank could conceal itself in a dense cloud of diesel exhaust, was also a minor quantum advance. Another advantage, first recognized in mid-1969, was that these tanks, because of their small size, were ideally suited to amphibious operations, meaning coming ashore from landing ships. This potential proved important in planning for the coming war.

Seen hypothetically, by using T-54/55 tanks the Israeli armed forces could capture ammunition, spare parts, and fuel in enemy territory and actually use them, which would not be possible with their Western tanks. Also possible were special missions in which the vehicles could go into action camouflaged as Egyptian, Syrian, or Iraqi tanks. Mastery of Soviet technology also opened for Israel the possibility of capturing further tanks and using them in future wars. The transfer of selected components to Western tanks by the Israeli weapons industry was also conceivable, in order to combine the best of both worlds in the vehicles.

A simple technical comparison of the tanks showed that the Soviet tanks possessed similar capabilities, and with only about two-thirds the weight. The T-54/55 tanks carried less fuel and ammunition, but their operational range was similar, and the performance of their suspensions was also not comparable to that of any other tank used by Israel. The Soviet tanks were smaller and thus more difficult to hit; however, a hit usually had fatal consequences for the crew. Despite their heavy armor, their general survivability was ranked lower than that of Western models, and the 100 mm gun was less effective than the 105 mm gun of the Shot and Magach tanks.

After several technical inspections and a thorough examination of all the captured tanks, the Israelis estimated that about 140 were suitable for use. However, a Western engine would have to be installed, and the Soviet gun replaced by the 105 mm weapon of the Shot. With regard to the international tank market of 1968 and without taking into account any diplomatic aspects, the financial advantage of using the reconfigured tanks was obvious: in 1967–68 the Israeli general staff estimated that the conversion into a Tiran tank would cost 35,000 Israeli pounds (then about $10,000). The price of a Centurion, however, was 440,000 Israeli pounds, and for an M48A3 Patton, 582,000 Israeli pounds.

The conversion of all 146 Tiran tanks therefore cost the equivalent of a company of Shot tanks or two platoons of Magach tanks.

Their estimated maximum service life, however, was just ten years, since from the beginning it was envisaged that the Tiran tanks would be removed from service after all the Israeli Shermans had been replaced by the new standard tanks, the Shot and the Magach. The Tiran was therefore to be employed as a second-class tank, like the M50 and M51 Shermans. Two decisive problems remained unsolved, however; namely, the acquisition of ammunition for the 100 mm gun and the procurement of spare engines and transmissions. It was clear to Israel Tal that the Tiran was only an interim solution, but at that time there was no alternative. The mechanics under Arkadi Timor immediately began development of a prototype for the conversion line that would turn the captured T-54/T-55 tanks into Tirans, and in the process deepened their knowledge about the tanks. In the following years, about a thousand tanks parts were copied and reproduced by the Israelis and civilian industry, stocks of spare parts for all Soviet tanks (including the T-34 and IS-3M) were gathered, technical manuals were created, and mechanics and technicians were trained to service and maintain the Tirans.

Among the most important changes were

- the replacement of the 7.62 mm PKT and 12.7 mm DShK machine guns by the Browning M1919 7.62 mm machine gun used by the Israelis, and the removal of the bow machine gun;
- the replacement of the communications system;
- an increase in fuel capacity from 216 to 255 US gallons (817 to 965 liters);

Tiran 1	T-54 in original configuration
Tiran 2	T-55 in original configuration
Tiran 3	T-62 in original configuration
Tiran 4	modified T-54 with original 100 mm gun, new track shields, new loader's hatch, and an M1919 7.62 mm machine gun
Tiran 4 Sharir	modified T-54 with 105 mm L7 gun (same as that in the Shot), new coaxial 7.62 mm machine gun, and new 12.7 mm cupola machine gun, plus many detail improvements (including fire control system, power supply, air-conditioning, communications system)
Tiran 5	modified T-55 with original 100 mm gun, new track shields, new loader's hatch, and a 7.62 mm M1919 machine gun
Tiran 5 Sharir	modified T-55 with 105 mm L7 gun (same as that in the Shot), new coaxial 7.62 mm machine gun, and new 12.7 mm cupola machine gun, plus many detail improvements (including fire control system, power supply, air-conditioning, communications system)
Tiran 6	modified T-62 with original 115 mm gun.

Overview of the versions of the Tiran tank

- an increase in ammunition capacity for the main gun from 33 to 44 rounds for the T-54 (Tiran 4) and from 43 to 59 for the T-55 (Tiran 5);
- an increase in ammunition capacity for the machine guns by 60 percent plus more hand grenades;
- the installation of an NBC defense system;
- the removal of the heating system in the engine compartment; and
- the maximum possible use of tools, lubricants, and spare parts to the standard of the Israeli armed forces, in order to achieve maximum logistical equality with the other types of tanks.

The first official test for the Tiran tanks came in late 1967 at a weapons display. The introduction process was just beginning, and the tanks were still in their original Soviet configurations (Tiran 1 and 2). Among those present was Defense Minister Moshe Dayan and an entourage of generals and government officials, including Chief of the General Staff Yitzhak Rabin and his future successor and deputy Chaim Bar-Lev, commander of the armored corps, plus Israel Tal.

The observers had high expectations, and they were indeed treated to a memorable spectacle: despite adjustments, the tanks taking part in the display missed their targets by several hundred yards. It later turned out that the crews had used the wrong ammunition, but the damage had been done. Dayan now became the greatest opponent to introduction of the Tiran, but Arkadi and Tal were not discouraged by this setback and continued to push for the introduction of the vehicles into service.

FORMATION OF THE TIRAN BRIGADE

By mid-1969 the Israelis had gained knowledge and experience with the Tiran, and the time was ripe for a final decision on its service entry. This decision was made by the chief of the general staff, Chaim Bar-Lev, at the end of June, when he requested the formation of a brigade with 140 Tiran tanks. This was a courageous decision, since within the Israeli armed forces these were still regarded as second-class tanks, and the shortages of ammunition and spare engines had not been overcome. The idea of forming a brigade had been born, however, and from then on it progressed steadily.

On the day after Operation Raviv, in which Israeli Tiran tanks and BTR-50 armored personnel carriers drove 28 miles (45 km) into Egypt, destroying infrastructure and military equipment, the order was finally issued to form the 274th Brigade. It was supposed to be conceived as a mechanized landing brigade. The planners were probably not yet aware of the scope of their idea at the time: if the Tiran brigade was actually to be used as an operational combat group, it also had to be provided with the appropriate — and in wartime

Tiran-1, Tiran-4 (T-54)	
Type	Battle tank
Manufacturer	Kharkov Locomotive Factory KhPZ, Ukraine (T-54) Uralvagonzavod, Russia (T-54A and later versions)
Service introduction	1947 (Soviet Union), 1968 (with the Israeli armed forces)
Number	35,000 (Soviet Union), 146 (with the Israeli armed forces)
Crew	4 (commander, gunner, loader, driver)
Combat weight	39.7 tons (36,000 kg)
Length	19 ft., 8 in. (6,000 mm; not counting barrel), 29 ft., 6 in. (9,000 mm; (with barrel)
Width	10 ft., 10 in. (3,300 mm)
Height	7 ft., 10 in. (2,400 mm)
Primary armament	Tiran 1, Tiran 4: D-10TG 100 mm gun (33 rounds T-54 and Tiran 1, 44 rounds Tiran 4) Tiran 4 Sharir: Royal Ordnance L7 105 mm gun
Secondary armament	1 × M1919 7.62 mm coaxial machine gun 1 × M1919 7.62 mm machine gun (3,000 rounds) 1 × M2HB 12.7 mm machine gun (600 rounds)
Fire control system	T-54: no stabilization T-54A: vertical plane stabilization T-54B: two-plane stabilization
Engine	V-54 12-cylinder diesel engine, 520 hp
Transmission	mechanical transmission (5 forward gears, 1 reverse)
Power-to-weight ratio	14.4 hp/ton
Ground clearance	16.7 in. (0.425 m)
Wading ability	55 in. (1.4 m)
Trench crossing	106 in. (2.7 m)
Obstacle	31.5 in. (0.8) m
Gradient	30%
Maximum speed	30 mph (50 kph) (on roads), 18 mph (30 kph) (off roads)
Fuel capacity	153 + 74 US gal. (580 liters + 280 liters; with external tanks)
Range	273 miles (440 km) (on roads), 180 miles (290 km) (off roads)
Protection	Armor steel structure (100–200 mm frontal, 80–150 mm on the sides) Smoke generator Tiran 4: NBC defense system

Tiran 2, Tiran 5 (T-55)	
Type	Battle tank
Manufacturer	Uralvagonzavod, Russia (T-54A and later versions)
Service introduction	1958 (Soviet Union), 1968 (with the Israeli armed forces)
Number	27,500 (Soviet Union), 146 (Israel)
Crew	4 (commander, gunner, loader, driver)
Combat weight	39.7 tons (36,000 kg)
Length	19 ft., 8 in. (6,000 mm; not counting barrel), 29 ft., 6 in. (9,000 mm; with barrel)
Width	10 ft., 10 in. (3,300 mm)
Height	7 ft., 10 in. (2,400 mm)
Primary armament	Tiran 2, Tiran 5: D-10T2S 100 mm gun (43 rounds T-55 and Tiran 2, 59 rounds Tiran 5) Tiran 5 Sharir: Royal Ordnance L7 105 mm gun
Secondary armament	1 × M1919 7.62 mm coaxial machine gun 1 × M1919 7.62 mm machine gun (3,000 rounds) 1 × M2HB 12.7 mm machine gun (600 rounds)
Engine	V-55 12-cylinder diesel engine, 580 hp
Transmission	mechanical transmission (5 forward gears, 1 reverse)
Power-to-weight ratio	16.1 hp/ton
Ground clearance	16.7 in. (0.425 m)
Wading ability	55 in. (1.4 m)
Trench crossing	106 in. (2.7 m)
Obstacle	31.5 in. (0.8) m
Gradient	30%
Maximum speed	30 mph (50 kph) (on roads), 18 mph (30 kph) (off roads)
Fuel capacity	180 + 105 US gal. (680 liters + 400 liters; with external tanks)
Range	341.75 miles (550 km) (on roads), 223 miles (360 km) (off roads)
Protection	Armor steel structure (100–200 mm frontal, 80–150 mm on the sides) Smoke generator Tiran 4: NBC defense system

Tiran 3, Tiran 6 (T-62)	
Type	Battle tank
Manufacturer	Uralvagonzavod, Russia (T-54A and later versions)
Service introduction	1962 (Soviet Union), 1974 (with the Israeli armed forces)
Number	22,700 (Soviet Union, export), 120 (Israel)
Crew	4 (commander, gunner, loader, driver)
Combat weight	40.8 tons (37,000 kg)
Length	19 ft., 8 in. (6,000 mm; not counting barrel), 30 ft., 10 in. (9,000 mm; with barrel)
Width	10 ft., 10 in. (3,300 mm)
Height	7 ft., 10 in. (2,400 mm)
Primary armament	U-5TS 115 mm smooth-bore gun (40 rounds)
Secondary armament	1 × M1919 7.62 mm coaxial machine gun (2,500 rounds) 1 × M2HB 12.7 mm machine gun (500 rounds)
Engine	V-55 12-cylinder diesel engine, 580 hp
Transmission	mechanical transmission (5 forward gears, 1 reverse)
Power-to-weight ratio	15.7 hp/ton
Ground clearance	16.7 in. (0.425 m)
Wading ability	55 in. (1.4 m)
Trench crossing	106 in. (2.7 m)
Obstacle	31.5 in. (0.8) m
Gradient	30%
Maximum speed	31 mph (50 kph)
Fuel capacity	254 + 105 US gal. (960 liters + 400 liters; with external tanks)
Range	404 miles (650 km) (on roads), 280 miles (450 km) (off roads)
Protection	Armor steel structure (120–240 mm frontal, 80–150 mm on the sides) Smoke generator NBC defense system

extremely valuable — resources, in particular direct support from the air force and navy.

It wasn't just the required operational support, since everything about this brigade was unusual. While the other armored brigades had seventy to one hundred tanks, the Tiran brigade was to consist of 146 tanks. While other brigades were under the command of the same armored divisions and had a combined logistics system, the Tiran brigade functioned as an independent brigade, which was under the direct command of the general staff and had its own logistics system at the division level.

Gideon Altshuler was named the first commander of this new brigade. It received its first operational assignment even before it was completely formed: the formation of two armored units as an intervention reserve. One brigade was to be stationed at Sharm El Sheik in the Sinai, and the other at Eilat. From that time on, the brigade was an official part of the Israeli armed forces, although there was still uncertainty as to how its capabilities should be employed.

Arkadi Timor, Israeli expert on Soviet tanks and head of the Tiran development department. *IDF*

Yaakov Lapidot was responsible for the introduction of the Tiran into the Israeli Armored Corps. During the Yom Kippur War in 1973, he commanded a Tiran brigade and was subsequently given command of the 440th Tiran Division. *IDF*

THE TIRAN BRIGADE IN ACTION

By the end of 1971 the Tiran brigade was operational and ready for action. As a reserve unit, however, its service was limited, since its tanks were in storage and only a handful of tank crews were in active service, in combat training, or on guard duty in the Sinai. To put this into perspective, however, it can be stated that the bulk of the Israeli armed forces at that time shared this low level of activity. At the beginning of the 1970s, tanks were not required to deal with security threats, which were usually countered with patrol vehicles and specialized antiterror units.

Israel's vigilance declined until even some of the border posts remained unmanned. These were the same posts from which the Egyptians on the banks of the Suez Canal were to be stopped in the event of an attack. A new war was in the air, even if Israel assumed that Egypt would not start it until it had received long-range tactical missiles and modern combat from the Soviets. The Israelis also believed that Syria would never go to war without Egypt, resulting in the deceptive impression that a two-front war was unlikely at this point.

The fronts were also so quiet that the Tiran brigade retained its unique status and continued its irregular activities. At the beginning of 1972, the Israeli armed forces decided to replace the Tiran's gun with the 105 mm Sharir model. This would at least solve the ammunition problem, since the Tiran's gun would now use the same ammunition as the Shot and Magach tanks.

Installation of the new gun resulted in the loss of the gunner's night vision device. At first this seemed of lesser importance, since none of Israel's other tanks had night vision equipment, but consequences of this action became apparent during the Yom Kippur War at the latest. The engine problem was solved, however. The Israelis purchased agricultural equipment from Romania that was powered by the same engine installed in the T-54/T-55.

In the years that followed, the Tiran brigade took part in several important actions. Probably the most important were the actions in support of the offensive against the Egyptian forces on the southern front during the Yom Kippur War in 1973, and the invasion of southern Lebanon in the first Lebanese War of 1982.

Chapter 16
The Yom Kippur War, 1973: The Southern Front (Fourth Arab-Israeli War)

> For if the front of a position is so strong due to entrenchments and obstacles that an attack becomes impossible, the enemy is forced to bypass it.
> — Carl von Clausewitz, *On War*

Under Anwar el-Sadat,[1] successor to the late president Gamal Abdel Nasser, there was a major change in the internal and foreign policies of Egypt. He skillfully began a political balancing act between Moscow and Washington, in the assumption that he could obtain weapons for a military decision in the Sinai from the Soviet Union and simultaneously force Israel to yield only through American influence.

In the meantime, the Soviet Union continued to reequip the Egyptian army, and in spring 1973, in addition to tanks and artillery, for the first time it also supplied R-17 Scud (SS-1c) medium-range surface-to-surface missiles. Capable of carrying conventional or nuclear warheads, these rockets had a range of up to 186 miles (300 km) and were thus capable of posing a direct threat to Israeli population centers such as Be'er Sheva.

With the addition of medium-range surface-to-surface missiles and after several years of arms deliveries from the Soviet Union, the Egyptian president now had the decisive arsenal of weapons for a war of destruction against Israel. In April 1973 he decided on a renewed campaign against the small coastal state and tasked Israel's defense minister, General Ahmed Ismail Ali,[2] with developing a plan of operation. Ismail Ali had commanded the Egyptian military in the Six-Day War and was most responsible for that defeat. He had analyzed the Israeli superiority and adapted his battle plan as follows:

The first strike should not be left to the Israelis but should be carried out by Egypt. Israel would be engaged in a two-front war against Egypt and Syria, with the forces of the surrounding Arab states acting as reserves. The attacks were to be made along the entire front of the Suez Canal and the ceasefire line on the Golan Heights.

The objective of this plan was to make it impossible for the Israelis to recognize the main thrust of the attacks in advance and possibly initiate rapid countermeasures. However, in any case a simultaneous attack by Syria east of the ceasefire line would tie up Israeli forces, not only on the Sinai Peninsula but also on the Golan Heights.

The Egyptians chose October 6, 1973, as the day for the attack, the tenth day of Ramadan and, that year, also the day of the Jewish Yom Kippur holiday. The Egyptians could thus be confident that many Israeli soldiers would not be in their garrisons, but on leave. The tides in the Suez Canal and the fact that there would be a full moon on the night of October 6 also contributed to the choice of this date for the attack.

The Egyptian high command originally planned for the attack to begin at 1800. This would place the sun at their backs, and the arrival of darkness soon afterward would enable them to throw up bridges during the night. The Syrians, on the other hand, scheduled their attack for 0800, when the sun rising in the east would blind the Israeli forces. The attackers finally agreed on a compromise and planned their attack for 1400.

The Israeli government, especially Prime Minister Golda Meir and the chief of the military intelligence service, Major General Eli Zeira,[3] were confident that after the War of Attrition (1968–70), the implementation of the ceasefire, the death of

---

[1] Anwar el-Sadat (1918–81) grew up in a simple village on the Nile River delta. He left the military academy in 1938 as a lieutenant and admired the successes of Rommel's tank army in North Africa during the Second World War. In the course of the 1952 revolution in Egypt, Sadat held the office of minister of the interior and, after Nasser's death in 1970, took over the reins of government as president. After losing the Yom Kippur War in 1973, Sadat worked with US president Carter to continue the peace process. He was the first Arab president to address the Knesset in 1977, negotiated the Camp David Agreement with Menachem Begin, and was awarded the Nobel Peace Prize in 1978. Sadat was assassinated by members of the Muslim Brotherhood during a military parade to honor those who died during the Yom Kippur War.

[2] Ahmed Ismail Ali (1917–74) graduated from the military academy in 1938, the same year as Nasser and Sadat. He fought in three Israeli-Arab wars and last led the Egyptian army as defense minister in the 1973 Yom Kippur War. He died of lung cancer in London in 1974.

Nasser, and the simmering civil war in Jordan, it would be a considerable time before Egypt and Syria would be prepared to launch a military strike against Israel.

Since taking command in January 1972, Chief of the General Staff David Elazar alone had repeatedly warned about the threat of an invasion of the Sinai by the Egyptian armed forces. In recent months there had been increasing signs of this. These included the transfer of ground units to the Suez Canal, the construction of tank ramps, and new access roads.

Elazar urged Defense Minister Moshe Dayan to at least partially mobilize the armed forces; however, he firmly refused. Despite this, Elazar ordered Major General Albert Mandler, commander of the 252nd Division, to immediately also place the 401st and 460th Armored Brigades in Sinai on alert, in addition to the 14th Armored Brigade, which was already at the Bar-Lev Line. The Israeli commander of the southern front, Major General Shmuel Gonen,[4] also endorsed a higher level of readiness and on October 2 visited the troops on the Bar-Lev Line.

Egyptian T-55 of an armored brigade of the 7th Infantry Division reaches the east bank of the Suez Canal. Within forty-eight hours the Egyptian army sent more than four hundred tanks across the canal. *Wikipedia*

---

[3] Eli Zeira (1928–) became known as the director of Aman, the military intelligence service of the Israeli armed forces. He was disgraced by the Agranat Commission, which investigated the failures of the Israeli leadership after the 1973 Yom Kippur War. Although the commission praised Zeira's exceptional intellectual abilities, he had to leave his post due to incorrect assessments and evaluations of the enemy situation.

[4] Shmuel Gonen (1930–91), born in Vilna, Poland, immigrated to Palestine during the British Mandate and served in the Haganah at a young age. He was wounded five times during the 1948–49 War of Independence. He commanded a tank company in the Sinai campaign of 1956 and later the first tank battalion with the newly acquired Centurion tanks. During the Six-Day War, he commanded the 7th Armored Brigade and in 1973 took over command of the southern front as Sharon's successor. During the 1973 Yom Kippur War, Chief of Staff Elazar Gonen relieved him of his command due to differences in strategy and replaced him with Lieutenant General Chaim Bar-Lev. After severe criticism of his leadership decisions in the report by the Agranat Commission, he left the Israeli armed forces and also the country and from then on lived in Africa. He never returned to his homeland and died in 1991.

After further disturbing reports about Egyptian troop movements at the Suez Canal were received by the Israeli military intelligence service, Golda Meir summoned her closest advisors for further consultation. In this "kitchen cabinet" — so-called because she liked to meet with her closest advisors at home in her kitchen — were Deputy Prime Minister Allon, Defense Minister Dayan, Chief of the General Staff Elazar, and the head of the intelligence service, Shalev. Chief of the Secret Service Major General Zamir was ill and unable to attend.

As before, the "kitchen cabinet" assessed the situation as threatening but again recalled the statements by the intelligence service in May, which described an Arab attack as unlikely. For the time being, however, Elazar's proposal to partially mobilize the armed forces prevailed. However, the cabinet decided to discuss further steps definitively on October 7.

CHAPTER 16: The Yom Kippur War, 1973: The Southern Front (Fourth Arab-Israeli War)

THE EGYPTIAN BUILDUP AND OFFENSIVE INTO THE SINAI PENINSULA

At dawn on October 5, Israeli observation posts in the Bar-Lev Line followed a buildup by the Egyptian army on the Suez Canal in unprecedented strength. The observed activities could not be regarded as one of the regular autumn maneuvers. Elazar therefore again recommended that the entire Israeli military be mobilized, but in the late afternoon, Meir again firmly refused. She explained her decision by declaring that Israel did not want to give the impression that it was preparing to launch a preventive strike. Under no conditions did she want to be seen as the aggressor.

In the morning hours of October 6, the Israeli general staff received further information from the military intelligence service that predicted with high probability an Egyptian-Syrian attack on the same day. Meir now revised her decision and directed Elazar to order mobilization at 0630. This was a very challenging logistical undertaking, since the Israeli population was celebrating Yom Kippur, the highest Jewish holiday. General Gonen ordered some units of the 252nd Division, which was already on a state of alert, to move into the western part of the Sinai.

In the Israeli defensive plan for the Suez Canal, about six hundred troops of the 16th Infantry Brigade occupied the positions of the Bar-Lev Line. Most of these bombproof defensive positions were manned at platoon strength and armed with mortars and machine guns.

The Bar Lev Line strongpoints themselves had no antitank weapons. This role was the responsibility of tank platoons of the 14th Armored Brigade, positioned in the rear, of which a total of eight platoons were at readiness on October 6. Of these, five manned the strongpoints in the northern sector between El Cap and Port Fuad, and one each for the strongpoints at the north end of the Great Bitter Lake and for the southern sector at Port Tawfiq. An additional armored platoon was at the coast road to Ras Sudra.

The remaining eight armored companies, with about ninety tanks of the 14th Armored Brigade, were supposed to provide concentrated resistance in the event of an attack by the enemy on the Bar Lev Line. Of these, an armored battalion with two companies was positioned at the Baluza–Tasa road, southeast of El Kantara. An armored battalion with three companies was gathered around Tosa, while another armored battalion with three companies was in position east of the exit from Gidi Pass.

Farther in the rear were six armored and mechanized infantry brigades, parts of the 143rd Division (under Major General Ariel Sharon), and the 162nd Division (under Major General Avraham Adan). Both divisions were reserve formations, some

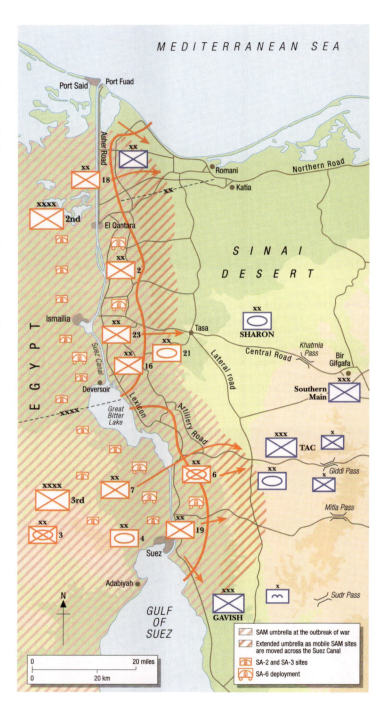

Map showing the occupation of the planned bridgeheads by Egyptian forces east of the Suez Canal. The deployment of the Type S-75 Dwina (SA-2) and S-125 Newa (SA-3) surface-to-air missile positions is also shown. *Osprey*

138 | THE ISRAELI ARMORED CORPS: History, Equipment, Operations, 1948 to 2024

Major General Shmuel Shonen (commander of the southern front) and Major General Ariel Sharon (commander of the 143rd Division) during planning to defend against the imminent Egyptian armored offensive in the Sinai. By that time, the enemy had already fortified their bridgeheads east of the Suez Canal. *Israel Government Press Office*

El-Shazly's plan of battle envisaged taking the Bar Lev Line by surprise, delaying Israeli's mobilization, forcing the enemy units into battle immediately with whatever reserves were available, and wiping them out one after another. The Egyptians were to regroup at the Bar Lev Line in order to be ready for a move deeper into the Sinai.

The achievement of Egyptian air superiority was based on an air defense system with surface-to-air missiles, consisting of the S-75 Dvina (SA-2 Guideline), the S-125 Neva (SA-3 Goa), and the SK12 Kub (SA-6 Gainful). Since the Israelis relied on their air force and on their tanks and their superior abilities in mobile warfare, an effective antitank defense was vital if the Egyptian attack was to succeed.

The first wave of attackers was equipped with the new RPG-7 rocket-propelled grenade launcher from the Soviet Union, with which they would engage close-range targets. This weapon weighed 14 pounds (6.3 kg) and had a rate of fire of four to six rounds per minute and a range of 383 yards (350 m).

The second attack wave was to be equipped with the 9K11 Malyutka (AT-3 Sagger) portable wire-guided antitank missile. Powered by a solid fuel rocket motor, this wire-guided antitank missile had a speed of 377 ft./sec. (115 m/sec.) and a 5.5-pound (2.5 kg) warhead and could be used against both hard and soft targets at ranges from 547 to 3,280 yards (500–3,000 m).

Since the 105-mile-long, roughly 656-foot-wide, and up to 59-foot-deep Suez Canal was a difficult natural obstacle, crossing it required careful planning and the use of modern technical aids. El-Shazly decided to conduct simultaneous crossings of the canal along its entire length. This was to minimize the effectiveness of Israeli countermeasures and force the enemy to disperse his defensive forces, especially the much-feared Israeli air force. High-pressure water cannon were used to make breaches in the sand wall of the Bar Lev Line. As well, ramps were constructed on the west bank that were higher than the artificial walls of the Bar Lev Line and were used as platforms for Egyptian direct-fire and antitank weapons.

of whose personnel first had to be mobilized should their units be sent into action. These units also had no supporting infantry.

The three divisions' tank strength consisted of a total of 588 M48A3s (Magach 3), 152 M60s (Magach 6), 234 T-54/T-55s (Tiran), and about 250 M50 and M51 Shermans. They also had M109 self-propelled 155 mm howitzers and M107s with 175 mm guns, Soltam self-propelled guns (artillery pieces mounted on M4 Sherman chassis), M3 half-tracks, and M113 APCs.

In charge of Operation Badr was the Egyptian chief of the general staff, Saad el-Shazly.[5] He knew that the Egyptian army, which was already in position, represented his greatest advantage. Israel, on the other hand, was dependent on the mobilization of its reserves in an emergency, which would take some time.

For the crossing of the canal, El-Shazly ordered two armies into attack positions between Suez and Kantara:
In the first echelon were the following:

- The Third Army, with the 7th Infantry Division at the south end of the Great Bitter Lake and the 19th Infantry Division at Suez. Echeloned to the rear was the 25th Armored Brigade.
- the Second Army, with the 18th Infantry Division north of the Great Bitter Lake in the Lahtzanit area, the 2nd Infantry Division at Hizayon, and the 16th Infantry Division at Ismailia

---

[5] Saad el-Shazly (1922–2011), born in the Nile River delta, became the youngest student to attend the military academy in Cairo in 1939. As a lieutenant, he witnessed the Israeli War of Independence in 1948–49 and founded the first Egyptian parachute battalion. He fought bravely and prudently as a battalion commander on the Sinai front in the 1967 Six-Day War, which earned him great respect and recognition. In 1971, he was promoted to chief of staff and commanded the Egyptian army in the 1973 Yom Kippur War. Following disagreements with Sadat over the conduct of the war after the formation of the Egyptian bridgehead on the eastern bank of the Suez Canal, El-Shazly fell out of favor and resigned from the army. During Mubarak's government, he was posthumously awarded numerous medals.

CHAPTER 16: The Yom Kippur War, 1973: The Southern Front (Fourth Arab-Israeli War)

Israeli M60A1 tanks of the 600th Armored Brigade of the Sharon Division moving up to the western front line to relieve the units of the exhausted 252nd Division, October 1973. *Israel Government Press Office*

- the 135th Infantry Brigade, at Port Said
- the 15th Armored Brigade, behind the seam between the 2nd and 18th Infantry Divisions at Mifreket

In the second echelon were
- the 6th Mechanized Infantry Division, west of Suez;
- the 4th Armored Division, southwest of the Great Bitter Lake on the Cairo–Suez rail line; and
- the 21st Armored Division and the 23rd Mechanized Infantry Division, west of Ismailia and north and south of the road to Cairo, respectively.

Other units included a battle group from the reinforced 130th Amphibious Brigade, southwest of Suez, at Cabrit on the Lesser Bitter Lake, and in the Port Said. This unit was to carry out surprise attacks with amphibious vehicles where possible.

The Egyptian armored divisions had each released an armored brigade to the infantry divisions and so, in addition to the usual two infantry brigades and one mechanized infantry brigade, had just one armored brigade and one artillery brigade. Both armies were also reinforced by two artillery brigades, a sapper brigade, and a battalion of commandos. Other commando forces were standing by to take part in surprise paratrooper actions in the enemy rear.

Altogether there were about 260,000 troops, 1,700 T-54/55 and T-62 tanks, 4,000 artillery pieces, 150 SAM positions, and 2,500 guided antitank weapons on the west bank of the Suez Canal, ready to attack.

At 1355 on October 6, 1,500 guns of the artillery batteries of the Egyptian Second and Third Armies opened up with preparatory fire on the Israeli strongpoints. In the first hour, more than 10,500 shells fell on the defensive positions of the Bar Lev Line.

At the same time, about 150 Egyptian aircraft, MiG-17 and MiG-21 fighters and Su-7 fighter-bombers, struck the Israeli forward airfields at Bir El Thamada and Refidem, the Tasa area, and the Israeli artillery positions in the northern and central sectors.

Although the Egyptian attack was not unexpected, the Israelis were surprised by the exact timing of the attack. The Israeli air force was able to scramble a few pairs of F-4E fighter aircraft and shoot down a number of Egyptian aircraft before lack of fuel forced them to return to their bases.

With the shifting of the preparatory artillery fire onto the Israeli rear, all five of the Egyptian infantry divisions on the west bank of the canal and the 135th Infantry Brigade, deployed on the left, began crossing on a broad front in eighty-two places.

In the first wave, infantry and artillery observers crossed the canal in inflatable and wooden boats. They negotiated the

The Egyptian leadership debating how to proceed after the failure of their major offensive in the Sinai on October 15, 1973. *From left*: Chief of Staff Saad el-Shazly, Prime Minister Anwar el-Sadat, Defense Minister Ahmed Ismail Ali. *Wikipedia*

raised banks with ropes and bamboo ladders, after which the Egyptian rapidly advanced about 1.25 to 2 miles between the Israeli positions.

The bulk of these forces consisted of squads armed with RPG-7s, AT-3 Sagger antitank guided missiles, or shoulder-fired SA-7 Grail surface-to-air missiles. At the same time, Egyptian tanks began moving onto the raised platforms on the west bank and opened fire, the effects of which were felt up to 2 miles east of the canal.

Within an hour, all the infantry battalions of the first wave successfully crossed the Suez Canal and secured the landing zones. The following infantry battalions moved through the secured landing zones and began encircling the Israeli strongpoints. The Israeli armored platoons that were supposed to provide a direct defense at the canal did not reach their firing positions in time and were surprised by the massed use of RPGs and antitank guided missiles by the Egyptians. Within a few minutes they destroyed about a third of the Israeli tanks moving toward the canal.

By the time darkness fell, the Egyptians had established three bridgeheads with a depth of up to 5 miles. These were situated between Port Tawfiq and Shallufa, at Deversoir and El Firdan, and south of El Kantara and El Cap. Fifty ferries were also operating, and the construction of six pontoon bridges had begun.

The Second Army now began sending tanks, artillery, and armored vehicles to the east bank in an organized way. The use of smoke was supposed to conceal the crossing of the canal. The Third Army was somewhat behind schedule, but during the night it was able to begin sending across heavy weapons, vehicles, and tanks. By morning the Egyptians had moved about 250 tanks into the bridgeheads on the east side of the canal.

The tank companies of the Israeli 14th Armored Brigade began moving toward their firing positions at the Bar Lev Line during the Egyptian preparatory fire. The Magach and Sherman tanks soon came under fire from the mobile RPG-7s and antitank guided weapons and suffered considerable losses. For example, just two tanks from the two Israeli armored companies deployed at El Firdan and Ismailia were left serviceable.

With the forces of the 14th Armored Brigade diminishing rapidly in this first phase, General Mandler directed both reserve brigades to the front line. The 460th Armored Brigade, with two tank battalions, advanced as far as Tasa and opened fire on the bridgeheads at El Kantara and El Firdan.

In fierce and confused fighting, which went on all night into October 7, several tanks of the 460th Armored Brigade succeeded in destroying an Egyptian crossing site. They broke into El Kantara and prevented a further expansion of the bridgeheads. But growing losses and the fact that Egyptian infantry was already in the brigade's rear finally forced the unit to withdraw.

The 401st Armored Brigade, which was acting as the second reserve brigade, drove west through the Gidi and Mitla Passes with two tank battalions and deployed one at El Kubri and Port Tawfiq, and the second against the southern end of the Bitter Lake. A fierce battle developed that raged all night, during which the tank companies repeatedly provided support to the threatened strongpoints of the Bar Lev Line, while also advancing through the Egyptian infantry to the bank of the canal in order to take the crossing sites under fire.

CHAPTER 16: The Yom Kippur War, 1973: The Southern Front (Fourth Arab-Israeli War)

On the morning of October 7, the 401st Armored Brigade had just twenty-three tanks still operational. When the Egyptian Third Army then began landing its first tanks east of the Suez Canal, this forced the Israeli armored units to pull back to defensive positions behind the Bar Lev Line. They were thus unable to prevent the expansion of the Egyptian bridgeheads. Only one of the strongpoints of the Bar Lev Line held out until the end of the war, and the others were either taken by the Egyptians or abandoned.

REINFORCEMENTS ARRIVE AND THE DEFENSIVE STRUGGLE

The huge losses suffered by General Mandler's 252nd Division in the night of October 7, the increasing Egyptian pressure to expand the bridgeheads, and the heavy losses among aircraft of the Israeli air force forced the rash mobilization of Israeli reserves in the form of the 143rd and 162nd Divisions.

The commander of the southern front, Major General Gonen, met with the commanders of the 143rd and 162nd Divisions and Chief of the General Staff Elazar in the corps command post in Refidim. There they determined the areas of responsibility and plan of attack for the coming battles:

- The sector of front between El Cap and Ismailia was in the 162nd Division's area of responsibility. Under its command were the 217th and 500th Armored Brigades and the newly attached 460th Armored Brigade. These units were to attack the Egyptian Second Army south of El Kantara from the northeast.
- In the sector between Ismailia and the crossing between the Great and the Lesser Bitter Lakes was the 143rd Division with the 600th and the newly attached 14th Armored Brigades. These were to stand by in reserve at Tasa and, in the event that the 162nd Division was successful, attack the Egyptian Third Army in the south.
- In the southern sector to the Gulf of Suez, the 252nd Division was to support the possibly successful advance to the south by the 143rd Division.

In the event of the seizure of the Egyptian bridges, Major General Sharon urged a crossing of the canal. General Gonen disagreed and argued that the Egyptian bridgehead had to be cleared completely before Israeli troops could cross to the west side of the canal.

By the afternoon of October 7, the Egyptian Second and Third Armies had moved five infantry divisions of the first operational echelon completely to the east bank of the Suez Canal,

Paratroopers of Force Shmulik and tanks of the 79th Armored Battalion (attached to Sharon's 143rd Division) in defensive action against the 25th Armored Brigade of the Egyptian Third Army, which was equipped with T-62 tanks. Thanks to the flanking attack by Adan's 162nd Division, by evening eighty-six of the ninety-six Egyptian tanks had been destroyed, October 17, 1973. *David Schiller Archive*

despite ongoing Israeli air attacks, so that by nightfall there were around four hundred tanks there.

While Egyptian engineers repaired several bridges over the canal that had been destroyed, on the Israeli side the armored brigades of the two divisions prepared for the attack. The 460th and 600th Armored Brigades left their forward positions and turned the responsibility for securing them over to the battalions of a mechanized infantry brigade. The 217th Armored Brigade was still widely spread out, approaching along the coastal road.

During the Israeli buildup, there were differences of opinion concerning combat and contingency planning, as well as Sharon's opinion that the canal should be crossed as quickly as possible, which led to misunderstandings between the commander of the southern front and the division commanders, which in turn led to considerable delays. General Elazar finally prevailed, which ended the debate between his commanders, and ordered both divisions to push on to the canal front.

The Israeli 600th Armored Brigade soon came under fire from highly effective antitank guns opposite El Kantara and was bombed by the Egyptian air force and was forced to halt its advance. The 460th Armored Brigade also engaged powerful infantry forces and, as a result of heavy losses to AT-3 Sagger antitank guided missiles, was also forced to halt its attack. An attempt by the 217th Armored Brigade to carry out a relief attack

in support of the 460th Armored Brigade also failed in the face of stubborn resistance by the enemy.

Several Israeli units nevertheless managed to advance to within proximity of the canal bank; however, they were thrown back by the Egyptian forces, which had now grown to eight hundred tanks and fifty thousand troops. This forced the command of the southern front to withdraw both divisions into defensive positions behind the front line.

The failure of the October 8 counterattack at the Suez Canal led the Israeli general staff to reconsider fundamental decisions. While Dayan presented a rather pessimistic picture of the overall situation to members of the press and even considered a withdrawal of the armed forces into the interior of the Sinai Peninsula as an option, Elazar and his staff were working on more-offensive scenarios.

In order to resolve the continuing differences between the commander of the southern front, Gonen, and the division commanders regarding the conduct of operations, Elazar appointed his predecessor, Lieutenant-General Chaim Bar-Lev, as the new commander of the southern front. As the most senior officer, Bar-Lev acted as Gonen's superior and exercised sufficient authority to bring about an agreement on the different tactical and operational views, above all being Sharon's position regarding a crossing of the canal.

On the same day, considerable differences of opinion arose in the Egyptian supreme command as to the further conduct of operations. Defense Minister Ismail insisted on a consolidation of forces on the east bank of the Suez Canal; the opening of the important Katmai, Mitla, and Gidi Passes; and a subsequent advance into the Sinai. Chief of the General Staff Shazly was unable to support this position. He believed that a push into the Sinai would be vulnerable to air attack, since it would take place outside the Egyptian surface-to-air missile screen. As well, such an attack would play into the hands of the Israeli tanks, which were waiting in higher defensive positions.

Sadat and Ismaili prevailed and ordered Shazly to make preparations for an attack in the Sinai, which was to take place on October 14. The 4th Armored Division was to support the Third Army, and the 21st Armored Division the attack by the Second Army.

While the Egyptian forces were preparing to attack, Bar-Lev and Sharon were planning the crossing of the canal. However, information concerning Egyptian reinforcements on the east bank forced a postponement.

On October 13, the Israeli command suffered a severe blow. Major General Mandler was in his M113 issuing orders when it was struck by an AT-3 Sagger missile fired by a group of Egyptian infantry. Mandler and his crew were killed. The major general, who was known as a very talented and circumspect leader, was replaced by Brigadier General Kalman Magen.

A short time later, El-Shazly ordered a combined assault by all the forces on the east bank of the Suez Canal. At 0600 on October 14, Egyptian artillery opened fire along the entire front line of the Egyptian Second and Third Armies. This was followed by airstrikes against the Israeli defensive positions. The attack that the Egyptian chief of the general staff wanted to avoid at any cost, which he had been unable to talk either Sadat or Ismaili out of, was met by a well-prepared enemy. This offensive would later turn the tide of the Yom Kippur War in Israel's favor.

The tank battles that now followed were of no less intensity than the Battle of Kursk in 1943, when the Wehrmacht attacked the defensive positions of the Red Army.

In the south the Egyptian 3rd Armored Brigade, with ninety-four T-55 tanks, two battalions of artillery, and two mechanized infantry battalions, moved out of the area northeast of the city of Suez through the wide valley of the Wadi Mab'ouk in the direction of Mitla Pass. To protect the 3rd Armored Brigade's right flank, the 22nd Armored Brigade supported the attack south of Port Tawfiq. The Israeli 401st Armored Brigade recognized the main direction of the Egyptian thrust, deployed a mechanized infantry battalion frontally to block it, and placed two armored battalions with Magach 3 tanks in flanking positions at Wadi Mab'ouk. In bitter fighting that lasted until midday, the Israelis largely wiped out both Egyptian armored brigades, destroying 140 tanks and forcing the rest to retreat. The Egyptian attempt to take the vital road leading to the pass, which would have enabled a secure advance into Sinai, failed.

The same thing happened to the Egyptian 7th Infantry Division, which, reinforced by the 25th Armored Brigade with about a hundred T-62 tanks, had set out in the direction of the Gidi Pass. An Israeli armored battalion with thirty M51 upgraded Shermans achieved a frontal defensive success there. An attempt by the 25th Armored Brigade to outflank the Israelis failed, and after the loss of twenty T-62 tanks, the Egyptian units withdrew in the direction of the canal.

In the northern sector of the Bitter Lake, the Egyptian 1st and 14th Armored Brigades encountered the Israeli 14th and 600th Armored Brigades of the 143rd Division. The former blocked the advance, while the latter outflanked the Egyptian units. The Israelis repulsed the attack and inflicted heavy losses on the Egyptian units.

The attacks by the Egyptian 24th Armored Brigade, positioned in the north toward the El Firdan area, and by the 15th Armored Brigade, from El Kantara, collapsed after a fierce delaying action by the Israeli 460th Armored Brigade. By midday the exhausted Egyptian units, having suffered considerable losses, returned to their starting positions. The Egyptian command was unable to make good this setback as the war continued. The loss of 260 tanks weighed heavily.

Shortly after he issued the order for a renewed attack, Major General Saad Mamoun, commander of the Egyptian Second Army, suffered a severe heart attack and died. This meant that a coordinated attack was no longer possible, and the Egyptian offensive, which had been launched in a scattered manner, was ultimately doomed to failure.

While El-Shazly raged, the Israeli command saw the opportunity to take the counteroffensive, and Elazar ordered Operation Gazelle, the crossing of the Suez Canal, the destruction of the remaining units of the Second Army to the west, and the severing of all links to the Third Army east of the canal.

Elazar's plan of operations was based on the following points:

Shot Kal tanks of the 217th Armored Brigade, part of the Bren Division, cross the Suez Canal during Operation Gazelle. Units of Sharon's 143rd Division provided cover for the crossing. October 1973. *Israel Government Press Office*

- The 143rd Division was to advance to the canal from the Tasa area, open the crossing site at Deversoir, establish bridgeheads east and west of the canal, and erect two bridges for the crossing.
- The 162nd Division was to stand by in the Tasa area, advance through the 143rd Division, expand the western bridgehead, and then drive south to the west of Bitter Lake.
- Using the crossing site, elements of the 252nd Division were to follow to the west bank and cover the right flank of the southward attack. Two brigades on the east bank were to prevent possible counterattacks by elements of the Egyptian Second and Third Armies.

Lieutenant-General Bar-Lev selected a location opposite Deversoir as the best place to cross the canal. Deversoir was in the sector of front held by the Egyptian Second and Third Armies, and Great Bitter Lake protected the left flank.

On the night of October 16, paratroopers of the 247th Brigade began crossing the canal in inflatable boats and formed a 650-yard-deep bridgehead. At the same time, the 14th Armored Brigade of the 143rd Division secured the road on the canal bank, allowing engineers and ferries to be moved in for the comprehensive preparation of the crossing.

The paratroopers on the west bank rapidly expanded the bridgehead, advanced along the canal against surface-to-air and artillery positions, and captured several poorly guarded ammunition dumps. The Israeli troops met little organized resistance. Indeed, for a long time the surprise crossing by the Israelis went unnoticed by the Egyptian command.

Sharon's 143rd Division began securing the approach routes to the crossing site in order to open a corridor. This led precisely through the positions of the Egyptian 16th Infantry Division and the 21st Armored Brigade. Both were in the area of the so-called Chinese Farm, an agricultural area with a Japanese-run research center for agriculture. The Egyptians recognized the Israeli intentions and with their combined forces tried to foil the planned crossing.

The Israeli 600th Armored Brigade, led by two armored battalions and supported by the 14th Armored Brigade, accepted battle around the "Chinese Farm." Both units became involved in fierce fighting. While the first Egyptian attacks were repulsed, Israeli reconnaissance discovered the approach of the 25th Armored Brigade. It was moving from south to northeast of Bitter Lake and had no fewer than ninety-five T-62 tanks.

The Israelis committed the 600th Armored Brigade frontally against the advancing Egyptian tanks, while the 460th Armored Brigade took up a flanking position. By late afternoon, eighty-six of the Egyptian T-62s had been destroyed. After bitter fighting, the Egyptian units around the "Chinese Farm" were finally defeated, and the vital corridor to the canal was opened.

Sharon's units also suffered heavy losses, and Dayan already began to doubt the success of Operation Gazelle, but Bar-Lev

stood firm and declared. "If we had known beforehand what high losses we would suffer, we probably would not have made the crossing of the canal. But now that we are on the other side, we will see the operation through to the bitter end."

In the meantime, the Israeli engineers completed the bridge crossings and the 162nd Division began the crossing with the 460th and 500th Armored Brigades. During the course of October 17, the Egyptian command realized the importance of the Israeli bridgehead on the west bank of the canal and dispatched the 23rd Armored Brigade and the 150th Paratrooper Brigade from the operational reserve from the Cairo area toward the canal. The Third Army moved the 2nd Armored Brigade, which was west of Bitter Lake, to the north, and the Second Army took up a defensive position at the village of Serapeum with elements of the 23rd Mechanized Division.

During October 19 the 162nd Division—with the 460th Armored Brigade on the right, the 500th Armored Brigade on the left, and the 217th Armored Brigade bringing up the rear—succeeded in advancing toward the Gineifa Hills in the area west of Bitter Lake, while the first brigades of the 252nd Division followed on the west bank.

The follow-up plan for the two divisional commanders, Avrahan Adan and Kalman Magen, called for a rapid expansion of the bridgehead and a breakout to the south to isolate the Egyptian Third Army. Ariel Sharon's orders were to proceed farther north toward Ismailia to destroy the SAM and artillery positions there and cut off the Egyptian Second Army.

El-Shazly recognized the seriousness of the situation and asked Sadat for permission to use at least four brigades of the Third Army east of the canal to take the pressure off the cutoff Second Army. Sadat refused to approve any withdrawal of troops to the western bank of the canal, since this would be tantamount to a retreat or surrender.

While Sharon's units advanced farther north and took out additional SAM positions, Adan and Magen energetically drove their units southward. On October 21 the Egyptian Third Army was finally cut off from its headquarters and its supplies on the west bank, trapping approximately 30,000 Egyptian troops in their defensive positions.

However, the guns were not to fall silent until October 25, since numerous units were cut off from headquarters and therefore did not receive the information about an imposed ceasefire. A little later, UN observers slowly began to position themselves along the front line.

As the counterpart of the Tank Museum at Latrun, there is a museum to the Ramadan War, as the Yom Kippur War was called by the Egyptian side, in Cairo. The painting provides a dramatic image of the crossing of the Suez Canal and the Egyptian attack on the Bar-Lev Line, with lanes being cut through the sand walls with the aid of high-pressure water cannon. *David Schiller Archive*

CHAPTER 16: The Yom Kippur War, 1973: The Southern Front (Fourth Arab-Israeli War)

Chapter 17
The Yom Kippur War, 1973: The Northern Front (Fourth Arab-Israeli War)

> We knew that the state of Israel was at stake. Every single person there on the front line was a hero. Everyone stood behind their rock and fought until they fell. Losing was not an option.
> — Zvika Greengold, leader of an armored company and holder of the Israeli Medal of Valor

In the 1960s the Syrians turned the Golan Heights bordering Israel into a dense network of military positions. For years, these seemingly invincible fortresses served the Syrian military as bases for hostile actions against Israeli settlements. They directed artillery fire at them and tried to divert the Jordan River to deprive Israeli agriculture of its most important source of water.

After the Syrian defeat in the Six-Day War in 1967, the local population and the Syrian army withdrew behind the ceasefire line, known as the "Purple Line." The name came from United Nations maps on which the ceasefire line was marked in the color purple. The United Nations maintained observation posts along this line and monitored the agreed-upon border demarcation.

From a geographical perspective, the Golan Heights are a high plateau between the Sea of Galilee and the Syrian capital, Damascus. The plateau, which is up to 1,000 m high, is bordered to the north by the Hermon mountain range (peak height 2,814 m) and to the south by the Yarmuk, a tributary of the Jordan. To the west is the Sea of Galilee, and to the east the gently sloping valley of the Wadi ar-Rukkad, on the Syrian side, forms a natural border. The north–south extent of the heights is around 65 km, the distance from west to east around 30 km. The largest Israeli-occupied town on the heights was Kuneitra.

From Israel's point of view, there was no alternative to installing a deeply echeloned defense immediately behind the ceasefire line to secure the course of the border up to the western break in the Jordan Valley, due to the limited depth of space available. In an emergency, this was intended to intercept an initial thrust and delay the enemy attack until the arrival of reserve units.

Israeli major general Yitzhak Hofi[1] was responsible for the northern front. He had taken over command from Major General Mordechai Gur, who had been appointed military attaché in Washington. Hofi analyzed the military challenges on the Golan Heights and recognized that the armies of Syria and Israel would be facing each other eye to eye in the event of a possible armed conflict on the open plain. There was no obstacle between the two parties that could have delayed the advance by an invading army. From a military perspective, this situation resulted in advantages in favor of the Syrian armed forces, which were trained according to Soviet doctrine.

The basic Israeli concept on the Golan was to maintain a front with relatively few troops at constant readiness, to build up defense operations based on air support, and to hold back reserve elements.

The Israeli fortification system south of the Hermon massif was supported by seventeen strongpoints, each manned by about a dozen infantrymen and protected by mines and wire entanglements. Nine armored platoons were distributed among the seventeen positions and were on standby. The Israelis also laid new roads to facilitate the movement of artillery and tank reserves in the event of a threat. In addition, the Israelis dug trenches at least 8–10 feet (2.5–3 m) wide all along the ceasefire line, laid minefields, and built firing positions on ramps for tanks to slow down an enemy attack.

Around seventy-five tanks from two tank battalions of the 188th Barak Tank Brigade and infantrymen from two infantry battalions of the 1st Golani Brigade defended the Israeli front to the west of the "Purple Line." These units belonged to the

---

[1] Yitzhak Hofi (1927–2014) joined the Haganah in 1944 and commanded a company during the 1948–49 War of Independence. He quickly rose to various leadership positions within the Israeli armed forces. In the 1973 Yom Kippur War, he was commander of the northern front and briefly took over as chief of staff in 1974. He then served in the Israeli secret service, Mossad. Among other things, he was responsible for Operation Entebbe. This was an operation to free Jewish hostages in Uganda who were being held captive by Palestinian and German terrorists in a hijacked Air France passenger plane.

36th Division, under the command of Major General Rafael Eitan. The trained paratrooper officer had taken command of the division on the Golan Heights only about a year before and moved into his headquarters in Nafakh.

The Syrian army also drew its conclusions from the defeat in the 1967 Six-Day War and installed a dense antitank defense system east of the "Purple Line" as far as Damascus. The Syrian general staff concentrated on laying prefabricated bridges and removing Israeli minefields. In the defensive lines themselves, the Syrians positioned dug-in Soviet-made T-34/85 tanks, 57 mm and 85 mm antitank guns, 100 mm multipurpose guns, and mobile units equipped with RPG-7 and AT-3 Sagger antitank weapons. In addition, there was a comprehensive air defense system comparable to that of Egypt, with surface-to-air missile batteries of the types S-75 Dvina (SA-2 Guideline), S-125 Neva (SA-3 Goa), and SK12 Kub (SA-6 Gainful) from Soviet production.

THE BUILDUP

In mid-September 1973 the Israeli air force intelligence service began reporting a threatening buildup of Syrian tank and artillery units at the ceasefire line. The Syrian surface-to-air missile system also seemed to be at a higher level of readiness.

On September 26, Defense Minister Moshe Dayan and his chief of general staff, David Elazar, visited the front line on the Golan. General Hofi explained the situation and added that Syrian medium artillery was being massed in the Jabah area, just a few kilometers east of the Syrian truce line—another indication they were planning an attack. In an interview, Dayan, who was accompanied by newspaper and television reporters, sent a warning to Syrian president Hafez al-Assad[2] to refrain from a further deployment of troops.

Since the Six-Day War, Assad had made great efforts to turn Syria into a superior military power with help from the Soviet Union. He saw this effort threatened by the small neighbor state Israel. He was thus interested not only in destroying Israeli, but

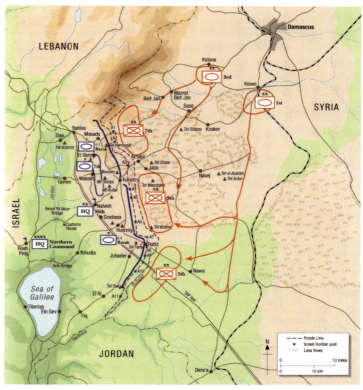

Positions of the Syrian and Israeli units shortly before the outbreak of war on the Golan Heights, October 1973. *Osprey*

in regaining the Golan Heights as well. He was convinced that Egypt and Syria together could defeat Israel in a two-front war.

The Israeli high command meanwhile placed the standing army at the highest state of alarm. South of Kuneitra, Eitan placed the 188th Barak Armored Brigade, under the command of Lieutenant Colonel Ben-Shoham, at readiness, with the 53rd Armored Brigade in the south and the 74th Armored Brigade in the north. He also ordered the immediate dispatch of the 7th Armored Brigade with the 71st, 77th, and 82nd Armored Battalions and the 75th Mechanized Infantry Battalion to the Golan as reinforcements.

This brigade was then at Be'er Sheva, in the south of the country, and was regarded as one of the best units in the Israeli military.

---

[2] Hafez al-Assad (1930–2000) belonged to the Alawite religious community and attended the military academy at a young age, where he was trained as a pilot. He joined the pan-Arabist-Socialist Baath Party in 1947. In 1963 he played a role in the Baath Party's seizure of power in Syria and was promoted to lieutenant general in the air force. With the loss of the Six-Day War in 1967, he gained further power, and after another coup in 1970, al-Assad had his rivals in government arrested and appointed himself president by plebiscite. Al-Assad shaped Syria into a dictatorship and crushed numerous popular uprisings. He died in 2000. His second son, Bashar al-Assad, became his successor at the age of thirty-four.

A few weeks earlier, its commander, Colonel Avigdor Ben Gal,[3] had greeted former members of the brigade at Latrun on the occasion of the twenty-fifth anniversary of the formation of the unit. Little did he know that just a few weeks later, his brigade would fight one of the fiercest tank battles in the history of the Israeli armed forces.

After the 7th Armored Brigade's arrival on the Golan Heights, the Israeli forces in the defensive positions numbered about 12,000 troops, with 180 tanks and numerous M113 armored personnel carriers and M3 half-tracks. The tanks were the Shot Kal Alef, upgraded Centurion heavy tanks with the 105 mm gun and the Continental diesel engine from the M48A3 Patton tank.

General Hofi, meanwhile, moved his headquarters to Camop Nafakh on the Golan Heights and ordered additional reserve units to prepare for mobilization. The staffs of the military administration at Kuneitra were withdrawn, and doctors and other medical personnel were transferred to the area. Furthermore, Hofi ordered the extension of existing antitank ditches and the laying of a large number of additional mines.

THE BATTLE OF THE GOLAN HEIGHTS

By October 6 the Syrian army moved no fewer than three infantry and two armored divisions with a total of about 70,000 troops toward the "Purple Line." Each infantry division consisted of two infantry brigades and one armored and one armored infantry brigade. The Syrian general staff envisaged the following plan for the campaign:

After the surprise attack by Syrian armored units, Shot Kal tanks of the 53rd and 74th Armored Battalions of the 188th Barak Armored Brigade move into firing positions, October 1973. *Israel Government Press Office*

- The 7th Division was to break through the northern sector at Kuneitra with the 68th and 85th Infantry Brigades, cross the Wasset road, and then swing north–south and link up with 9th Division.
- The 9th Division was to break through the central sector with the 33rd and 52nd Infantry Brigades and the 1st Armored Division at Tel Hara to Kuneitra, in order to advance toward the main link on the Golan plateau in the direction of Khushniya-Nafakh.
- The 5th Division, with the 61st and 112th Infantry Brigades, was to support the attack by the 9th Division, break through the "Rafid gap," and block the road to the Sea of Galilee.
- Simultaneous landings by paratroopers were to seize and keep open the Jordan bridges, in support of the advance to Galilee by the two armored divisions.

Each infantry brigade also included an armored battalion with thirty tanks, while each armored infantry brigade had an armored battalion and two mechanized infantry battalions. The three committed divisions had a total of 540 T-54/T-55 tanks, while the two armored divisions had 460 of the more modern T-62 tanks. The Republican Guard—also called the Assad Brigade—stationed at Katana, was to protect Damascus, the nation's capital and the seat of government. It was also equipped with T-62 tanks and BMP-1 armored personnel carriers. Including

---

[3] Avigdor Ben Gal (1936–2016) grew up in Lodz, Poland. After the Wehrmacht's invasion of Poland, he fled to Russia with his family. After the death of his parents, he migrated to Tel Aviv and joined the Israeli Defense Forces. He gained his first combat experience during the Suez Crisis in 1956 and in the Six-Day War 1967, where he was responsible for logistics in the staff of a brigade. In 1973 he took command of the 7th Armored Brigade and was promoted to brigadier general at the same time. After the Yom Kippur War in 1973, he commanded the northern front. After retiring from the military, he chaired the board of directors of Israel Aerospace Industries and the Israeli think tank International Policy Institute for Counter-Terrorism at the Interdisciplinary Centre Herzliya. He passed away in February 2016.

On the Israeli side, on the morning of October 6, 1973, General Hofi summoned all of his brigade commanders to report to Nafakh, to the base camp of the Golan forces. He showed them aerial photos of the situation on the ground, and intelligence information indicating that the Syrians were going to attack that day. The Israeli foreign intelligence service, Mossad, assumed that the attack was to be expected at about 1800.

But at 1350, the ominous sound of Syrian aircraft and ear-shattering explosions shook the Israeli positions. Simultaneously the guns of the Syrian 7th, 9th, and 5th Infantry Divisions opened fire on the enemy strongpoints all along the ceasefire line. After the artillery fire shifted farther forward, three Syrian infantry divisions led by armored brigades deployed in breadth attacked along the entire front line. The Israeli armored platoons immediately moved into their prepared positions and opened fire. While the Israelis were still concerned with the Egyptian invasion of the Sinai, the Syrian intervention in the north turned the Yom Kippur conflict into a two-front war.

In the north the Syrian 7th Infantry Division, with the 68th Infantry Brigade right and the 85th Infantry Brigade left, attacked from the area south of Hadr in the direction of Masada. Through the dust, the commander of the Israeli 74th Armored Brigade, Lieutenant Colonel Yair Nafshi, made out the telltale outlines of hundreds of armored vehicles, mine-clearing tanks, and trucks. He immediately ordered his armored companies' Shot Kal Alef tanks onto the ramps, and they opened fire from long range. The Israelis in fact succeeded in smashing the leading enemy unit right at the antitank ditch, delaying the advance by the Syrian 68th Infantry Brigade. The Shot Kal Alef tanks concentrated their fire on the bridge-laying and mine-clearing tanks and the armored vehicles of the engineers.

At the same time, the Syrian 9th Infantry Division attacked from the Kudne area, with the 52nd Infantry Brigade advancing on Kuneitra and the 33rd Infantry Brigade heading toward Tel Hazeika. Despite effective defensive fire from the Israeli 53rd Armored Brigade, by 1600 the 33rd Infantry Brigade penetrated to Tel Aksha and sent an armored battalion through Tel Hazeika from the southwest against Kuneitra. This breach of the front

Repairs are carried out on a Shot Kal tank near the ceasefire line, October 1973. *Israeli National Collection*

the previously mentioned dug-in T-34s, the Syrians had about 1,500 tanks available for the offensive. The Syrians thus enjoyed an eight-to-one numerical superiority in tanks over the Israelis.

The Syrian army also deployed numerous rocket systems such as the 9M21 (Frog 7) with a fragmentation warhead or cluster munitions, which had a range of up to 44 miles (70 km). This weapons system made it possible to attack targets far beyond the front, with no danger to the Syrian air force. For air defense, like the Egyptian armed forces the Syrians deployed the ZSU-23-4 Shilka. This antiaircraft tank weighed 20.5 tons and was armed with four ASP-23 liquid-cooled 23 mm cannon. These systems augmented the familiar antiaircraft batteries.

The Syrian army was under Defense Minister Major General Mustafa Tlas,[4] and the mobilized forces were commanded by Chief of the General Staff Youssef Chakkour.

---

[4] Mustafa Tlas (1932–2017) grew up in ar-Rastan, Syria. He studied at the military academy near Homs and became friends with the later Syrian prime minister Hafiz al-Assad at an early age. After the Baath Party coup in 1963, Tlas was appointed to the party's military committee and was given command of the 5th Armored Brigade. During the Six-Day War in 1967, he commanded the Syrian reserve and later served as chief of staff. In 1972 he became minister of defense. After the death of Hafiz al-Assad, Tlas remained a close confidant of Prime Minister Bashar al-Assad for a long time, until he retired from the Syrian military in 2004.

It quickly became clear to the Israeli general staff that the overwhelming might of the Syrian army could not be stopped by the two armored brigades of the 36th Division, under the command of Major General Rafael Eitan. In the photo, Major General Yitzhak Hofi (commander of the northern front) and Chief of Staff David Elazar discuss sending further reserve units to the Golan Heights, October 1973. *Israel Government Press Office*

was alarming, and General Hofi realized that the 188th Armored Brigade was overburdened with leading the defensive battle. He ordered the 82nd Armored Battalion of the 7th Armored Brigade, which had meanwhile arrived on the Golan, to move into the southern sector of front to take some of the pressure off the 53rd Armored Battalion. The 74th Armored Battalion, which was already engaged in fierce defensive fighting, was attached to the newly arrived armored brigade.

Brigadier General Ben Gal now sent all available units to the front line: in the far north was the 71st Armored Battalion, south opposite Kuneitra was the 77th Armored Battalion, and in the middle was the 75th Mechanized Infantry Battalion. The three Syrian infantry divisions continued to advance, taking heavy losses, along the entire front line, and the T-54/T-55 tanks, guns blazing, broke into the Israeli defensive positions one by one.

The Syrians exploited numerous breakthroughs against the 33rd Infantry Brigade on the southern front line and sent the 1st Armored Division through the open flank at Al Rafeed. At the same time, the 15th Mechanized Infantry Brigade of the 3rd Armored Division broke through gaps in the front at Kudne and sent units against the northern front line of the Israeli 7th Armored Brigade. The powerful Syrian air defenses, with their numerous SAM batteries, made life difficult for the Israeli air force.

The observation strongpoint on the south peak of Mount Hermon, which was held only by about two platoons of Israeli infantry, was seized by elements of the Syrian 82nd Paratrooper Battalion in the afternoon.

As darkness fell, the Syrian units began preparing for night action. Their tanks were equipped with infrared searchlights and night vision devices. This gave the Syrians a considerable tactical advantage over the Israelis, who neither had similar equipment nor assumed that in the event of an enemy attack, it would continue under cover of darkness. For this reason, the Israeli armed forces also acquired too few artillery illumination rounds and parachute flares for lighting the battlefield — a mistake that would come back to haunt them on the Golan Heights. Even support from the air force, which dropped flares, and the fact that at least a few tank commanders had night vision binoculars were of little help.

In the southern sector the enemy forced the hard-fighting units of the 188th Armored Brigade farther and farther back. Almost unopposed, the Syrian 51st Armored Brigade, with about a hundred T-54/T-55 tanks, moved powerfully along the front line toward the Israeli headquarters in Nafakh. The looming catastrophe was, however, forestalled by the courage of Lieutenant Zvika Greengold.[5] The twenty-one-year-old tank officer with his few armored platoons held out against the Syrian attackers for twenty hours, changing tanks six times after they were hit, and, in an extraordinary display of skill, destroying about forty armored vehicles of the Syrian army.

In the northern sector too, the battle raged relentlessly. At 0300 a tank commander reported from his disabled Shot Kal Alef the approach of the Syrian 78th Armored Brigade, which

---

[5] Zvika Greengold (1952–) grew up in the kibbutz Lohamey HaGeta'ot. At the age of twenty-one he joined the Israeli Armored Corps and was sent to the Golan front immediately after the outbreak of the Yom Kippur War in 1973. He is regarded as a hero in Israel since, leading a few Shot Kal Alef tanks and in an almost hopeless situation, he defeated numerous armored vehicles of the Syrian 51st Armored Brigade. After the war, he managed various companies in the food and chemical industries.

The tide turned and the Israeli army launched a counteroffensive across the ceasefire line into Syrian territory. The photo shows Shot Kal tanks of the 146th Reserve Division under Major General Moshe Peled, October 1973. *Israel National Collection*

was accompanied by elements of the 85th Infantry Brigade. These two units were supposed to attack the 7th Armored Brigade's open south flank and take out the Shot Kal Alef tanks on the tank ramps. If this plan had succeeded, both the northern and southern sector defenses would have been destroyed. Ben Gal subsequently ordered an armored company under the command of Captain Meir Zamir to meet the dangerous flanking attack. With his ten battle tanks, Zamir selected firing positions on both sides of the so-called road and waited in hiding. These Israeli tanks also had no night vision devices, so Zamir ordered the tanks to switch off their engines. Then they waited until the Syrian tanks were within firing range. Only then did a Shot Kal Alef switch on its searchlight, illuminating the battlefield. The rest of the Israeli tanks moved into firing position and in a short time knocked out about thirty T-54/T-55 tanks.

The commander of the 77th Armored Battalion, Lieutenant Colonel Avigdor Kahalani,[6] had a similar experience. After the commander of the 71st Armored Battalion was put out of action, he assumed responsibility for the unit. In the ghostly moonlight, he saw thousands of blinking colored lights advancing toward the firing positions of his two battalions. He ordered his tanks to hold their fire, while his tank commanders watched the infrared lamps of the approaching Syrian tanks through night vision binoculars. When the tanks moved nearer, the gunners were also able to make out the silhouettes of the Syrian armored vehicles under the guidance of their tank commanders. Kahalani first ordered the drivers to move toward the firing ramps and finally gave the order to open fire. Within a matter of minutes, numerous Syrian tanks were in flames, since the tank battle was fought at very close range. At one point, Kahalani saw that his tank was being illuminated by a Syrian infrared lamp, but by backing up at the very last second, he was able to cause the shot to miss by a few inches.

---

[6] Avigdor Kahalani (1944–) grew up in Nes Ziona, on the edge of the Judean hill country of Shefela, and studied history at Tel Aviv University. He joined the Israeli armed forces in 1962 and became an officer in the armored corps. In 1964 he was part of a delegation that evaluated the M48 Patton heavy tank in West Germany. In the 1967 Six-Day War, he led a tank company of the 79th Tank Battalion in the battles for Jerusalem, and in the 1973 Yom Kippur War he led the 77th Tank Battalion of the 7th Armored Brigade. He was awarded the Israeli Medal of Valor for his heroic service during the fighting in the "Valley of Tears." After ending his military career, he became an author (*The Heights of Courage: A Tank Leader's War on the Golan*) and politician. He was a member of the Labor Party and later minister of internal security during Netanyahu's presidency.

A Shot Kal tank moves out of Nafek in the direction of Kuneitra, October 1973. *Israel Government Press Office*

The defensive battle against the powerful Syrian opponent had begun. Both parties began a pause in the firing at 0100; however, they reorganized their units and took time to rearm and refuel. The scene, with burning and exploding tanks and the sight of crews fleeing and marked by shock, was like an inferno. Medical vehicles came forward to evacuate the dead and wounded, while workshop units recovered damaged tanks from the firing ramps. More than 130 Syrian tanks burned that night. The battlefield before the Israelis had become a tank graveyard and was later to go down in history as the "Valley of Tears."

On the southern front the Syrians resumed their successful battle at dawn with the 46th, 51st, and 43rd Armored Brigades and advanced energetically with about five hundred tanks at the exit from the Al Rafeed and Kwdana narrows. The Israelis were intercepting Syrian radio messages, which in the rush of victory reported, "We can see down to Galilee!" A Syrian breakthrough toward the hills bordering the Jordan seemed imminent.

On the Israeli side, the 53rd Armored Battalion had just twelve vehicles left. While they continued to defend bravely, they were hardly enough to stop the overwhelming Syrian force. Desperate, General Eitan ordered Colonel Ben-Shoman to immediately pull back toward Rafakh with the exhausted remains of the 188th Armored Brigade. However, the 115 mm guns of the T-62s of the Syrian 1st Armored Division continued smashing the Israeli defensive positions. The brigade lost more tanks, and Ben-Shoman was badly wounded when his tank took a direct hit.

Surprisingly, the Syrian command now decided to stop the advance by all its units on the southern Golan, to reorganize for a further offensive, and to move up reserve units. With their questionable order, however, the Syrians worsened a failure in the north rather than exploiting their success in the south.

Dayan and the Israeli general staff recognized the serious situation south of Kuneitra and sent two more powerful reserve divisions to the Golan: the 146th Division (Musa) with the 4th, 9th, 70th, and 205th Armored Brigades, under Major General Moshe Peled,[7] and the 240th Division (Laner) with the 17th and 679th Armored Brigades, under Major General Dan Laner.[8] The two divisions were to close the broken front south of Kuneitra so that Eitan's 36th Division could concentrate on the sector north of Kuneitra.

On the third day of fighting, October 8, the 7th and the 188th Armored Brigades were still in their firing positions, fighting at heavy cost against units of the Syrian 7th Infantry Division and elements of the 3rd Armored Division. The Syrians now also began trying to break the defense lines from the side with AT-3 Sagger antitank guided missiles and guided weapons fired from helicopters. In the north, between Hermonit and Bukata, there were just seven operational tanks of the 71st Armored Battalion, and farther south a few remaining tanks of the 77th Armored Battalion, while what was left of the 74th and 82nd Armored Battalions defended the front lines at Kuneitra.

After almost four days of nonstop fighting, without sufficient sleep or food and under continuous fire from tanks, artillery, and warplanes, the Israeli tank crews were completely exhausted.

---

[7] Moshe Peled; see portrait on page 160.

[8] Dan Laner (1922–88) grew up in Vienna and immigrated to Palestine with his parents in 1938 before the annexation of Austria by the German Reich. After serving with Yugoslav partisans in World War II, he joined the Palmach as an officer and took over the 1st Infantry Battalion of the Yiftach Brigade during the during the 1948–49 War of Independence. In 1950, Laner took over the Golani Brigade and was promoted to colonel. During the Six-Day War in 1967, as a brigadier general and deputy commander of the northern front, he was instrumental in planning the counteroffensive on the Golan Heights. After his important mission to stabilize the southern front line on the Golan Heights in the 1973 Yom Kippur War as commander of the of the 240th Division, he alternated between command and staff functions until his retirement from the army.

Soviet-made Syrian T-62 tank of the Assad Brigade. The T-62 was armed with the powerful 115 mm smooth-bore gun, which could penetrate the Israeli Shot tank at medium distances. The Syrian army employed more than 450 T-62 tanks in the fighting on the Golan Heights. Many were captured by the Israeli during the war, and after the war they were placed into service in special Tiran battalions as the Tiran 3 and Tiran 6. In the photo, one can see the sandbags used to protect the external fuel tanks. *Osprey*

The few remaining Shot Kal Alef tanks were able to decide the duels against the T-54/T-55s in their favor and halt the advance, but now, in the final hours of this decisive battle in the "Valley of Tears," the Israelis found themselves facing about a hundred T-62 tanks of the 81st Armored Brigade with their powerful 115 mm guns.

In this desperate situation, Lieutenant Colonel Kahalani radioed his crews of the 71st and 77th Armored Brigade to give them courage: "I don't know what's happening to us. It's just the enemy we've always known. We are stronger than he. Move forward and form a line with me. I will lead the way. Follow me!"

The Shot Kal Alef tanks slowly started moving, drove up the tank ramps, and simultaneously opened up with a precise barrage. With their strength fading and little ammunition, the Israeli crews fought off and finally stopped the attack by the Syrian 81st Armored Brigade. The crews of the surviving Syrian tanks turned their vehicles around and fled in panic.

Meanwhile, the Israeli reserve units were reaching the Golan Heights in ever-larger numbers, and the brigade commanders reorganized their frontline units to drive the Syrian forces back to the "Purple Line." In the south, the units of Peled's 146th Division established contact with Qatsrin and attacked enemy-occupied Khushniya. At the same time, the units of Laner's 240th Division pushed up the Yehudiya Gorge and fought a fierce battle with the Syrian 1st Armored Division. Since a breakthrough in the now-reinforced southern sector had become more difficult for the enemy, the Syrians planned to break through the front lines north of Kuneitra with the help of the 3rd Armored Division. These efforts failed, however, as a counterattack by the 7th Armored Brigade, which had been brought back up to strength, foiled the attack.

The Israelis now had to take advantage of the enemy's weakened situation and launch a counterattack on Syrian territory, especially since the Israeli military intelligence service was already reporting the approach of reinforcements in the form of Iraqi units. Nevertheless, as early as October 10, the Syrian general staff considered the campaign on the Golan a failure. It was now faced with the problem that the capital, Damascus, was in acute danger should the Israelis decide to advance into Syria.

THE COUNTERSTRIKE

On October 10, there was a meeting of the Israeli general staff to weigh an advance only as far as the "Purple Line," versus an attack deeper into Syrian territory. Defense Minister Moshe Dayan struggled with both options and was concerned about a possible reaction on the part of the Soviet Union. Chief of the General Staff Elazar, on the other hand, advocated an advance of about 12 miles (20 km) into the interior of the country, to limit Syria's conduct of the war and exert pressure on Egypt.

Prime Minister Meir finally ended the debate and decided in favor of Elazar's proposal. Two invasion routes were up for discussion, one of which offered advantageous terrain for tanks and led in a wide sweep to the southeast through the 18-mile-wide opening between the Lava Lake and the Jebab-Abab hills. This would cut off all access routes for Iraqi and Jordanian reinforcements. However, since the armored forces required for a large-scale offensive were not available, the Israeli leadership considered it safer to choose a more northerly route. This area was now the worst possible option, since an advance along the Hermon massif led through impassable terrain. However, there the Israelis had protection for their flank and a good view of the terrain ahead. In addition, this route also formed the route to Damascus.

However, the plan required a frontal attack to open the road from Kuneitra to Damascus. It was a demanding task for the exhausted Israeli crews, since this advance would go straight through the deeply entrenched Syrian defenses, with extensive minefields, dug-in tanks, and antitank positions.

General Eitan was to command the advance along the northern axis, with the 7th and 188th Armored Brigades in the lead. General Laner, with the 679th Armored Brigade and the 17th Mechanized Infantry Brigade, was to follow about two hours later the heavily fortified main road to Damascus. The mission of Peled's 146th Division was essentially to secure the entire southern wing of the Golan Heights, 10 km south of Kuneitra, pin down the Syrian 5th

Lieutenant Colonel Avigdor Kahalani, commander of the 77th Armored Battalion, led a heroic defensive battle against the onrushing Syrian armor. He described his leadership principles in his book *The Heights of Courage: A Tank Leader's War in the Golan*. In the photo, the acting chief of the general staff, Mordechai Gur, congratulates Lieutenant Colonel Kahalani on receiving the Medal of Valor, the highest Israeli military decoration. Sitting to the left of Gur is the Israeli president Yitzhak Rabin. Jerusalem, 1975. *Israel Government Press Office*

Infantry Division on the "Purple Line," and, where possible, support Laner's advance.

The Syrian 7th Infantry Division took up defensive positions north of Kuneitra up to the Hermon mountain range. Between Tel Hermon, Majdal Shams, and Beit Jinn, it posted the 68th Infantry Brigade on the right and on both sides of the Kuneitra–Arnabeh road. The 121st Mechanized Infantry Brigade was on the left. The 78th Armored Brigade took up defensive positions in the Tel Sha'ar area, and the 65th Armored Brigade was in reserve near Sa`sa. The latter was on standby, to provide support in the direction of Beit Jinn or Mashara if necessary. A Moroccan expeditionary corps was also located in this area and took up position at Beit Jinn.

After the bombardment of the Syrian positions by Israeli artillery, the 7th Armored Brigade, reinforced with two tank battalions from the 188th Armored Brigade, crossed the ceasefire line toward Masada at 1100 on October 11. The paratrooper brigade followed close behind. The Israeli attack took the Syrian 7th Infantry Division by surprise at its weakest point. It succeeded in penetrating the Syrian positions and pushing back the 68th Infantry Brigade by around 10 km by nightfall.

At about 1300, Laner's 679th Armored Brigade and the 17th Mechanized Infantry Brigade attacked on both sides of Kuneitra. Both units ran into the antitank forces of the Syrian 121st Mechanized Infantry Brigade, which from elevated positions inflicted considerable losses on the attackers. Only with combined forces did they finally succeed in forcing the passage of Kuneitra and the continuation of the attack in the direction of Khan Arnabeh, where the Syrian defense, with a combined system of guided antitank missiles, recoilless antitank guns, and targeted counterattacks, proved extremely effective in delaying the Israeli units.

But the situation was about to get worse for the attacking Israelis: the king of Jordan bowed to pressure from the Arab states involved in the conflict and decided to provide direct support to the Syrian armed forces, sending the Jordanian 40th and 92nd Armored Brigades. In combination with the two Iraqi armored brigades that were on the way, there was the possibility of forming a new powerful force with which to counter the Israeli attack.

On October 12, the Israeli 7th Armored Brigade attacked again on two main axes, and its northern group was able to break through to Beit Jinn and Mazraat Beit Jinn. In a fierce battle lasting more than six hours, they succeeded in capturing the villages and surrounding hills in that area. In the process, the Israeli troops also encountered the Moroccan battle group but quickly smashed it and, as night fell, assumed a defensive posture.

The southern units of the 7th Armored Brigade pushed through Hales along the main road to Damascus, but despite several outflanking attempts by two armored battalions, they were unable to achieve success against the defensive positions of the Syrian 78th Armored Brigade.

At the same time, units of Laner's 240th Division advanced in the direction of Cancar. As the Syrian defense skillfully held up the attack, General Hofi briefly attached the 20th Armored Brigade from Peled's 146th Division to Laner's division. This combined force succeeded in overcoming the Syrian defense.

General Elazar ordered his Israeli units to secure the areas of Syrian ground that had been taken, and to establish a defensive position on the new front line, Hader-Beit Shan-Masarat-Hales-Tel Shams. By then the Syrian forces were no longer capable of offensive action, and elements of the Arab coalition forces that had been requested to provide support had either halted during their approach or had already been wiped out in combat.

While the Israeli units were reorganizing, General Laner saw a huge dust cloud on the southern horizon in the direction of Tel Mashara. What he was seeing was the approach by the leading elements of the Iraqi 3rd Armored Division, with about 130 T-55 tanks and a mechanized infantry brigade with another sixty tanks. Two more armored brigades from the Khita-Sheikh Maskin area were following close behind. Later the Syrian 9th Infantry Division, with around two hundred tanks, was in the Sassa-Kisweh area, while the battered 1st and 3rd Armored Divisions took up defensive positions northwest of Damascus. Both divisions were resting and were in the process of receiving replacements in the form of crews and new T-62 tanks delivered directly from the Soviet Union.

Mossad estimates put the strength of the enemy forces facing the Laner Division on October 11 at about 1,300 tanks. Once again, the Israeli forces found themselves facing a tremendous challenge.

To fend off the immediate Iraqi threat on the southern flank, Laner's plan was to use the 679th Armored Brigade, under Brig. Gen. Ori Orr,[9] to initially attack the enemy at the foot of the ridge of Tel A-Sha`ar and Tel Ayouba. At the same time, the 17th Mechanized Infantry Brigade, to the east, and the newly 205th Armored Brigade, from Peled's division to the west, were to encircle and destroy the enemy.

In fact, the enemy units walked straight into the ambush. The Israeli tanks opened concentrated fire on the Iraqi tanks from 330 yards (300 m). Within minutes, the well-organized Israeli mechanized units destroyed parts of the Iraqi 3rd Armored Division, delaying their advance. Although the encirclement of the Iraqi battle groups inflicted losses, it could not prevent the withdrawal of these forces toward Tel Hara. Finally, the Jordanian 40th Armored Brigade arrived and took up defensive positions west of the Iraqi units. At the same time, from firing positions east of the Hermon slopes, Syrian artillery also succeeded in blocking the advance by the Israeli supply columns on the roads toward Saasa and Beit Shan. Thus, the Syrian front succeeded in fending off an Israeli pincer attack and avoided a total collapse of the front.

A Magach 3 tank during the counteroffensive into Syrian territory. The upgraded Israeli version of the M48A3 Patton with a 105 mm gun and Continental twelve-cylinder diesel engine proved very successful. October 1973. *IDF*

---

[9] Ori Orr (1939–) grew up in Kfar Haim and attended the University of Tel Aviv. He joined the Israeli armed forces in 1957 and commanded a tank company in the 7th Armored Brigade as a captain during the Six-Day War in 1967. In the 1973 Yom Kippur War, he led the 679th Armored Brigade. After the war, he took command of a division stationed on the Golan Heights in 1976 and later became chief of staff of the central front command. During the invasion of Lebanon in 1982, he commanded the units of the northern front. After thirty years of service in the army, in 1988 he took over positions in various companies and later became a member of the board of directors of Israel Aircraft Industries. In the 1990s, he served under the Peres presidency in various political functions in the Knesset.

By midday on October 15, the Syrian-Iraqi forces had regrouped and, as a result, stabilized the defensive front, especially between the slopes of Mount Hermon and Saasa to the southeast:

- The Syrian 7th Infantry Division secured the area between Mount Hermon and Kafr Shams. Its 81st Armored Brigade fortified the area around Beit Shan, while the 65th Armored Brigade occupied defensive positions west of Saasa, and the 62nd Armored Brigade secured the area around Cancar.
- The 9th Infantry Division took up position between Kafr Shams and Um Butna, with its front facing north.
- From Um Butna to the south was the 5th Infantry Division. In the rear were what was left of the Jordanian 40th Armored Brigade and elements of the Syrian 1st Armored Division and the 15th Armored Brigade east of Al Mal.
- South of El Mal were elements of the Iraqi 3rd Armored Division, while the bulk of the Iraqi 1st Armored Division was sent in the direction of Damascus and in the days that followed took up position in the area east of Al Mal.

In order to eliminate the threat posed to the Israeli invasion zone by the remaining parts of the Iraqi 3rd Armored Division, in the early afternoon of October 15, an Israeli thrust was launched from three directions against the Iraqi formations. By nightfall, the Israeli armored forces succeeded in wearing down the enemy, destroying numerous tanks and armored vehicles and thus largely eliminating the Iraqi reserve.

In the meantime, the Jordanian 40th Armored Brigade reorganized itself and joined the Iraqi 1st Armored Division. At the same time, the Syrian 7th Infantry Division also concentrated its infantry and mechanized units in the Sa`sa area. On October 19, all units from the Sa`sa area and the area east and south of Al-Mal launched an attack against the Israeli front line.

The attack began at sunrise. In fierce fighting, the Syrian 7th Infantry Division gained ground at Tel Shams, as did the Iraqi 1st Armored Division in front of El Mal. Despite this, however, elements of the Israeli 146th Division maintained control of the El Mal area and repulsed several waves of enemy forces, consisting of Iraqi, Syrian, and Jordanian units.

The battles for Mashara and El-Mal lasted into the night before the attacking armored forces withdrew to their starting positions. Apart from small-scale advances, there were no further tank battles in this area. In contrast, the fighting in the Tel Shams-Sa`sa area continued until October 21. Although the Israeli units initially had to retreat a few miles, they were eventually able to stabilize the situation again and finally advance to the outskirts of Sa`sa.

General Elazar now decided on one more operation: the recapture of the observation strongpoint on Mount Hermon. He gave the job to the Elisha and Hezi Paratrooper Battalions of the 37th Paratrooper Brigade and two infantry battalions of the Golani Brigade. The air force supported the operation, with CH-53G helicopters transporting the reserve paratroopers to the northeast peak of Mount Hermon. The Syrian commandos near the landing zone were taken by surprise and quickly overcome, while five Israeli artillery batteries kept heads down in the enemy positions on the peak.

In the last light of October 22, the battalions of the Golani Brigade took the area around the south peak of Mount Hermon. The Israeli special commandos ultimately forced the decision in hand-to-hand combat. Syrian resistance diminished at about noon, and a short time later the south peak with the observation station fell back into Israeli hands.

THE END OF THE WAR AND LESSONS FROM BOTH FRONTS

When the tide began to turn in Israel's favor on the battlefields along the Suez Canal and the Golan Heights, Moscow began pushing for a quick ceasefire. In particular, the Soviet head of state, Leonid Brezhnev, feared the loss of influence on the Nile and the Suez Canal. In order to emphasize his wishes, Brezhnev sent his prime minister, Alexei Kosygin, to Cairo on October 16. At the same time, US president Richard Nixon also sent his secretary of state, Henry Kissinger, to Moscow for negotiations.

After the Israeli armed forces continued their advance toward Suez on October 23, despite ongoing ceasefire negotiations, the Soviet Union threatened to intervene. Combat troops were to be deployed to Damascus and the Suez Canal, and SCUD medium-range missiles would be deployed east of Cairo and demonstratively equipped with nuclear warheads. Nixon responded to this threat by increasing the level of defense readiness to DEFCON 3.

As a result, the Soviet Union did not make good on its threats, and a confrontation between the nuclear powers was avoided. Both later jointly enforced a ceasefire in UN Security Council Resolution 338, which led to the deployment of a peacekeeping force, Israel's withdrawal from the west bank of the Suez Canal and Syria, and the immediate start of direct negotiations between the warring parties.

Both sides, Arab and Israeli, suffered considerable casualties in the Yom Kippur War of 1973. Egypt and Syria lost about 2,100 tanks, 850 armored personnel carriers, 550 artillery pieces, and 340 warplanes. Israel's losses included about 400 tanks and 102 combat aircraft. The Arab side lost about 16,000 killed, Israel 2,520.

Despite the generally high tank losses on both sides, caused mainly by the opposing armored forces and by the air forces and various guided weapons and rockets, in this war too, the tank remained the most dangerous antitank weapon.

In the first days of the war, the Israelis came to the realization that the operational doctrine of tanks leading the way against fortified targets, followed by supporting infantry and artillery, which had brought success in the Six-Day War of 1967, would no longer lead to success. The Israelis subsequently changed their method of advance, attacking with tanks and infantry combined, supported by the air force and thoroughly planned artillery and mortar fire. In the process, infantry units were given the task of eliminating enemy antitank guided weapons.

Israeli armored units always tried to first take possession of hills or ridges or to encircle or outflank enemy positions. They soon discovered, however, that the Arabs had adapted to this tactic and placed infantry with antitank guided weapons both on the commanding hills and the intervening ground.

The Shot Kal Alef tank, equipped with the powerful 105 mm gun and the Continental engine of the M48A3 tank, with automatic transmission, was assessed by the crews, especially on the Golan Heights, as the most reliable armored vehicle of the war. On occasion the armored battalions were mixed in such a way that Magach tanks provided covering fire from fixed positions while the Shot Kal Alef units carried out the attack. Where possible, aimed fire from a stopped tank was preferred over stabilized fire from a moving tank, in order to increase the probability of a hit.

For the Syrian crews of the Soviet T-62, with its smooth-bore gun and folding-fin-stabilized hollow charge ammunition, it was much more difficult to hit targets at ranges in excess of 1,960 yards (1.8 km). It could open fire from about the same distance with armor-piercing, fin-stabilized, discarding sabot ammunition. Wherever conditions allowed, the Israeli tanks, which had the advantage of having optical rangefinders, opened fire with HEAT ammunition from 4,375 yards (4 km).

That the Israeli armored units were able to maintain their dominant position in the Middle East in this war as well was less due to the superiority of the Shot Kal Alef and Magach tanks over the Soviet T-54/55 and T-62 than to the higher level of training of their crews. With precise and rapid fire, they were able to stop a massed advance by hundreds of Syrian tanks. Ammunition was loaded into the Israeli tanks not only during breaks in the fighting, but also during the ongoing battle. It is also worth noting that the Israelis aimed to use more than one crew per tank, since experience had shown that losses of tanks were proportionally lower than those of crews.

Although all the Syrian and Egyptian tanks were equipped with infrared and in some cases residual light amplifiers of British origin, the fighting — with a few exceptions — ceased at night on both fronts. The fact that the Arab units did not attack at night, although they would have been technically capable of doing so, could be related to their inadequate level of training. The Israelis lacked active infrared equipment and were lucky to have been involved in only two night battles on the Golan. The Israeli crews found an interim solution of using a single tank with a white-light spotlight to illuminate the battlefield, while the others were able to open up with targeted fire.

The massed use of the Malyutka infantry antitank guided weapon, better known as the AT-3 Sagger, came as an unpleasant surprise to the Israelis. On the second day of the canal crossing, there were no tank-versus-tank duels as Mandler, for example, had planned. Instead, his tanks encountered enemy infantry, in position with their antitank guided weapons far in front of the Egyptian tanks. The Israeli forces therefore had to learn to hit these positions with directed artillery and infantry. Only after they had been eliminated could the classic tank duels follow, in which the Israelis recorded numerous successes.

But there were other cases of negligence on the Israeli side: little attention was paid to available secret-service information, for example, concerning the use of the new antitank guided weapons or about the timing of the attack at the Suez Canal and on the Golan Heights. This is all the more astonishing because the Israelis had the complete Egyptian plan of attack but nevertheless failed to draw from this material for operational planning.

Despite the Israeli victory, the so-called Agranat Commission later investigated the failings by the political leadership, the secret service, and the general staff. The results, which were made public in April 1974, led to decisive personal consequences:

- Chief of the General Staff David Elazar was to bear direct responsibility for the failures on the eve of the war, both in the assessment of the situation and in the mobilization of the army, despite his intelligent and forward-looking leadership in battle. Elazar immediately submitted his resignation to the government.
- The commission accused Major General Shmuel Gonen of failing to fulfill his duties. As commander of the southern front, he had remained inactive despite reliable intelligence reports on enemy activities. Gonen also left the Israeli army and immigrated to Africa.
- Finally, the commission also accused the head of military intelligence, Major General Eli Zeira, of ignoring numerous warnings and of incorrect evaluations of situation reports. He resigned from his position in 1974.

According to the report, Prime Minister Golda Meir behaved correctly in the critical prewar days, used her authority wisely, and led Israel prudently during the war. Although Meir subsequently managed to win the elections in December 1973, her coalition lost further seats, making a majority in parliament impossible. She announced her resignation in April 1974.

The report was similarly positive about Defense Minister Moshe Dayan, since he had already warned the government about a possible war in May 1973. Nevertheless, public protests led to his resignation. It was not until Begin's government in 1977 that he returned to politics as foreign minister.

Finally, Egypt, though militarily inferior, emerged from the war as the political victor, since it led to the return of the Sinai and a lasting peace with Israel. In Israel, on the other hand, the war left an ambivalent impression on the population, even though the armed forces were victorious on an operational level, achieving a brilliant feat of arms with the encirclement of the Egyptian Third Army and the advance deep into Syria. After the resounding success in the 1967 Six-Day War, the Israelis had not expected such a strong military commitment from the Arabs.

THE AT-3 SAGGER ANTITANK GUIDED MISSILE

In 1958, the Soviet Union began development of antitank guided missiles and in 1960 placed the first production version, the 3M6 Shmel (AT-1 Snapper), into service with the Red Army. Introduced in 1964, the 3M11 Falanga (AT-2 Swatter) had improved speed and range and was the first Soviet guided missile that could also be fired from helicopters. Both the AT-1 and AT-2 could be used only from vehicles.

The requirement for a portable infantry version was finally explicitly included in the technical specifications for the subsequent model, primarily to strengthen the antitank capability of the Red Army's motorized rifle regiments. In 1965, the introduction of the 9K11 Malyutka (AT-3 Sagger) represented a milestone in the development of antitank guided missiles.

The Malyutka was first used in combat in April 1972 by units of the North Vietnamese army in Quang Tri Province, taking out an American M48A3 tank in the process. A year later, the Israeli armed forces also learned about the effectiveness of the Malyutka when hundreds of Israeli tanks were destroyed by Egyptian antitank guided-missile teams within a few days during the 1973 Yom Kippur War.

It was only with the advent of reactive armor that somewhat slowed the triumphal march of the Malyutka. Although the Red Army introduced the 9M111 Fagot (AT-4 Spigot) and the 9M113 Konkurs (AT-5 Spandrel), more-modern second-generation guided missiles with semiautomatic guidance from 1970, the Malyutka remained a central antitank system of the Warsaw Pact armed forces until the collapse of the Soviet Union and is still in use today in many Third World countries—sometimes in modernized versions.

The Soviet army's Malyutka teams consisted of three men: two to carry the rocket and launching system, and a team leader who was responsible for the periscopic sight and the control mechanism. After the missile was fired, it was controlled by means of a joystick connected to it by means of wire. A red light on the missile's rocket engine served as an aiming aid for the operator. While the probability of a hit was only in the 50 to 60 percent range, with an effective range of 2,734 yards (2,500 m) and great penetrative ability, the Malyutka was superior to all other antitank weapons then available to the infantry. In particular, it was much more accurate than the 105 mm guns of the Centurion and M48 Patton tanks. *David Schiller Archive*

Compared to other systems of that time, this novel guided antitank weapon was relatively light (the rocket weighed 24 pounds [11 kg] and the firing and control mechanisms 68 pounds [30.9 kg]) and, with its ability to penetrate 400 mm of armor steel, was capable of penetrating all known types of armor. Most importantly, the system could be assembled and made ready to fire in less than a minute. Using the periscopic sight, the missile could be guided from cover (trenches, foxholes, bunkers) without exposing the operator as an easy target. *David Schiller Archive*

Original designation	9K11 Malyutka
NATO designation	AT-3 Sagger
Service introduction	1963
Length	2 ft., 10 in. (860 mm)
Diameter	5 in. (125 mm)
Weight	24 lbs. (10.9 kg)
Rocket engine	single stage, solid fuel
Speed	377 ft./sec. (115 m/sec.)
Guidance	wire guided, MCLOS (manual command to line of sight)
Range	547–3,280 yards (500–3,000 m)
Warhead	5.7 lbs. (2.6 kg), hollow charge

The AT-3 Sagger Antitank Guided Missile

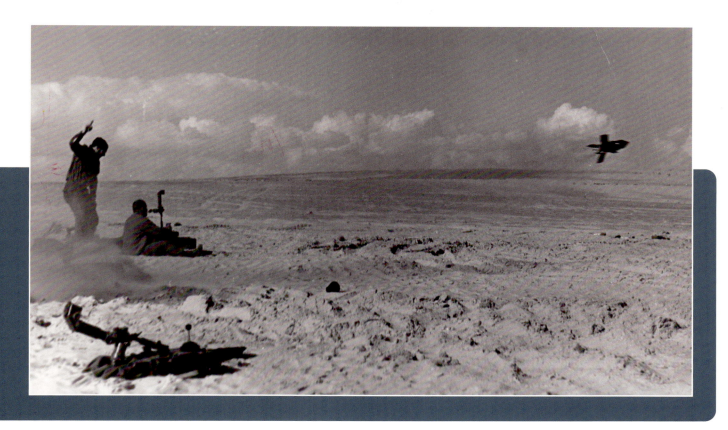

CHAPTER 17: The Yom Kippur War, 1973: The Northern Front (Fourth Arab-Israeli War)

PORTRAIT OF MOSHE PELED

Moshe Eisenberg (later Peled) was born in Ein Ganin, east of Tel Aviv, in 1925. He served in the Palmach as a young man and acted as a platoon leader and company commander in the Golani Brigade during the fighting around Upper Galilee and in the Jordan Valley during the War of Independence in 1948–49. Peled also took part in the fighting for Umm Rashrash, present-day Eilat, and was wounded there. After the war, he left the army and worked as a farmer in Nahalal, a village west of Nazareth.

Brigadier General Chaim Bar-Lev recalled Peled in 1956 on the occasion of the Suez Canal, and he was to take over an armored company. In 1962, Peled completed command training at the Army Armor Center at Fort Knox in the United States. After his return to Israel in 1964, he first commanded an armor battalion with the rank of major and later an armored regiment as a colonel. When the Six-Day War broke out in 1967, he served as deputy to Major General Elad Peled, the commander of the 36th Division. He played a leading role in the fighting in the Jerusalem sector and later also saw action in the capture of the southern sector of the Golan Heights.

Between 1968 and 1970, Peled formed the 670th Mechanized Infantry Brigade during the War of Attrition and, in his capacity as deputy commander, led the armored units in the Sinai. At the outbreak of the Yom Kippur War in 1973, he was promoted to major general and took command of the 146th Division. He led it as a reserve division to the Golan in order to support the delaying action by Rafael Eitan's 36th Division against the numerically superior Syrians. With the arrival of further reinforcements, the Syrian attack was halted, and a large-scale counteroffensive was launched east of the ceasefire line in Syrian territory. Syrian resistance soon waned, and on October 22, 1973, the guns fell silent.

After the Yom Kippur War, Peled assumed command of the Israeli Armored Corps. Against the background of the enormous materiel and personnel losses in the armored corps, it was his task to restore the striking power of the corps, compensate for the losses, and integrate new armored formations.

Peled doubled the number of armored divisions and with Israel Tal demanded the development of an Israeli tank—the Merkava. He also adapted the doctrine of the armored corps to take greater account of combined arms combat—that is, the interaction of infantry, tanks, artillery, and air force—in future. This decision was based on experience from past Israeli-Arab conflicts.

Peled's doctrine was first implemented in rudimentary form as part of Operation Litani, then applied to the full during the First Lebanon War in 1982.

During his service as a career officer, Peled studied history and economics at the University of Tel Aviv.

In 1980, he left the Israeli army and served, among other things, as managing director of the security company Elul Technologies and the defense company Rafael Advanced Defense Systems Ltd. He died in April 2000 and is buried in Nahalal.

Today, Moshe Peled is honored as one of the five most capable armor commanders in military history at the General George Patton Museum of Leadership at Fort Knox, alongside Erwin Rommel, Creighton Abrams, George Patton, and Israel Tal.

Major General Moshe Peled during his time as commander of the Israeli Armored Corps, June 1976. *Israel Government Press Office*

PORTRAIT OF AVRAHAM ADAN

Avraham Eidelson (later Adan) was born in 1926 in Kfar Giladi in Palestine. He joined the Palmach in 1943 and served during the War of Independence in 1948–49 as a captain in the 8th Infantry Battalion of the Negev Brigade. His infantry company was instrumental in the conquest of Umm Rashrash, today's Eilat.

The photo that captured the raising of the Israeli victory flag on the Red Sea on this occasion soon gained legendary fame and was compared to the raising of the American flag on Mount Suribachi on the island of Iwo Jima during the Second World War.

During the invasion of the Sinai and the battles against the Egyptian forces during the Suez Crisis of 1956, Adan led the 82nd Armored Battalion of the 7th Armored Brigade. After the war, he served as operations officer of the Israeli Armored Corps and later, after promotion to colonel, as commander of the 7th Armored Brigade.

In the 1967 Six-Day War, he served as deputy to the commander of the of the 31st Division, Avraham Yoffe, and once again fought against Egyptian units in the Sinai. After the war, he succeeded Israel Tal as commander of the Israeli Armored Corps and was promoted to brigadier general.

Adan served as commander of the 162nd Division on the Sinai front during the Yom Kippur War in 1973. After initial setbacks by his division on the Bar-Lev Line, the counteroffensive not only succeeded in crossing the canal north of the Great Bitter Lake but also achieved the destruction of numerous surface-to-air missile sites and the encirclement of the Egyptian Third Army. Even after the proclamation of the ceasefire, Adan and his unit continued to fight until October 25.

After the war, he served as Israeli military attaché in Washington from 1974 to 1977. In his 1980 book, *On the Banks of the Suez*, he impressively described the battle on the Suez Canal during the Yom Kippur War. Adan died in September 2012.

Avraham Adan, major general and commander of the 162nd Division, explains to Defense Minister Moshe Dayan the situation of his forces during the Yom Kippur War, October 1973. *Israel Government Press Office*

Chapter 18
Revolution in Tank Design: The Merkava

While the tanks of the NATO and Warsaw Pact nations were designed to be employed in the widest range of climatic conditions around the world, with the Merkava tank Israel took its own path in the 1970s. The armored vehicle was uncompromisingly tailored to the operating conditions in the Middle East and to Israeli operational principles. The Merkava Mark IV was the first combat vehicle to be fitted with a hard-kill active protection system. At almost 72 tons, it is still considered the heaviest and probably the best-protected series-produced battle tank in the world.

DEVELOPMENT

Shortly before the outbreak of the Six-Day War on June 2, 1967, the French government imposed an arms embargo on Israel, after which France ceased to be a reliable arms supplier. During the war, the Israeli armed forces fought with AMX-13, M50 Shermans, and Centurions against the Arab T-34/85 and M48 Patton. After the war, an agreement was reached with Great Britain for the purchase of obsolete Centurions from British stocks and the construction of a production line for the new Chieftain tank in Israel, from which the British withdrew under pressure from the Arab states in 1969. As a result, Israel realized that it had to become independent of the major powers in the field of weapons technology.

Development of the Merkava began in 1970 under the leadership of Major General Israel Tal, an experienced tank officer and intelligent project manager. Engineers, designers, and mechanics did not work separately in different offices and workshops, but together in a single large room—with the prototype under construction in the center.

The design of the new tank was to be specifically adapted to the operating conditions in Israel. The engineers also placed emphasis on a high level of protection for the crew, as well as the possibility of economic, largely independent production in Israel. In order to fulfill the first criterion, the engine was mounted at the front, in contrast to other main battle tanks. This provided additional protection against frontal attacks, especially with hollow-charge weapons. The hatch in the rear also allowed easier access to the crew compartment under enemy fire. Finally, the narrow turret reduced the frontal silhouette and thus the probability of enemy hits. Most of the ammunition was stored in the hull to reduce the risk of fire in the event of a hit on the turret. Protection at the expense of mobility was also given top priority in the design of the suspension: by dispensing with a torsion bar suspension, it was possible to simplify the design of the hull floor and, compared with other main battle tanks of the same generation, to significantly reinforce it for protection against mines and booby traps. If damaged (e.g., by mines and booby traps), the external autonomous swing arm assemblies can be replaced individually with little effort.

Apart from the protection, the Merkava has been consistently designed for use in Israel and neighboring countries. The air filters are optimized for use in the desert, the tracks lack the usual rubber pads, and there is no deepwater-wading equipment. Since the ground is mostly hard and stony and the troops did not require the vehicle to be transported by rail or air, there were no specific weight limits. As a result, the Merkava Mark I weighed an impressive 63 tons when it was launched. By comparison, the Leopard 2A4 weighed 55 tons and the M1A1 Abrams 57 tons.

The first prototypes from 1974 were still based on Centurion assemblies for testing purposes. The first official picture of a dedicated Merkava prototype appeared in the *American Armed Forces Journal* on May 4, 1977. Series production finally began in 1978 under the responsibility of MANTAK (Merkava Tank Office), which is part of the Israeli Ministry of Defense. The first Merkava Mark I was handed over to the troops in April 1979, and the new tank began supplementing the existing fleet of Centurions and M60s.

The first combat experience with the new tank, gained during the Lebanon War of 1982, flowed into the design of the Merkava Mark II, production of which began in 1983. In addition to modification of the 60 mm mortar—which could now be loaded from the fighting compartment without the loader exposing himself—a new Israeli-made transmission and a larger fuel tank were installed. There were also minor adjustments to the fire control system.

After the Merkava tank entered service in 1978, about seventy vehicles left the production line each year. Shortly after the Lebanon War of 1982, production slowed to about fifty tanks per year, as the authorities concentrated on overhauling and increasing the combat effectiveness of existing vehicles. The photo shows a Merkava Mark I from the first production batch, with typical exhaust system and turret stowage basket on the rear and sides of the turret. November 1978. *IDF*

The Merkava Mark II was the result of lessons learned in the Merkava's first combat use in the war in Lebanon in 1982. It featured enhanced armor, fire control, and propulsion systems. Survivability was also improved through the introduction of an explosion suppression system in the crew compartment. Heat sensors, combined with inert gas bottles, immediately extinguished fires. In the photo is a Merkava Mk II B Dor Dalet with added armor. The heavy and massive layout of the armor is especially evident on the bow plate element. *IDF*

Probably the most obvious change was the heavy chains on the rear of the turret, which was supposed to prevent antitank missiles from reaching the turret ring or detonate them prematurely. There were three subvariants of the Merkava II: the II B, with thermal-imaging device and upgraded fire control system; the II C, with supplemental armor on the turret roof; and the II D, with modular composite armor.

The Merkava Mark III entered service in 1989. Compared to the Merkava II, it had a more powerful engine, the hydraulic turret drive was replaced by electric motors, and the steel armor was replaced by composite armor. A minor but not insignificant change was the installation of a telephone on the rear of the hull, which enabled accompanying infantry to communicate directly with the tank's crew.

The most important innovation, however, was the introduction of the IMI (Israeli Military Industries) 120 mm smoothbore gun, which significantly increased the Merkava's combat capability. The numerous changes did, however, result in an increase in weight to 65 tons. There were also three subvariants of the Merkava III: the III B, with improved armor; the III Baz, introduced in 1995 with automatic target tracking, a backup camera for the driver, an air-conditioning system, and a modified NBC system; and the III D, with modular composite armor, improved tracks, and an autonomous weapons station.

The current production version, the Merkava IV, has been in production since 2003. The hull was completely redesigned to accommodate the new drive system (MTU 883 engine, Renk RK 325 transmission). A new fire control system includes an independent thermal-imaging system for the commander, a 360-degree camera system enables the crew to observe the immediate area around the vehicle, and the command-and-information system as well as the laser-warning system (Elbit Systems) have also significantly improved the tactical overview (locations of own and detected enemy units).

Due to losses to antitank guided weapons in the Second Lebanon War of 2006, starting in 2009 all Merkava Mark IV tanks were upgraded to Mark IV M Windbreaker standard with the Rafael Advanced Defense Systems Ltd. active defense system. The system not only automatically defends against incoming antitank missiles and guided weapons, but it also informs the crew of the location of the enemy that fired the weapon. The Merkava IV is thus the first production battle tank with a hard-kill active defense system.

In total, 2,270 Merkavas have been produced since 1979 (250 Mark Is, 580 Mark IIs, 780 Mark IIIs, and 660 Mark IVs). The local Israeli armaments industry has produced more than 90 percent of the components of the Merkava; thus, production of the tank is almost independent of foreign subcontractors.

CHAPTER 18: Revolution in Tank Design: The Merkava

TECHNICAL DETAILS

The Merkava has a crew of four: driver, gunner, loader, and commander. As well, up to six troops can be carried inside the tank at the cost of the ammunition stock.

The tracks and the six road wheels were taken from the Centurion, whose suspension had proved itself on the stony ground of the Golan during the Yom Kippur War. The road wheels are individually sprung with coil springs, and the first and last pairs of road wheels also have hydraulic shock absorbers. Not only does the coil spring suspension allow the same speeds as a torsion bar suspension, but it is also considerably less expensive, and damage caused by mines and IEDs can be repaired quickly. The rubber pads present on the tracks of most Western tanks were dispensed with, which led to relatively low manufacturing costs and simple maintenance, but at some cost in maximum speed.

The twelve-cylinder diesel engine (Teledyne Continental AVDS-1790-6A) installed in the Mark I produced 900 hp, which gave the 63-ton tank a relatively poor power-to-weight ratio of 14.3 hp/ton. The transmission (Allison CD-850-CBX) had two forward gears and one reverse gear; power was transmitted by means of mechanical superimposed steering. Fuel capacity was 370 US gallons, which gave the Merkava a range of 186 miles (300 km) (off roads) or 310 miles (500 km) (on roads).

In the Mark II the transmission was replaced with a hydromechanical automatic transmission (Ashot Ashkelon) with four forward and three reverse gears. The Mark III brought a more powerful but likewise air-cooled twelve-cylinder diesel engine (Teledyne Continental AVDS-1790-9AR) producing 1,200 hp, which gave the tanks, with its increased combat weight of 65 tons, a power-to-weigh ratio of 18.5 hp/ton.

The Mark IV introduced a liquid-cooled twelve-cylinder diesel engine (MTU 883) producing 1,500 hp, and a hydromechanical transmission (Renk RK 325) that "drives, steers, and brakes." As a result, the Merkava has a power-to-weight ratio similar to that of the Leopard 2A6M and a maximum speed of 40 mph (64 kph).

The hull floor is comparatively thick and—atypical for a battle tank—slightly V shaped, to better deflect the shock waves from exploding mines and improvised explosive devices (IEDs). The seats are decoupled from the vehicle floor so that the acceleration does not directly affect the crew in the event of an explosion. The fuel tanks are self-sealing to prevent fires, and from 1981 a fire suppression system was installed in the fighting compartment and a fire-extinguishing system in the engine compartment (both halon based).

In terms of armor, the Mark I and II lagged behind the state of the art—Israel still relied on armor steel in their construction,

Development of the Merkava Mark III began in August 1983. It underwent a fundamental change with respect to ballistic protection, firepower, and mobility. The tank's hull was lengthened by 18 inches (45.7 cm), and it had interchangeable additional armor modules and the new 120 mm MG251 L44 gun. Made by IMI, the gun is a copy of the German 120 mm weapon of the Leopard 2 and can fire all types of NATO 120 mm munitions. This enables Israel to quickly acquire ammunition from foreign suppliers in the event of war. In the photo is a Merkava Mk III D Dor Dalet. *IDF*

A Merkava Mark III during maneuvers. *IDF*

Merkava Mark I	
Type	Battle tank
Manufacturer	Merkava Tank Office (MANTAK)
Service introduction	1978
Number	250
Crew	4 (commander, gunner, loader, driver) + 6 infantry
Combat weight	67.2 tons (61,000 kg)
Length	24 ft., 7 in. (7,500 mm; not counting barrel), 27 ft., 3 in. (8,300 mm; with barrel)
Width	12 ft., 2 in. (3,700 mm)
Height	8 ft., 10 in. (2,700 mm)
Primary armament	M64 L17A 105 mm gun (62 rounds)
Secondary armament	1 × 12.7 mm coaxial machine gun and 2 × FN MAG 58 7.62 mm machine guns (10,000 rounds) SOLTAM 60 mm mortar (30 rounds) 2 × 6 smoke grenade launchers (24 rounds)
Fire control system	Knight Mark 1
Engine	Teledyne Continental AVDS 1790-6A 12-cylinder diesel engine, 900 hp
Transmission	Allison CD-850-6BX (2 forward gears, 1 reverse)
Power-to-weight ratio	14.8 hp/ton
Ground clearance	21.6 in. (0.55 m)
Wading ability	55 in. (1.4 m)
Trench crossing	118 in. (3.0 m)
Obstacle	39 in. (1.0 m)
Gradient	60%
Maximum speed	28.5 miles (46 kph) (on roads)
Fuel capacity	237.75 US gal. (900 liters)
Range	248 miles (400 km) (on roads)
Protection	Armor steel structure (cross-wall construction) NBC defense system Mark 1B: turret chains (against antitank weapons)

Merkava Mark II	
Type	Battle tank
Manufacturer	Merkava Tank Office (MANTAK)
Service introduction	1983
Number	580
Crew	4 (commander, gunner, loader, driver) + 6 infantry
Combat weight	68.3 tons (62,000 kg)
Length	24 ft., 7 in. (7,500 mm; not counting barrel), 27 ft., 3 in. (8,300 mm; with barrel)
Width	12 ft., 2 in. (3,700 mm)
Height	8 ft., 10 in. (2,700 mm)
Primary armament	M64 L17A 105 mm gun (62 rounds)
Secondary armament	1 × 12.7 mm coaxial machine gun (2,500 rounds), 2 × FN MAG 58 7.62 mm machine guns (10,000 rounds) SOLTAM 60 mm mortar (30 rounds) 2 × 6 smoke grenade launchers (24 rounds)
Fire control system	Knight Mark 2
Engine	Teledyne Continental AVDS 1790-7A 12-cylinder diesel engine, 950 hp
Transmission	Renk RK 304 (4 forward gears, 4 reverse gears)
Power-to-weight ratio	15.6 hp/ton
Ground clearance	21.6 in. (0.55 m)
Wading ability	55 in. (1.4 m)
Trench crossing	118 in. (3.0 m)
Obstacle	39 in. (1.0 m)
Gradient	60%
Maximum speed	34 miles (55 kph) (on roads)
Fuel capacity	237.75 US gal. (900 liters)
Range	310 miles (500 km) (on roads)
Protection	Armor steel structure (cross-wall construction) NBC defense system Mark II C: improved roof protection Mark II D: composite armor on the turret sides

while other main battle tanks of the time, such as the T-64, the T-72, the Leopard 2, and the M1 Abrams, already had modern composite armor. The frontal silhouette of the turret was kept very narrow. The turret sides were of bulkhead construction and allowed the cavities to be used as additional storage spaces for material and ammunition (12.7 mm). With the Mark II D version, additional composite armor was mounted on the outside of the vehicle to at least partially compensate for the tank's technical deficit. With the Mark II, steel chains were attached to the rear of the turret, which were intended to cause approaching projectiles to explode prematurely before they penetrated between the turret and the hull—this system was later retrofitted to the Mark I B as well.

It was not until the Mark III version that a modular composite armor system called "Kasag" was introduced, in addition to the complete redesign of the turret. The protection modules are designed in such a way that they could be replaced quickly and easily in the event of battle damage without having to cut open the turret. The hull armor remained unchanged on the Mark III. As with the Mark I and II, the engine at the front served as additional mass to increase the penetration distance of impacting projectiles.

The introduction of the new engine with the Mark IV also required an adaptation of the hull design, which included a changeover of the hull armor to composite materials. The turret of the Mark IV was again completely redesigned. In contrast to many other main battle tanks, in which the focus of the armor was placed primarily against a frontal threat of ±30 degrees while the flanks are relatively poorly armored, the Mark IV has consistently strong turret armor in the ±90-degree range, as well as very strong roof protection.

Since the Mark I version, the Merkava's active components have included a smoke-discharging system with six smoke grenade launchers on each side. With the Mark IV M Windbreaker, the Trophy hard-kill active protection system was also introduced. The latter uses a four-facet distributed phased-array pulse Doppler radar (Elta ELM-2133) to monitor the area around the tank, detect and identify approaching projectiles, calculate their predicted trajectory, and neutralize them with explosively formed projectiles before they strike the vehicle; the system has an automated reloading feature. If the predicted trajectory will not strike the vehicle, no countermeasure is activated. In any case, however, the crew is shown the location of the enemy shooter, and, if necessary, the turret can be automatically rotated toward the target.

By injecting diesel into the exhaust gas jet, the Merkava can conceal itself with smoke at any time. From the Mark III BAZ version onward, the tank also has a laser-warning system (Amcoram LWS-2).

The Marks I and II were originally armed with a 105 mm L71A M64 (license-produced version of the Royal Ordnance L7 M68) gun. Ammunition capacity was sixty-two rounds, of which six rounds were ready ammunition in a revolver magazine in the turret, the rest in the rear of the hull. The Matador 1 fire control system was equipped with a laser rangefinder. The gunner could select magnification factors of 1 and 8 on his sight (from the Mark II B version also with thermal imaging); the commander, factors of 4 and 20 on his periscope.

Beginning with the Mark III, the 105 mm gun was replaced by an IMI type L44 120 mm smooth-bore gun, which had the same performance parameters as the 120 mm smooth-bore guns used by Western battle tanks (e.g., Leopard 2, M1 Abams, Leclerc) and also fired the same ammunition. The larger caliber did, however, result in a reduction in ammunition capacity to forty-eight rounds. The also new Knight Mark 3 fire control system enabled the Merkava to fire while on the move. The commander was also given a new periscope with magnification factors of 4 and 14 and could also use the gunner's optical gunsight, which was stabilized in two planes (fivefold magnification by day, twelvefold by night). The Mark III BAZ also introduced a target tracking system, which automatically placed the hold point on the target.

The Mark IV received the Knight Mark 4 fire control system, with fully stabilized commander's periscope including thermal-imaging device, giving the Merkava full hunter-killer capability at night as well.

Merkava Mark III	
Service introduction	1989
Number	780
Crew	4 (commander, gunner, loader, driver) + 6 infantry
Combat weight	70 tons (63,500 kg)
Length	24 ft., 11 in. (7,600 mm; not counting barrel), 29 ft., 6 in. (9,000 mm; with barrel)
Width	12 ft., 2 in. (3,700 mm)
Height	8 ft., 10 in. (2,700 mm)
Primary armament	MG251 L44 120 mm gun (46 rounds)
Secondary armament	1 × 12.7 mm coaxial machine gun (2,500 rounds), 2 × FN MAG 58 7.62 mm machine guns (10,000 rounds) SOLTAM 60 mm mortar (30 rounds) 2 × 6 smoke grenade launchers (24 rounds) Mark 3D: Remotely Operated Weapon Station (R-OWS)
Fire control system	Knight Mark 3: hunter-killer capability, target tracking
Engine	Teledyne Continental AVDS 1790-9A R12-cylinder diesel engine, 1,200 hp
Transmission	Renk RK 304 (4 forward gears, 4 reverse gears)
Power-to-weight ratio	19.7 hp/ton
Ground clearance	17.7 in. (0.45 m)
Wading ability	55 in. (1.4 m)
Trench crossing	118 in. (3.0 m)
Obstacle	39 in. (1.0 m)
Gradient	60%
Maximum speed	37 miles (60 kph) (on roads)
Fuel capacity	290 US gal. (1,100 liters)
Range	310 miles (500 km) (on roads)
Protection	Composite armor Mark III D: added protection module hull + turret

An FN MAG 7.62 mm × 51 machine gun is mounted coaxially. Two other weapons of this type are mounted on the commander's and loader's hatches. Ammunition capacity for the machine guns is 10,000 rounds. From the Mark III version onward, a Browning M2 12.7 mm heavy machine gun can also be mounted on the gun mantlet for improved penetrative ability against lightly armored targets.

As an additional weapon, the Merkava also has a 60 mm mortar. In the Mark I, this still worked on the muzzle-loading principle (i.e., the commander had to expose himself to load the weapon), but from the Mark II onward, the mortar can be loaded from the fighting compartment by the loader. The mortar fires explosive, smoke, and flare rounds, with an ammunition supply of thirty rounds.

A rearview camera was introduced with the Mark III BAZ, and from the Mark IV version onward, the Merkava has a 360-degree camera system, which enables the crew to observe the area around the tank without gaps and automatically with the help of image-processing algorithms. The combination of the command-and-information system also introduced with the Mark IV and the Trophy active protection system provides the crew of the Merkava with a comprehensive situational picture that is currently unique for a series-produced main battle tank.

The Merkava Mark IV Barak currently represents the pinnacle of modern battle tank design, bringing together Israel's extensive combat experience and technological expertise. This latest addition to the Merkava series is more than just an armored vehicle; it is a fully integrated combat system designed to meet the multifaceted challenges of the modern battlefield.

A significant feature that sets the Merkava Mk. IV Barak apart is the integration of artificial intelligence (AI) into its operating systems. This AI assists in threat identification and decision-making processes and can prioritize targets in real time, significantly reducing the cognitive load on the crew. The result is a faster, more accurate response to threats, which increases both the tank's lethality and the survivability of its crew.

This protection has been supplemented by an improved version of the Trophy active protection system and a modular additional protection concept. The latter primarily heightens the protection provided by the vehicle floor against mines and IEDs.

With the Iron Vision "see-through" helmet-mounted display, the crew can see their immediate surroundings virtually without having to expose themselves. This is achieved by capturing and transmitting real-time images from the outside to the crew's helmet displays, creating a 360-degree field of view around the tank. This technology marks a significant advance in armored warfare, since it greatly improves the situational awareness of the crew in a closed-hatch armored-vehicle environment.

Merkava Mark IV	
Service introduction	2003
Number	360
Crew	4 (commander, gunner, loader, driver) + 6 infantry
Combat weight	71.65 tons (65,000 kg)
Length	24 ft., 11 in. (7,600 mm; not counting barrel), 29 ft., 6 in. (9,000 mm; with barrel)
Width	12 ft., 2 in. (3,700 mm)
Height	8 ft., 10 in. (2,700 mm)
Primary armament	MG253 L44 120 mm gun (48 rounds)
Secondary armament	Remotely Operated Weapon Station (R-OWS) 1 × 12.7 mm coaxial machine gun (2,500 rounds), 2 × FN MAG 58 7.62 mm machine guns (10,000 rounds) SOLTAM 60 mm mortar (30 rounds) 2 × 6 smoke grenade launchers (24 rounds)
Fire control system	Knight Mark 4
Engine	General Dynamics GD883 12-cylinder diesel engine, 1,500 hp
Transmission	Renk RK 325 (5 forward gears, 2 reverse gears)
Power-to-weight ratio	24.6 hp/ton
Ground clearance	17.7 in. (0.45 m)
Wading ability	55 in. (1.4 m)
Trench crossing	118 in. (3.0 m)
Obstacle	39 in. (1.0 m)
Gradient	60%
Maximum speed	40 mph (64 kph) (on roads)
Fuel capacity	370 US gal. (1,400 liters)
Range	310 miles (500 km) (on roads)
Protection	Composite armor NBC defense system Mark IV M: Rafael TROPHY active defense system Mark IV M: Amcoram LWS-2 laser warning system

The IDF is committed to future-proofing the Merkava Mk. IV Barak. Continual upgrades to sensors, armor, and armament are planned, as well as the integration of unmanned systems and robotics. These advances will ensure that the Barak remains at the forefront of tank technology to successfully meet the challenges of the future.

The next step in the evolution of the Merkava tank was the Mark IV. This new vehicle was to be a fully digitalized main battle tank combining electronics, sensors, and computers in a single battle management system. Real-time information on the situation can be exchanged among the crew of a tank as well as between tanks. This allows a better overview of the battlefield and thus increased survivability. With the option of saving situation maps, these can later be used for debriefing or training purposes. The picture shows an armored platoon with Merkava Mk IV P tanks during maneuvers in the Negev desert. *IDF*

A Merkava Mark IV tank equipped with the Trophy active defense system developed by Rafael Advanced Defense Systems Ltd. A radar system mounted on the tank with 360-degree all-around coverage locates an approaching projectile, calculates its azimuth and elevation angle, as well as the speed, distance, and time of impact, and initiates a countermeasure in the form of an exploding charge shortly before impact. *IDF*

IN ACTION

The Merkava had its baptism of fire in the First Lebanon War in 1982, where it proved itself superior to the Syrian T-62 and largely immune to antitank weapons (AT-3 Sagger and RPG-7). Despite several losses, the Israeli Armored Corps regarded the new tank as a significant improvement over the Centurion.

During the Second Intifada in February 2002, a Merkava Mark III was destroyed by an explosive device with an estimated 220 pounds (100 kg) of TNT, killing all four crew members. Two more Merkavas were destroyed in March 2002, and five crew members lost their lives.

In the Second Lebanon War in 2006, the Hezbollah employed more than a thousand antitank rockets and guided missiles, including the more modern, Russian-made RPG-29 Vampir, 9K113 Konkurs, 9K115-2 Metis-M, and 9K135 Komet. This resulted in minor damage to eight Merkavas, the temporary unserviceability of forty-two more (primarily Mark IIs and IIIs), and the complete destruction of five Merkavas (2 Mark IIs, 1 Mark III, and 2 Mark IVs). On twenty-one of these vehicles, it was later found that the armor had been completely perforated, fifteen by antitank weapons and six by IEDs and antitank mines.

During the Israeli Operation Cast Lead in Gaza from December 27, 2008, to January 18, 2009, the Israeli forces committed a total of 140 Merkavas (Marks II, III, and IV). By adapting their tactics and training on the basis of experience in the Second Lebanon War of 2006, the tanks were used more successfully, and not a single Merkava was lost during the hostilities.

In December 2010, Hamas fired a type 9K135 Komet antitank guided missile at a Merkava III stationed at Al-Bureij, on the Gaza-Israel border. The warhead perforated the tank's armor but caused no harm to the crew.

As a result of this attack, Israel decided to deploy the first armored battalion equipped with the Merkava Mark IV M along the Gaza Strip. On March 1, 2011, a Merkava Mark IV M was attacked by Hamas, and the approaching missile was neutralized by the active defense system, making this the system's first operational success.

The 401st Brigade, which was equipped with the Merkava Mark IV M, was committed during the Israeli Operation Protective Edge from July 8 to August 26, 2014, whose target was the Hamas tunnel network in the Gaza Strip. During the intensive fighting, the Trophy active defense system proved itself under real-life conditions for the first time, since dozens of antitank weapons were intercepted and not a single Merkava was destroyed by enemy rockets/missiles.

A Hotchkiss H-39 next to a Merkava Mark I during the Israeli independence day celebrations, Jerusalem 1978. *Israel Government Press Office*

THE IRON VISION SYSTEM BY ELBIT SYSTEMS

The Iron Vision system by Elbit Systems is a helmet-integrated vision system for tank crews. Designed to increase the situational awareness and combat effectiveness of armored vehicles, Iron Vision provides a seamless 360-degree panoramic view of the battlefield without the crew needing direct visual contact with the outside world. This system is part of the next generation of combat vehicle technologies and overcomes the traditional limitations of armored vehicles by using virtual-reality technologies to feed information about the immediate environment directly into the crew's field of vision.

Iron Vision combines different technologies into an effective complete system:

- **Helmet-mounted display** (HMD): Iron Vision uses an HMD system that enables the crew to see information and data in real time directly in front of their eyes. The information is projected onto the helmet visors, enabling intuitive and immediate situation analysis.
- **360-degree vision**: With cameras and sensors mounted all around the vehicle, Iron Vision provides a complete all-round view. This enables crew members to identify hazards and targets without having to physically move outside the protection of the vehicle.
- **Augmented reality** (AR): Iron Vision integrates AR technology to overlay real images with additional information. This can include marking targets, highlighting threats, or displaying navigation routes.
- **Integration with other systems**: The system is designed to interact seamlessly with other onboard computer systems and sensors in the vehicle. This allows data from reconnaissance drones, satellite images, and other information sources to be fed into the user's field of vision.

This offers tank crews the following advantages, among others:

- **Improved situational awareness**: The comprehensive view increases the crew's ability to perceive their surroundings and react quickly to threats.
- **Crew protection**: Since crew members do not have to leave the vehicle to observe the battlefield, Iron Vision improves protection against enemy fire and environmental influences.
- **Faster decision-making**: Real-time visualization and data integration enables faster analysis and decision-making under combat conditions.
- **Night combat capability**: The high-resolution cameras and sensors allow the tank to operate in all lighting conditions, including night operations.

ISRAEL TAL:
THE PRACTICE OF ARMORED WARFARE

(Speech by Israel Tal to the symposium of the Swiss War Technology Society, 1984)

INTRODUCTION

The views set out below are based on combat experience from the Middle East wars from 1956 to 1982, in which up to 1,200 modern and older tanks, of both Eastern and Western origin, were deployed simultaneously. Combat was conducted with the aid of state-of-the-art communications and reconnaissance equipment, with the air force providing direct support for the armored advances. Especially in the First Lebanon War in 1982, both warring parties also used combat helicopters in large numbers.

Experiences of the Israeli army:

- The operational decision was brought about with armored units as the decisive offensive element. They generated the decisive effect in large, concentrated formations. The use of small numbers of dispersed tanks always resulted in failures. Experience shows that attacking tanks suffer heavy losses. When leading a battle, it is therefore constantly a question of where the losses are to be accepted so that the decision can be forced. For this reason, key decisions must be made early on in the battle.
- Mounted armored infantry have never been a success. The best armored personnel carrier is always a poor battle tank. Battle tanks should therefore always be used for combat operations that would allow mounted infantry to fight. The armored personnel carrier gives the armored infantry mobility and splinter protection in the approach.
- Infantry can decide an action only at the tactical level.
- Close air support: The development and deployment of portable surface-to-air missiles is increasingly diminishing the capability of employing the air force to provide direct support. Therefore, in the future, large numbers of combat helicopters will take over the role of "flying artillery."
- Reconnaissance must seek and maintain contact with the enemy. Through the use of modern reconnaissance assets, like remotely controlled drones carrying cameras, information is acquired and forwarded faster and more securely. With this, senior command quickly obtains a good picture of the situation, whose evaluated findings can be quickly transmitted to subordinate units.

THOUGHTS ON THE DESIGN OF A NEW BATTLE TANK

Overriding Considerations

As described above, tanks are employed en masse in concentration. For Israel this creates the requirement to procure tanks in large numbers, and they must therefore be inexpensive and correspondingly simple in design. Since tanks never fight alone, different tanks and their effect in combination should be compared. The evaluation of the technical specifications of an individual tank is therefore only of moderate importance. Individual tanks put out of action are not significant from this point of view.

Hits and Their Effect

Most hits penetrate the tank. The projectiles that enter the tank generally inflict enormous damage. On average, one dead and two wounded must be expected from each hit. In 20–40 percent of cases the wounded suffer primarily from burns. Older-type tanks have a high probability of exploding when hit. The latest type of vehicles are likely to take 50 percent of hits without exploding. Losses are primarily attributable to hits in the ammunition storage and hydraulics.

The following main design requirements have emerged on the basis of these findings:

- Separation of the ammunition and hydraulics. Or replacement of the hydraulics with a hit-resistant power transfer system.
- Separation of the crew from the ammunition and hydraulic components

Armor and Fire Protection

The evaluation of damaged tanks reveals that the 60-degree frontal area is most at risk. Approximately 50 percent of hits were found in this area. Furthermore, the hits are evenly distributed between the turret and the hull. Even on the most-modern tanks, the armor protection is concentrated in the front area and corresponds to that of a good, armored personnel carrier. Since essential subsystems are also located in the hull, this distribution is considered inadequate. There is therefore a need for more balanced armor protection.

In the interior, the protection of the crew can be considerably increased by clever compartmentalization in line with the main design requirements mentioned above. Since powder fires cannot be extinguished and powder self-ignites at a temperature of approximately 170 degrees Celsius (338 degrees Fahrenheit), chain reactions must be prevented, and the resulting pressure must be released to the outside. The designer is also faced with the problem of how to achieve maximum protection for the crew by optimally arranging the armor and vehicle components. In the Merkava tank, we have been able to use 70 percent of the vehicle's weight to protect the crew.

Tank Dimensions
The size of a tank is not so important in itself. A small turret silhouette is decisive. A tank should not be "small" and compact. Experience with small, well-armored Eastern vehicles showed that in 95 percent of cases, they were "mobile bombs" when hit.

Internal Power Transfer
To date, no nonflammable hydraulic oil has been found. For this reason, protection against burns caused by defective hydraulics is particularly important. A good result was achieved with the Merkava tank by separating the crew from the hydraulic components as consistently as possible and by design measures that immediately interrupt the flow of oil in the event of a defect. In the First Lebanon War in 1982, for example, no Merkava crew was lost due to hits to the hydraulics.

President Levi Eshkol (*with binoculars*) and Major General Israel Tal (*right*) observe a maneuver by the Israeli Armored Corps, 1966. *Israel Government Press Office*

Firepower
Not only the gun and fire control system are of great importance. If one side runs out of ammunition at a critical moment in the battle, the number of available rounds of ammunition had a decisive influence on success.

Mobility
The mass of the tank should also be considered in this regard. Combat experience shows the following:

- The mobility of a tank is first and foremost a function of the psychological status of the driver and tank commander.
- The individual tank must never be faster than the mass of tanks.
- The ability to negotiate obstacles is more important than maximum speed.
- A particularly high acceleration is not essential.
- Good climbing speed is required: 12 mph (20 kph) on a 10 percent gradient, 3 mph (5 kph) on a 60 percent gradient.

Overall, a power-to-weight ratio of 17–20 hp per ton is sufficient.

Repair Service
The crew should be able to repair technical defects itself.

Close-Range Defense of the Tank
When at readiness, the tanks should be able to be protected by their own crews. For this reason, and because a certain reserve of personnel is necessary in the tank itself during combat, the crew should have a minimum of four men.

Author's comments: The Merkava tank began leaving the production line in 1978, experienced its baptism of fire in the First Lebanon War in 1982, and still today forms the backbone of the Israeli Armored Corps.

Chapter 19
Operation Peace for Galilee: The Lebanon Offensive, 1982

BACKGROUND

Throughout the period of diplomatic efforts following the 1948–49 War of Independence, hostilities between Israel and the surrounding Arab states continued uninterrupted, and the Palestinian paramilitary organizations continued to be active. For a solution to the so-called Palestinian problem could probably have been found within the ceasefire limits of the UN Partition Plan of November 1947, but with the founding of the Israeli state and the attacks on Israel by the Arab states, such possibilities once again receded into the distance.

Past Israeli victories, particularly the Six-Day War and the resulting territorial gains, had exacerbated the situation with the Palestinians, since much of the Palestinian population came under Israeli occupation and administration as a result. This triggered an ongoing refugee movement, with the surrounding Arab states interning their Palestinian brothers in refugee camps.

In this context, underground organizations such as the guerrilla organization Fatah, which carried out attacks on Israel, also gained strength. Its founder, Yasser Arafat,[1] saw armed struggle as a suitable means of achieving Palestinian independence. This idea was not new but was in line with contemporaneous revolutionary thought and the related experiences from Cuba, Vietnam, China, and Algeria. The Fatah founders were particularly impressed by the Algerian example of the struggle by the Front de Libération Nationale (FLN) against the French colonial rulers. While the FLN was unable to defeat the far-superior French forces in the Algerian war of 1962, it was able to force France to seek a political solution to the conflict.

This successful struggle for independence by supposedly inferior forces against the superior oppressors had achieved exactly what the founders of Fatah dreamed of for Palestine. Algeria subsequently became the most important supporter of Fatah, supplying weapons and even trained Fatah fighters — called Fedayeen.

Egyptian president Gamal Abdel Nasser also recognized the political and military potential of the young Palestinians living in refugee camps. Nasser finally commissioned his confidant Ahmed Shuqairi in January 1964 with the founding of the so-called Palestinian Liberation Organization (PLO), which initially recruited mainly from the refugee camps. The organization's goal was to liberate Palestine, but under the supervision of the other Arab states. Well financed, with a broad base of support, the PLO was not only a rival but also an existential threat to Fatah. To avoid losing potential Palestinian fighters to the PLO, Arafat now saw a stepping up of the armed struggle against Israel as the only way to raise Fatah's profile.

Fatah fighters carried out about fifty attacks against Israeli civilian installations between September 1967 and January 1968. These actions failed, however, to spark a mass uprising against the Israelis among the Palestinians, and so Fatah withdrew its fighters into Jordan and Lebanon. Fatah established its military and political base in the Jordanian border city of Karameh in the Jordan Valley, where many Palestinians had fled to after the Six-Day War.

The Israeli defense minister, Moshe Dayan, reacted immediately to this retreat, which he saw as an opportunity to destroy Fatah. He ordered units of the 7th and 60th Armored Brigades plus the 35th Paratrooper and 80th Infantry Brigades, including five battalions of artillery, to the west side of the Jordan at the Allenby and Damia Bridges. Major General Uzi Narkiss, commander of the central front during the Six-Day War, was to lead the Israeli force. Jordanian military intelligence, however, recognized the buildup

---

[1] Yasser Arafat (1929–2004), born and raised in Cairo, became involved in the Arab national movement in Palestine from an early age. Arafat studied at Cairo University in the 1950s, served as a lieutenant in the Egyptian army, and fought against the allied nations in the Suez War in 1956. Arafat founded the Movement for the Liberation of Palestine (al-Fatah) in 1957, served as its chairman in 1968, and later became leader of the Palestine Liberation Organization (PLO). After the defeat in the Israeli campaign in Lebanon in 1982, Arafat fled to Tunisia. As a result of the autonomy agreement, Arafat returned to Palestine in 1994 after twenty-seven years in exile and founded the Palestinian Authority. In December 1994, he won the Nobel Peace Prize, together with Shimon Peres and Yitzhak Rabin. In 2000, Arafat negotiated with Israeli prime minister Ehud Barak and American president Bill Clinton at Camp David on the creation of a Palestinian state. Arafat died in 2004. His wish to be buried on the Temple Mount in East Jerusalem was firmly rejected by the Israeli government.

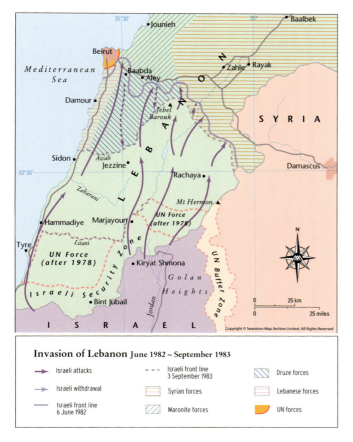

Invasion of Lebanon June 1982 – September 1983
- Israeli attacks
- Israeli withdrawal
- Israeli front line 6 June 1982
- Israeli front line 3 September 1983
- Syrian forces
- Maronite forces
- Druze forces
- Lebanese forces
- UN forces

of troops in March 1968 and interpreted it as a threat to the capital city of Amman. Two brigades of the Jordanian 1st Infantry Division supported by tank units subsequently moved out and took up positions east of the Jordan bridges.

The Israeli battle plan called for a frontal attack on Karameh by one battle group, while another carried out an encirclement, plus an airborne landing, which were to result in its fall. On March 21, 1968, the Israeli force, with about 15,000 troops, crossed the Jordan River and attacked.

The crossing of the Allenby Bridge and the landing by the paratroopers were successful. The secondary thrust, however, met fierce Jordanian and Palestinian resistance, despite which the Fatah camp was destroyed. The attempt to encircle the city failed, however, and the Israeli forces withdrew back across the Jordan before nightfall.

Since the Fatah camp in Karameh had been destroyed, the Israeli command considered the operation a success. The Jordanians, on the other hand, saw their successful defense of the city as a triumph, and Fatah believed that the fighting had destroyed the myth of Israeli invincibility.

The Arab world also celebrated the clash as a great victory, which restored Arab honor tarnished by defeat in the Six-Day War. The battle also confirmed Fatah's path and led to its takeover of power within the PLO. Fatah quickly grew to become its largest faction, and in February 1969 the central committee of the Palestinian Liberation Organization elected Yasser Arafat as its chairman.

While Fatah established good contacts with most Arab governments after coming to power, relations with Jordan remained strained. After the expulsion of 1948, the kingdom was home to the largest Palestinian exile community, with around 750,000 members. After the Six-Day War in 1967, they were joined by around 250,000 additional Palestinians, most of whom were accommodated in refugee camps along the east bank of the Jordan River.

From Arafat's point of view, Jordan appeared to be the most natural starting point for guerrilla operations, as well as the ideal base for the entire Palestinian resistance and a secure headquarters for its leaders. The Fatah leadership armed thousands of refugees who entered Karameh and formed their own security forces to control both the camps and life outside. Heavily armed, they moved freely and shaped the street scene in many places, even in the capital, Amman. Between 1968 and 1970, the Palestinian resistance movement continued to expand its power in Jordan. In the north of the country, the Jordanian government temporarily lost control of entire towns and regions, while the PLO was able to establish a sort of "state within a state."

From the point of view of Jordanian king Hussein, the Palestinian resistance movement in Jordan thus became an uncontrollable power factor that not only would bring down massive Israeli retaliatory strikes but would also call into question the authority of the royal family and thus threaten Hussein's rule.

This simmering conflict escalated in September 1970. The catalyst was the plan for a peace agreement among Israel, Jordan, and Egypt, which was presented by American secretary of state William P. Rogers. This document, known as the "Rogers Plan," also contained stricter conditions for the Fedayeen, including, for example, a ban on weapons in cities. However, the plan did not take into account the Palestinian demand for a separate state and was therefore tantamount to a declaration of war to the Palestinians. The Palestinians carried out several assassination attempts on King Hussein and hijacked American passenger planes, which they blew up in the Jordanian desert after evacuating all the passengers.

For the Jordanian king, these attacks were acts of war. On the morning of September 17, the Jordanian army therefore began attacking the PLO and the huge refugee camps in Karameh

After the attack on an Israeli bus in which thirty-seven Israelis lost their lives on March 14, 1978, three Israeli infantry brigades accompanied by armored units marched into southern Lebanon in an operation code-named Litani. In the photo is a Shot Kal Bet tank providing support to the advancing infantry at Nabatäa, June 1982. *Israel Government Press Office*

and the surrounding area of Amman. The conflict between the approximately 65,000 well-equipped Jordanian soldiers and the almost 20,000 militarily far inferior and poorly organized guerrillas lasted a total of ten days. Around 1,000 armed resistance fighters, 2,500 civilians, and 300 Jordanian soldiers lost their lives in the bloody battles of what became known as "Black September."

Defeated, the surviving Fatah fighters withdrew into the north of the country. Under Nasser's protection, Arafat himself fled to Cairo, from where he negotiated a ceasefire on September 27. Despite this, in July of the following year, King Hussein, with American support, ordered his forces to attack the Palestinian military positions in the north of the country and drive out the remaining guerrillas.

Hussein celebrated a great victory and at the same time restored his authority in Jordan. For the Palestinian resistance fighters, however, a new diaspora began, and "Black September" and the attacks in July represented another painful and costly defeat. After the expulsion from Jordan, many observers forecast the end of the Palestinian resistance movement and the PLO. However, thanks to the network of supporters built up by the Fatah leadership over the years, many of whom were based outside the Arab world, it was possible to keep the resistance alive and establish a new base in Lebanon.

Lebanon was home to the second-largest Palestinian exile community, with around 300,000 members. After the PLO's defeat in Jordan, around 100,000 more joined them. The groups set up new military bases in the Arkub Mountains in the south of Lebanon and, as in Jordan, established a "state within a state," which became known as "Fatah Land." These bases were the ideal starting point for guerrilla attacks against Israel.

There were now increasing confrontations between the PLO and Israel in southern Lebanon. The Israeli-backed Lebanese militias under the command of Major Saad Haddad were unable to prevent the Palestinian fighters from attacking northern Israel.

On March 14, 1978, a Palestinian terror squad carried out an attack on a bus near Haifa in which thirty-seven Israelis lost their lives. The Israeli response was swift, and the attack provided the pretext for an Israeli invasion. Eight days later, three Israeli infantry brigades accompanied by armored units, a total of about 20,000 troops, marched into Lebanon under the code name Operation Litani, supported by heavy attacks by naval and air forces.

The Israeli air force bombed the Palestinian refugee camp at Tyros and numerous Lebanese border villages. Armored units and infantry occupied southern Lebanon up to the Litani River. The costs of the Israeli invasion included at least two thousand dead Lebanese civilians plus approximately two hundred thousand Lebanese and sixty-five thousand Palestinian refugees and many wrecked villages.

On March 19, 1977, the United Nations Security Council passed Resolution 425, which instructed Israel to withdraw from southern Lebanon. A UN peacekeeping contingent (UNIFIL) was formed and stationed in the area between the Litani River and the most southern part of Lebanon, controlled by the Christian militias. However, complete surveillance of the security zone by the approximately seven thousand UN soldiers proved to be very problematic in the difficult terrain, with the result that PLO commandos repeatedly succeeded in penetrating into Israel.

In April 1981, elements of the Syrian units stationed in east-central Lebanon—the 76th and 91st Armored Brigades, the 58th Mechanized Brigade, and the 62nd Infantry Brigade, plus ten independent "commando" battalions with a total strength of about 30,000 troops with powerful supporting artillery—attacked the bases of the Christian militias in the area around Zahle, on the most important road linking Damascus with Beirut. Starting in the spring of 1979, there were also increasing aerial engagements between Syrian fighters and Israeli fighters escorting reconnaissance aircraft.

With the growing number of artillery strikes by the Palestinians against residential areas in northern Israel, a fierce border war developed. Further Israeli mechanized incursions into southern

A column of Shot Kal Gimel tanks of the 211th Armored Brigade advancing in the direction of Sidon, June 1982. *IWM*

Lebanon and a Syrian intervention did not result in longer-lasting ceasefires. Israeli prime minister Menachem Begin[2] and his defense minister, Ariel Sharon, visibly lost faith in a peaceful solution to the conflict. A retaliatory strike by the Israelis was thus only a matter of time.

Sharon planned a military offensive into Lebanese territory in the spring of 1982. Its objectives were to destroy the PLO infrastructure, liquidate its command centers, and drive the Syrian forces, which were supporting the Palestinians, out of the southern part of the country. A new Lebanese government would subsequently be installed to prevent the return of the PLO.

[2] Menachem Begin (1913–92) grew up in Brest-Litovsk, Russia (now Belarus). He studied law at the University of Warsaw and fled to Soviet-occupied Vilnius after the outbreak of the Second World War in 1939. As part of his military service with the Free Polish army, he was sent to Palestine. There he joined the Zionist underground organization Irgun and became its leader in 1943. Begin was responsible for the bomb attack on the King David Hotel in Jerusalem in 1946. After the declaration of independence in 1948, he founded the Cherut party, which later became the leading force in the Likud bloc. He then served in various posts under the Levi Eshkol government and rose to become Israel's sixth prime minister in 1977. In November of the same year, he held a historic meeting with Egypt's president Anwar el-Sadat, which led to the Israeli-Egyptian peace agreement with the help of US president Jimmy Carter. Begin and Sadat were awarded the Nobel Peace Prize for the Camp David Accords. In 1982, he decided to invade Lebanon as part of "Operation Peace for Galilee." Begin unexpectedly resigned from all his posts on September 15, 1983, and died in Tel Aviv in March 1992.

CHAPTER 19: Operation Peace for Galilee: The Lebanon Offensive, 1982

While three brigades of the 91st Division advanced west along the coast in the direction of Damour, the 96th Division carried out an amphibious landing, cleared the coastal strip, and covered the Israeli advance. In the photo, M113 armored personnel carriers come ashore near Sidon, June 1982. *Osprey*

Defense Minister Ariel Sharon explains Israeli progress in Operation Peace for Galilee during a press conference, June 1982. *Israel Government Press Office*

THE STATE OF THE ISRAELI ARMED FORCES

The opening setbacks in the Yom Kippur War in October 1973 had forced the Israeli military to revise its tactics. Israel recognized the necessity of employing combined arms operations—infantry, mechanized units, artillery, and air forces—and these would be employed in Lebanon. The associated consequences for the command of operations were incorporated into the tactics used by future senior commanders and the training of the troops.

The Israeli tank arsenal was also changing. Some of the older British-made Shot tanks and the Magach 3 tanks, based on the M48 Patton, were replaced by more-modern Magach tanks, based on the American M60. In the Yom Kippur War of 1973, the Magach had been successful in the fighting in the Sinai Peninsula against Egyptian Soviet-made T-54/55 and T-62 tanks, primarily on account of its powerful 105 mm gun. The new Merkava tank was to receive its baptism of fire in the campaign against the PLO fighters and Syrians in Lebanon, where Syrian T-72 tanks supplied by the Soviet Union were deployed for the first time, at the gates of Beirut.

THE TERRAIN

Lebanon comprises an area of 4,015 square miles (10,400 km^2) and geographically can be divided into four longitudinal strips of land running from north to south. The western strip along the coast is bordered by the Mediterranean and the Lebanon Mountains. The mountain range that runs along the eastern edge of the coastal strip dominates the entire surrounding area. It is about 100 miles (160 km) long and has a width of about 15.5 miles (25 km). The mountain peaks rise to heights of about 9,800 feet (3,000 m). The mountains' eastern flank consists of steep, dry, and narrow valley gorges. The western flank, by contrast, slopes somewhat more gently. East of the Lebanon Mountains is the Beqaa Plain. It is about 75 miles (120 km) long and 6 miles (10 km) wide and in the east is bordered by the Anti-Lebanon Mountains, which rise to a height of 8,200 feet (2,500 m).

The country's most important road runs from Beirut to Damascus. It crosses the Beqaa Valley at the Rayak airport and passes through the town of Zahle. The Beirut to Sidon road, on the other hand, winds its way through the southern mountain slopes and meets the coastal road at Sidon. Farther north, another road crosses the high ridges to reach Jounieh, a small, strategically important port north of Beirut. The two roads running north–south are the aforementioned coastal road from Tripoli to the Israeli border and the road through the Beqaa Valley.

The Litani River makes it difficult to cross in an east–west direction due to its, in places, gorge-like valley in the south of Lebanon and is therefore of strategic importance. Other key positions that considerably restrict military movements are located in the Lebanon Mountains.

M113 armored personnel carriers of the 211th Armored Brigade clearing streets in Sidon, June 1982. *Israel Government Press Office*

The terrain presented some new challenges for the Israeli armed forces. While the armored units had primarily been organized and trained for fast, mobile operations over long distances, the situation in Lebanon was completely different. The terrain was in stark contrast to the wide-open spaces of Israel. Apart from isolated actions in built-up and mountainous areas, the Israelis had fought mainly in hilly desert terrain, where long-range visibility and the range of its weapons could be exploited. Now they had to be prepared to fight in rugged mountainous terrain, on the one hand, but also in cramped and crowded urban centers — so-called urban fighting — on the other hand.

On June 3, 1982, a Palestinian terrorist carried out an assassination attempt on the Israeli ambassador in London — the casus belli for a renewed war in the Middle East. The Israeli chief of staff, Rafael Eitan, instructed the commander of the northern front, Major General Avigdor Ben-Gal, to deploy seven divisions with 75,000 troops and 1,250 tanks into attack positions and to launch Operation Peace for Galilee, the invasion of Lebanon.

THE OFFENSIVE

Ben-Gal's plan envisaged an advance by three battle groups, roughly equal in strength:

- In the west, along the coast, the 91st Division (Brigadier General Yitzhak Mordechai), with amphibious support from the 96th Division (Brigadier General Amos Yaron), was to advance from northern Galilee via Tyrus, Sidon, and Damour to Beirut; clear the coastal strip; and destroy the enemy forces in Beirut.
- In the center, the 36th Division (Brigadier General Avigdor Kahalani) and the 162nd Division (Brigadier General Menachem Einan) were to advance from northern Galilee across the Litani River to Nabatiye and to a position abeam Beirut, in order to block the Beirut–Damascus road and thus cut the flow of supplies to the Syrian forces from the east.
- In the east, the 252nd Division (Brigadier General Immanuel Sakel) and the 90th Division (Brigadier General Giora Lev) were to advance from the Golan Heights through Hasbaya to the Beqaa Valley and destroy the enemy in so-called Fatah Land.
- The 880th Division (Brigadier General Yom-Tov Tamir) was to stand by in reserve to support the eastern battle group in the area of the Beqaa Valley.

Yasser Arafat organized his 25,000 fighters into three brigades and, with these, occupied the following defensive positions:

- The Yarmouk Brigade was positioned in the west on the Tyros–Sidon–Damur axis.
- The Kastel Brigade took up position in the south in the Beaufort-Nabatiye-Jezzine position.
- The Karameh Brigade was positioned in the east in the area of the Hermon massif in "Fatah Land."

As early as 1981 the Fatah command began receiving Soviet-made arms, which were primarily paid for by Libya. These included a total of twenty T-54/55 medium tanks, sixty T-34 medium tanks, ninety towed M-46 130 mm guns, eighty BM-21 multiple rocket launchers, and large numbers of mortars and antiaircraft guns. There was no shortage of small arms, with countless RPG-7s and numerous type 9K32 Strela 2 (SAM-7 Grail) shoulder-launched surface-to-air missiles augmenting the antitank and antiaircraft capabilities of the PLO.

With thirty thousand troops; six hundred T-55, T-62, and T-72 tanks; and numerous artillery positions, the Syrian forces were concentrated mainly in two geographical areas:

- In the west was the 7th Infantry Division, with the 68th and 85th Infantry Brigades and the 51st Mechanized Brigade.
- In the east was the 1st Armored Division, with the 76th and 91st Armored Brigades and the 62nd Infantry Brigade in the Beqaa Valley.

After a fierce battle involving all three Israeli divisions and the reorganization of forces in the Damour-En Dara-Sultan Yakoub area, the first armored units reached Beirut. The picture shows a Merkava Mark I tank of the 36th Division entering the southern part of the city, August 1982. *Israel Government Press Office*

The Syrians also installed a comprehensive network of SAM batteries of the types S-75 Dvina (SA-2 Guideline), S-125 Neva (SA-3 Goa), and 9K33 Osa (SA-8 Gecko).

THE ATTACK

On the morning of June 6, 1982, the Israeli 91st Division (Mordechai), with the 211th Armored Brigade and the 375th and 769th Mechanized Brigades, attacked along the coast, regrouped in Tyrus, and the next day reached the outer suburbs of the city of Damour. At the same time, Palestinian positions were bypassed, both by an Israeli amphibious operation, in which a mixed brigade of the 96th Division (Yaron) landed north of Sidon in the area of the mouth of the Awali River, and by the 1st and 211th Armored Brigades.

The advance by the two western battle groups along the coastal road was extremely rapid. On the second day of fighting, the units of the 91st Division linked up with those of the 96th Division in the Sidon area. South of Damour, however, the Israelis halted their attack because of fierce opposition from large PLO units that had entrenched themselves in the city.

In the central sector, the 36th Division (Kahalani) and the 162nd Division (Einan) drove from northern Galilee to the Arnoun Mountains and took the town of Nabatiye. At Jezzin they encountered units of the Syrian 1st Armored Division, reinforced by the PLO's Kastel Brigade. After fierce fighting, the point unit broke through the defensive positions to the north and finally reached the high ground southeast of Beirut. A battle group from the Golani Brigade turned east to take the heavily fortified Beaufort Castle built by the Crusaders. For years the PLO had been directing artillery fire onto settlements in northern Israel from there. The fortress fell on the night of June 7.

The third Israeli battle group, made up of the 90th Division (Lev) and the 252nd Division (Sakel), was supposed to advance from the western Golan Heights, along the western slope of the Hermon massif in the direction of Hasbaiya, and farther into the southern part of the Beqaa Valley; however, both units met heavy resistance in "Fatah Land" and the surrounding villages. There was house-to-house fighting against armed Palestinians and Syrians in well-fortified positions, which had to be taken one by one. The Israeli troops suffered considerable losses when clearing the houses, and the tanks advancing on the few main roads also came under heavy flanking fire from antitank weapons.

Fierce battles against the Syrian 1st Armored Division developed into the Battle of the Beqaa Valley, where the Merkava tank saw action for the first time. The combined use of tanks, infantry, artillery, and air forces finally allowed the Israelis to gain the upper hand. The heavy fighting left about two hundred Syrian tanks and several hundred light armored vehicles burning on the battlefield.

On June 10, the leading group of forces from the western battle group was south of Beirut, where heavy fighting was expected against the Syrian 85th Infantry Brigade. Meanwhile, the central battle group reached the village of En Dara, near the road linking Beirut with Damascus. There it became involved in a firefight with the Syrian 62nd Infantry Brigade; however, it was quickly decimated by Israeli attack helicopters.

In the east, however, armed Syrian helicopters attacked Israeli armored units and inflicted significant losses with their HOT antitank missiles. The 12.7 mm heavy machine guns carried by the Israeli tanks proved largely ineffective, since the helicopters for the most part remained out of range.

In the evening, an Israeli armored battalion equipped with Magach tanks was surrounded by the Syrian 58th Mechanized Brigade and several commando battalions in the village of Sultan Yakoub. While the crews were able to break through to the Israeli lines, they were forced to abandon most of their tanks and other vehicles. Israeli combat aircraft restored the situation with tactical air support and also shot down twenty-five Syrian fighters and four helicopters.

The three battle groups reached their interim objectives on the fifth day and reorganized on the line Damour-En Dara-Sultan

The Israeli M109 self-propelled howitzer, acquired from the United States, received its baptism of fire in the Yom Kippur War in 1973. Upgraded M109 A1 Rochev Alef and M109 A2 Rochev Bet self-propelled howitzers saw action during the First Lebanon War. In the photo, an M109 A1 Rochev Alef with longer gun, additional 7.62 mm machine gun, and additional side stowage space, outside the city of Beirut, July 1982. *Israel Government Press Office*

Yakoub. The western and central battle groups attacked south of Beirut. The eastern battle group, however, drove on through the Beqaa Valley and secured the eastern high ground to prevent Syrian forces from moving into "Fatah Land." There followed fierce tank battles between Merkava and Syrian T-72 tanks. The Merkava proved itself superior in action and knocked out many T-72s, a number of which were captured.

The final battle round about Beirut broke out from June 22 to 25. The Israeli units sealed off the western and southern parts of the city, blocked the road to Damascus, and pounded the northern part of the city with artillery fire. West Beirut, where, in addition to 10,000 PLO fighters, the PLO leadership was located, was completely surrounded. Having achieved their military objectives for the time being, the Israelis went from a war of movement to a state of siege.

The use of military means now alternated with political activity. West Beirut was under frequent artillery fire, and the PLO forces replied mainly with Soviet BM-21 multiple rocket launchers.

CHAPTER 19: Operation Peace for Galilee: The Lebanon Offensive, 1982

The suffering of the civilian population, but also the desperation of the PLO and the Syrians, ultimately led to political negotiations strongly influenced by the US. These brought about a cessation of all hostilities, and by September 3 about 10,000 PLO fighters left by sea for various Arab states, taking their small arms with them.

Israeli losses totaled 370 killed and 2,400 wounded, and more than sixty tanks were destroyed. During the course of the Israeli offensive, the PLO lost at least a thousand fighters, and eight thousand were captured. The Israelis succeeded in destroying or capturing almost all of the PLO's tanks as well as its antiaircraft and artillery systems. The Syrian forces recorded 1,200 killed and about 3,000 wounded, plus the loss of about ninety combat aircraft, twelve helicopters, and a large percentage of their armored vehicles, which were either destroyed or captured by the Israelis.

CLOSING REMARKS

The Israeli leadership had drawn the consequences for the invasion of Lebanon from the tactical lessons of the Yom Kippur War of 1973. For the first time in their history, the Israelis consistently implemented joint operations across all branches of the armed forces. The tank, which was used in all three battle groups, once again proved its worth as a central weapons system, this time also in difficult terrain. However, the use of tanks was pointless if they were not used in a concentration to bring about operational decisions.

The exploitation of the tanks' maneuverability and mobility in the terrain was another factor in the success of the Israelis. Despite the upgrading of their T-62 and T-72 tanks, the Syrians tended to halt before firing. The Israelis, on the other hand, were constantly on the move and used this advantage to take Syrian tanks from the flank or even from the rear.

Israeli military officials believed that tanks should be heavy in order to provide better protection both for the crew and the ammunition through stronger armor. When modern antitank weapons penetrate the main armor, crew casualties and material damage are the result. This led to even more effective reinforcement of the armor protection at the front or sides and naturally resulted in a greater overall weight of the tank.

The turret should also not be too low, since in many cases the tank has to move too far out of cover in order to gain the necessary visibility. The firepower and autonomy of a tank depend to a large degree on the amount of ammunition carried, so that the availability of sufficient ammunition often determines the outcome of battles. The requirement to carry as much ammunition as possible has not been affected by modern fire control systems and the higher first-hit probability of modern tanks.

Israeli major general Israel Tal considered the tendency to reduce the number of crew members from four to three by using automatic loaders to be wrong and a misguided development. With only three men, operational capability, maintenance, and the possibility of self-defense are too limited. Even more serious was the fact that if just one crew member were disabled, the entire tank would be out of action for the rest of the battle.

The Merkava tank's baptism of fire was a success. It proved itself due to its great mobility in terrain, excellent protection for its crews, and a good hit rate. The Merkava proved to be more survivable in combat than the Magach and Shot tanks. Ongoing improvements to the Merkava's chassis, turret, armor, and cannon continue to the present day.

From the perspective of the terrain alone, as well as the ability to prepare for defensive battles, the advantage was clearly on the Syrian side. The Israeli chief of staff, Rafael Eitan, repeatedly pointed out that the T-72 tank in particular was one of the most modern battle tanks extant and that its fighting power should not be underestimated. Tank battles no longer took place exclusively as duels between individual vehicles, but in interaction with combat helicopters, artillery, and antitank weapons.

Artillery in particular has undergone a significant improvement since 1973 through the development and introduction of modern fire control and reconnaissance systems and ultimately also a quantitative increase. In Lebanon the artillery proved its worth in the rapid suppression of antitank positions, as well as in combat in the mountains.

Israeli-Lebanese talks, which took place in January 1983 under American leadership and focused on a peace settlement, provided for an Israeli troop withdrawal and the creation of a 19-to-25-mile-wide (30–40 km) security zone on Israel's northern border, as well as the establishment of normal diplomatic relations. On May 17, 1983, the Lebanese and Israeli governments signed a troop withdrawal agreement. The Israelis withdrew about 12 miles (20 km) to the south, to the Awali River.

Over the years, the American contingent of the multinational peacekeeping force became increasingly involved in battles with Syrian forces, which were growing in strength, and was soon withdrawn again. In the 1990s, Syrian forces with at least 30,000 soldiers occupied central Lebanon. However, the south of the country was completely under Israeli control until the year 2000.

Despite the occupation, or perhaps because of it, the influence of radical Islamic militias in southern Lebanon grew steadily.

Syrian T-62 tanks captured by the Israelis. Syrian T-62s first saw action on the Golan Heights during the Yom Kippur War in 1973. Successor to the T-55, this tank was armed with a U-STS L55 115 mm smooth-bore gun and was powered by a W-55W V12 diesel engine. Unlike the T-55, the fume extractor was farther to the rear, and the distance between the first two road wheels was less. Later models had Kevlar protective mats and a simple fire-extinguishing system. The Syrians lost more than five hundred T-62 tanks during the Israeli offensive in Lebanon. *IDF*

Hezbollah became the most powerful and influential of these militias. Supported by Iran, it gradually succeeded in destroying the militias allied with Israel as early as the late 1990s. Through constant attacks on Israeli troops in southern Lebanon and in Israel itself, it gained almost complete control over southern Lebanon despite the establishment of a security zone and the presence of the UNIFIL force. As a result, a sustainable peace does not seem to be in sight.

CHAPTER 19: Operation Peace for Galilee: The Lebanon Offensive, 1982

Chapter 20
The 2006 Lebanon War and the Fighting in the Gaza Strip

In the First Lebanon War of 1982, the Israeli army forced the withdrawal of Palestine Liberation Organization (PLO) fighters by advancing as far as Beirut and, after a partial withdrawal of its own, retained military control of a strip of territory between the Litani River and the Israeli border 15 miles (25 km) away. From then on, the predominantly Shiite Hezbollah ("Party of God") terrorist organization fought against the Israeli troops stationed there.

This paramilitary organization was formed as a merger of various Islamist groups immediately after the First Lebanon War. Its goal was the liberation of Lebanon from the occupying power Israel and the establishment of an Islamic republic based on the Iranian model.

In the first few years after the establishment of the security zone, Hezbollah carried out only a few attacks on Israeli forces. Over the years, however, the number of attacks on patrols and armored vehicles increased, with numerous Israeli soldiers being injured or killed.

The high number of casualties prompted the Israeli general staff to take action. Combat tactics from the First Gulf War in 1991 and the conflict in Bosnia in 1995 convinced the Israeli leadership that a war from a distance with increased use of artillery and targeted airstrikes would be far more effective than ground offensives with tanks, infantry fighting vehicles, and mechanized infantry. Ehud Barak,[1] who served as defense minister under Shimon Peres in 1996 and as prime minister from 1999, was also convinced of this.

In 2000, the prime minister ordered his chief of staff, Sha'ul Mofas,[2] to evacuate Israeli ground troops from the security zone in Lebanon. This withdrawal was accompanied and coordinated by United Nations troops. After the withdrawal, Hezbollah took advantage of the situation and built hundreds of bunkers and gun emplacements in the area close to the border and set up extensive, decentralized weapons depots that were connected to each other by a sophisticated tunnel system. This tunnel system increasingly resembled that used by the North Vietnamese army and the Vietcong during the Vietnam War.

When they withdrew, the Israelis left an impressive arsenal of weapons behind for the South Lebanese army. It failed to maintain the defense of southern Lebanon, however, and slowly withdrew. As a result, Hezbollah was able to capture large quantities of weapons and arm its troops with them. In the following years, Hezbollah also installed numerous BM-21 Katyusha rocket launcher systems, known to the Germans as "Stalin's Organs" during the Second World War, produced in Russia. Multiple launchers were largely replaced by smaller, mobile single launchers with ranges of up to 25 miles (40 km). The batteries were supplied from Iranian stocks via Syria.

In addition to the considerable arsenal of weapons, the uneven terrain in southern Lebanon also offered decisive advantages for the defender. It consists largely of valleys with

---

[1] Ehud Barak (1942–) grew up in the kibbutz Mishmar haSharon and studied mathematics and physics at the Hebrew University in Jerusalem. Barak joined the Israeli armed forces in 1959, served as commander of the elite Sajeret Matkal unit, and commanded a reconnaissance company during the Six-Day War in 1967. In the 1973 Yom Kippur War, he led an armored battalion during the Egyptian invasion of the Sinai Peninsula. After the war, he was major general in command of the central front and became lieutenant general and chief of staff in 1991. After his military career, Barak was appointed to the cabinet by Yitzhak Rabin in 1995, where he pursued a stellar political career, first as interior minister and later as foreign minister. In 1999, he was elected prime minister of Israel in a head-to-head election against Benjamin Netanyahu. When the opposition leader Ariel Sharon visited the Temple Mount in September 2000 and the Second Intifada broke out as a result, Barak felt that his policies had failed, and he was defeated by the Likud-Kandi in February 2001. Today, Barak is a partner in the investment company SCP Private Investment Partners.

[2] Sha'ul Mofas (1948–) grew up in Tehran, Iran, and immigrated to Israel in 1957. After high school, he served in an Israeli paratrooper brigade and took part in the Six-Day War, the Yom Kippur War, the Lebanon War, and Operation Entebbe as a member of the elite Sajeret Matkal unit. He was promoted to brigadier general in 1988 and to major general in 1994. Three years later, he took over the office of chief of staff as lieutenant general. Following the outbreak of the Second Intifada and the associated emergence of guerrilla fighting in the occupied territories, Mofas refocused the Israeli armed forces on asymmetric combat. In 2002, he joined Sharon's cabinet and became minister of defense. In January 2015, he announced his retirement from politics.

Merkava Mark IV heavy tanks on the move in Lebanon during Operation Change of Direction, August 2006.
Israel National Collection

hollows and ditches as well as hilly highlands, with Tyre as the only major city in the region. The nature of the landscape severely restricts the ability of armored forces to maneuver and deploy, and channels advances onto easily recognizable and exposed roads. This provided ideal opportunities for the defensive force to take appropriate antitank measures, lay ambushes, and lay mines in narrow passages.

However, Hezbollah used not only the terrain to its advantage, but also a special kind of warfare against the Israeli armed forces, equipped with conventional weapons systems. Guerrilla tactics and asymmetric warfare such as ambushes; symmetric warfare such as ambushes, surprise attacks, and rapid retreats; acts of sabotage; and fighting in overbuilt, confusing areas were intended to slow down and thwart Israeli attacks.

Estimates indicated that there were about 10,000 active Hezbollah fighters in southern Lebanon — in the Nabatieth region and south of the Litani River. Hezbollah's headquarters were in the southern part of Dahiye, in the Shiite quarter of Beirut. Their commander, Hassan Nasrallah,[3] divided his forces in southern Lebanon into several sectors, each of which included twelve to fifteen villages, so that all sectors were connected to one another to secure the chain of command. If communications were severed, the affected sector continued fighting autonomously.

---

[3] Hassan Nasrallah (1960–) grew up in the village of Bassouriyeh in the south of Lebanon. After completing his high school education, he moved to Najaf to study at Hauwza, a Shiite university. After the Israeli invasion of Lebanon in 1982, he joined Hezbollah. Following the assassination of Hezbollah leader Sayyid Abbas al-Musawi, Nasrallah was elected as the new political leader by the central committee at the age of thirty. After the start of the Second Lebanon War in 2006, he threatened an "open war" against Israel.

CHAPTER 20: The 2006 Lebanon War and the Fighting in the Gaza Strip

The Hezbollah fighters were divided into a paramilitary-organized army and a guard organization consisting of so-called militias for the villages. Its forces wore military uniforms and consisted of experienced, well-trained, and well-disciplined fighters, who were usually organized in squads or platoons and were mainly responsible for operating artillery, surface-to-air missile batteries, and antitank weapons.

The militias, on the other hand, were experienced guerrilla fighters and responsible for defending the villages in the event of an enemy incursion. Dressed as civilians, these fighters also brought with them a high level of motivation and training, formed defensive rings, and harbored a mobile arsenal of AK-47 assault rifles, light machine guns, RPGs, AT-3 Sagger antitank missiles, and 9K32 Strela (SA-7 Grail) shoulder-fired antiaircraft missiles. The Hezbollah also had the Russian-made 9K135 Kornet (AT-14 Spriggan) mobile antitank weapons system. This portable guided-weapons system, with a tandem hollow-charge warhead, could be used against both hard and soft targets at ranges up to 6,015 yards (5,500 m).

On the morning of July 12, 2006, the Hezbollah militia opened fire on Israeli positions near the southwestern border between Israel and Lebanon with mortars to divert attention from an ambush on a border patrol in the area of Aita ash-Shaab. A squad of Hezbollah fighters broke through the border fence and subsequently destroyed two armored vehicles with RPGs, killing three Israeli soldiers. Two wounded were taken prisoner and spirited into southern Lebanon.

The Israelis immediately gave chase with a platoon of armored infantry and a Merkava Mark IV tank of the 7th Armored Brigade. Shortly after crossing the border, the tank drove over a large IED. Five Israeli soldiers lost their lives.

When Israeli prime minister Ehud Olmert,[4] who had taken over the position after Ariel Sharon's stroke, learned of the incident, he ordered a comprehensive military strike against Hezbollah. The first Israeli combat aircraft took to the air in the early afternoon on July 12, 2006, and began a massive bombing campaign against all important access roads and bridges in southern Lebanon, as well as the capital, Beirut, and the international airport. The Israelis also initiated a naval blockade to prevent the arrival of additional weapons systems and Hezbollah militias.

Olmert instructed Defense Minister Amir Peretz[5] and the chief of the general staff, Dan Chalutz,[6] to work out a battle plan for Operation Change of Direction, the attack in southern Lebanon. Peretz, who had little military experience, relied completely on the decisions made by his chief of the general staff, who outlined them as follows:

[4] Ehud Olmert (1945–) comes from a family of Russian immigrants who immigrated to the British Mandate of Palestine in 1933. Olmert served in the Golani Brigade during the Yom Kippur War, where he was a military correspondent on Ariel Sharon's staff. After the war, Olmert was first elected to the Knesset for the Likud Party, where he became the youngest member of parliament at the age of twenty-eight. He held numerous political offices and committees. In 1999, Olmert challenged Ariel Sharon for the chairmanship of the Likud Party but was defeated in the party's internal elections. During Sharon's government, he was appointed minister of industry and trade and deputy prime minister. After Sharon's stroke in January 2006, Olmert took over his duties. The Winograd Commission, which investigated the events of the Second Lebanon War, accused Olmert of serious leadership failure. In addition, investigations into corruption and bribery forced Olmert to resign in 2008. An early government election was held in March 2009, allowing Benjamin Netanyahu to form a new government. Olmert was charged with corruption by the public prosecutor's office and ultimately sentenced to fines and imprisonment after a lengthy trial.

[5] Amir Peretz (1952–) grew up in Morocco and immigrated to Israel with his parents at the age of four. He completed his military service in the artillery from 1970 to 1972 and, after completing his officer's course, joined the paratrooper brigade as an ammunition officer. In 1974, as a result of a serious traffic accident in the Sinai, he was discharged from the army as unfit for service. He entered politics in 1983 and became a member of the Knesset in 1988 and chairman of the Histadrut trade union federation in 1995. Under Prime Minister Ehud Olmert, he took over as minister of defense in 2006. The Winograd Commission's final report also accused him of serious shortcomings in his leadership during the Second Lebanon War in 2006, which ultimately made Peretz politically unacceptable. He was voted out of office but ran again for the post of Labor Party leader in 2011. He was finally reelected in 2015, and his term of office ended when Naftali Bennett's government took office in June 2021. Peretz was considered a pioneer of the "Iron Dome" protective shield, the mobile ground-based defense system against enemy rockets, artillery, and mortar shells.

[6] Dan Chalutz (1948–) immigrated to Israel from Iran with his parents. He grew up in the Sharon Valley and studied economics at Tel Aviv University. He joined the Israeli air force in 1966, graduated from fighter school in 1968, and served in the first F-4 Phantom squadron in 1969. He flew numerous combat missions during the 1968–70 War of Attrition and the 1973 Yom Kippur War. In 1982, he was retrained on the new F-16 Fighting Falcon fighter aircraft, and in 1986 he led the Phantom squadrons. In 1993 he was promoted to brigadier general, and in 1998 to major general and head of the operations department of the general staff of the Israel Defense Forces. This was followed in 2000 by his appointment as commander of the Israeli air force. He introduced new combat aircraft such as the F-15 Strike Eagle; improved cooperation between the air force, the ground forces, and the domestic intelligence service Shin Bet; and became chief of staff of the Israeli army in June 2005, when he was promoted to lieutenant general. He also admitted to misconduct in leadership during the Second Lebanon War and submitted his resignation in January 2007.

M109A2 Rochev Bet self-propelled howitzer of a reserve artillery battalion supporting the Israeli attack in Lebanon from positions in northern Galilee. *Israel National Collection*

- Demand for the release of the two abducted Israeli soldiers and their unconditional return to Israel
- Entry of military forces into southern Lebanon to destroy Hezbollah's artillery and rocket-launching positions as well as its command infrastructure
- Creation of a naval and air blockade to prevent Syria and Iran from delivering further weapons to Hezbollah
- The application and implementation of United Nations Resolution 1559, which called for the disarmament and withdrawal of all Hezbollah militias from the south of Lebanon and the deployment of the Lebanese army along the border with Israel

The Israeli general staff then ordered visibly smaller incursions by ground forces into southern Lebanon. The military used drones to locate enemy positions but also struck Hezbollah positions with warplanes and helicopters. The enemy did not respond to the initially hesitant attacks by the Israelis. Despite the Israeli bombing, Hezbollah succeeded in firing hundreds of Katyusha rockets into northern Israel daily. Several rockets also struck the Israeli port city of Haifa, which was about 24 miles (40 km) from the Lebanese border.

Israeli air defenses and artillery were helpless against this type of threat. The time between the spotting of an enemy rocket position by Israeli reconnaissance and the launch was as a rule too short for it to be engaged by fighter-bombers or artillery.

CHAPTER 20: The 2006 Lebanon War and the Fighting in the Gaza Strip

The Israeli leadership during the Second Lebanon War in 2006. *From left*: Chief of Staff Dan Chalutz, President Ehud Olmert, and Defense Minister Amir Peretz. *Israel National Collection*

Despite this, the Israeli air force flew more than nineteen thousand combat sorties during the war and attacked more than seven thousand enemy targets—far more than in the Golan Heights and the Sinai during the Yom Kippur War.

When the firing of rockets by Hezbollah went on undiminished, the Israelis launched their first major ground operations on July 19, 2006. Chief of the General Staff Chalutz waited too long—much too long—to take this step. He came to the decision that only an invasion by mechanized forces and infantry could put an end to the continuous rocket fire by Hezbollah.

On July 23, the 51st Infantry Battalion of the Golani Brigade, the 101st Battalion of the 35th Paratrooper Brigade, and several tank companies of the 7th Armored Brigade attacked Hezbollah positions at Bint Jbeil, a larger village near the Lebanese border. The plan called for an ambush-like strike into the village from the north to eliminate as many Hezbollah fighters as possible, followed by a withdrawal from the region. But Chalutz changed his mind and ordered the attack to come from the south and a complete clearing or occupation of the area. Contrary to expectations, the Israelis encountered heavy resistance and lost about a dozen soldiers in bloody fighting. After days of fighting, the Israelis withdrew, without taking Bint Jbeil.

The government subsequently ordered the call-up of 15,000 reservists between July 28 and 31, 2006, in order to undertake an even more comprehensive ground attack into southern Lebanon.

Chalutz ordered the commander of the northern front, Major General Udi Adam,[7] and the chief of staff of the operations section, Major General Gadi Eizenkot,[8] to work out plans for a large-scale attack. Four divisions were to take up offensive positions on the border with Lebanon and stand by for a comprehensive ground offensive:

- The 91st Division "Galilee Formation," under the command of Brigadier General Gal Hirsch, was heavily weighted with infantry brigades, an armored brigade, and an artillery battalion. The division was to advance to the west and attack and secure the area around Bint Jbeil and Maroun al-Ras.
- The 162nd Division "Steel Formation," commanded by Brigadier General Guy Tzur, with the 401st Armored Brigade, the Givati and the Nahal Brigades, and an artillery regiment, was to cross the river in the Wadi Saluki, east of the seam with the 91st Division, attack

the suburbs of the towns of al-Khiam and Marula, and advance to the Litani River.

- The 366th Division "Pillar of Fire Formation," led by Brigadier General Erez Zuckermann, was heavily equipped with mechanized infantry and was to occupy the towns of al-Khiam and Marjayoun east of the boundary to the 162nd Division and support the drive on Marula by that division.
- The 98th Paratrooper Division "Fire Formation," commanded by Brigadier General Eyal Eisenberg, was to move into the towns of Zarit, Yatar, Rashaf, and Dbil, west of the 91st Division's sector boundary, destroy the enemy, and advance farther west to Tyre.

The Israelis also deployed the upgraded Merkava Mark IV for the first time. It combined all new telecommunication systems, electronics, sensors, and computers in an advanced fire control system. In addition to the traditional vision blocks and periscopes, it predominantly uses electro-optical systems. In this way, information can be exchanged not only between members of the crew, but between the individual tanks. This data integration gave the tank commanders a better overview of the battlefield and, with it, decisive advantages against opposing tanks, whose coordination was still based on the usual visual contact. With the new system the crew no longer required direct visual contact to transmit the position of the enemy. Instead, the situation maps are presented in real time on flat screens inside the tank.

The Merkava Mark IV also has an improved power-to-weight ratio thanks to its MTU MT 883 diesel engine, developed in Germany, which produces 1,500 hp. An improved suspension system and a new barrel recoil mechanism for the 120 mm gun also gives its kinetic-energy penetrator ammunition a higher muzzle velocity.

Israeli for the first time employed the Iron Dome system for defense against enemy rockets. It is a mobile, ground-based rocket defense system capable of defeating short-range rockets and artillery shells at all times of day and in all types of weather. The system consists of a radar unit, a control center, and a launcher with twenty interceptor missiles. In an emergency, the radar detects an approaching enemy rocket, calculates its trajectory, and sends the information to the control center, which determines the time of impact and automatically triggers a countermeasure by firing the defensive missile. An Iron Dome battery can defend an area of 58 square miles (150 km²), at ranges of up to 40 miles (70 km), and can engage up to six targets simultaneously. The Israeli army currently has several Iron Dome systems in use and achieves success rates of up to 80 percent. IDF

THE GROUND OFFENSIVE

In the meantime, the United Nations Security Council called for an end to the fighting in the south of Lebanon and set a ceasefire date of August 14, 2006. On August 11, Major General Udi Adam began the ground offensive into Lebanon against Hezbollah—knowing full well that the Israeli forces had only sixty hours until the previously agreed-on ceasefire. After heavy artillery fire on numerous suspected Hezbollah positions, the four Israeli divisions marched toward the Litani River.

Units of the 366th Division moved north and soon reached the first suburbs of Marjayoun. The division's point battalion

---

[7] Udi Adam (1958–) grew up in Tel Aviv and studied at Bar-Ilan University and the École militaire in Paris, among others. He joined the Israeli Armored Corps in 1976. During the Lebanon War in 2006, Adam was commander of the northern front. However, Chief of Staff Dan Chalutz assigned him Major General Moshe Kaplinski as his superior, as Chalutz was not satisfied with the leadership of the northern front command. Adam announced his resignation in September 2006. In April 2016, Moshe Yaalon, then minister of defense, appointed Udi Adam as director general of the Israeli Ministry of Defense.

[8] Gadi Eizenkot (1960–), the son of Moroccan immigrants, grew up in the Israeli port city of Eilat and studied history at Tel Aviv University. He served in the Golani Brigade, took over its command as a brigadier general in 1997, and later led the 366th Armored Division, a reserve unit of the Southern Command. In 2005, he headed the operations department as chief of staff and took over command of the northern front in 2006, following the resignation of Udi Adam as commander. In February 2015, Eizenkot was promoted to chief of staff, succeeding Benjamin Gantz.

drove between the towns of al-Khiam and Marjayoun, where they encountered Hezbollah fighters. An Israeli supply convoy and several Merkava IV tanks were hit by 9K135 Kornet antitank guided missiles. The Israeli battalion commander then ordered a comprehensive rescue action, ignoring the order to advance on Marjayoun. The following engagement between the 366th Division and the Hezbollah fighters produced no decision, however, and the Israelis therefore withdrew their units back to the assembly area beyond the Lebanese border.

In a preliminary action, parts of the 55th Paratrooper Brigade of the 98th Division occupied the town of Dibil, south of Rashaf. Hezbollah reconnaissance units discovered the paratroopers hiding in buildings and opened fire with artillery and guided missiles, killing nine soldiers and wounding thirty-one. At the same time, other units of the division occupied Rashaf to the north and attempted to open and secure a supply route. However, this plan did not succeed here either prior to the ceasefire, due to the sustained enemy fire.

The action by the 35th Paratrooper Brigade was not to be crowned with success either. It had been ordered to land north of Yatar, near Jabal Amil, since several rocket batteries were suspected there. However, for unexplained reasons the paratroopers were dropped much farther south than originally planned, and during the landing the unit was ambushed by Hezbollah, whose fighters fired their shoulder-launched Strela guided surface-to-air missiles. A Sikorsky CH-53 Sea Stallion helicopter immediately caught fire. Brigadier General Eyal Eisenberg immediately stopped further landings of troops a short time later, thereby aborting the operation.

The 91st Division quickly advanced to the outskirts of the town of Bint Jbeil but was stalled by Hezbollah's extensive system of bases, barriers, and long-range antitank weapons. The towns of Bint Jbeil and Maroun al-Ras were not captured. Brigadier General Gal Hirsch broke off the attack and also withdrew his unit behind the Israeli border.

The 162nd Division was ordered to reach the Litani River, which forms the natural border with southern Lebanon. The division was to move along the Wadi Saluki, a narrow dry valley on the main Qantara–Ghanduriyah axis, whereby the march required crossing the river of the same name. The hilly and stony terrain did not permit a detour. The wadi was lined with surrounding hills, which allowed the enemy to set up excellent firing positions.

Even before the outbreak of the war, Hezbollah recognized that the road between Qantara and Ghanduriyah was an important access route for the invasion forces and that Wadi Saluki was a bottleneck along this road. Hezbollah therefore established heavily fortified firing positions on the hills and prepared for a possible Israeli attack.

Brigadier General Guy Tzur deployed his two infantry brigades to initially occupy the heights along the Wadi Saluki but encountered fierce resistance from Hezbollah. Conflicting Israeli communications between the two infantry brigades meant that the order to march now also reached the armored battalions of the 401st Armored Brigade, under the assumption that the wadi was secure and the passage was open. This proved to be a grave mistake.

The battalions moved their tank companies through the narrow wadi in column formation, with less than 20 m between tanks. The wind dispersed the clouds of smoke produced by the grenades in front of them to conceal their approach in a matter of minutes. When the first tanks reached a bridge over the Saluki River, wire-guided AT-3 Sagger antitank guided missiles opened fire on the worthwhile targets. The leading vehicles of the companies received direct hits, and another Merkava IV was badly damaged and swept down an embankment. The attack slowed down the entire armored column, and Hezbollah launched a comprehensive strike with all the weapons at its disposal.

The tank commanders desperately called for air and artillery support by radio. However, the calls for help went unheard, since their radio equipment's range was limited by the complex terrain. The crews were thus left to their own devices and tried to coordinate their fire, while the infantrymen of the Nahal and Givati Brigades began to storm the firing positions on the hills. During the course of the day, a reserve battalion of the 401st Armored Brigade moved up and used recovery vehicles to evacuate the disabled tanks on the bridge.

The Israelis finally succeeded in eliminating numerous Hezbollah firing positions, clearing the roads, and putting the attackers to flight. General Tzur reorganized his division and actually captured the Ghanduriyah heights on the morning of August 13. After the first Merkava Mark IVs of the 401st Armored Brigade crossed the Saluki River on the night of August 14, the Israeli general staff called off the attack into Lebanon and ordered a withdrawal back to Israel. Despite various partial successes, the Israeli general staff was unable to achieve the defined objectives.

The ceasefire took effect at 0800 on August 14, 2006. Resolution 1701 of the United Nations Security Council regulated the postwar order, in which Israel undertook to withdraw behind the Israeli-Lebanese border—the so-called Blue Line. The Lebanese army was to station 15,000 soldiers in the south. In return, the Hezbollah militias laid down their weapons and were to hand over control of the area south of the Litani River to the Lebanese armed forces and UN troops. Despite this compromise peace, the presidents of both warring parties loudly proclaimed victories.

Chief of Staff Benjamin Gantz monitors strikes by the Israeli air force against targets in the Gaza Strip during Operation Pillar of Defense in November 2012. *IDF*

Israel lost a total of 120 soldiers and forty-one civilians killed. A further 750 soldiers were wounded. The army lost sixteen tanks and five aircraft. Hezbollah in turn lost 650 fighters, but 1,181 civilians also lost their lives. There was no victor in this war.

ANALYSIS OF THE OFFENSIVE AND ITS CONSEQUENCES

The reasons for Israel's failure can be explained and evaluated as follows:

- The Israeli government's war aims were insufficiently formulated and could not be achieved with the available means and the planned deployment of the armed forces.
- The Israeli chief of staff, Dan Chalutz, waited too long before deploying ground troops, since he believed that he could eliminate the rocket batteries with air and artillery strikes and thus wear down Hezbollah.
- The infantry and tank crews were poorly prepared for the war and received no specialized training. The commanders and troops were familiar only with police actions in the Palestinian areas of the West Bank and the Gaza Strip. A combined arms battle, as practiced in the First Lebanon War of 1982, against a heavily armed and well-prepared opponent was too much for the Israelis.
- Despite having the latest technology, the Israeli intelligence service failed to identify the Hezbollah positions and interfere with the enemy's communications network.
- Hezbollah learned from previous mistakes, studied the enemy's fighting methods, and, on this basis, developed new forms of guerrilla warfare.

The Israeli army not only had to take relatively heavy losses in men and materiel in this war but, more importantly, lost its aura of invincibility. After the conventional wars of 1948, 1956, 1967, 1973, and 1982, the Israeli armed forces had earned the reputation of being able to develop unbelievable striking power to win wars despite its numerical inferiority.

The Arab world, especially Hezbollah, already regarded the Israeli army's withdrawal from southern Lebanon in 2000 as a victory against the "Zionist enemy." This view was again strengthened by the outcome of the most recent Lebanese war: despite massive military pressure, Hezbollah had been able to hold out; it remained capable of fighting and inflicted significant losses on the Israelis, both on the battlefield and in civilian targets in the enemy rear, which were struck by rocket fire.

As it had done with the Agranat Inquiry after the 1973 Yom Kippur War, the Israeli government directed a commission headed by former judge Eliyahu Winograd to investigate the political and military leadership during the Second Lebanon War. This report ultimately proved not only the mistakes of the government and the general staff, and the unclear war aims, but also the lack of communication between the government and the military and the hesitant execution of the ground offensive. The minister of defense and the chief of general staff were primarily responsible for these serious mistakes. As a result of the investigation, Amir Peretz and Dan Chalutz drew personal conclusions in the first half of 2007 and resigned.

Nasrallah later revealed in an interview that he had never expected a war of this magnitude after the first skirmish with the Israelis.

On a military-tactical level, the Second Lebanon War in 2006 can serve as a real lesson in the clash between two very different opponents: on the one hand, the Israeli armed forces as a modern and at least to some extent network-oriented high-tech armed force, and, on the other hand, Hezbollah as a comparatively simply armed and organized guerrilla force.

As a result of the war, the Israeli general staff re-evaluated combined arms combat and increasingly practiced cooperation between the various branches of the armed forces.

HAMAS AND THE CONTINUOUS FIGHTING IN THE GAZA STRIP

In 1987, an uprising broke out among the Palestinian Arabs against the Israeli occupying power in the West Bank — the First Intifada. In its course, the radical organization Hamas, which emerged from the Palestinian branch of the Muslim Brotherhood, grew in importance. This paramilitary organization fought primarily for the establishment of an Islamic-Palestinian state in the entire area of the former British Mandate in Palestine and the subsequent destruction of the state of Israel. In response to the escalation of violence, the PLO's National Council, meeting in exile in Algiers in November 1988, called for an independent Palestinian state in the territories occupied by Israel. This step became possible after Jordan renounced the West Bank in favor of the PLO in July 1988. In doing so, the PLO implicitly recognized the state of Israel and thus its willingness to accept a future two-state solution, whereby Yasser Arafat was to govern the new Palestinian state. The General Assembly of the United Nations recognized Palestine as a de facto autonomous state but never gave it voting rights.

After the end of the Second Gulf War in 1991, there were increasing signs that the originally irreconcilable positions of the two parties would soften. Under the chairmanship of US president George H. W. Bush and the former Soviet president Mikhail Gorbachev, bilateral rounds of negotiations and direct talks between the parties took place for the first time in September 1993. Under Norwegian mediation, the two sides agreed on mutual recognition of the partial autonomy of the Palestinian Arabs in the Gaza Strip and the Jericho area.

The so-called expanded-autonomy agreement of September 24, 1995, was then referred to as the Oslo II Agreement. It specified the structure and self-administration of the Palestinian autonomous territories and the division of the West Bank into three zones: Zone A comprises the major cities with the exception of Hebron and is fully controlled by the Palestinians. Zone B is under joint administration. Zone C comprises the Jewish settlements and uninhabited areas with military bases. It is under the command of Israel.

However, Palestinian terrorist attacks, on the one hand, and continued Israeli settlement activity, on the other hand, have pushed the original goal of the two Oslo Accords a long way off. Therefore, and due to the delayed Israeli troop withdrawal, further negotiations became necessary, which led to the Hebron Agreement in 1997, the Wye Agreement in 1998, and the Sharm El Sheik Agreement in 1999.

In July 2000, a summit meeting scheduled by US president Bill Clinton between Israeli president Ehud Barak and Palestinian leader Yasser Arafat seemed to bring a final settlement within reach. Ultimately, however, these talks also ended without result. The future state of Palestine was to encompass the entire Gaza Strip and over 95 percent of the West Bank and connect both parts of the territory via a transit route. Jerusalem was to be divided up again. In the end, however, the Clinton plan also failed, primarily due to the core issues of securing Palestinian statehood under international law, as well as the definition of borders, the status of Jerusalem, the question of the right of return of the 1948–49 refugees, and the future of the approximately 200,000 Israeli settlers in the Gaza Strip and the West Bank.

In the fall of 2000, the Second Intifada broke out. Following a visit to the Temple Mount in Jerusalem by former defense minister and opposition leader of the right-wing Likud bloc, Ariel Sharon, violence broke out between Israeli security forces and Arab demonstrators. The unrest spread from Jerusalem to the entire Israeli-controlled territories; namely, Ramallah, Nablus, Hebron, and Gaza. Hamas also gained strength in the wake of numerous Palestinian attacks on Israeli civilians, established its stronghold in the Gaza Strip, and actively supported these actions.

The Gaza Strip is a coastal area on the Mediterranean Sea, approximately 25 miles (40 km) long and between 5 and 9 miles (8 and 15 km) wide. It borders Israel and Egypt and, together with the West Bank, forms the Palestinian Autonomous Territories. The borders with Israel are under Israeli control. The most-important cities in the Gaza Strip are the city of Gaza in the northeast, the city of Rafah in the southwest, on the border with Egypt, and the smaller town of Khan Yunis to the east. The landscape consists mainly of sand and dunes, so that only a few parts of the country are suitable for agriculture. This means that the approximately 1.8 million inhabitants are mostly dependent on supplies from the United Nations Relief and Works Agency Relief and Works Agency (UNRWA).

The so-called Qassam Brigades form the military arm of Hamas. Organized in cells, these militia units, in contrast to Fatah's al-Aqsa Brigades, are under a centralized command. Several cells are in the West Bank, but the majority of the Qassam Brigades are stationed in the Gaza Strip. In 2007, Hamas violently overthrew Fatah in the Gaza Strip and took over control there.

Its arsenal of weapons ranges from simple small arms, machine guns, mortars and explosive charges, RPG-7 antitank weapons, and AT-3 Sagger wire-guided antitank missiles to the man-portable 9K135 Kornet antitank guided-missile system (AT-14 Spriggan). For more-distant targets, Hamas developed its own surface-to-surface rockets, the "Kassam rockets," which can carry 11 to 33 pounds (5 to 15 kg) of explosives, depending on the variant. The rockets have ranges of up to 15 miles (24 km), and some sources even speak of ranges of up to 25 miles (40 km). The surface-to-surface rockets are usually fired from the city of Beit Hanun, east of Gaza City.

OPERATION CAST LEAD, 2008

Despite the withdrawal of the Israeli occupying power in August 2005 as part of the so-called Sharon Plan, the removal of Israeli settlements from the Gaza Strip, and the ceasefire arranged by Egypt, Hamas continued firing rockets deep into the Israeli heartland. For the Israeli defense minister Ehud Barak, it became impossible to go on standing by idly in the face of these actions, and so he decided on an attack into the Gaza Strip.

The M113 APC received its baptism of fire in the Vietnam War. The Israeli armed forces placed the vehicle into service in 1972, prior to the outbreak of the Yom Kippur War, and gave it the name Nagmash. Israeli acquired the impressive total of about six thousand of these vehicles. The M113 earned the reputation of being mechanically reliable and highly maneuverable. The war in Lebanon in 1982 revealed its vulnerability due to its inadequate armor protection. Over the years, numerous modifications were made to improve its protective capabilities. In the photo is an M113 of the 460th Armored Brigade near the border with the Gaza Strip. *IDF*

CHAPTER 20: The 2006 Lebanon War and the Fighting in the Gaza Strip | 191

Merkava Mark 4 on the move during Operation Protective Edge, July 2014. *IDF*

To this end, Barak said, "There is a time for peace and a time for battle; now is the time for battle!," and he instructed his chief of staff, Gabriel Ashkenazi,[9] and the commander of the southern front, Major General Yoav Galant,[10] to draw up a plan of attack, which was given the name Operation Cast Lead.

The lessons learned in the unsuccessful operation in the Second Lebanon War of 2006 would now be applied, and Hamas's asymmetric conduct of warfare would be countered by the use of combined arms and a networked operational command. Hamas's military striking power in the Gaza Strip was to be weakened by surprise airstrikes, followed by a ground offensive with tanks and mechanized infantry. Logistics, communications centers, and weapons dumps were to be destroyed in a comprehensive way, and tunnel systems, which guaranteed the terror organization's supply chain, were to be taken out. Furthermore, Hamas leaders and operation staffs as well as its security services were to be neutralized.

However, the Israeli general staff was faced with a challenge, since Hamas was not prepared to fight in the open. It waged a

[9] Gabriel Ashkenazi (1954–) grew up in Chagor, northeast of Tel Aviv. He studied political science at the University of Haifa and joined the Israeli armed forces in 1972. He served in the Golani Brigade in the Sinai during the Yom Kippur War, fought as deputy commander of an infantry battalion during Operation Litani in southern Lebanon in 1978, and finally took over command of the Golani Brigade during the First Lebanon War in 1982. Promoted to brigadier general, he was later transferred to the armored corps and commanded an armored division. In 1996, he was promoted to major general and commander of the northern front. After serving as deputy chief of the general staff, the Israeli cabinet appointed him chief of general staff in February 2007.

[10] Yoav Galant (1958–) studied economics and financial management at the University of Haifa. He joined the Israeli navy in 1977 and served in the 13th Flotilla. In 1999, he changed branches and took command of the Gaza Division and later, as major general, commanded the southern front. Galant was intended to succeed Gabriel Ashkenazi as chief of the general staff. Due to suspicion of preferential treatment in the sale of land, his appointment was withdrawn by President Benjamin Netanyahu. He entered politics on behalf of the social-conservative Kulanu Party in 2015 and won a seat in the Knesset. During Netanyahu's presidency, he was minister of immigration and integration and later minister of education.

guerrilla war similar to that of Hezbollah, hiding in densely populated cities, and tried to strike unexpectedly. With the decision in favor of an Israeli military operation under these circumstances, it was accepted that casualties among the civilian population were inevitable.

The trauma of the Second Lebanon War caused the Israeli military to realize that their own casualties could very quickly undermine trust in the political and military leadership. It was therefore important to further improve the safety of the soldiers and thus keep Israeli losses as low as possible. This was, however, a major challenge in a ground operation carried out in a densely populated area such as the Gaza Strip.

The coming military operation therefore required thorough preparation: Combat pilots trained in various attack scenarios, and the foreign intelligence service Mossad obtained information about rocket batteries, logistics installations, arms dumps, and tunnel systems, while the Israeli Armored Corps and mechanized infantry practiced operating against an opponent operating asymmetrically. Phosphorus was to be used to create smoke screens within minutes, to enable the tanks and infantry to advance under cover.

The Israelis benefited from having controlled the Gaza Strip until their withdrawal in 2005 and were therefore very familiar with the nature of the terrain, street networks, and the urban area. Furthermore, Egypt completely sealed its border with the Gaza Strip during the military operation.

Operation Cast Lead began on a Sabbath, December 27, 2008, at 1130. Airstrikes in the central and northern Gaza Strip targeted arms depots, factories, and other critical Hamas infrastructure. In the first hours, about a hundred combat aircraft and helicopters struck more than 250 tactical targets, dropped more than 100 tons of bombs, and in the process destroyed many Hamas tunnel systems.

In the second wave, the warplanes, particularly the F-15I Ra'am, destroyed numerous rocket batteries and munitions dumps, while a third wave targeted command and communications facilities. Taken by surprise, Hamas called these airstrikes the "Black Saturday Massacre" and replied by firing type 9K51 Katyusha rockets at the Israeli port city of Ashdod, more than 12.5 miles (20 km) away.

After a week of airstrikes and artillery strikes, Major General Yoav Galant ordered the 35th Paratrooper Brigade, the Golani and Givati Brigades, and the 401st Armored Brigade of the 162nd Division—a total of six thousand to eight thousand troops—to prepare to attack. The general staff organized the force, which together formed the Gaza Division, into three areas of operations and assigned each brigade a corresponding autonomous area of operation:

- In the west, near the Egyptian border, rocket and arms smuggling routes were to be identified and attacked.
- In the south, Hamas training areas and arms dumps were to be destroyed.
- In Gaza City, the crippling of command facilities and communications installations had top priority.
- In the north, rocket batteries were to be put out of action.

In addition, each brigade was assigned its own warplanes, attack helicopters, and drones, the use of which was coordinated by an air liaison officer and the brigade commander when necessary. Thus, the brigade commander was for the first time given freedom of action over another branch of the armed forces. Drones flying ahead of the advancing units were to collect real-time images of the terrain and other reconnaissance information and thus provide the command with an enhanced image of the situation at all times.

Under covering fire from a heavy artillery barrage, on January 3, 2009, the four brigades moved into the Gaza Strip. The troops divided the main axis in the Gaza Strip, the Salaheddin Road, and thus the entire area into three parts. The 35th Paratrooper Brigade moved from the east through Atratra, west of Beth Lahia, to the outskirts of Gaza City. The Golani Brigade pushed on three axes from the northwest to the south in the direction of Beit Lahia, Jabalia, and Beit Hanun, from where most of the Qassam rockets were fired. The Givati Brigade moved from the south to the northeast and advanced toward Zeitun, while the 401st Armored Brigade linked up south of Gaza on the grounds of the former settlement of Netzarim, sealing off the encircled capital from the south as well.

Fierce airstrikes on the road between Khan Yunis and Rafah preceded the advance from the south into the settlement of Moraj. This was also supposed to cut Gaza and Khan Yunis off from access to Egypt via Rafah. The Israeli forces advanced rapidly, in most cases led by armored Caterpillar D7 and D9 bulldozers. Attack helicopters and reconnaissance drones accompanied the advancing tanks and armored personnel carriers.

The attack force did not always follow the classic road network, since these were largely mined, but instead took alternative routes prepared by the armored bulldozers and in some cases broke into built-up areas directly through the houses. Most of the Israeli advances were made at night, exploiting Hamas's lack of night-fighting capabilities and training.

In contrast to Hezbollah, which fought stubbornly for every inch of ground during the Second Lebanon War, Hamas showed little will to face the overpowering Israeli forces. The IEDs placed

Achzarit armored personnel carriers accompanied the mechanized advance during Operation Protective Edge. The Achzarit is a converted T-54/55 tank whose turret has been removed, additional armor installed, and a 7.62 mm machine gun fitted. Photo taken in 2014. *IDF*

beside the streets and roads had little to no effect on the Merkava IVs with their added armor. The interruption of Hamas communications also produced quick results: The Qassam Brigades soon found themselves unable to communicate in order to perhaps stop or at least delay the attacker. Hamas quickly withdrew into the urban areas, mixed with the population, or disappeared into bunkers and tunnels. Most of the fighters discarded their uniforms to remain unrecognized.

Although details about the Gaza Division's campaign remain secret, rapid progress was made by the ground forces. There were repeated engagements until January 5, but the battle was clearly dominated by the Israelis as a result of Hamas's reluctance to openly exchange blows with the Israelis. The drones and the Israeli intelligence network continued to do good work and enabled the brigades to locate and largely destroy targets such as rocket-firing bases, tunnel systems, arms dumps, and command facilities.

The Israeli air force also continued its precision strikes, taking out many Hamas leaders. The Hamas Ministry of the Interior did report successes, including the capture of numerous Israeli soldiers. Meanwhile, protests developed in Palestinian-dominated towns and cities. In Ramallah, for example, hundreds of people demonstrated against the bloodshed. Major protests also developed in Hebron and other cities in the West Bank. They were echoed a little later in rallies in Western capitals, where demonstrators called on the governments in Paris and London to demand a ceasefire.

After the units of the Gaza Division had largely achieved their attack objectives and the captured Hamas defensive positions had been secured, the Israeli general staff drew additional reserve units into the fighting. These took over the secured sectors and thus enabled the units of the Gaza Division to advance farther.

However, as the war continued, foreign criticism of the harsh actions by the Israeli armed forces grew louder and louder, not least because it became clear that the civilian population in particular was suffering from the war. In fact, the number of civilian casualties increased with each day of the military action, and more and more Western governments called for an immediate ceasefire.

The Israeli government finally bowed to this pressure. A planned third phase of the war, in which a further advance into the city of Gaza and fierce house-to-house fighting with high casualties on both sides were expected, did not materialize. Even Chief of Staff Gabriel Ashkenazi also decided against a third phase of the offensive and had Operation Cast Lead declared over. The official ceasefire took effect on January 18, and the Gaza Division began its withdrawal from the Gaza Strip.

The strategic aftereffects of the 2008–09 Gaza war, which lasted twenty-two days and claimed at least 1,200 Palestinian and thirteen Israeli victims, are remarkably small from today's perspective. Even though Hamas suffered major losses, neither the balance of power in the Middle East nor the domestic political conditions in Israel and the Palestinian territories have fundamentally changed.

For Israel, the results of the operation were ambivalent. The adaptability of the Israeli military leadership with regard to asymmetric warfare can initially be seen as positive. In reaction to the Second Lebanon War against Hezbollah, the Israeli armed forces adapted operational planning, command structures, troop training, and equipment to the conditions of irregular warfare.

The Merkava Mark IV tank, which was also adapted to the requirements of asymmetric warfare, proved to be the backbone of the Israeli Armored Corps. In the complex urban environment, tank crews had to expect attacks from any direction. The armored vehicles were engaged by antitank guns and guided missiles from close range, which concentrated on their vulnerable top and rear areas. Mines and roadside IEDs also posed a great threat to the tanks and their crews.

To meet such threats, the Merkava Mark IV was given upgraded turret roof armor, much thicker than that standard on battle tanks. The commander's hatch is so thick and heavy that it can be opened and closed only by electric motors. If the electric motors fail, the hatch can be opened manually by means

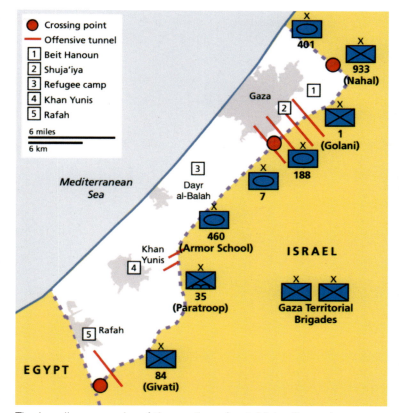

The Israeli commander of the southern front, Major General Shlomo Turgeman, moved his three divisions into attack position around the Gaza Strip shortly before the start of Operation Protective Edge. The map shows the positions of the corresponding brigades, July 2014. *RAND Corporation*

of a threaded jack. The loader's hatch has been deleted, since fewer openings in the roof armor area compromise the integrity of the total armor less.

The necessity to better protect the roof area of the turret against attacks from above has affected its shape. Compared to the wedge-shaped turret of earlier versions of the Merkava, it now has a striking stepped silhouette. As a result, the Merkava Mark IV has a larger signature and is thus a better target.

Mines will pose a much-greater threat in the wars of the near future. In the past, mine damage was limited mostly to the chassis of tanks and could be repaired relatively quickly. Around 50 percent of the Israeli tanks damaged by mines in the Yom Kippur War were repaired within twenty-four hours. Today, improvised mine traps and modern roadside IEDs are much more dangerous. With its side skirts made of special armor elements attached to robust suspensions, the Merkava was always quite well protected on the sides, with the Merkava Mark IV using the side skirts already familiar from the Merkava Mark III. However, some Merkava Mark IVs are seen with very long side skirts, which protect the return rollers and the chassis as a whole. The rear part of the side skirts is often removed, both to prevent the accumulation of dirt and debris in this area as well as to save weight.

Despite the ballistic shape of the hull bottom, the Merkava Mark IV's protection against mines is relatively modest. Additional floor plates were used on the Merkava Mark III. Despite this, close cooperation with infantry and engineers remains essential to counter the threat posed by hidden IEDs.

The low casualty figures on the Israeli side can be explained primarily by these technical adaptations, the detailed planning in the run-up to the attack, and the uncompromising deployment and combination of all the weapons systems used. From a purely military perspective, the considerably impaired deterrence of the Israeli military caused by the conflict in Lebanon was completely restored.

Nevertheless, Israel was still being bombarded by rockets, and so the minimum objective of the war must be considered to have been missed. The initial euphoria of military success was soon followed by disillusionment that after the war, the Gaza Strip basically only returned to the status quo antebellum.

In any case, soon after the withdrawal of the first Israeli units, radical Islamists reappeared in the destroyed streets and claimed victory for themselves.

OPERATION PROTECTIVE EDGE, 2014

Hamas rocket fire on Israeli population centers continued even after Operation Cast Lead. This was especially true as Hamas benefited from the new Islamist regime in Egypt. Whereas the toppled Egyptian president Husni Mubarak had closed the border to Gaza, the newly elected Mohammed Mursi kept it open so that Iranian weapons such as the Fajr-3 and Fajr-5 artillery rockets reached Hamas unhindered.

These surface-to-surface rockets were a development of the Chinese WS-1 multiple rocket launcher system and could be fitted with fragmentation or incendiary warheads or with bomblets (cluster munitions). Unlike the Qassam rockets, they were capable of striking not only Be'er Sheva, Ashkelon, or Ashdod, but also targets in the southern suburbs of Tel Aviv.

Hamas also succeeded in acquiring a number of MILAN antitank missiles with the MIRA (MILAN infrared adapter) thermal sight. This system locates heat sources and guides the missile to targets up to 1.8 miles (3 km) away.

In 2012, the number of clashes between Israeli patrols and Hamas fighters grew steadily. Hamas continued to fire rockets from the border region of the Gaza Strip at the Israeli towns of Ashkelon and Ashdod, and the Israelis responded with targeted airstrikes. Ultimately the hostilities intensified, and Israel made ready for another incursion into the Gaza Strip.

After Ahmed Jabari,[11] leader of the military wing of Hamas, was killed in a drone strike, Israeli chief of staff Benjamin Gantz[12] launched Operation Pillar of Defense on November 12, 2012. This was another large-scale airstrike by the Israelis similar to Operation Cast Lead, aimed at destroying the enemy's infrastructure, rocket positions, and Hamas leadership. Hamas responded with furious counterattacks on the towns of Holon and Rishon Lezion, south of Tel Aviv, but in Tel Aviv too, the sirens howled for the first time since January 1991.

For the first time, Israel used its ground-based missile defense system — the so-called Iron Dome. But the unrest did not subside. The Hamas rocket fire on Israeli settlements continued, and for sustainable protection against the strikes of the Israeli air force, the terrorist group even expanded its tunnel system. These tunnels were used to hide supplies but also led into Israeli territory for the launching of targeted attacks against settlements. In June 2014, the kidnapping and murder of three Israeli teenagers once again triggered a military escalation.

As a result, violent demonstrations shook both the West Bank and East Jerusalem. These riots eventually spread to the Gaza Strip, with Hamas intensifying its rocket fire on Israel.

---

[11] Ahmed Jabari (1960–2012) was considered one of the five most important military leaders of Hamas. He served in Fatah at a young age, and after the defeat in the Lebanon War, he was sentenced to thirteen years in prison for his involvement in terrorist actions against Israel. After his release, Jabari became a member of the Hamas leadership in 1995. At the height of the Second Intifada, after the death of Salah Mustafa Muhammad Shehade, the commander of the Qassam Brigades, Jabari became his successor. In 2006, Jabari became the supreme commander and one of the leaders of Hamas. He died during Operation Pillar of Defense when a missile launched from an Israeli drone struck his vehicle.

[12] Benjamin Gantz (1959–) grew up in the Kfar Chaim moshav in the Emek Chefer region of central Israel. He joined the paratroopers in 1977, was promoted to officer in 1979, and led numerous air force units. In 1994 he was promoted to brigadier general and served in the Judea Division and later in the Samaria Division. After six years, he took over as commander of the Judea Division and was promoted to major general at the same time, and beginning in 2002 he commanded the northern front. The Israeli government finally elected Gantz to be chief of staff of the Israeli armed forces in 2011. Gantz retired from the military in 2019 and has since pursued a political career. He is currently serving in the Bennett-Lapid cabinet as minister of defense.

The Israeli general staff commissioned the commander of the southern front, Major General Shlomo Turgeman,[13] with the preparation of a new renewed incursion into the Gaza Strip under the code name Operation Protective Edge. The experience from the previous operations and the military intelligence situation led to the assumption that between 25,000 and 30,000 Hamas fighters, divided into divided into six brigades, were in the Gaza Strip.

However, planning the operation proved difficult, since the Israeli general staff could not agree on whether the entire Gaza Strip should be conquered, or where exactly the Hamas tunnels were located and how civilian casualties could be avoided to the extent possible. There was also disagreement about the duration of the operation. In the end, the decision was made in favor of a comprehensive operation involving the air force and naval forces.

The Israeli command assigned the following units to the operation:

- the 36th Division, with the 1st Golani Brigade, the 7th and 188th Armored Brigades, the 35th Paratrooper Brigade, and the 282nd Artillery Brigade
- the 162nd Division, with the 933rd Nahal Brigade, the 401st Armored Brigade, and the 215th Artillery Brigade
- the 643rd Gaza Territorial Division, with the 84th Gavati Brigade, the 460th Armored Brigade, and two territorial brigades

In peacetime, each branch of the armed forces within a brigade usually trained independently. During operations, however, the branches waged combined arms warfare within the brigade. An example of this is the 401st Armored Brigade, which had single tank, infantry, artillery, and logistics battalions. This structure can also be found at battalion level, where, for example, the infantry battalion of the 84th Givati Brigade also had an armored company in addition to infantry companies. This mix of combat units is accompanied by clear advantages, since operations in the Gaza Strip are dominated by fighting in built-up areas.

The infantry units were to go ahead of the armored units, remove mines and barricades, clear streets, and secure and keep open road junctions. These advance actions were intended to protect the advancing armored units from surprise fire from enemy RPGs and guided missiles and, overall, to detect the enemy's actions early and, if possible, thwart them.

Only a few of the combat units mentioned were close to the Gaza Strip, and they therefore had to be moved from the central and northern fronts to the south. In particular, moving the Merkava Mark IV tanks and Caterpillar D9 armored bulldozers proved to be a logistical challenge due to the limited number of transport vehicles available.

The Israeli army mobilized no fewer than 84,000 reservists for Operation Protective Edge. The units, especially those located on the Golan Heights, underwent brief training in order to be prepared for the requirements for deployment in the Gaza Strip. The force finally took up position on the border with the Gaza Strip. The 162nd Division was located northeast of Gaza City and Beit Hanun, the 36th Division was in the central part, and the 643rd Territorial Division was in the southwest at Khan Yunis-Rafah.

A comprehensive airstrike on around 220 targets in the Gaza Strip opened Operation Protective Edge on July 8, 2014. During the first week of the operation, the Israeli air force flew more than 1,700 sorties, mainly targeting logistical facilities, arms depots and surface-to-surface rocket batteries, and Hamas command and control facilities. Although the initial successes looked promising, the enemy rocket fire decreased somewhat, and even an Egyptian ceasefire proposal was accepted by Israel, Hamas continued to invade Israeli territory via its tunnel system. On July 17, when Hamas fighters with assault rifles and RPG-7 antitank weapons emerged from a tunnel and launched a surprise attack on Kibbutz Sufa, an Israeli ground offensive seemed inevitable.

Then, on July 17, the three Israeli divisions crossed the border of the Gaza Strip. In the first phase, the Hamas tunnel system was to be largely dug up and destroyed. This operation proved very challenging, since first the tunnels had to be located, then cleared, and finally blown up. In general, the Israelis avoided fighting in the tunnels and instead sent in their special Jahalom Unit. It was an engineering unit whose personnel were equipped with breathing and communications equipment and explosives, in order to allow them to operate successfully in the special tunnel environment.

The second phase called for the destruction of the most-important rocket-launching batteries, located in the Shuja'iya district in Gaza City. The Israeli secret service had learned that

---

[13] Shlomo Turgeman (1964–) was born in Marrakesh, Morocco, immigrated to Israel with his family at an early age, and grew up in Ashkelon. In 1982, Turgeman joined the Israeli army and served as a platoon commander in the 401st Armored Division and company commander in the 460th Armored Brigade. After serving as a battalion commander, he took over the 500th Armored Brigade in 1999. Four years later, he was promoted to brigadier general and took command of a reserve division on the northern front. In 2004, he led the Israeli Armored Corps for two years, was promoted to major general in 2009, and took command of the southern front in 2013.

there were more than eight hundred Hamas fighters in the area. This task fell to two infantry battalions of the 1st Golani Brigade. It was decided not to use an armored unit, since the heavily built-up area meant that it would be an infantry operation, and numerous tunnel systems were expected. Coordination problems between the southern front's command and the general staff delayed the entry into the city by a day, which gave Hamas additional time to prepare.

On July 19 the two infantry battalions entered the city quarter. Other units of the 36th Division moved along the border with Gaza as a deception and diversionary maneuver. But the effort to deceive Hamas failed. The two advancing infantry battalions were soon under heavy fire from small arms, antitank guns, and mortars. Armored personnel carriers that escorted the infantry — mostly older American-made M113 APCs, with only a few Israeli-made Namer vehicles — took numerous hits, and most were knocked out along with their crews.

The situation in the Shuja'iya quarter deteriorated visibly for the Israelis, since recovery of the disabled armored vehicles proved more than difficult. The infantry suffered heavy casualties in house fighting, and the location and elimination of the tunnel systems led to precarious situations. The brigade commander and both battalion commanders were wounded and put out of action during the fighting.

The leaders of the 1st Golani Brigade saw no other choice but to force Hamas to give up with heavy airstrikes and artillery strikes. These were carried out on July 20 and finally brought the battle for Shuja'iya to an end.

Due north of the 1st Golani Brigade, the 162nd Division, with the 933rd Nahal Brigade and the 401st Armored Brigade, found itself facing significantly less resistance in the Beit Hanoun and Beit Lahia areas. The unit encountered numerous nests of resistance, fought tunnel battles, and repulsed a Hamas attack on a school run by the United Nations aid organization (UNRWA). The two brigades also increasingly fought against snipers and Hamas squads armed with antitank guided missiles, with the Merkava Mark 4's active defense system proving its effectiveness against the latter.

In the center was the combat zone of the 7th and 188th Armored Brigades. Analogous to Operation Cast Lead, the former was to advance to the coast and divide the Gaza Strip into two parts, to hamper command as well as communications and supply by Hamas. During the operation, however, the 7th Armored Brigade's orders changed, and it was directed to locate and neutralize tunnel systems. In the process it entered towns such as Deir al-Balah, looked for tunnel openings, and took part in fierce house-to-house battles.

The 188th Armored Brigade, which was east of the 7th Armored Brigade, was supposed to support the units of the 1st Golani Brigade in the battle for Shuja-iya. However, its advance was further delayed by unexpectedly fierce resistance from Hamas fighters and the breaking down of many older Merkava tanks.

The Israeli fighting units operating in the south also soon found themselves in action and regular street battles with Hamas. The 35th Paratrooper and the 460th Armored Brigades entered the city of Khan Yunis, while the 84th Givati Brigade, on the one hand, guarded its southern flank and, on the other hand, attacked Hamas in the city of Rafah, near the border. The troops of the Givati Brigade benefited from having maintained border posts in the region in the months leading up to the operation and were thus very familiar with the area. The battalions advanced, riding in their Namer and M113 armored personnel carriers by day and operating on foot during the night.

The Israelis succeeded in locating and blowing up several of the Hamas tunnel systems, including in the south, while eliminating numerous Hamas fighters; however, they also suffered heavy casualties. While the fighting in the Gaza Strip was still raging, the governments of the warring parties began negotiating a ceasefire with mediation by Egypt. It was not until August 26, 2014, that an open-ended agreement took effect and the guns fell silent for the time being.

CONCLUDING REMARKS

Although the Israeli war objective of Operation Protective Edge — namely, to stop Hamas rocket fire — was in fact achieved, Israel's armed forces were unable to bring about the destruction of the tunnel systems and the elimination of Hamas leadership facilities. During Operation Protective Edge, the Israeli armed forces deployed a total force of 571 Merkava tanks in the Gaza Strip. These tanks, which were used mainly in offensive operations, fired a total of 22,269 rounds, including the M339 multipurpose tank ammunition. This ammunition, specially designed for the 120 mm smooth-bore gun, is suitable for engaging bunkers, urban structures, unarmored and lightly armored vehicles, and dismounted infantry.

Once again, the Merkava tanks played a key role during the operation, since they provided the all-important protection for the crews and at the same time enabled a high degree of mobility. The Israelis used the tank in particular to secure outlying urban areas and support the infantry during the seizure of tunnel systems and houses in densely populated areas. The tank was of great importance there due to its

precise fire support. The Merkava tanks equipped with the Trophy active protection system proved to be decisive in combating Hamas's antitank weapons. In fact, no Merkava tank was irreparably destroyed, since the active protection system successfully intercepted numerous antitank missiles.

The Israeli armored units recorded fourteen killed and 241 wounded. The use of the obsolescent M113 APCs, which dated from the days of the Vietnam War, was much criticized, since they provided little protection for their crews.

Hamas acted more effectively and aggressively than in previous conflicts. Although the Israelis won most of the close battles, the Hamas fighters inflicted considerable losses on even the best infantry and armored units. Israeli soldiers later stated that they experienced a far more heavily armed and better-organized Hamas in this operation than in Operation Cast Lead. It seemed as if Hamas had adopted many of Hezbollah's experiences and tactics from the fierce house-to-house fighting during the 2006 Lebanon War. They used the complex urban area to their advantage, laying numerous antitank ambushes, burying mines to protect tunnel systems, and installing booby traps to block the entrances to houses.

Nevertheless, Operation Protective Edge impressively proved the importance of armored vehicles for combat in built-up areas. While in recent years the Israeli military invested heavily in missile defense systems and its air force, it is now once again placing increasing emphasis on the technical advancement of its armored forces.

After successfully outfitting the Merkava Mark IV with the Trophy active defense system, in 2017 the Israelis introduced the Elbit vision system. Successfully tested in the F-35 Lightning combat aircraft, the system provides tank crews with a 360-degree picture of the combat area without having to open the hatches. Numerous cameras are mounted around the tank, which transmit images to the Elbit vision system, which combines the images into an all-around view and projects the result directly onto the helmet visors of the tank crew.

Deliveries of the upgraded Merkava Mark IV Barak tank to the armored battalions will begin in 2023. It is equipped with an expanded Trophy defense system, 360-degree cameras for vision by day and night, a sight for the tank commander analogous to those in modern combat aircraft, additional sensors for target acquisition, and updated software for electronic warfare.

Map of the Gaza Strip. *Wikipedia*

NO PEACE IN THE GAZA STRIP: OPERATION GUARDIAN OF THE WALLS

The armed conflict between Hamas and Israel was never going to end, as mutual skirmishes and border conflicts continued to flare up despite the ceasefire. Against the backdrop of the Palestinian parliamentary elections being canceled once again and further clashes between Israeli security forces and Palestinians around the Temple Mount, a series of rockets fired from Gaza on May 10, 2021, triggered another Gaza war. The continuous launching of rockets against Israel ended only on May 20, 2021, with the Israeli Iron Dome ground-based short-range defense system intercepting around 90 percent of the 4,360 rockets fired. Both Hamas, which operates from the Gaza Strip, and the terrorist militia Islamic Jihad, which had established itself in the

West Bank, claimed responsibility for the rocket attacks. While Hamas hardly had any rockets with a range of more than 75 km in the last Gaza war seven years earlier, the renewed rocket attacks clearly demonstrated that it now had better systems capable of reaching as far as Tel Aviv and Jerusalem. Hamas deliberately hid its military positions and launching bases near civilian facilities and therefore misused the Palestinian population as human shields. The terrorist organization also expanded its tunnel system into an extensive underground network. In addition to bunkers, there were also weapons workshops and storage rooms that were connected to supply and transportation routes.

Retaliation was not long in coming, and the incumbent Israeli prime minister Benjamin Netanyahu[14] ordered airstrikes and artillery strikes on rocket positions, command centers, and the tunnel system. The Israeli army, which had been better prepared since the last Gaza war in 2014, thwarted tactical surprise attacks by the Qassam Brigades, Hamas's elite units, on Israeli territory at an early stage. The standoff weapons for precision target engagement became more effective, destroying numerous launching bases and putting pressure on the tunnel system and rocket production sites. The elimination of top Hamas cadres such as the leader of the military apparatus, Mohammed Deif,[15] proved less successful. However, Chief of General Staff Benny Gantz refrained from a ground invasion due to the general threat situation. Mediated by Egypt and the UN, the warring parties finally agreed to a ceasefire. On the night of May 20, 2021, the guns fell silent for the time being.

2023. THE WORLD HOLDS ITS BREATH: GAZA AGAIN BECOMES A WAR ZONE

Exactly half a century to the day after Egypt and Syria attacked Israel in what would become the Yom Kippur War, Hamas unexpectedly invaded Israel from the Gaza Strip on October 7, 2023, breaking through the 52-kilometer-long and 600-meter-wide cordon along the border. In the nearby kibbutzim of Re'im, Kfar Aza, and Be'eri, as well as in the city of Sderot, the terrorist militia indiscriminately shot civilians and soldiers on the streets and in houses. At the same time, the cities of Ashkelon, Tel Aviv, and Jerusalem were hit by an incessant, unprecedented rocket barrage of over five thousand projectiles. Meanwhile, Hamas kidnapped around two hundred civilians and soldiers and took them to Gaza, dispersing them in the densely populated coastal strip to make their liberation more difficult.

The Kassam Brigades, conservatively estimated at around 30,000 men, managed to achieve the element of surprise in this way. Their commander, Mohammed Deif, issued his orders verbally, and his men silently moved into their attack positions on the night of October 7. Advancing through tunnels, sometimes without lighting or radio communication, lightly equipped infantry forces awaited the signal to attack. In fact, Deif briefed only a few Hamas commanders on the plans for the operation. Israel was in shock — after all, the country was experiencing its worst attack in five decades. One of Israel's ironclad rules is the doctrine of taking the war to the enemy's territory wherever possible. In 1956, 1967, and 1973, as well as in both Lebanon and four Gaza wars, battles raged on the enemy's territory. In 2023, however, the enemy struck Israel's heartland for the first time since the 1948–49 war of independence. Israel was spared a two-front war, since the Lebanese Hezbollah militia, which is closely allied with Iran and Hamas, refrained from intervening in the war for the time being.

The extent of the coordinated and apparently long-planned attack became apparent after just a few days: Israel mourned the loss of more than six hundred dead and two thousand injured — far more than in all four Gaza wars combined. On the same day, Prime Minister Netanyahu declared a state of war,

---

[14] Benjamin Netanyahu (1949–) grew up in Jerusalem. While he was attending high school, the family moved to Cheltenham in the state of Pennsylvania. Netanyahu studied architecture at the Massachusetts Institute of Technology (MIT) and political science at Harvard University. After returning to Israel, he served in the special unit Sayeret Matkal. He was discharged from active service in 1972 with the rank of captain. After various jobs in the private sector, he finally switched to politics, becoming Israel's deputy ambassador in Washington, DC, in 1982; a member of the Knesset in 1988; and head of the Likud Party in 1993. As the leading candidate, he won the 1996 parliamentary election against Shimon Peres but lost the 1999 election to Ehud Barak, following allegations of corruption, and stepped down from the political stage for the time being. It was not until 2002 that Prime Minister Ariel Sharon reactivated Netanyahu and appointed him foreign minister. After Likud emerged as the second-strongest party in the 2009 parliamentary elections and was tasked with forming a government as part of a coalition, Netanyahu was elected prime minister. Apart from a short break from office in 2021–22, he has held this post to this day. His older brother Jonathan, also a member of the Sayeret Matkal, was killed in action during Operation Entebbe in 1976 and is considered a war hero in Israel.

[15] Mohammed Deif (1965–) grew up in the Khan Yunis refugee camp in the Gaza Strip. He joined Hamas in 1990, worked his way up through the ranks, and became the top military commander of the Qassam Brigades in 2002. Little information is known about Deif. He apparently lost his wife and child during Operation Protective Edge in 2014 and other family members during Operation Swords of Iron in 2023.

mobilized his military reserves, and declared that the goal was the complete destruction of Hamas. In the days that followed, the Israeli army succeeded in quickly defeating the enemy on its own territory, deploying troops to the south, completely sealing off the Gaza Strip, and launching the first airstrikes against Hamas positions. UN secretary-general Antonio Guterres convened a special summit, while US secretary of state Lloyd Austin ordered two carrier battle groups around the aircraft carriers USS *Gerald R. Ford* and USS *Dwight D. Eisenhower* to the eastern Mediterranean to provide the Israelis with all the support they needed. Just a few hours after the attack, Netanyahu formed a war cabinet to strategically plan the retaliatory strike and the destruction of the terrorist militia. The operation was now launched under the noble code name Swords of Iron.

In addition to the prime minister, the war cabinet consisted of

- Benny Gantz, politician and former minister of defense (2020–22);
- Gadi Eizenkot, politician and former chief of general staff (2015–19);
- Yoav Gallant, current minister of defense and former commander of the southern front; and
- Gideon Sa'ar, Likud member of the Knesset and former minister of justice.

Galant subsequently entrusted his chief of staff, Herzi Halevi,[16] with the task of drawing up an operational plan with the following objectives:

Frontline report by the Israeli army leadership on the activities of the Hezbollah militia on the border with Lebanon. *From left*: Brigadier General Shai Klapper (commander of the 91st Territorial Division), Chief of Staff Herzi Halevi, Defense Minister Yoav Gallant, and Major General Ori Gordin (commander of the northern front). *IDF*

- Neutralization and destruction of Hamas's military infrastructure by means of airstrikes, and the elimination of its political leadership
- Clearing the Gaza Strip by means of a subsequent ground offensive, locating and destroying underground command and logistics facilities and eliminating pockets of resistance
- Withdrawal of forces and establishment of a security structure to prevent a resurgence and border incursions by Hamas

Halevi was expecting a difficult task, since he knew that Israel had not faced such a threat since 1948–49. In addition, difficult, built-up terrain awaited him in the Gaza Strip, where Hamas would operate mostly covertly from tunnels. Furthermore, Israel's army had to be considerate of the hostages still in enemy hands. Deif, on the other hand, anticipated a major attack by the IDF and reinforced his position, which consisted of three defensive lines around Gaza City: the first line was in the open terrain between the city and the border with Israel, a second barrier was on the outskirts of the city itself, and a third was inside the city.

---

[16] Herzi Halevi (1967–) grew up in Jerusalem and studied at the Hebrew University in Jerusalem from 1995 to 1998 and at the National Defense University in Washington from 2004 to 2005. He is a trained paratrooper, served in a paratrooper brigade, and moved to the management of the Israeli military academy in 2004. After commanding the Sayeret Matkal counterterrorism unit, Halevi was appointed head of the Aman military intelligence service in 2014. In 2018, he took command of the southern front as a brigadier general. Then prime minister Yair Lapid appointed Halevi as the thirty-sixth chief of general staff in 2022, promoting him to lieutenant general.

Halevi took more than two weeks to prepare his troops for the battle plan and the training associated with this operation. He formulated his plans as follows:

- In a first phase, the 98th Paratrooper Division, under the command of Brigadier General Dan Goldfuss,[17] with the 89th Commando Brigade, the 35th Paratrooper Brigade, and the 214th Artillery Brigade, were to conduct reconnaissance in force to destroy combat infrastructure and antitank positions close to the border in the northern Gaza area.
- In a second phase, the 162nd Armored Division, under the command of Brigadier General Itzik Cohen,[18] with the 401st Armored Brigade, the 933rd Infantry Brigade, and the 215th Artillery Brigade, were to penetrate the northern Gaza area to finally seek out and eliminate the enemy in the Gaza City area.
- In a third phase, the 36th Armored Division (belonging to the northern front command in peacetime), under Brigadier General Dado Bar-Kalifa, with the 7th and 188th Armored Brigades and the 1st Infantry Brigade Golani and the 6th Infantry Brigade Etzioni, were to cross the border, quickly push to the coast, cut the Gaza Strip in half, secure it to the north, and then advance farther south.
- The 252nd Armored Division, under Brigadier General Moran Omer, with the 10th and 14th Armored Brigades and the 84th Infantry Brigade Givati, were to stand ready as a reserve to support the units fighting in the north or advancing to the south.
- The advance of the ground troops was to be supported by preparatory artillery fire. At the same time, parts of the special units Sayeret Matkal, Shayetet 13, and Shaldag were to seek out and mark tunnel shafts to enable selective airstrikes.

Halevi immediately ordered his forces into attack position. The Gaza force was to be led by the commander of the southern front, Major General Yaron Finkelmann.[19] For the first time since the Lebanon War in 2006, the Israeli army command again deployed an armored division as a reserve element in the Gaza Strip. "An important and, for the 252nd Armored Division, decisive deployment, to form powerful striking forces with the neighboring units with which to decisively wear down the enemy — until victory," explained Finkelmann. On the nights of October 27 and 28, the first units of the Givati Brigade advanced into the Gaza Strip to conduct reconnaissance in force. On the evening of October 28, the war cabinet prepared the people for a long ground war. Around midnight, the air force and artillery launched further strikes. Then the Israeli armored corps rolled into battle with Merkava Mk. IV tanks and Namer and Eitan APCs and infantry fighting vehicles.

The 36th Armored Division took the fifth generation Merkava Mk. IV Barak into action for the first time. Its modernization compared to the Mk. IV type focused in particular on improved command capabilities and an updated fire control system. The combat helmets incorporated the Iron Vision system from Elbit, with head-up display. This provides the tank commander with an intuitive, conformal image of the world outside the tank, as well as relevant fire control data, through a fusion of camera images, sensor values, and other data. Hostile targets can thus be recognized more quickly and better identified, and possible action scenarios can be displayed. This increases the survivability of the tank and therefore of the crew. In addition, the Trophy active protection system developed by Rafael Advanced Defense, or its Israeli version WindGuard, has also been updated.

The Eitan armored fighting vehicle also experienced its baptism of fire in the current conflict. Developed as the successor to the M113 APC, this 8×8 wheeled infantry fighting vehicle is lighter and faster than the Namer armored personnel carrier, based on the chassis of the Merkava Mk. IV. A specially made underbody protects the Eitan very effectively against land mines and booby traps. The vehicle has an improved NBC protection system and integrates WindGuard. The modular design enables the use of numerous weapon systems such as a 30 mm cannon, mortar, or rocket launcher. The first series-produced vehicles of the 933rd Infantry Brigade Nahal, which is part of the 162nd

---

[17] Dan Goldfuss (1976–) grew up in Jerusalem as the son of South African Jews. He joined the IDF at an early age, rose to lieutenant colonel in the Shayetet *13* antiterrorist unit, and fought in the Gaza Strip in 2008–09 during Operation Cast Lead. In 2019, he was promoted to brigadier general, taking over the infantry corps. In 2022, he became commander of the 98th Paratrooper Division.

[18] Itzik Cohen (1977–) joined the IDF in 1995 as an infantryman and served in the 84th Givati Infantry Brigade as a company commander, later as a battalion commander, and finally as commander in chief, with the rank of brigadier general. He experienced all four Gaza Wars as commander and took over command of the 162nd Armored Division in 2023.

[19] Yaron Finkelmann (1975–) is a trained paratrooper and joined the IDF in 1993. He led a paratrooper reconnaissance battalion of the 35th Paratrooper Brigade in the Second Gaza War in 2008–09, during Operation Cast Lead. Promoted to brigadier general, he took command of the 98th Paratrooper Division in 2017 and commanded the southern front as a major general in 2023.

Launching of a Stunner guided missile from the David's Sling air defense and missile defense system. This system is used primarily to combat long-range artillery rockets and short-range ballistic missiles. The targets can be engaged from heights of a few meters above the ground up to an altitude of 15 km at speeds up to Mach 7.5.

Armored Division, saw action the first time on October 7, 2023, in the battle for Zikim, near Gaza City.

The 36th and 162nd Armored Divisions advanced out of Erez from the northern Gaza border on two axes through the intermediate objectives of Beit Lahia and Beit Hanoun and reorganized their formations in the Jabalia area, north of Gaza City. Hamas put up fierce resistance in the Beit Hanoun area, but this was overcome despite heavy Israeli losses. At the same time, the 252nd Armored Division advanced from the eastern border of the Gaza Strip south past Gaza City to the coast. In doing so, it drove a wedge from east to west through the enemy's territory, dividing the entire strip in the same way as the Protective Edge offensive during the 2014 Gaza War. In the combined arms battle, battalions of the 84th Givati Infantry Brigade supported the heavy artillery along the border, while the air force also provided cover for the advancing armored units. The IDF thus completely sealed off the northern part of the Gaza Strip. Then infantry units and special forces advanced into Gaza City and began to locate tunnel shafts, clean out the Hamas-occupied al-Shifa hospital, and open humanitarian corridors for the transportation of the sick and wounded and civilians. The Israeli army spokesman, Brigadier General Daniel Hagari, showed the main entrances to the Hamas tunnel system underneath the hospital, sometimes on camera. Underground command posts as well as weapons and ammunition depots were found there.

Jabalia was considered the largest refugee town in the entire Gaza Strip. Israel's domestic intelligence agency, Shin Bet, discovered the command post of Hamas general Ibrahim Biari — who was responsible for the attack and the massacres in all the

CHAPTER 20: The 2006 Lebanon War and the Fighting in the Gaza Strip | 203 kibbutzim to the north—under the town. An F-16 squadron under the direct command of air force commander Major General Tomer Bar then destroyed Biari's command post with a targeted airstrike using blockbuster bombs. The six 900 kg bombs tore terrible craters in the refugee city, killing numerous Palestinians, including women and children. While a wave of sympathy for the Jewish state swept through the world in the first days of the war, this slowly began to crumble with the bombs on Jabalia. Hamas fueled anti-Israel sentiment even further with unverifiable, horrendous casualty figures. From then on, the Gaza force suffered from the contradiction of its strategic goals. The first objective, the destruction of Hamas, came into conflict with the second objective, the liberation of all hostages. The beleaguered Hamas was tempted by the release of individual hostages, which it offered via Qatar in return for a ceasefire, although Galant and Halevi recognized the dilemma: if Israel agreed to a ceasefire, its own army would lose the momentum that had carried it to a breakthrough in northern Gaza. In addition, the decimated enemy could recover, reorganize its forces, and smuggle its own supplies into Gaza by means of the four hundred or so humanitarian truck deliveries every day. However, if the military cabinet were to delay or even reject the ceasefire, the political leadership under Netanyahu would come under even more pressure, which the families of the hostages have already been vociferously exerting on the streets, in the media, and in front of the government building in Jerusalem. The military cabinet finally gave in to the pressure, however, and a ceasefire followed on November 24, 2023, during which a prisoner exchange took place.

With the ceasefire, Hamas took the law of the land out of the Israelis' hands, which is why the IDF resumed its offensive with all the more unprecedented force after the ceasefire on December 1, 2023. Halevi shifted the campaign to southern Gaza and concentrated part of his forces on the city of Khan Yunis. The army intelligence service, Aman, suspected that cadres from the top Hamas leadership were at the center of these units. It deployed the 98th Paratrooper Division and parts of the 252nd Armored Division against the city. The 35th Paratrooper Brigade, which conquered the Wailing Wall from the Mount of Olives in the 1967 Six-Day War—one of the great moments in recent Israeli history—served as the leading element. After consolidating the remaining units in the North Gaza front, Halevi moved the Israeli armored forces to central Gaza, where the sprawling city of Deir al-Balah and the al-Burej refugee camp are located. Since the base of another Hamas brigade was apparently located here, the first fierce battles soon began. In the process, the air force constantly pinned down the enemy and destroyed its infrastructure and command posts. The Israeli ground forces fought with extreme caution to spare the civilian population as much as possible. Under the ground, specialists regularly blew up shafts and tunnels when it was certain that there were no more hostages in the tunnel network.

Halevi's frontline report of January 14, 2024, read as follows:

- In northern Gaza, operations are now taking place only with low intensity. Sporadic pockets of resistance are being suppressed by elements of the 162nd Armored Division, and newly discovered tunnel entrances with a decentralized enemy command structure are being engaged.
- In central Gaza, the 36th Armored Division is fighting with high intensity. The two refugee camps al-Burej and al-Maghazi have been captured and brought under control. Under the ground, the tunnel battle continues, as large weapons factories have been identified.
- In southern Gaza, the battle for Khan Yunis also continues with high intensity. The 98th Paratrooper Division continues to fight four reinforced Hamas battalions with parts of the 252nd Armored Division. Goldfuss reports the city is completely surrounded and the northern battalion largely destroyed, the eastern battalion badly battered, the western battalion greatly reduced, and the southern battalion still largely intact.

Since the outbreak of the war, Lebanese Hezbollah on the border had visibly intensified its strikes against Israel. In January 2024, the attacks reached another peak, with around seventy rockets fired from positions south of the Litani River striking towns in northern Galilee, realistically bringing a real two-front war within reach.

As a result of the intensification of the Hezbollah attacks, the Israeli general staff placed the 36th Armored Division back under the command of the northern front commander, Major General Ori Gordin,[20] as support.

The Iron Dome system intercepted the short-range missiles, but it was the David's Sling air defense system that engaged the medium-range missiles that were launched from sites farther north in the area between the Litani Mountains and the Beirut–Damascus road. While the Iron Dome missile defense system intercepts missiles with a range of less than 70 kilometers, David's Sling closes the gap to the Arrow 2 long-range defense system and combats missiles with a range of 70 to 300 km. The system, which was developed by the Israeli company Rafael Advanced Defense Systems, is based on the most-advanced radar technology and guided interceptor missiles and underwent its baptism of fire in 2017.

At the end of October 2023, after mechanized reconnaissance in force, the first Merkava tanks of the 36th and 162nd Armored Divisions launched a ground offensive in northern Gaza. *IDF*

In mid-February 2024, the Biden administration discussed a comprehensive peace plan for the postwar phase, which envisages the creation of a Palestinian state, and called on the Israeli army leadership to agree to a further ceasefire. According to the latest information, before this book went to press, the Israeli cabinet rejected a further ceasefire as well as a two-state solution, especially since Israel wants to conduct the political negotiations itself and rejects mediation via third parties. In the military arena, the IDF will probably also win the now fifth Gaza war. However, even after this conflict in the Middle East, a sustainable solution at a political level is unlikely to emerge. The world continues to hold its breath.

[20] Ori Gordin (1969–) grew up in San Diego, California, where his parents attended university. In 1971, the Gordin family returned to Israel, where Ori joined the special unit Sayeret Matkal as an infantryman in 1988. After serving in the Lebanon War in 2006, he took over the leadership of the Sayeret Matkal in 2007. As a colonel, he led the 55th Paratrooper Brigade in 2011 and the 98th Paratrooper Division as a brigadier general in 2015. In 2020, he was promoted to major general and took over Home Front Command during the Gaza War in 2021. One year later, he took over command of the northern front.

Chapter 21
The Transformation of the Israeli Armed Forces

Over the past ten years, the Israeli armed forces have fundamentally changed the structure and priorities of their war-fighting organization. The ground forces—infantry, armor, and artillery—have been reduced and instructed to make structural and doctrinal changes to equip them for anticipated further future conflicts against nonstate actors such as Hamas and Hezbollah.

THE TRANSFORMATION

This transformation was driven by a conscious decision by Israel's political and military leadership to strengthen the country's defensive formations and prioritize cyber and intelligence capabilities. The current Israeli defense minister, Benjamin Gantz, explained the reasons for this as follows:

> *The purpose was to create a smaller but more powerful army capable of confronting nonstate adversaries in complex environments and on multiple fronts. Achieving this goal depends first and foremost on the ability to gather accurate intelligence, process it effectively, analyze it, and then disseminate it to the fighting forces in real time. I state unequivocally that I have prioritized cyberspace and intelligence over infantry and tanks. Unlike the threat of ground invasion, the threat of cyberattacks is real.*

The structural and doctrinal changes in the Israel Defense Forces were, by and large, the operational and organizational response to the gradual transformation of Hamas and Hezbollah from local resistance movements to powerful militant organizations.

Within twenty-five years, Hamas has transformed itself from a grassroots socioreligious movement into a political regime with a military wing consisting of more than 30,000 fighters and an arsenal of around 20,000 rockets that can reach targets up to 125 miles (200 km) away.

Hezbollah underwent an even-greater organizational change, transforming itself from a grassroots political movement into what many experts consider to be the most powerful nonstate military force in the world. It is estimated to have over 60,000 fighters and more than 100,000 missiles. Hezbollah's tactical capabilities have developed dramatically as a result of its experience in the Syrian civil war, and it is now able to carry out attacks beyond Lebanon's borders.

The fighting experience, firepower, and self-confidence of Hamas and Hezbollah have raised their status in the eyes of the Israeli military leadership, so that the two organizations are now regarded as one of the greatest military threats to Israel's security.

THE NEW STRUCTURE OF THE GROUND FORCES

In the summer of 2015, under then chief of staff Benjamin Gantz, the Israelis launched the Gideon multiyear plan (GMYP) to downsize, modernize, and reform the Israeli army in order to counter asymmetric, nonstate threats, which now took political precedence over traditional conventional warfare between states. The Israeli Defense Forces reduced both its combat and support forces, both active and reserve.

In the professional formations, 10 percent of officer posts were abolished, and the number of troops was reduced from 45,000 to 40,000, while the duration of military service for conscripts was shortened by four months. The reserves were hit hardest by the transformation: 100,000 of the 300,000 reservists were retired.

Perhaps the most far-reaching change proposed by the GMYP was the reorganization of the combat troops. Since its foundation, the division had been the central operational structure. However, after the 1973 Yom Kippur War, the decline of conventional warfare and the emergence of nonstate adversaries led to a hollowing out of the divisions.

Over time, the Israeli armed forces operated in smaller areas in the West Bank, the Gaza Strip, and southern Lebanon, in which large combat groups could not be deployed, let alone stationed. The task was no longer to occupy vast areas of an enemy state, but instead to gain operational control over geographically limited enemy areas and eliminate local threats such as rocket launchers and weapons-smuggling tunnels.

Merkava Mark IV heavy tank of a company of the 7th Armored Brigade fording a stream in the tank-training area on the Golan Heights, 2016. *IDF*

The capabilities of the nonstate actors against which the armed forces were increasingly deployed—disorganized militias in southern Lebanon and local Palestinian terror cells in the West Bank and Gaza Strip—were advanced but did not justify the deployment of entire divisions.

In 2011, the Israelis began implementing a new operational doctrine that envisioned brigades as independent operational structures, each capable of planning and executing ground maneuvers without divisional support. The new brigades each consisted of six battalions, including infantry, armored, artillery, and engineer troops, as well as an independent headquarters. In addition, each battalion was empowered to communicate directly with the air force and navy regarding exfiltration and fire support.

Israel assumes that its future conflicts will be characterized by dynamic opponents who constantly change their structures and methods and acquire new techniques and weapons. The switch to smaller battle groups with the combined capabilities of different types of troops and the ability to plan and execute battles independently increases effectiveness and flexibility. This reform, in turn, had a profound impact on the organization of the individual branches of the armed forces.

INFANTRY

In recent years, the combat infantry forces have been downsized, and instead the security forces, which guard Israel's borders and the occupied territories, have been expanded. In 2005, the Israelis founded Kfir, a new infantry brigade specializing in these security tasks. The purpose of this unit was to maintain a permanent presence in the West Bank in order to carry out routine

CHAPTER 21: The Transformation of the Israeli Armed Forces | 207

security missions, protect Israeli settlements, and prevent infiltration attempts into Israel. Between 2004 and 2017, the Israelis set up four more battalions to carry out these tasks.

After the infantry units had to accept a considerable reduction in personnel following the decision to shorten the period of compulsory military service, they began to focus their training on fighting a guerrilla war and preparing for future conflicts against Hezbollah and Hamas.

The basic training of infantry units is divided into two parts: general training and special training. The first part of basic training focuses on fundamental skills such as the preparation, use, and maintenance of a personal weapon; marching over long distances with heavy packs; battle formations; and military sign language.

The second part of the basic training is carried out after the soldiers have been assigned to their individual specializations: squad leader, sniper, machine gunner, mortarman, antitank gunner, medic, or rifleman. In the past, special training focused on techniques of warfare in open terrain. Urban warfare was rarely practiced, and underground warfare and combat techniques in tunnels and underground fortifications were completely excluded from the training plan of standard infantry units.

The most important principle with regard to underground facilities and urban areas was simply to avoid them. However, from 2014 onward, specialized training focused on urban warfare and introduced underground warfare as a new concept with its own combat doctrine. Open-field warfare practices, such as the occupation of Syrian and Egyptian fortifications, were removed from specialized training.

ARMORED FORCES

Historically, the two basic principles of the armored corps were mobility and speed. The logic behind these principles was to use the unique mobile capabilities of the tank to minimize its vulnerability. Israeli forces used these capabilities to achieve decisive victories against conventional enemy forces, such as in 1956 during the Suez Crisis, 1967 during the Six-Day War, and 1973 during the Yom Kippur War. In all these conflicts, fighting took place in the open, and the guiding principle for urban warfare at the time was to avoid it unless it was essential to the mission.

The 2006 Lebanon War showed that armored units are less effective in urban areas and in asymmetric warfare. During the first three weeks of fighting, the armored corps and the rest of the ground forces waited in remote areas while the air force fought Hezbollah. When the ground invasion finally began, only two of four active armored brigades took part. The tasks assigned to the armored units in Lebanon also

THE ARMORED CORPS OF THE ISRAELI ARMED FORCES TODAY

Current commander in chief (2022): Hisham Ibrahim

Current Structure (2022)
36th Armored Division "Ga'ash"
(active, northern command)
    7th Armored Brigade "Saar me-Golan" (active)
    75th Armored Battalion "Romach" (Merkava Mark III)
    77th Armored Battalion "Oz" (Merkava Mark IV)
    82nd Armored Battalion "Gaash" (Merkava Mark II)
    603rd Armored Engineer Battalion "Lahav"
    188th Armored Brigade "Barak" (active)
    53rd Armored Battalion "Sufa" (Merkava Mark III)
    71st Armored Battalion "Reshef" (Merkava Mark IV)
    74th Armored Battalion "Saar" (Merkava Mark IV)
    605th Armored Engineer Battalion "haMahatz"
    263rd Armored Brigade "Merkavot ha-Esh" (reserve)

162nd Armored Division "Utzvat HaPlada"
(active, southern command)
    401st Armored Brigade "I'kvot Ha-Barzel" (active)
    9th Armored Battalion "Eshet" (Merkava Mark IV)
    46th Armored Battalion "Shelah" (Merkava Mark IV)
    52nd Armored Battalion "Ha-Bok'im" (Merkava Mark IV)
    601st Armored Engineer Battalion "Asaf"
    37th Armored Brigade "Ram" (reserve)
    460th Armored Training Brigade "Bnei Or" (active)
    195th Armored Training Battalion "Adam" (Merkava Mark II)
    198th Armored Training Battalion "Ezuz" (Merkava Mark III)
    532nd Armored Training Battalion "Shelah" (Merkava Mark IV)
    196th Armored Training Battalion "Shahak"
    (tank commander training)
    Armored Training Battalion "Magen" (
    tank instructor training)

252nd Armored Division "Sinai"
(reserve, southern command)
    10th Armored Brigade "Harel" (reserve)
    14th Armored Brigade "Machatz" (reserve)

319th Armored Division "Ha-Mapatz"
(reserve, northern command)
    4th Armored Brigade "Kiryati" (reserve)
    205th Armored Brigade "Iron Fist" (reserve)

340th Armored Division "Idan"
(reserve, central command)
    847th Armored Brigade "Merkavot HaPlada" (reserve)

Other Armored Brigades
    8th Armored Brigade (reserve)
    679th Armored Brigade "Yiftah" (reserve)

Disbanded Armored Brigades
    211th Armored Brigade "Yishai"
    500th Armored Brigade "Kfir"

differed significantly from those in Israel's previous conflicts. Instead of penetrating deep into southern Lebanon and crushing the enemy, the armored forces carried out attacks against suspected Hezbollah units near the border, restricting their freedom of movement by means of patrols and checkpoints or securing logistical supplies.

As a result, the Israeli Armored Corps has significantly reduced its size and changed its structure to adapt to the new security requirements. According to the former deputy chief of staff, Yair Naveh, more than ten reserve brigades have been abolished in the past ten years, and this downsizing is expected to continue.

In addition, the remaining armored brigades will no longer be equipped with four to six armored companies per battalion, but with three armored companies, two infantry companies, and one engineer company. With this new composition, the armored units can now operate independently as small battle groups, fulfill a wider range of missions, and operate more effectively in urban combat. As a result of this reform to the structure of the armored corps and its integration into the new combat units, the armored units were significantly more effective in Operation Protective Edge 2014 than in previous conflicts against nonstate actors.

For the first time in thirty-two years, all four active armored brigades were deployed during the operation, meaning that around five hundred tanks were involved in the fighting.

The armored corps suffered fourteen fatal casualties during the operation, but all of them were caused by mortar fire outside the Gaza Strip or by sniper fire against personnel outside their vehicles; not a single tank was destroyed by enemy fire!

Armored engineers in action. In the right foreground is a Puma armored combat engineering vehicle, based on the chassis of the Centurion, with the turret removed. In addition to numerous other modifications, its most-striking features are the side skirts and suspension from the Merkava tank, as well as attachment points for various engineering equipment on the front of the vehicle. The tank being recovered in the center of the photo is a Merkava, probably a Mark I. In the far rear is an M88A1 recovery vehicle, based on the chassis of the M48A2 Patton. The Chiluz has been used in recovery missions and rescue operations in the Gaza Strip, the West Bank, and southern Lebanon. *IDF*

ARTILLERY

In the early decades, the role of artillery was to provide fire support for the maneuvering units. Accordingly, artillery played a key role in Israel's armed conflicts in the 1960s and 1970s. However, like the armored corps, the artillery corps has lost importance in Israel's modern conflicts with the decline of conventional warfare. No foreign forces have attempted to invade Israel since the 1973 Yom Kippur War, and the Israeli armed forces have conducted ground maneuvers with several divisions only once since then, during the First Lebanon War in 1982.

The great effective range of artillery shells, combined with the inability to hit targets with sufficient precision, increased the risk of friendly fire and excessive collateral damage in built-up areas. The artillery corps therefore also began to reform itself in order to cope with the changed operational environment.

Shortly after the turn of the millennium, two new, secret units were therefore set up within the artillery corps in order to remedy the discrepancy between the traditional capabilities of artillery and the requirements of an urban battlefield. Instead of artillery weapons, the new units are equipped with drones to carry out attack and reconnaissance missions. The attack drone unit (Unit 5252 or Zik), operates the Israeli Hermes 450 multirole tactical drone, which can carry out precise strikes at long distances with precision-guided munitions, thereby minimizing collateral damage.

The reconnaissance drone unit (Unit 5353 or Sky Rider) operates the Israeli Skylark I, II, and III drones, which are small enough to be carried by an infantryman and deployed within minutes. The drone is equipped with advanced communication capabilities and can transmit high-resolution real-time video day and night over a distance of 25 miles (40 km). The collected tactical information is delivered directly to the commanding officers on the battlefield in real time. In 2014, another new unit was set up with the task of tracking the trajectories of enemy rockets. With the help of sensors at different altitudes, precise meteorological data such as air pressure, humidity, wind, and temperature are collected, which are crucial for ballistic calculations. These data are then forwarded to the relevant weapon systems that rely on the information (including artillery pieces, drones, and missiles), thus ensuring a general increase in accuracy.

As a result of the reform, the personnel structure of the artillery corps has been significantly reduced, and the armed forces currently have four active artillery brigades and four reserve battalions.

RESTRUCTURING OF THE OTHER BRANCHES OF SERVICE

AIR FORCE

In the first decades of Israel's existence and in its first military conflicts, the Israeli air force (IAF) had the task of supporting the ground forces. Because of its numerical inferiority, the IAF followed two principles: surprise and concentration of forces.

In the Six-Day War the IAF carried out surprise attacks, first against targets in Egypt, then in Syria and Jordan, destroying much of the enemy air forces, at the cost of twenty-four men killed and forty-six combat aircraft. In the Yom Kippur War, the IAF found itself facing the reverse situation: it first had to defend Israeli airspace against a surprise attack before it could take the offensive—and then had to confront the Soviet air defense systems operated by the Egyptians and Syrians. Losses were therefore significantly higher: ninety-two killed and 103 combat aircraft.

The air force's capabilities were greatly improved by the acquisition of the F-15A Eagle and the F-16 Fighting Falcon in 1978. During the First Lebanon War, in ninety days of operations the IAF destroyed the Syrian air defense system and several hundred of its aircraft without loss. However, as Israel became increasingly involved in low-intensity conflicts against the PLO, Hamas, and Hezbollah, which operated in small groups and hid among the civilian population, the operational role of the IAF diminished. While IAF operations were still efficient and lethal during the First and Second Intifadas and the Second Lebanon War in 2006, they no longer had a tangible impact on the outcome of the conflicts. As a result, the IAF began to prioritize precision strike capability and stealth technology over air-to-air and air-to-ground attack capabilities.

To this end, it procured the F-35 Lightning II and C-130J Super Hercules transport and aerial-refueling aircraft. Perhaps the highest national priority for the IAF was to maintain and demonstrate the capability to attack and destroy hardened nuclear facilities in remote geonomic areas from the air. However, the modern weapon systems strained the IAF's budget and forced it to deprioritize other capabilities and disband several fighter squadrons (F-15, F-16, and AH-1 Cobra gunships).

NAVY

Due to its small population and limited natural resources, Israel has always been dependent on imports from overseas for its self-sufficiency. The Mediterranean and the Red Sea alone account for 98 percent of Israel's imported goods. Over 80 percent of Israel's population is spread along the 197 km coastline, which is particularly vulnerable to attack. In addition, much of the critical infrastructure is located near or along the Israeli coast.

The protection of trade routes, the defense of Israeli territorial waters, and the guarding of the coastline have therefore been the most-important missions of the Israeli navy. It was developed to defeat the Egyptian and Syrian navies, operating destroyers, missile boats, patrol boats, and two submarines. In the Yom Kippur War the Israeli navy was able to largely neutralize both opposing navies and capture twenty-four enemy vessels without loss. After the war, however, the decreased probability of major engagements against enemy naval forces and the increasing tensions with nonstate actors led the Israeli military command to invest more resources in maritime security missions, to prevent attacks against Israeli citizens. As a result, all the navy's destroyers and large missile boats were decommissioned, and patrol boats and smaller missile boats were acquired to replace them.

Joint maneuver by the 7th Armored and Givati Brigades, 2015. *IDF*

These changes had a price, however, and the navy in particular was criticized for having made an insufficient contribution to the Second Lebanon War in 2006. An investigating commission after the war concluded that the navy had largely lost its ability to conduct offensive military operations because of its emphasis on policing tasks.

In 2007, however, the navy took over responsibility for blockading the Gaza Strip, and in 2011 it acquired the new role of defending the newly discovered natural-gas fields in the Mediterranean. Also in 2011, Israeli acquired three more submarines capable of carrying nuclear weapons from Germany, doubling its fleet to six boats, whose primary role is nuclear deterrence against Iran.

SPECIAL-OPERATIONS FORCES

The special units can be divided into four groups:

- Special forces: General Staff Reconnaissance Unit (Sayeret Matkal), Navy Commandos (Shayetet 13), Air Force Commandos (Shaldag) and the technical special unit (Yahalom)
- Commando units: Egoz, Maglan, and Duvdevan
- Reconnaissance units: Paratrooper Reconnaissance Battalion, Golani Reconnaissance Battalion, Givati Reconnaissance Battalion, Nahal Reconnaissance Battalion, 7th Reconnaissance Battalion, and 401st Reconnaissance Battalion

Merkava Mark IV tank of the 7th Armored Brigade with infantry during urban combat training, 2017. *IDF*

- Specialized units: air-supported search and rescue unit (669), Canine Unit (Oketz), HUMINT Intelligence Unit (504), and unit for precision-guided missiles (Moran)

Despite the number of special-forces units, in only two cases have elite units made significant contributions to the outcome of a war: during the Suez Crisis in 1956, when paratroopers landed behind the enemy lines at Mitla Pass in the Sinai, and during the Six-Day War in 1967, also in the Sinai, when paratroopers landed at Abu Ageila. In Israel's other conflicts, they either were assigned minor and insignificant, albeit complex, missions or were attached to an operational brigade.

After Israel's twenty-four years of continual limited-intensity conflicts in southern Lebanon, the West Bank, and the Gaza Strip, the ability of the special forces to make a decisive contribution to major military operations reached its nadir. The committee looking into the Second Lebanon War of 2006 concluded that the Israelis had not effectively deployed their special forces, because they had been scattered over the entire armed forces and placed under different commands.

The commission went so far as to claim that several of the special-forces units had been formed for specific operational requirements that no longer existed. Pride prevented these units from shifting their focus and entering into cooperations to retain their relevance.

As part of the lessons learned from the Second Lebanon War, in 2011 the Israelis created the so-called Depth Corps, at whose core was the new Commando Brigade, which united the three commando units (Egoz, Maglan, and Duvdevan) under a unified command and made it the most important force in the battle against Hamas and Hezbollah.

Israel plans to acquire further examples of the tried-and-tested Namer armored personnel carrier for integration into armored battalions and mechanized infantry battalions. It is based on the Merkava Mk IV chassis, weighs 60 tons, offers the same level of protection as the Merkava with modular composite armor, and is powered by a 1,200 hp V-12 diesel engine from Teledyne Continental. In addition to three crew members, the vehicle can accommodate a further eight armored infantrymen. The picture shows a Namer of the 13th Mechanized Infantry Battalion of the Golani Brigade during a maneuver on the Golan, August 2012. *Michael Mass Photography*

An antitank company and an engineer company were removed from each reconnaissance battalion and were replaced by two additional reconnaissance companies, with the new focus being placed on underground warfare and combat in built-up areas. Even after the restructuring, the elite units worked autonomously from the other special units and were further expanded and professionalized—at the cost of the conventional battle groups.

INTELLIGENCE SERVICES

The Israeli military intelligence service is divided into four core units:

- Signals Intelligence (SIGINT, Unit 8200), responsible for gathering intelligence in the electromagnetic sphere
- Photo or Visual Intelligence (VISINT, Unit 9900), responsible for mapping of terrain and the evaluation of satellite images and other photographic material
- Human Intelligence (HUMINT), responsible for recruiting and employing human resources for open and undercover intelligence gathering

CHAPTER 21: The Transformation of the Israeli Armed Forces | 213

- Research Unit, responsible for preparing threat analyses (possible hostile intentions and operations)

In the past, traditional military targets included primarily military bases, troop concentrations, defense installations, dams, power plants, bridges, and other fixed infrastructure. Because of their size and status, and the absence of civilian populations, as a rule these targets required no precise intelligence gathering. The intelligence process (gathering, evaluation, dissemination) could take months or years. Over time, as the probability of a conventional war diminished and the threat from nonstate actors grew, the focus of military intelligence shifted. Instead of determining the capabilities and intentions of nations, the focus of the military intelligence services shifted to monitoring the military activities of nonstate hostile entities.

The SIGINT unit was expanded by the addition of a cyber unit, which specialized in the hacking and sabotage of electronic systems, and by the Hatsav Unit, which gathered information from social media platforms. The most significant expansion was the formation of the so-called Operational SIGINT Battalion, which is temporarily attached to a combat unit for specific operations and supplies it with real-time information.

In 1988, Israel became the eighth nation in the world to launch its own surveillance satellite into orbit. In the following three decades, eight more satellites were successfully put into orbit. The until-now-latest Israeli surveillance satellite has been in service since 2016. The VISINT Unit has perforce also grown, to be able to process the constantly growing stream of visual data in ever-shorter times.

In addition to reorganizations within the units, there have also been interorganizational changes. In the past, the groups within the research, SIGINT, VISINT, and HUMINT units had always been organized by geographical areas or specific phases of the intelligence process. Now the groups concentrate on organizational or ideological targets, such as Islamic Jihad and ISIS. The change from a geographical paradigm to a capability or organizational paradigm required additional reforms in the military intelligence service. After the Arab Spring, the Israeli armed forces realized that they had failed to predict the scope of the uprisings and the resulting regional instability. Aviv Kochavi, then director of the Military Intelligence Service, therefore set up a regional department within the research unit, whose mission is to examine and monitor the economic, social, and political developments, particularly in the Middle East, and to provide early warning of potential geopolitical shifts of strategic importance to Israel. It is hoped that the formation of multidisciplinary ad hoc teams will make it possible to react quickly to time-critical threats. Finally, the intelligence service also

The leaders of the Israeli armed forces in 2022. *From right to left*: Defense Minister Benjamin Gantz, Prime Minister Yair Lapid, and Chief of Staff Aviv Kochavi. *IDF*

established a new Targeting Department to create a target data bank with the aid of Deep Learning algorithms and Big Data. If a target is confirmed by a human analyst, the algorithm learns, making it more efficient with time.

CYBER FORCES

The Israelis formed their first cyber units in 2011. At first, Shin Bet, Israel's civilian security service, was responsible for protecting the critical cyber infrastructure. When the cyber threat then quickly expanded beyond the capacity of the resources of a single authority to a strategic dimension, the armed forces began to concede the cybersecurity priority and assume responsibility for the protection of the military and civilian infrastructure. Cyber activities were divided into two departments: the Intelligence Directorate, which is responsible for gathering of information and offensive cyber operations, and the Computer, Information Technology and Cyber Defense Directorate, which is responsible for defensive cyber operations and protection of the infrastructure.

The Cyber Defense Division is the supreme entity for cyber defense and is led by a brigadier general, which reflects its importance (staff departments are usually led by colonels). The organizational structure of the Cyber Defense Division is modular and allows the soldiers to work both as part of a large task force within the department as well as independently in small teams directly attached to a combat unit.

The formation of these organizations and the setting of priorities for cyber defense represent a significant cultural change.

The obsolete M113 APC is being replaced by the Eitan armored fighting vehicle. Named after the former chief of the Israeli general staff Rafael Eitan, this 8×8 wheeled vehicle weighs about 35 tons, offers the well-known composite armor known as the Iron Fist defense system, is powered by a 750 hp diesel engine, and has room for a crew of three and up to nine armored infantry. This AFV is capable of carrying a variety of weapons systems; for example, an Mk. 44 30 mm cannon, a coupled 7.62 machine gun, and smoke grenade launchers. A digital fire control system enables networked battlefield communications and data synchronization with other combat vehicles. *IDF*

The Israeli military has a long tradition in which the fighting units have priority over all others in the competition for qualified personnel and financial resources. New recruits were first sent to the combat units, and only those who had to be classified as unsuitable for combat were sent to the support units. Since the prioritization of cyber defense, recruits, even if suitable for combat, are sent directly to the cyber units if they meet their requirements. Finally, in 2015 — while the fighting units experienced a considerable loss in personnel — the cyber units were once again augmented by several hundred positions (in addition to the 10,000 existing positions).

THE FUTURE

In the center of the military transformation is a new defensive concept. Roughly at the end of the 2010s, the Israel perception of its military objectives in a conflict changed dramatically. Israel no longer strove for the total defeat of its enemy and instead tried to defend itself against possible threats by means of highly developed defense infrastructure and technology and — where necessary — to preventively neutralize potential future threats by means of targeted precision strikes.

Israeli not only surrounds itself with fences and concrete walls along its borders but has also integrated advanced technologies to increase the effectiveness of these physical barriers.

Over the years, the Israeli border barriers were fitted with day and night vision cameras, contact sensors, and motion detectors.

These measures were enhanced by military patrols, concealed observers, and sand-filled areas near the fence, which could be searched by military tracking dogs for footprints. In some places, Israel has replaced its border fence with concrete-and-steel walls, especially in areas with a higher risk of infiltration or sniper fire.

In 2017, Israel began replacing the 80-mile-long border fence with Lebanon with a 29-foot-high concrete wall topped by a further 10 feet of steel fence. A year later, Israel began construction of a new barrier between Israel and the Gaza Strip. The 20-foot-high barrier is made of galvanized steel, and after its completion it will stretch along the border between Israel and the Gaza Strip.

Under the Israel-Gaza barrier, the Israelis are constructing an underground concrete wall to protect against infiltration tunnels. The underground wall is to extend for 65 km between Israel and the Gaza Strip. The barrier will be made of concrete and steel and extend up to 100 feet (30 m) deep in the ground. In 2018, Israel also decided to construct a sea barrier along the sea border with the Gaza Strip. The barrier consists of three layers (a regular breakwater, reinforced concrete, and barbed wire), all equipped with intelligent fences with alarm systems and contact sensors, day and night vision cameras, and motion detectors.

Israel has an active multilayer missile defense system that offers protection against both hostile states and militant organizations. This includes the Arrow 3, Arrow 2, David's Sling, Iron Dome, and Iron Beam — a newly developed active defense system that uses focused laser beams to intercept small objects such as mortar rounds and small drones.

There are, however, critics of this doctrine of self-isolation. A nation that shows mental weakness makes it easier for the enemy to defeat it. Major General (ret.) Yitzhak Brick, who, as chief ombudsman, investigated the operational readiness of more than a thousand soldiers, is a fierce critic of the current doctrine. He is critical of the political and military leadership for tailoring its planning for the armed forces to the engaging of nonstate entities and ignoring the possibility of a conventional war in the future: "The current misconception of the military leadership is that there will be no more major [conventional] wars. It doesn't consider the possibility that the Middle East will change . . . that the Syrians will recover, and the Egyptians will change their attitude. Just a small military for two theaters [the Gaza Strip and Lebanon]."

Brick believes that with the current doctrine, Israel will have even more difficulties defeating the nonstate foes. "The next war will be a multifront war against Hamas in the Gaza Strip [and] Hezbollah in Lebanon, and simultaneously we will be confronted with rocket attacks from Syria and perhaps from Iraq. Israel will be attacked with 1,500 to 2,000 rockets per day, including some with 1,300-to-1,550-pound (600–700 kg) warheads. Israel faces a serious problem, for at present it is not capable of defeating such heavy, coordinated attacks. As well, the air force alone is not in the same position we saw in the most recent campaigns in Gaza. Our missile defense systems are not sufficiently developed to deal with such a large number of rockets."

High-ranking officers have stated that the only effective defense against such massive and destructive rocket fire is to occupy the areas from which the rockets are being fired, by means of a major ground operation to occupy the Gaza Strip, in Lebanon and in Syria, and, if necessary, to extend this control into Iraq and Iran. This challenge cannot be met with cyber forces alone.

Who knows, perhaps the Israeli Armored Corps will be strengthened again in the near future?

There is a memorial plaque at the Latrun Tank Museum commemorating all the fallen tank crews since the War of Independence. *Marc Lenzin Archive*

CHAPTER 21: The Transformation of the Israeli Armed Forces

VISIT TO THE 188TH ARMORED BRIGADE

In August 2022, the author and the writer of the prologue had the opportunity to visit an armored brigade of the Israeli armed forces. The choice fell on the 188th Armored Brigade, which together with the 7th Armored and 1st Infantry Brigades forms the 36th Division, an independent formation of the northern front. We drove by car from Herzliya, north of Tel Aviv, through the Sharon Valley, Galilee, and across the Jordan River up to the Golan Heights. After passing Nafakh, after a short drive we arrived at Aleika, home to the headquarters of the 188th Armored Brigade.

Even before the Six-Day War there was a Syrian military camp there, probably occupied by an armored or a mechanized infantry brigade. The barracks, which served as quarters, offices, and rations and recreation spaces, have in part remained unchanged from the war of 1967. We were welcomed by a major who was the unit's operations officer and, as part of the brigade's operations staff, was directly under the brigade commander. Acting as a hub, he coordinates the links to reconnaissance, the combat elements, the fire support units, the engineers, and logistics, similar to a chief of staff in western European armies.

In a short presentation he explained to us the unit's role in the event of emergency. The brigade trains for possible missions in built-up areas against the asymmetrically operating Hezbollah in southern Lebanon or Hamas in the Gaza Strip. It also trains for classic tank warfare, either in the extended plains of the Goland or in the Negev desert. The brigade's principal weapon of war is the proven Merkava tank.

In order to meet the demanding combat scenarios, the crews and commanders of the armored battalions are either in training in standard situations or in combat operations along the Israeli border. This combination makes it possible to maintain a high level of training, on the one hand, and to acquire combat experience against possible opponents, on the other hand.

Combat in built-up areas is practiced in villages built to resemble those of the enemy. Training is carried out with live ammunition inside the village. Tanks, however, practice firing live rounds while securing and keeping open the entrances and exits of the village.

The companies are made up of regular soldiers and reservists. The former do their basic service, which is a regular duration of two years and eight months. The latter, on the other hand, take part in an annual refresher course to maintain their operational readiness. The soldiers regularly go on a short leave on the day before Shabbat (the seventh day of the Jewish week and a day of rest).

A Shot Kal Alef tank next to a memorial stone at the entrance to the headquarters of the 188th Armored Brigade. *Marc Lenzin Archive*

Our visitors program included the opportunity to watch a mock battle by one of the armored companies. However, the event was canceled after a routine security assessment of the situation on the Golan border. At the same time, Israeli forces, in cooperation with the Shin Bet domestic intelligence service, killed Taisir al-Jabari, a high-ranking member of Islamic Jihad. This action led to a counterattack by Islamic Jihad with rockets aimed at Israel's infrastructure and civilian population, whereupon the Israelis activated their Iron Dome missile defense system.

The operations officer subsequently described his experiences during Operation Protective Edge in 2014. Israel learned from reliable sources that Hamas had occupied a UNRWA hospital in Gaza City and had probably hidden large quantities of arms there. Two armored platoons of the 188th Armored Brigade and an Israeli special unit were sent to destroy the Hamas forces and uncover the weapons dump.

The operations officer, who was then still a common soldier, was the gunner in a tank. Massive fire from the tanks kept the enemy's heads down while the special unit entered the hospital. One of the Hamas members set off an IED, inflicting several fatal and numerous other casualties on the rescue force.

This action demonstrates emphatically that every Israeli armored unit — at any time and in any place — can be called to action in an emergency and must therefore be kept at a high state of readiness.

Visit to the 188th Armored Brigade

188th Armored Brigade memorial on the Golan Heights. In addition to a memorial stone, there is a knocked-out Syrian T-62 tank. In the background is the Valley of Tears, where the fiercest tank battles took place in 1973. *Marc Lenzin Archive*

188th Armored Brigade memorial on the Golan Heights. The memorial is dedicated to the men of the brigade who gave their lives during the Yom Kippur War. Before the war started, the 188th Armored Brigade spread its two armored battalions along the entire ceasefire line. The troops defended a total of seventeen strongpoints, each in platoon strength. These two armored battalions were responsible for slowing the assault by the Syrian tank units and giving the 7th Armored Brigade time to position itself behind the battalions of the 188th Armored Brigade as a second defensive position to destroy the enemy forces that had broken through. *Marc Lenzin Archive*

Silent witnesses to a past war. The photo was taken at a spot called Tel Saki, located at the south end of the Golan Heights. Here, too, there is a memorial stone to the Israeli troops who gave their lives at this fiercely defended strongpoint during the Yom Kippur War. *Marc Lenzin Archive*

CHAPTER 21: The Transformation of the Israeli Armed Forces | 219

THE TANK MUSEUM AT LATRUN

The Israeli museum of the armored forces is one of the most outstanding and interesting military museums in the world. It is in Latrun, close to the highway between Jerusalem and Tel Aviv, and has the official name Yad La-Shiryon, or the Armored Corps Memorial Site and Museum.

The central museum building is a police fort built by the British during the Mandate period. In the War of Independence in 1948–49, the Arabs occupied the building and thus blocked the vital communication link to the encircled population of Jerusalem. In the so-called Latrun offensive, despite numerous attacks the Israelis failed to take the fort during the war. Not until the Six-Day War in 1967 and the resulting Israeli territorial gains was the fort finally taken.

On the initiative of veterans, a memorial to the fallen soldiers of the Israeli tank corps and a tank museum were established at this historic site in 1982. The collection of tanks on display is quite impressive. All the tanks that served or are serving with the Israeli armed forces, as well as armored personnel carriers and support vehicles, can be found in the collection.

On display are the first armored trucks, the so-called sandwich trucks, half-tracks, and jeeps with mounted machine guns from the time of the War of Independence. Alongside them are the Hotchkiss H-39, the Cromwell Mark IV, and the AMX-13, plus the Sherman, Shot, and Magach tanks with their numerous variations. Also on display are several special pieces, including a wooden model of a Merkava Mark I and parts of bridges used to cross the Suez Canal, and an observation tank on a Sherman chassis deployed along the Bar-Lev Line during the Yom Kippur War with an 88-foot-tall lifting platform. The four marks of the Merkava tank complete the Israeli tank arsenal.

Syrian and Egyptian tanks from the Arab-Israeli conflicts are also on display. The future visitor will also find T-54/T-55 and T-62 tanks that were captured by the Israelis and modified into the Tiran series. Many other foreign tanks—including several from the Second World War—round out the collection of about 160 vehicles.

At Latrun, the commemoration of the history of the armored corps and the memory of the fallen is writ large. In addition to a memorial, which honors the allied troops of the Second World War, opposite it there is a memorial to all the Jews who died while serving under the Allied flag in the same war—be it as members of British units or in the independent Jewish Brigade.

An American-made M60 Patton tank that was converted into the Israeli Magach 7 Gimel version is just one of many impressive examples among the armored vehicles on display at the Latrun Tank Museum. This tank was upgraded with added reactive armor, side skirts, and improved fire control system, based on that in the Merkava. It served with the 401st Armored Brigade, including in Operation Protective Edge in 2002. *Marc Lenzin Archive*

All the armored vehicles that have served or currently serve with the Israeli armed forces are displayed at the Latrun Tank Museum. *Marc Lenzin Archive*

The Tank Museum at Latrun

Another memorial stone honors the service of Major General Israel Tal, the creator of the Israeli Armored Corps. An impressive, very long plaque finally commemorates all those who served in the armored corps and fell in one of the Israeli-Arab wars.

The interior spaces, with numerous models, portraits of all commanders of armored corps, and multimedia presentations on the creation of the Israeli tank arm and the Merkava tank, round out a visit to the museum, making it an unforgettable experience.

The memorial to Major General Israel Tal, creator of the Israeli armored doctrine, who was also responsible for the Merkava tank, developed in Israel. *Marc Lenzin Archive*

In August 2022, a solemn ceremony was held at the Latrun Tank Museum to mark the appointment of the new Israeli Armored Corps commander. *Marc Lenzin Archive*

The newly named commander of the Israeli Armored Corps, Brigadier General Hisham Ibrahim, with author Marc Lenzin. *Marc Lenzin Archive*

CHAPTER 21: The Transformation of the Israeli Armed Forces | 221

Epilogue

Since tanks first appeared on the battlefield in 1916, they have combined firepower, protection, and mobility. Their tradition is rooted in the cavalry of the commanders Alexander and Hannibal, both of whom delivered the mortal blow to their opponents, the Persians and the Romans, with their mounted right wings.

Tanks have been and are of singular importance to the security and existence of Israel. The Negev and Sinai deserts are suitable for wide-ranging operations, as are the more closely chambered Golan Heights with their basalt rock. The Gaza Strip and the West Bank also lend themselves to armored attacks.

A SOLID FOUNDATION

For a long time, there was no monograph in German about Israel's armored forces. Then the historically knowledgeable armored infantryman Marc Lenzin and the analytical Leopard 2 commander Stefan Bühler got together in Bern. They set themselves the task of writing a book on the history and the current state of the Israeli armored forces. It is a theme of epic breadth. The two Bernese threw themselves into the literature and the sources. They held discussions, examined tactics and techniques — and have now produced a work that has a solid foundation. It covers everything that makes up Israel's armored force.

Stefan Bühler expertly outlines the sandy path from the early Hotchkiss via the warhorses the Sherman, Centurion, and Patton to Israel Tal's inspired Merkava. He knows the tactical and technical detail and presents them in such a way that even those who don't have caterpillar tracks on their feet can understand.

General Tal addresses what gives Israel's armored forces their quality. He trained the armored corps, he won wars, and he forced progress. Tal refused to tolerate negligence in training. He exposed bluff. In 1967, he led his *Ugda* on the Via Maris to the Suez Canal. In 1973, he prepared the decisions in the general staff that allowed General David Elazar to make the right decisions after returning from the front and to command victoriously.

FROM A JEEP

On June 5, 1967, Israel launched the most successful preemptive strike in military history, with brilliant generals. In the Sinai, the armored strategist Yeshayahu Gavish led the *Ugda* commanders Tal, Ariel Sharon, and Avraham Yoffe — three officers made of gnarled wood.

- Tal commanded his division from a jeep — direct, deliberate, precise.
- Sharon fought the decisive breakthrough battle at the fortress of Abu Ageila. In a single night he coordinated his tanks and armored personnel carriers, the paratroopers, the infantry, the engineers, and the heavy fire of the artillery so masterfully that, before the morning dawned, he had opened the lane for Yoffe's division to drive to the Suez Canal.
- In turn, Yoffe, a massive, rustic Falstaffian figure, skillfully outmaneuvered the helpless Egyptians. By June 8, he too had reached the Suez Canal.

David "Dado" Elazar, the skilled tank officer, directed the armored units on the Golan Heights. Up the slopes and then across the plateau, he led his six brigades to what became the demarcation line. In doing so, he drove away the Syrian guns that had so brutally shelled the kibbutzim in Galilee since 1948.

BAR-LEV'S STEADY HAND

On October 6, 1973, the tableau of generals in the Sinai was not quite as convincing. Shmuel Gonen, the commander of the southern front, failed. Not until Moshe Dayan replaced him with the steady Chaim Bar-Lev did order come to the defense. Bar-Lev, with *Ugda* commanders Sharon, Adan, and Mandler, turned the page: on the night of October 15–16, Sharon crossed the Suez Canal and decided the war on the southern front.

In the north, General Yitzhak Hofi commanded the Golan front. The divisions under Rafael Eitan, Moshe Peled, and Dan Laner put up heroic resistance to the onrushing Syrians. This authors of this book were honored to have the foreword written by Ambassador Aviv Shir-On. Few could describe more grippingly what was going on in Israel's young, armored cadres at the time.

Israel's armored corps abruptly changed tactics on the night of October 8–9. It was, in the midst of the defensive battle, like changing wheels on a moving train. In 1967, the tank commanders had roared through the desert in pure battle tank advances. But now the triumph of those six days had evaporated. Now they had to fight against the enemy's wire-guided Sagger missiles in a battle of combined arms.

ISRAEL TAL'S INSPIRED MERKAVA TANK

After the war, Israel Tal invented the revolutionary new Merkava tank, the Israeli combat vehicle par excellence. In 2022, half a century later, it is still the backbone of the Israeli army.

The words that General Tal spoke to his 84th Division in 1967 are legendary: "Everyone attacks; everyone breaks through; everyone looks forward; no one looks back. In 1956, we broke through in thirty-six hours. This time we have twenty-four. We will suffer casualties. It will be a fight to the death. We will never give up, regardless of the losses."

On June 5, 1967, Tal completed the task that General Gavish had given him in four instead of twenty-four hours.

THE ELITE

Tel chef, telle troupe ["Like leader, like troop"] — is especially true of Israel's armored corps. Young Israelis still aspire to join the tanks, just as they wish to serve in the special forces, the paratroopers, and the air force. Tank officers and soldiers see themselves as an elite, and they are. In all wars, in every campaign, they have had an outstanding effect.

In the first Gaza wars of 2008–09, 2012, and 2014, they unleashed their full force. In all three operations, they divided the enemy territory in two. When the politicians applied the handbrake in May 2021, they remained on the border. They provided fire support from their own territory, but they were not allowed to exploit their mobility. So, the government denied the army a resounding success.

But the armored force can do more. General Aviv Kochavi restructured the armed forces, but no army can do without the firepower, protection, and movement of its tanks — least of all in the embattled state of Israel.

Dr. Peter Forster
Colonel of the artillery
Editor in chief of *Bulletin-1.ch*

Directory of Chiefs of the General Staff and Commanders in Chief of Armored Corps

Directory of Chiefs of the General Staff and Commanders in Chief of Armored Corps			
Period	Chief of staff	Commander in chief	Historical events
1947–49	Yaakov Dori	Yitzhak Sadeh	Arab unrest
			War of Independence, 1948–49
1949–52	Yigael Yadin	Moshe Pasternak	
1952–53	Mordechai Maklef		
1953–58	Moshe Dayan	Yitzhak Pundak	Battles against Jordanians and Egyptians in the West Bank and Gaza Strip, 1953–56
		Chaim Laskov	Suez Crisis, 1956
		Uri Ben-Ari	
1958–61	Chaim Laskov	Chaim Bar-Lev	
1961–64	Tzvi Tzur	David Elazar	
1964–68	Yitzhak Rabin	Israel Tal	Conflicts with Syria over the water resources of the Jordan River, 1964–67
			Six-Day War, 1967
1968–72	Chaim Bar-Lev	Avraham Adan	War of Attrition between Israel and Egypt, 1968–70
1972–74	David Elazar		Yom Kippur War, 1973
1974–78	Mordechai Gur	Moshe Peled	Israeli invasion of southern Lebanon and war against the PLO during Operation Litani in 1978
1978–83	Rafael Eitan	Amnon Reshef	First Lebanon War: Operation Peace for Galilee
		Moshe Bar-Kochba	
1983–87	Moshe Levi	Amos Katz	
1987–91	Dan Shomron	Yossi Ben Hanan	First Intifada: Fighting against the Palestinians in the West Bank and the Gaza Strip
1991–95	Ehud Barak		
1995–98	Amnon Lipkin-Shahak		Intensive fighting against Hezbollah in southern Lebanon
1998–2002	Shaul Mofaz	Ehud Shani	Withdrawal of Israeli troops from Lebanon
			Start of the Second Intifada—fighting against Palestinians in the West Bank and Gaza Strip
			The Israeli army enters the West Bank: Operation Defensive Shield, 2002
2002–05	Moshe Yaalon	Sami Turgerman	Numerous terrorist attacks in the West Bank and Gaza Strip
2005–07	Dan Chalutz		Withdrawal from the Gaza Strip, 2005
			Second Lebanon War—Operations Just Reward and Change of Direction, 2006
2007–11	Gabriel Ashkenazi		Israeli troops invade the Gaza Strip: Operation Cast Lead, 2008–09
2011–15	Benjamin Gantz		Israeli troops invade the Gaza Strip: Operation Protective Edge, 2014
2015–19	Gadi Eisenkot	Guy Hasson	
2019–	Aviv Kochavi		Israeli troops invade the Gaza Strip: Israel-Gaza conflict, 2021
2022–		Hisham Ibrahim	

Directory of Israeli Armored Vehicles

Directory of Israeli Armored Vehicles						
Model	Type	Service Entry	Number	Active (as of 2022)	Country of Origin	Original Designation
Renault R-35	light tank	1948	3	–	France	Renault R-35
Hotchkiss H-39	light tank	1948	10	–	France	Hotchkiss H-39
A27M Mk. IV Cromwell	cruiser tank	1948	2	–	Great Britain	Cromwell
AMX-13	reconnaissance tank	1956	400	–	France	AMX-13
M50 Sherman	medium tank	1956	300	–	Israel (USA)	M4A1 Sherman (basis)
M51 Sherman	medium tank	1962	180	–	Israel (USA)	M4A1 Sherman (basis)
Shot Meteor	battle tank	1959	1,080	–	Great Britain	Centurion
Shot Kal	battle tank	1967	390	–	Israel (Great Britain)	Centurion (basis)
Magach 1	battle tank	1965	200	–	USA	M48A1
Magach 2	battle tank	1965	150	–	USA	M48A2C
Magach 3	battle tank	1970	540	–	USA	M48A3
Magach 5	battle tank	1975	2,069	–	USA	M48A5
Magach 6	battle tank	1971	360	–	USA	M60, M60A1, M60A3
Magach 7	battle tank	1986	1,040	–	Israel (USA)	M60 (basis)
Tiran 1, Tiran 4	battle tank	1968	146	–	USSR	T-54 (basis)
Tiran 2, Tiran 5	battle tank			–	USSR	T-55 (basis)
Tiran 3, Tiran 6	battle tank	1974	120	–	USSR	T-62 (basis)
Merkava Mk. I	battle tank	1978	250	–	Israel	–
Merkava Mk. II	battle tank	1983	580	–	Israel	–
Merkava Mk. III	battle tank	1989	780	160	Israel	–
Merkava Mk. IV	battle tank	2006	660	330	Israel	–
Nagmash (Bardelas, Zelda)	armored personnel Carrier (APC)	1973		500	USA	M113
Achzarit	APC	1989	215	215	Israel (USSR)	T-54 (basis)
Nagmashot	APC	1984			Israel (Great Britain)	Centurion (basis)
Nagmachon	APC	1988			Israel (Great Britain)	Centurion (basis)
Nakpadon	APC	1994			Israel (Great Britain)	Centurion (basis)
Namer	APC	2008		120	Israel	
Puma	armored engineering vehicle	1991			Israel (Great Britain)	Centurion (basis)
Tagash	bridge layer	1967		10	USA	M60 ABLV
Chiluz	recovery vehicle	1967		25	USA	M88A1

Tank Markings of the Israeli Armed Forces

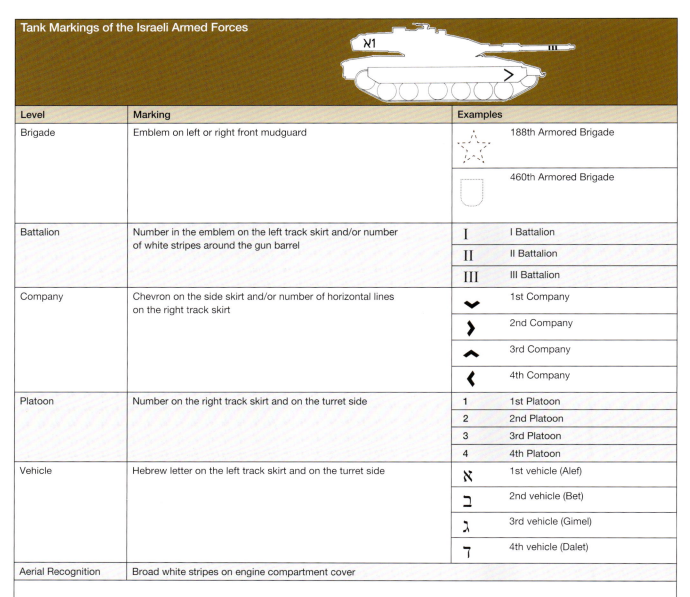

Level	Marking	Examples	
Brigade	Emblem on left or right front mudguard	☆	188th Armored Brigade
			460th Armored Brigade
Battalion	Number in the emblem on the left track skirt and/or number of white stripes around the gun barrel	I	I Battalion
		II	II Battalion
		III	III Battalion
Company	Chevron on the side skirt and/or number of horizontal lines on the right track skirt	⌄	1st Company
		⟩	2nd Company
		⌃	3rd Company
		⟨	4th Company
Platoon	Number on the right track skirt and on the turret side	1	1st Platoon
		2	2nd Platoon
		3	3rd Platoon
		4	4th Platoon
Vehicle	Hebrew letter on the left track skirt and on the turret side	א	1st vehicle (Alef)
		ב	2nd vehicle (Bet)
		ג	3rd vehicle (Gimel)
		ד	4th vehicle (Dalet)
Aerial Recognition	Broad white stripes on engine compartment cover		

Example: Magach 7,
2nd Battalion, 2nd Company, 3rd Platoon

Example: Merkava Mark IV,
2nd Battalion, 1st Company, 2nd Platoon

Example: Merkava Mk IV,
3rd Battalion, 2nd Company, 1st Platoon

Bibliography

Adan, Avraham. *On the Banks of the Suez*. London: Presidio, 1980.

Allon, Yigal. *. . . und David ergriff die Schleuder*. Berlin: Colloquium Verlag Otto H. Hess, 1971.

Barker, Arthur J. *Der Sechs-Tage Krieg*. Munich: Moewig Verlag, 1981.

Begin, Menachem. *The Revolt*. Los Angeles: Nash, 1972.

Ben Gurion, David. *Israel: Years of Challenge*. New York: Holt, 1963.

Blum, Howard. *Ihr Leben in unserer Hand: Die Geschichte der Jüdischen Brigade*. Munich: Econ Verlag, 2002.

Campbell, David. *Israeli Paratroopers, 1954–2016*. Oxford: Osprey, 2018.

Chamberlain, Peter, and Chris Ellis. *British and American Tanks of World War II*. London: Arms and Armour, 1969.

Charlwood, David. *Suez Crisis, 1956*. South Yorkshire, UK: Pen & Sword Military, 2019.

Churchill, Randolph S. *. . . und siegten am 7. Tag*. Munich: Scherz Verlag, 1967.

Däniker, Gustav. *Israels Dreifrontenkrieg*. Frauenfeld, Germany: Verlag Huber AG, 1967.

Dayan, Moshe. *Diary of the Sinai Campaign*. London: Weidenfeld & Nicolson, 1966.

Dayan, Moshe. *Die Geschichte meines Lebens*. Munich: Verlag Fritz Molden, 1976.

Dunstan, Simon. *The Centurion Tank in Battle*. Oxford: Osprey, 1981.

Dunstan, Simon. *Centurion vs. T-55: Yom Kippur War, 1973*. Oxford: Osprey, 2009.

Dunstan, Simon. *Israeli Fortifications of the October War, 1973*. Oxford: Osprey, 2008.

Dunstan, Simon. *The M113 Series*. Oxford: Osprey, 1983.

Dunstan, Simon. *The Six Day War, 1967: Jordan and Syria*. Oxford: Osprey, 2009.

Dunstan, Simon. *The Six Day War, 1967: Sinai*. Oxford: Osprey, 2009.

Dunstan, Simon. *The Yom Kippur War, 1973: The Golan Heights*. Oxford: Osprey, 2003.

Dunstan, Simon. *The Yom Kippur War, 1973: The Sinai*. Oxford: Osprey, 2003.

Eitan, Rafael. *A Soldier's Story: The Life and Times of an Israeli War Hero*. New York: Shapolsky, 1991.

El Shazly, Saad. *The Crossing of the Suez*. San Francisco: American Mideast Research, 1980.

Eshel, David. *Chariots of the Desert*. London: Brassey's Defence, 1989.

Eshel, David. *Israel's Armor in Action*. Tel Aviv: Eshel-Dramit, 1978.

Eshel, David. *The Lebanon War, 1982*. Tel Aviv: Eshel-Dramit, 1982.

Eshel, David. *The Yom Kippur War*. Tel Aviv: Eshel-Dramit, 1978.

Farquhar, Scott C. *Back to Basics: A Study of the Second Lebanon War*. Fort Leavenworth, KS: Combat Studies Institute Press, US Army Combined Arms Center, 2009.

Fey, Will. *Panzerkampf im Bild*. Osnabrück, Germany: Munin-Verlag GmbH, 1987.

Finkel, Meir. *Studies in Generalship: Lessons from the Chiefs of Staff of the IDF*. Stanford, CA: Hoover Institution, 2021.

Fletcher, David, and Richard C. Harley. *Cromwell Cruiser Tank, 1942–50*. Oxford: Osprey, 2006.

Forster, Peter. *Fällt Jerusalem?* Frauenfeld, Germany: Verlag Huber, 2001.

Gabriel, Richard. *Operation Peace for Galilee*. New York: Farrar, Straus and Giroux, 1985.

Gal, Reuven. *A Portrait of the Israeli Soldier*. New York: Praeger, 1986.

Gannon, Tom. *Israeli Shermans*. Essex, UK: Barbarossa Books, 2001.

Gannon, Tom. *Tanks of Early IDF*. Surrey, UK: Trackpad, 2019.

Gannon, Tom. *War of Independence: A Pictorial History*. Surrey, UK: Trackpad, 2021.

Gelbart, Marsh. *A History of Israel's Main Battle Tank*. Erlangen, Germany: Tankograd, 2005.

Gelbart, Marsh. *Modern Israeli Tanks and Infantry Carriers, 1985–2004*. Oxford: Osprey, 2004.

Grove, Eric. *Zweiter Weltkrieg Panzer*. London: Orbis, 1975.

Gur, Mordechai. *The Battle for Jerusalem*. New York: Popular Library, 1978.

Halle, Armin. *Panzer: Illustrierte Geschichte der Kampfwagen*. Bern, Switzerland: Scherz Verlag, 1971.

Herzog, Chaim. *The Arab-Israeli Wars*. New York: Random House, 2010.

Herzog, Chaim. *Entscheidung in der Wüste*. Berlin: Verlag Ullstein GmbH, 1975.

Higgins, David R. *Cromwell vs. Jagdpanzer IV*. Oxford: Osprey, 2018.

Hirsch, Gal. *Follow Me: Eighteen Essential Lessons on Leadership*. London: Gefen, 2020.

Kahalani, Avigdor. *The Heights of Courage: A Tank Leader's War on the Golan*. London: Greenwood, 1984.

Kahalani, Avigdor. *A Warrior's Way*. New York: S.P.I. Books, 1993.

Karsh, Efraim. *The Arab-Israeli Conflict*. Oxford: Osprey, 2002.

Katz, Samuel. *Armies in Lebanon, 1982–84*. Oxford: Osprey, 1985.

Katz, Samuel. *Israeli Defence Forces: 1948 to the Present*. London: Arms & Armour, 1985.

Katz, Samuel. *Israeli Defence Forces since 1973*. Oxford: Osprey, 1986.
Katz, Samuel. *Israeli Tank Battles: Yom Kippur to Lebanon*. London: Arms and Armor, 1988.
Katz, Samuel. *Israel's Armor Might*. Hong Kong: Concord, 1989.
Katz, Samuel. *Israel's Merkava I, II, III: Israel's Chariot of Fire*. Hong Kong: Concord, 1992.
Konzelmann, Gerhard. *Die Schlacht um Israel*. Munich: Verlag Kurt Desch, 1974.
Kuster, Matthias. "Der Libanon-Krieg 2006 aus militärstrategischer Sicht." *Military Power Revue*, February 2009.
Laffin, John. *The Israeli Army in the Middle East War, 1948–73*. Oxford: Osprey, 1987.
Lenzin, Marc, and Stefan Bühler. *Panzerfahrzeuge der Schweizer Armee seit 1921*. Stuttgart: Motorbuch Verlag, 2021.
Lenzin, Marc, Stefan Bühler, Fred Heer, and Peter Forster. *Die großen Panzerschlachten*. Stuttgart: Motorbuch Verlag, 2020.
Levy, Ma'or. *T-34 and the IDF: The Untold Story*. Tel Aviv: Desert Eagle, 2018.
Levy, Ma'or. *T-54/55 to IDF Tiran 4/5: The Birth of a Bastard Tank*. Tel Aviv: Desert Eagle, 2020.
Manasherob, Robert. *The First IDF Sherman Tanks*. Lion & Lioness 5. Jerusalem: SabingaMartin, 2010.
Manasherob, Robert. *M50 and M51*. Vol. 1. Lion & Lioness 2. Jerusalem: SabingaMartin, 2012.
Manasherob, Robert. *M50 and M51*. Vol. 2. Lion & Lioness 3. Jerusalem: SabingaMartin, 2015.
Manasherob, Robert. *Shot*. Centurion Tanks of the IDF 1. Jerusalem: SabingaMartin, 2011.
Manasherob, Robert. *Shot Kal Gimel*. Centurion Tanks of the IDF 7. Jerusalem: SabingaMartin, 2014.
Marshall, Samuel L. A. *Men against Fire*. New York: William Morrow, 1947.
Marshall, Samuel L. A. *Sinai Victory*. New York: William Morrow, 1958.
Mass, Michael. *Merkava Mk. 3 in IDF Service*. Tel Aviv: Desert Eagle, 2007.
Mass, Michael, and Adam O'Brien. *Magach 3 (M48A3) in IDF Service*. Tel Aviv: Desert Eagle, 2019.
Mass, Michael, and Adam O'Brien. *Magach 6A/6B (M60A1) in IDF Service*. Tel Aviv: Desert Eagle, 2019.
Mass, Michael, and Adam O'Brien. *Magach 7 & 7 Gimel in IDF Service*. Tel Aviv: Desert Eagle, 2022.
Matzken, Heino. *Ewiger Krieg im Nahen Osten*. Norderstedt, Germany: Books on Demand GmbH, 2011.
McNab, Chris. *Arab Armour vs. Israeli Armour: Six Day War, 1967*. Oxford: Osprey, 2021.
McNab, Chris. *Sagger Anti-tank Missile vs. M60 Main Battle Tank*. Oxford: Osprey, 2018.
Meir, Golda. *Mein Leben*. London: Hoffmann & Campe, 1975.
Morse, Stan. *Modern Military Powers: Israel*. London: Aerospace Publishing, 1984.
Myszka, John. *Israeli Improvised Armoured Vehicles & Jeeps, 1947–1949*. Deakin, Australia: Mouse House, 2012.
Narkis, Uzi. *The Liberation of Jerusalem: Battle of 1967*. London: Vallentine Mitchell, 1983.
Nordeen, Lon, and David Isby. *M60 vs. T-62: Cold War Combatants, 1956–92*. Oxford: Osprey, 2010.
Orr, Ori. *These Are My Brothers: A Dramatic Story of Heroism during the Yom Kippur War*. Tel Aviv: Yedioth Books, 2003.
Peres, Shimon. *Battling for Peace: Memoirs*. London: Random House, 1995.
Peres, Shimon. *David's Sling*. London: Weidenfeld & Nicolson, 1970.
Rabin, Yitzhak. *The Rabin Memoirs*. Berkeley: University of California Press, 1996.
Rodman, David. *Combined Arms Warfare in Israeli Military History*. Chicago: Sussex Academic, 2020.
Rothenberg, Gunther E. *The Anatomy of the Israeli Army*. New York: Hippocrene Book, 1979.
Sadat, Anwar. *In Search of Identity: An Autobiography*. New York: Harper and Row, 1978.
Seehase, Hagen. *Libanon-Syrien-Feldzug, 1941*. Salzburg, Austria: Österreichischer Milizverlag, 2022.
Segev, Tom. *Die ersten Israelis: Die Anfänge des jüdischen Staates*. Munich: Siedler Verlag, 2008.
Segev, Tom. *Es war einmal ein Palästina*. Munich: Siedler Verlag, 2005.
Segev, Tom. *1967: Israels zweite Geburt*. Munich: Siedler Verlag, 2009.
Sharon, Ariel. *Warrior: An Autobiography*. London: Simon & Schuster, 1989.
Teveth, Shabtai. *The Tanks of Tammuz*. London: Weidenfeld & Nicolson, 1968.
Trost, Ernst. *Die Schlacht um Israel, 1967*. Vienna: Verlag Fritz Molden, 1967.
Tucker-Jones, Anthony. *Armoured Warfare in the Arab-Israeli Conflicts*. South Yorkshire, UK: Pen & Sword Military, 2021.
Uhlmann, Ernst. *Israels Blitzkrieg gegen die Araber*. Zurich, Switzerland: Verlag Neue Zürcher Zeitung, 1967.
Varble, Derek. *The Suez Crisis, 1956*. Oxford: Osprey, 2003.
Wallach, Jehuda. *. . . und mit der anderen hielten sie die Waffe*. Koblenz, Germany: Bernard & Graefe Verlag, 1984.
Zaloga, Steven J. *Armour of the Middle East Wars, 1948–78*. Oxford: Osprey, 1981.

Zaloga, Steven J. *French Tanks of World War II*. Vol. 1. Oxford: Osprey, 2014.

Zaloga, Steven J. *French Tanks of World War II*. Vol. 2. Oxford: Osprey, 2014.

Zaloga, Steven J. *Israeli Tanks and Combat Vehicles*. London: Arms & Armour, 1983.

Zaloga, Steven J. *Red SAM: The SA-2 Guideline Anti-aircraft Missile*. Oxford: Osprey, 2007.

Zaloga, Steven J. *Scud Ballistic Missile and Launch Systems, 1955–2005*. Oxford: Osprey, 2006.

Zaloga, Steven J., and Jim Laurier. *The M47 and M48 Patton Tanks*. Oxford: Osprey, 1999.

Zideon, Ofer. *Israel's Front Line Armor*. Jerusalem: Wizard, 2012.

Zideon, Ofer. *Train Hard: Fight Easy*. Jerusalem: Wizard, 2013.

Authors' Biographies

MARC LENZIN

Born in Bern, Switzerland, in 1967. Postgraduate studies in business management at the Private University of Applied Sciences in Zurich. Member of the management board of an international IT manufacturer. Military training as an armored infantryman, as a first lieutenant deputy commander of an armored infantry company, and as a captain intelligence officer (S2) in the staff of a Bernese armored battalion. Historian who has written books on military history and tank battles. Works on the correspondence staff for the military journal *Schweizer Soldat* ("Swiss Soldier") and is a member of the European Military Press Association (EMPA).

STEFAN BÜHLER

Born in Thun, Switzerland, in 1984. Apprenticeship as a design engineer, further training as a mechanical engineer FH. Worked for seven years as a project manager in the field of tank construction and defensive systems in the defense industry and has been an explosive-ordnance-disposal officer with the Swiss armed forces since 2013. Military trained tank driver and commander (Leopard 2), platoon leader, and commander of Armored Company 12/1. Currently chief of operations (S3) in a tank battalion. Works as a correspondent for the military journal *Schweizer Soldat* and is a board member of the Officers' Association of the Armored Forces (OG Panzer).

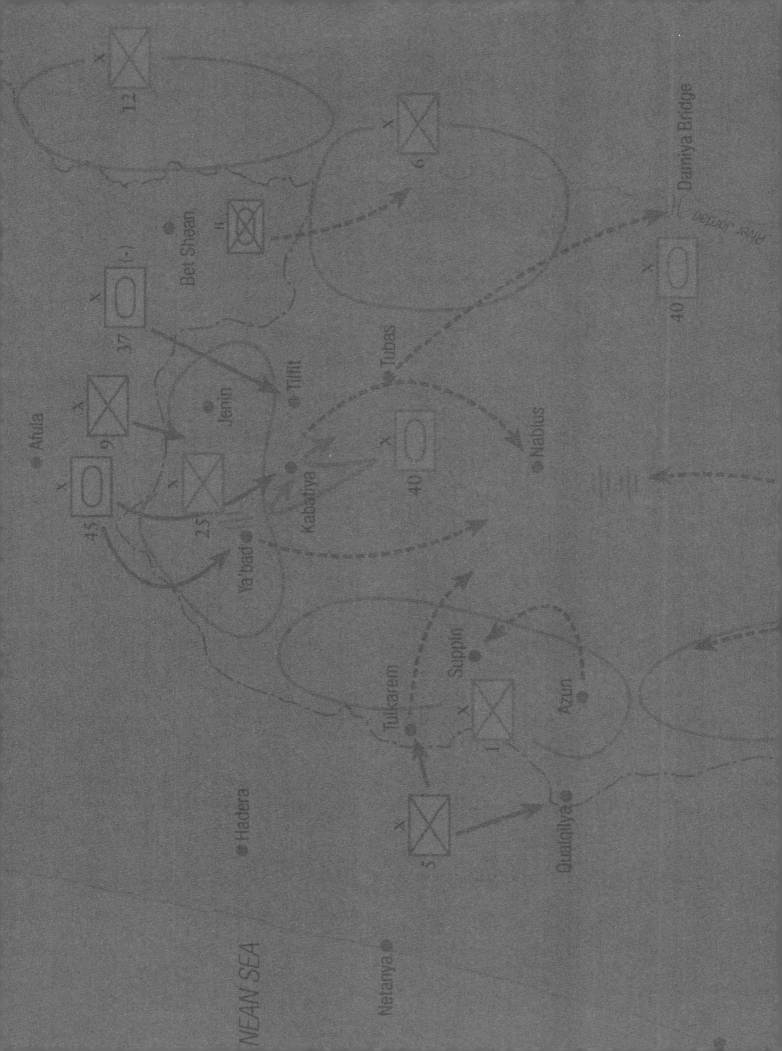